This comprehensive book deals with the full complexity of sexual and gender related issues of HIV/AIDS as they occur in the lives of Ghanaian men and women. Discussions of sex and gender, previously taboo subjects, have become possible as a result of the growing HIV/AIDS pandemic, not only in countries with much higher prevalence rates, but also in Ghana. The way the book engages these topics provides an understanding of key HIV/AIDS risk factors and a basis for facilitating appropriate and effective inter-related socio-cultural, and individual behavioral, transformations of gender roles, sexuality and related issues. Such changes should not only lead to diminished risk for HIV/AIDS but since, to be effective, they are encompassing and must of necessity lead in the direction of greater equity, they will also forge broader benefits. This book is to be praised for showing us the complexity and interrelationships of these issues and for so clearly making us understand that an attack on this most important of current public health problems can not be focused narrowly.

Gender roles, social transformation, poverty, mobility, communication, socialization, changing (popular and "high") cultural norms, anxiety, aggression, frustration and exploitation, and what is called sexual panic are all interwoven in a clear, yet nuanced manner, in this very important book which will serve as a watershed in our understanding of gender roles and sex in the Ghanaian context, and in the effort at combating HIV/AIDS in Ghana.

The book should prove of great interest and relevance for the general public, but especially for public health professionals and students, for anthropologists, for development workers and, especially, for those directly engaged in the urgent efforts of shaping and implementing interventions to combat the HIV/AIDS pandemic in Ghana, and elsewhere. The editors and authors are to be congratulated for producing a book which will clearly serve as a crucial springboard for how this can be done.

H.K. Heggenhougen
Professor
Department of International Health
Boston University School of Public Health
And Centre for International Health
University of Bergen (Norway)

Sex and Gender in an Era of AIDS

GHANA AT THE TURN OF THE MILLENNIUM

Sex and Gender in an Era of AIDS
GHANA AT THE TURN OF THE MILLENNIUM

Edited by:
Christine Oppong, M. Yaa P. A. Oppong and
Irene K. Odotei

SUB-SAHARAN PUBLISHERS

RA
643. 86
G 4
S 49
2006

First published in 2006 by
SUB-SAHARAN PUBLISHERS
P.O. BOX LG358,
LEGON, ACCRA, GHANA
for Historical Society of Ghana

ISBN 13: 978-9988-550-55-4
       10: 9988-550-55-3   call

FOREWORD

The National Commission on Culture, with a generous grant from the Royal Netherlands Embassy in Ghana, is instituting a publication series to be known as the Culture and Development Series. This is to enable the general public to access and use the results of research, analytical and literary works from Ghanaian scholars and writers.

Books published in the series will be selected and published on merit by an Editorial Committee of the University of Ghana. Their hall-mark will be originality, creativity, style, lucidity and contemporary relevance.

It is hoped that the series will stimulate thought and discussion on a wide range of issues of public concern, and offer insights, if not suggestions of solutions, to problems of culture, development and good governance.

The first selected works appear to meet these criteria; and it is our hope that they would set the bench marks for future publications. The forthcoming publications are:

1. Chieftaincy in Ghana – Culture, Governance and Development. Edited by Irene K. Odotei and Albert K. Awedoba.
2. Sex and Gender in an Era of Aids.
   Edited by Christine Oppong, Yaa Oppong and Irene Odotei
3. Religion and Leadership in Ghana
   Edited by Rev. A. A. Akrong and Rev. Elom Dovlo

The contemporary relevance of these collections of essays is quite evident. The National Commission on Culture and the Royal Netherlands Embassy are proud to sponsor the publication of the series.

SIGNED

CHAIRMAN
NATIONAL COMMISSION ON CULTURE

AMBASSADOR
ROYAL NETHERLANDS EMBASSY

Contents

EDITORS' NOTE AND ACKNOWLEDGEMENTS

The editors owe a great debt of gratitude to the patience and forbearance of the several contributors of essays to this volume, as this work has had a very extended gestation period.

It began as a germ of an idea when the first editor, Christine Oppong, was a Fellow at the Netherlands Institute for Advanced Study (NIAS), Wassenaar, near the Hague in 2000-2001 – hence the original Dutch connection and contributors and the focus on the turn of the millennium. Editing continued among other work during a subsequent period as Visitor to the same Institute in the spring of 2003.

Yaa Oppong worked on the volume and in particular, the writing of the epilogue, during her various assignments on population and development, while a Fellow and Research Associate at the Harvard University Centre for Population and Development. Irene Korkoi Odotei played a judiciously supportive and advisory role from the beginning and then took the work under her wing to guide it to a successful finish.

Publication of this work, and the whole series of which it forms an initial part, was actually spearheaded in the beginning by the Historical Society of Ghana, under its President, Professor Odotei. Then the production was financially facilitated by the visionary generosity of the Dutch Embassy in Accra, through the good offices of the Ambassador, His Excellency Arie Van der Wiel. Ultimately the series is coming into print under the auspicious aegis of the Commission for Culture, and under the sympathetic direction of its Commissioner, Professor George Hagan.

The editors' final debt of gratitude goes to the wise and dedicated Sub-Saharan Publishers, whose patient, practical work at long last resulted in the successful completion of the present volume you are holding in your hand.

EDITORS' PREFACE

For women and men, sex is a source of pleasure, expression of love, purpose of partnerships, path to procreation and creator of kinship. But it is also for some individuals a means to survival and accumulation; to feeding their children, making money and amassing wealth. However it may in addition be a terrible harbinger of disease and death. Moreover its negotiation and expression are deeply engendered, depending to a great extent on cultural norms moulding behaviour, circumscribing communication and affecting female or male access to required resources and power. For relative autonomy, power and resources profoundly affect ability and opportunities to communicate and negotiate and establish harmonious and fulfilling sexual relationships.

Prior to the advent of the HIV/AIDS epidemic in Ghana, matters relating to sex were rarely issues for public debate or discussion. Expressions of love and open displays of affection and sexual attraction were similarly a private affair. Kissing and even holding hands in public were virtually taboo. Now in contrast sex and the potential consequences of unprotected sexual relations are a matter of great public discussion. Moreover the often explicit advertisements and admonitions of the HIV/AIDS campaigns of recent years, on billboards and television screens and on radio programmes, have been seen and heard by a large proportion of Ghana's population, in their homes and on the streets and in public gatherings. In this current climate, sexual activity is increasingly viewed as a potentially 'risky' as well as exciting or pleasurable enterprise, and now patterns of infection make visible, track and mirror, hitherto private and intimate activities and their associated networks. For example the recent statistics from the Ghana Demographic and Health Survey (GDHS 2003) show clearly that being in a stable marriage partnership protects people from risk.

In an era of HIV/AIDS and the associated escalation in morbidity and mortality, promoting understanding of the contexts and contents of sexual relationships and the differential power relationships and 'bargaining' positions between men and women has taken on a new urgency. Greater attention is being paid to the need for more descriptive and in-depth case studies, which explore, nuance and untangle the political, economic and social contexts within which sexual encounters and relations occur.

This volume of essays seeks to explore and place before the reader matters pertaining to sex and sexuality in the context of changing gender roles and relations in Ghana, with a view to situating some of the socio-cultural dimensions of the sexual transmission of disease and death.

The case studies presented here take perspectives ranging from macro-level analysis of national policies and programs, to studies of inter-personal relations and analysis of individual life experiences. They include recorded conversations with individual men and women, examination of traditional institutions and how they are changing at the present time, observations of passing phobias and analysis of artistic representations of sex and gender roles as portrayed in novels and popular culture – songs and films. Some essays deal overtly with issues of sexuality, vulnerability, health risks, migration and the material bases of sexual relations in contemporary Ghana as well as in the past. Others, while still treating some of these topics, deal more explicitly with gendered identities and gender roles and relations.

The first essay is overtly historical and traces links between labour migration, sex and the spread of sexually transmitted infections in the twentieth century. The next two essays focus on transformations in traditional institutions in two southern culture areas (initiation rites and marriage and related rituals), indicating potential associations between rural underdevelopment, relative economic deprivation, population mobility and the risks of rapid spread of HIV. The fourth examines the impacts of frequent mobility and separation on the coastal families of fishermen and the kinds of risks involved. Chapters 5 and 6 are concerned with communication and behaviour in sexual relationships both inside and outside marriage and among commercial sex workers, including power relations and decisions about safer sexual practices. Chapter 7 is about school children and their socialization and lack of knowledge and sources of advice on sex, love and relationships and implications for school girl conception and abortion, not to mention the spread of sexually transmitted disease. Chapter 8 is about an elderly Kwahu woman's reminiscences on love and sex in her past life. Chapter 9 focuses on historical evidence of changing gender relations and apparent associations with altering witchcraft beliefs and practices in the Northern Mamprusi traditional kingdom. The next two chapters take apart and examine perceptions and portrayals of women in novels, songs and films, illuminating ambiguity, aggression and exploitation. Chapter 12 documents a wave of sexual panic which swept through the country and the rest of the region in the late nineties.

Thus, while some of the chapters deal with issues of sexuality, vulnerability, health risks, migration and the material bases of sexual relations in contemporary Ghana as well as in the past, the remainder focus more on identities and gender roles and relations, which are seen to be often fraught with frustration and anxiety.

The epilogue looks in detail and over time at governmental and non governmental responses to the AIDS epidemic in the country, outlining the various programs which have been designed and set up to counteract the real and escalating dangers to the population, young and old. Here again, gender issues are salient and pervasive, affecting perceptions both about the cause of the spread of the disease and the reactions to the various programs designed.

An overview of the chapters in this volume – and an indication of the themes that bind them together follows in the introduction, which also seeks to depict however briefly the historical, cultural, demographic and economic contexts of the case studies.

1

INTRODUCTION

Christine Oppong

The chapters in this volume portray aspects of changing gender roles and sexual relationships in Ghana in the last decades of the millennium now past, especially during the most recent period of the nineteen eighties and nineties, when the scourge of sexually transmitted disease and death, that is HIV/-AIDS, was first introduced and began to spread in Ghana's population. At the crux of the pictures portrayed and the matters discussed is the fact that customary norms shaping sex and gender roles have been altering and becoming prone to difference and conflict while traditional customs shaping sexual behaviour, in particular, those beliefs, sanctions and rules compelling sexual restraint and supporting abstention are breaking down and new contraceptive practices are being tried and advocated. The result has been that sexual behaviour is becoming more a matter of individual opportunity and choice for some; possibly involving partner discussion and sometimes including bargaining while for many it is being subtly and brazenly influenced by unequal power relations and resources between women and men.

Relationships and roles of women and men, girls and boys, are depicted in the essays that follow, as observed and described by writers from several disciplines, including anthropology, demography, history, geography and the arts. Accounts are presented of conversations, behaviour, ritual activities, songs, beliefs, fictional accounts and norms and of how traditional institutions and ways of life have been altering. The portraits painted, of people, places, situations, relationships and historical events are set within the wider context of profound political, economic and demographic transformations going on.

Some of the essays in this volume deal overtly with issues of sexuality, vulnerability and health risks. They indicate how rising risks seem often to be linked to migration for money by women and men, for survival or accumulation of material things. They demonstrate the frequent material bases of sexual contacts, in both the recent and historical past. Some provide examples of how traditional sexual regimes, often imposing restraint and chastity, both inside and outside marriage, appear to have been seriously disrupted in recent times.[1] Others focus on heterosexual communication and negotiations and power struggles between women and men. Yet others deal more explicitly with gendered identities and perceptions and beliefs about gender roles and portrayals of manhood and womanhood in songs, films and fiction and their assumed spiritual and moral attributes.

This introduction first briefly examines some pertinent facts about the national contexts of these studies, namely, aspects of Ghana's changing social, economic and political past up to the end of the millenium. Secondly, it provides a short overview of the chapters in the volume indicating the gist of their contents and noting some of the themes that link them together and differentiate them; but first, a word about the meanings attributed here to the terms sex and gender.

Sex and Gender: Attributes, Activities, Roles and Relations

The perspective assumed here is that biological differences, particularly parts played in physical reproduction by females and males in begetting and bearing the next generation, are more or less universal and globally, fairly similar. However, the several social roles females and males play in societies, including mating, marriage and parenthood, differ quite markedly. Moreover, they are prone to change historically over time, sometimes quite radically.[2] For these roles are socially constructed, culturally interpreted, economically constrained and supported, and may be environmentally impacted or politically motivated and controlled. They are accordingly very different, in different locations and social spaces, and in varying cultural contexts and time periods, altering either slowly or quickly from one time period to the next.

Gender is now a very popular and widely used term, denoting a social category which refers to these differences in female and male roles and the interlocking systems in which these roles are embedded. In fact, it is often unfortunately used in popular parlance as a synonym for sex, – that is the biological category of being female or male, thus apparently serving to blur distinctions between biological and social or cultural difference. It is a concept that denotes the varied and changing facets of the roles of females and males, as well as being used to describe the socio-cultural, economic and political systems of which they are a crucial part. Several indicators are commonly used to assess and compare women's positions in their own societies as compared with men. Among the frequently used indicators of women's position are women's control over and access to various resources and assets compared to those of men; the degree of their autonomy from men, disparities in human development indicators (for example health status) between men and women or other aspects of their privileges or oppression, intrinsic in social and legal institutions (C. Oppong & Wery 1994: 7). In the recent past, scholars of various disciplines have paid much attention to trying to understand the ways in which gender roles differ over the life course[3] and change through historical time, as economic and demographic transformations occur. They have also examined how changes in these roles impact developmental outcomes, both human development and economic development.[4]

The Changing National Context

The Republic of Ghana is on the West Coast of Africa. The Gulf of Guinea lies to the south and three francophone countries form its borders – Burkina Faso is to the north, Togo to the East and La Côte d'Ivoire to the West (see Map). The country is mainly low lying with a sandy coastline and low coastal plain, a forested middle belt and western region while the north is savannah, watered by the Black and White Volta rivers. The Volta Lake, one of the largest artificial lakes in the world, was created after Independence by the Akosombo dam, built for the generation of hydroelectricity under the visionary leadership of the first President of Ghana, Osagyefo Dr Kwame Nkrumah.

The population comprises several ethnic groups including the Akan (49%), the Mole Dagbane (17%), the Ewe (13%) and the Ga/Adangme (8%). There are also other smaller cultural and linguistic groups in different parts of the country (GSS 2004),[5] which is currently divided into 10 administrative regions – Western, Central, Greater Accra, Volta, Eastern, Ashanti, Brong Ahafo, Northern, Upper East and Upper West. These regions are subdivided into 138 districts. Accra is the administrative and political capital with a population of 1.7million. Ghana is a constitutional democracy and now operates a multi-party democratic presidential system of government. The country has an Executive President elected for four years with a maximum of two terms and parliament is also elected every four years. The judiciary is independent and the media – newsprint, radio stations and television stations are very active and closely followed.

For two or more decades, agriculture, mining, logging and retail trade have been the most important economic activities, with agriculture employing about half of the population. Most people work in the informal sector and are mainly self-employed in farming, petty processing and retail trade. The biggest export items remain cocoa, gold and timber. Recently fruits, tubers and nuts are also being exported.

Given the low levels of living prevalent among the majority of the population, the pressing aim of the Government's economic development program is poverty reduction and improved welfare for the population. In the mid nineties, a 2020 Vision strategy for development was articulated, with the goal of making Ghana a middle income country by that date. This emphasized economic growth, rural development, employment promotion and improved access to basic public services (education, health care, water and sanitation and family planning).

Ghana has a rapidly expanding and youthful population. In the 1960 Census, the population was 6.7 million, in 1970 it was 8.6 million, in 1984 12.3 million and by 2000 it had grown to 19.8 million. Thus, the population density per square kilometre more than doubled from 36 people in 1970 to 79 in the year 2000. At the same time, the percentage urban grew rapidly from 29% in 1970 to 44% in 2000. Meanwhile, over 30 years, the sex ratio has fallen from 98.5 males per 100 females in 1970 to 97.9 in 2000. The deficits of males in the population, especially in the age groups twenties and forties (as found in the GDHS 2004), may be the result of massive out migration, a global diaspora of men and women seeking a better life. During the same period, there was a decrease in the proportion of the population under 15 years to 41% and an increase in those 64 years and above to 5%, indicating the persistence of a high burden of dependency, especially of the youth for the adult population. There were also increases in life expectancy at birth during the same decades. (In 1984, for men, it was 50 years rising to 55 years in 2000 and among females it rose from 54 to 60 years in the same period). In addition, there were signs of declining fertility and improvements in health, at least in some sectors of the population. However, by the end of the millennium, a number of population issues were considered prejudicial to the Ghana's development, both human and economic. These included the persistently high levels of fertility and maternal mortality and under 5 morbidity, mortality and under nutrition, which were particularly prevalent in some regions. In addition, there was the continued spread of HIV/AIDS.

At the same time as enjoying rich cultural diversity in terms of different languages spoken and traditional, political and familial institutions, including modes of descent reckoning, (matrilineal, ambilineal, patrilineal, dual), customary marriage rites and patterns of domestic organization, there is much shared political and economic experience which unites the population. Ghanaians share a common history of British colonialism (which left behind a commonly used and widely spoken language, English). They united in the struggle for independence and after achievement of nationhood, they have endured shared shocks and suffering experienced during a sequence of various political upheavals and sometimes associated violence. The latter events, which were unfortunately often associated with economic decline, escalating pauperization, widespread uncertainty and anxiety, frequently frustrated aspirations (see Appendix p.327).

Not only has Ghana's internal population been growing at a fast pace but so also has the population of international migrants, now estimated at more than three million – comprising searchers after "greener (economic) pastures", often well-educated people, including medical doctors and nurses with rising expectations nourished by the formerly effective (British modelled), still functioning education system. This massive outward migration has occurred in the face of a stagnating economy and political uncertainty during the last decades of the twentieth century. By the end of the millenium, the remittances from individuals in this global diaspora were noted to have formed a highly significant proportion of national and household incomes and to have contributed among other things, to the building of salubrious suburbs in the big cities.

On March 6 1957, Ghana[6] became the first country in Sub-Saharan Africa to gain independence from the British. On 1 July 1960, a Republic was created by plebiscite within the British Commonwealth of Nations and Osagyefo Dr Kwame Nkrumah became Ghana's first president. At the time of Ghana's independence, the expectations for Ghana's successful development were high. However, the political road proved difficult and the ambitious targets envisioned for education, health and prosperity have often remained elusive. Since Independence, Ghana has been through four Republics, with intermittent and sometimes brutal military rules, in its short and turbulent post-independence existence[7]. Governments have come and gone and several times in the past military intervention has bedeviled the nation, shattering great hopes entertained for Ghana (Ofori-Atta 1988:17). Indeed, in the post independence years, there has been what has been described as a succession of disheartening crises,-a morale crisis, a moral crisis, a social crisis, a religious crisis, an economic and financial crisis and a political and constitutional crisis (op.cit. p 21).

In this work, what we seek to show evidence of is the idea of an emerging gender crisis. This is partly viewed as attributable to dislocation of populations and disruptions in sexual regimes and productive regimes. It is with the former disruption that we are particularly concerned here. It has involved the breakdown of traditional protective and socialization mechanisms, the overthrow of customary constraints to partner selection and sexual congress and related practices and the casting away of culture. Accordingly, some attention is first paid to cultural norms and traditional institutions shaping gender roles and relations.

Cultural Norms and Traditional Institutions

The gendered divisions of labor in homes, markets and farms in Ghana have traditionally been fairly clear-cut, with women and men playing distinct roles. They have different responsibilities for different activities and face very different constraints. Women bear primary responsibility for childbearing, child-rearing, much food production and most food processing, food preparation, washing and fuel wood and water collection. Furthermore, relations between males and females in Ghana are to some extent culturally and contextually specific in different regions and among different ethnic and language groupings, as these have varied marriage rites and rules of partner choice, different types of traditional architecture and domestic residence patterns and organization, child rearing practices and rituals surrounding infant naming, betrothal and funeral ceremonies. The largest of these cultural groupings is the matrilineal Akan, which comprises several sub populations including the Ashanti, Brong, Fanti, Akwapim, Kwahu and Akyem. The neighbouring Nzima in the south east also trace descent and membership of kin groups matrilineally. Other groups include the Ga Adangme and Krobo in the Greater Accra and Eastern Regions and the Ewe speaking people and other linguistic groups in the Volta Region. To the north of the Brong are the Gonja speaking people and in the Northern Region are the Dagbane speaking people of the kingdom of Dagbon, and to their north, the traditional kingdom of Mamprussi, which is surrounded and partly inhabited by several acephalous peoples. (See map).

In general, in the past, Ghanaian systems of kinship and marriage have been characterized by relatively weak and sometimes fragile conjugal ties and strong permanent and solidary lineage bonds. Filial and sibling ties have traditionally been likely to be more trusted and enduring than ties by marriage. These traditional systems of family relationships have been described as they existed in the pre and post colonial eras in a number of by now classic ethnographies.[8] In several traditional systems, spouses spend much, if not most of their married life living in separate domestic groups (as among the Akan and Ga) and polygyny has remained a desired norm for many men, which has often been achieved at least in later life, a pattern which the latest Ghana Demographic and Health Survey 2003 shows as continuing widely until today. And there is still widespread emphasis upon the values and practices supporting male sexual potency and female high fertility as the essay on fishing communities by Irene Odotei illustrates. Meanwhile for several decades, ethnographic studies have shown the diversity and complexity of domestic group organization, stressing the openness of such systems and the widespread customary segregation of conjugal role relationships in terms of interests, activities and management of resources. In such situations, the conjugal autonomy of women is often marked and domestic groups maintained and "headed" by women are common.[10]

The Economic Base: Fluctuating Livelihoods and Impacts of SAPS

Over the decades, Ghana's economic fortunes have fluctuated with alternating periods of boom, 'mediocrity' and bust (Leith 1996: 4). Indeed, 'Ghana stands out among African countries as holding the unenviable record of decline from a very strong economy .It had one of the very highest per capita incomes in the continent in the early 1960's, [but] by 1982, it was ranked twenty-first out of forty-four African countries (Canagarajah and Mazumdar 1997). The country had by then clearly suffered some sharp shocks, including oil price increase[s] and severe droughts in 1975-77 and again in 1980-81. However, some economic observers blamed the massive involvement of the state in economic affairs; its mismanagement and excessive public spending as being the root cause of the decline' (ibid.)

Through the various economic ups and downs, trade and agriculture have remained the mainstays of the livelihoods of the majority of the people both female and male. Trade, involving travel with desirable commodities, has been a prominent feature of the economy since time immemorial. And the peopling of the area in the past has been attributed as much to the country's geographical position or space relations within the vast network of West

African and European trade, as to its coveted resources in gold, ivory, kola and slaves (Dickson 1969: 32). For both men and women, trade continues to be an important source of livelihood and market trading, often involving travel, is a well established and still culturally accepted occupational activity for women in much of the country (eg. Newman et al. 2003: 31). It has its own perceived advantages and attendant risks to health and survival.

The agricultural sector, which still employs the bulk of the population in small scale farming, includes five major sub-sectors: crops,[11] cocoa, livestock, fisheries and forestry.[12] The most significant is cropping and includes small-scale indigenous methods, such as shifting cultivation, bush fallow (land rotation) and larger scale systems, such as the plantation system (Gyasi 1996). Ghana's main agricultural exports include cocoa, timber and pineapples. The traditional bush fallow system is the most common system of agricultural land use in Ghana.[13] However, with ever-increasing population growth, urbanization, infrastructural development and growing demand for cash crops, the traditional bush fallow system has been put under extreme pressure in many areas of the country and an increasing proportion of Ghana's cultivable land is being developed.

In 1983, under strong pressure from outside and with her economy already in dire straits, Ghana committed to a program of macroeconomic reform under a Structural Adjustment Program (SAP). This entailed a cut back of public services and retrenchment of the civil service, divestiture of state enterprises, removal of subsidies and an emphasis on export crops and privatization. However, relatively few large private enterprises were eventually set up and some apparently successful ones, for one reason or another, collapsed. Moreover, in spite of optimistic attempts to talk up the situation by international economic advisers, the downward economic slide continued till the end of the millennium.

Some have argued that impacts of the SAP were experienced most acutely by women and children (Manuh 1994). Women who were export farmers in the 1970's (and who had retreated to subsistence farming as a result of the economic crisis) now found themselves (under the Structural Adjustment Program) faced with rising costs for health care and other social services (as the government retreated from subsidizing these services) and demanded that people should pay as they went (eg. see Mikell 1990). Under SAP prenatal care, childbirth and infant health care had to be paid for. Therefore, 'the bulk of women's available cash from the sale of produce such as vegetables [was]... being used to pay doctors' fees and to buy medicines. This occurred at a time when women's available cash [was] at its lowest or non-existent' (Mikell 1990: 26). These conditions of increasing insecurity were coupled with, rising unemployment and inequality, migration and the intensification of women's workloads and sense of insecurity (Avotri et al. 1999).

An example of a series of changes in public policy (under Structural Adjustment) which adversely affected women's roles and responsibilities vis-à-vis men is provided by the case of agricultural extension. Following the agricultural sector reforms – as part of Structural Adjustment – women farmers, 'clearly lost...some of the provision of extension services they previously enjoyed and (we)re now being marginalized by more active and wealthy male farmers (Brown et al. 1997: 13 – 14). Another telling example is provided by the case of the education sector. Increases in schooling costs – under Structural Adjustment – also had gendered impacts in that, women appeared to bear the main costs of educating children. A study of two villages documented the male/female contrast. Whereas no man was solely respons-ible for the costs of education, 75 percent of women bore sole responsibility for meeting such costs (Brown et al 1997: 24). Moreover, access to higher education showed a marked male bias from puberty onwards. Boys and young men got far more access to secondary, tertiary and professional and technical training, which then meant that they were the ones equipped to get the best paid jobs. (See Table 1).

A decade after SAP, there were commentators who praised the country's economic performance even labeling it as Africa's star performer (Brown et al. 1997:5).[14] An analysis of Ghana's average annual growth of GDP purported to show that, compared to many of her neighbors and the majority of countries in the region, her macro economic performance had been relatively steady and sustained. However as many of the country's inhabitants knew well this 'star performance' came at a significant cost to the ordinary citizens of the country, including in particular, Ghana's women and children. For the SAP 'demand[ed] economic sacrifices from people, currency devaluation and rising unemployment levels.' (Mikell 1990: 26).

TABLE 1: AGE SPECIFIC ENROLMENT RATES (GDHS 1998 p. 140)

Age	Percent Enrolled F	M
14	76	76
15	64	69
16	49	63
17	34	45
18	18	29
19	16	27
20	5	20
21	6	16
22	5	14
23	3	11
24	1	9

It is apparent that from colonial times to the recent past (the period in which these essays are set) fluctuating economic fortunes, coupled with political uncertainties, have significantly and inequitably impacted the lives of Ghanaian men, women and children. These crises have undoubtedly affected the lives of the people depicted in these essays – the decline of public services,[15] the escalating pauperization and under and unemployment, – all have taken their toll, making many people ready to travel anywhere and do anything to improve their own and their children's lot in life. For Ghanaians have suffered unduly – and men and women have been affected in different ways.

In the year 2000, the **Report on the State of the Economy** described the continuing economic deterioration until that date, attributing this partly to external factors of low commodity prices and high crude oil prices; admitting also the part played by fiscal imbalances and excessive money supply (ISSER 2001). The economy was then described as characterized by high inflation, high interest rates, rapid depreciation of the cedi and a high debt overhang and a high incidence of poverty (op. cit. p.1). Earnings from cocoa and gold had fallen. Indeed the production of cocoa was still below the level of output achieved in the 1960s. However, despite the economic stress in 2000 – a period when the inflation rate rose from 15 to more than 40% – Ghana successfully underwent a national population and housing census and parliamentary and presidential elections. These events and successes showed the world Ghana's solid adherence to democracy and progress, in spite of everything.

Nevertheless an outcome of the policies and programs pursued was that by the end of the millennium more than 60% of Ghana's population still remained rural, poor and engaged in agriculture. Some 80% of agricultural production was still produced by smallholder farmers on family farms, engaged in back breaking work using the most primitive tools (hoes and cutlasses) and without access to machines or sources of energy other than human labour. Two out of five of these farmers were women and were mainly growing food. And till the end of the millennium agriculture still represented the most important sector in the economy, not only in terms of employment but also with respect to its contributions to the country's GDP and foreign exchange earnings. It also remained a major source of raw materials for manufacturing.

Changing Gender Roles:
Adversity, Male Bias, Mobility and
Increasing Female Autonomy and Responsibility

Ghana has been remarkable among all countries for the high levels of female as well as male economic activity, undertaken at all ages. By the end of the millennium, women in Ghana were observed to be, 'increasingly active in non farm economies' (Newman et al. 2000: 2). In view of their heavy and even escalating workloads, it is not surprising that a recent study of women's work and its consequences on their health, documented the increasing stresses being placed on Ghanaian women. These are stresses which have intensified as a result of, 'new forms of agricultural production, the economic crises of the 1980's and Structural Adjustment Programmes...[which have in turn] reduced employment opportunities for some women, increased work-loads and intensified women's sense of insecurity (Avotri et al. 1999: 1124). As some of the essays here will indicate, such economic anxiety and stress and responsibility for dependents has in some cases prompted women to leave the farms or refuse agricultural labour and engage in forms of migrant cash earning even more highly detrimental to their health.

Unfortunately, in spite of women's core responsibility for the maintenance of their families, they enjoy less access to productive resources. Not only do they have less higher education and training as noted above, but they also have less access to health care, leisure, rest and credit, as well as having limited control over productive resources such as land, livestock and tools (eg Avotri et al. 1999: 1124). (See Box 1 below).

Box 1 : Persisting Gender Inequalities

Adult illiteracy rates were 47 percent for women in 1995 and 24 percent for men.

In 1994, girls comprised 47 percent of primary school students, 35 percent of senior secondary students, and only 26 percent of tertiary school students.

In the eighties the incidence of the human immunodeficiency virus (HIV) and acquired immunodeficiency syndrome (AIDS) were three times higher among women than men. General morbidity levels for women were higher than for men.

Parents were more likely to seek health care for boys than for girls.

Discrimination in household nutrition and health care resulted in female infant mortality rates 10 percent higher than they would be if such discrimination did not occur.

Women worked longer hours than men—15 to 25 percent longer, when unpaid household work is accounted for.

Women had relatively poor access to, and control of, agricultural inputs, including land, fertilizer, machinery, and labor (including their own). They also had extremely limited access to agricultural extension services.

Women had less access to credit from formal channels than men do although, given the available data, the extent of the gender gap in credit is difficult to determine. Lack of collateral—partly because of weak land tenure rights—may exacerbate women's difficulty in getting as much credit as they need from formal sources.

World Bank **No. 145 October 1999**

Meanwhile changing residential patterns indicate increasing female autonomy and sole responsibility for children. As early as the sixties – a period of relatively rapid economic growth, the proportion of households recorded as headed by a woman, rose significantly (Lloyd et al. 1993:116). This situation has continued and by the end of the decade of the eighties, nearly one in three households were female headed, 'roughly one million more [such] households than would have been the case had the prevalence of female-headed households remained at the level of 1960' (ibid.). Not only had the proportion of households headed by women increased, but their marital situations had changed significantly as well over time with more women widowed or divorced and increasing numbers never married, a phenomenon which has continued to escalate to the present day. The growing proportions of Ghanaian women 'heading' households implied, 'their increasing primary economic responsibility and their growing vulnerability' (Lloyd et al. 1993:131). The rising numbers of women who were divorced or widowed was assessed as being particularly disadvantaged (ibid).

In view of policies and practices which have continued to lead to deterioration in women's economic opportunities and resources, a serious and escalating phenomenon has been the growing propensity of impoverished women, both young and more mature, to migrate alone or with others to look for wage labour and sometimes all they have found in saturated urban labour markets, and with their lack of training, is commercial sex work.

In the past, Ghana was lauded by feminist researchers as a place of relative gender equality and conjugal autonomy and in an era of sibling solidarity and strong ties of cooperation and collaboration between female kin, such relative gender equality and female conjugal autonomy could prevail, at least in southern Ghana, occupied by the Akan and Ga-Adangme, where even separate residence of spouses was the traditional norm. But in an era of spatial scattering of lineage members and rejections of sibling responsibilities and thus dwindling kin support, the opposite side of the coin has been that growing numbers of women have found themselves alone, with no husbands or kin to depend upon. This is occuring even during the most vulnerable period of their life cycle – the child bearing and rearing phase – when the multiple burdens of responsibility and physical work (both infant and child care and maintenance, domestic and subsistence work and cash earning) become too hard for a women alone to cope with.

Furthermore, not only is support of kin dwindling but sanctions brought to bear by kin are also waning. Whereas in a previous era, sexual customs such as *post partum* abstinence of mothers and pre-pubertal chastity of adolescents were closely watched, monitored and governed by co-resident kin, now such sanctions have collapsed. Beliefs and associated practices concerning harsh punishments for adulterous wives, or fines for their paramours have lost their sting and widely fallen into disuse. Taboos regarding the timing and location of sexual activity are ignored. Chaperones are avoided. Protective rules are forgotten. Fear of the supernatural sanctions brought to bear by ancestors has evaporated. The protection customarily afforded by co-resident fathers, uncles and brothers, or indeed husbands, to young nubile girls and married women, from the sexual overtures of importunate, irresponsible men, including older *"sugar daddies"* – is often not available. Labour migration, as we shall see, has separated many females from their traditional protectors.

The patterned sequence of events, marriage exchanges, rituals and transfers, preceding a publicly recognized sexual relationship between two individuals and the cementing of the set of affinal relationships between two sets of kin, and heralding the commencement of sexual congress and consequent births has been jettisoned in many cases. Consequences include the rising tide of abortions, the birth of unplanned, unwanted infants more at risk of under nourishment and deprivation, the rise in numbers of children with no known father, and the kinds of social, economic and psychological deprivation this entails.[16]

The levels of relative gender equality and female autonomy, for which Ghana was famous in the past, appear to have been disturbed by a series of socio-political events and economic fluctuations and demographic dislocations and transformations. The gendered divisions of labor have become more skewed and biased to such an extent that the wellbeing of much of the population is being put at risk. In addition, several of the essays in this volume demonstrate that shifts have occurred from moral and gift economies, based on kinship solidarity and long term reciprocity and care, to the cash nexus and commodification of life essentials, including sex. Traditional complementarities in gender roles appear to be increasingly breaking down and strain, conflict and disputes are more and more in evidence.[17]

Some of the kinds of economic and demographic transformations witnessed during the sixties and seventies have further intensified during the last two decades of the millennium, and form the ever changing backdrop for consideration of more recent evidence on changing gender roles in production and reproduction. Energy supplies have been under increasing strain and the numbers using household fuelwood have apparently increased – aggravating women's workload in finding and head loading fuel (local production of electricity has become increasingly problematic and costs of imported fuel have soared). Rural development has in many places been negligible or programs not infrequently, less than successful (eg. Kofie 1999). Much of agriculture has still remained unmechanized. Deindustrialization has set in (house building is now a major part of activity categorized as manufacturing).

A study in Ghana, carried out as part of a World Bank exercise of listening to the voices and problems of the poor, discovered a number of changes taking place in gender relations, in contexts in which environmental degradation, low wages, unemployment and massive labour migration have seriously impacted local communities. (see Narayan and Petsch 2002; Kunfaa et al. 2002). Coping strategies included diversification of livelihoods, taking on several jobs simultaneously and shouldering too heavy work burdens. In addition it was admitted or claimed that women might use sex or witchcraft to obtain money. The survey revealed that the decade of the nineties was a particularly difficult time, when problems of access, costs and dissatisfaction with services led to a marked drop in the numbers seeking or obtaining public health care. The Voices study concluded that despite their earnings, most Ghanaian women in both urban and rural communities concluded that overall they were worse off than in the past because, men were less responsible towards their families and were drinking more and because it was more difficult for everyone to earn a living. Meanwhile, indications were provided of more widespread violence against women, including forced sex, perpetrated by frustrated men, unable to fulfill their economic responsibilities to their wives and children.

Migration: Impacts on Gender Roles

Certain changing statistics provide the overall parameters of the speed of demographic transformations ongoing during the period. Migration in particular escalated. Migration has been a feature of Ghanaian life and economy since time immemorial. As Caldwell noted, 'Ghanaians have been conspicuously mobile for most of the [past] century' (Caldwell 1968: 362). In the post World War 1 period, the growth of the urban population was 'rapid,' partly fuelled from within but also from without (Caldwell 1968: 361). Indeed by 1960, 'almost a fifth of the urban population was of foreign origin' (ibid.) During the 1980's and 1990's migration flows (from, to and within Ghana and Sub-Saharan Africa) increased considerably, fuelled by, 'economic impoverishment; environmental degradation and alterations in the natural resource base; climatic change (including droughts) and population pressure' (C.

Oppong & Wery 1994: 19). As a result, people were forced to migrate in search of, 'often elusive and mainly insecure and poorly paid employment' (ibid).

The rapid rate of rural-urban movement is attested by the speed of urbanization which continues at a very fast rate in Ghana, as elsewhere in the region (percent urban – 29% in 1970; 36% in 1995 and an estimated 48% in 2015). However, movement is not all towards urban areas nor is it necessarily predominantly or even half male. In the past, male rural urban migration left a predominance of females in some rural areas as in the rest of the region with serious implications for agricultural labour and women's part in it. But women are now also increasingly mobile and at least one analysis has shown that in the late eighties to nineties there were more female than male migrants and the majority were in agricultural related activities (Canagarajah & Thomas 1997). Autonomous female migration may even outnumber associa-tional migration. More younger females are moving longer distances and going directly to Accra compared to thirty years ago (eg. Seljflot 1999). Clearly, each decade has its own unique patterns of movement linked to prospects and opportunities for jobs and incomes. A cumulative change appears to be the rising ability and propensity of younger, single women (the ones likely soon to be mothers) to move alone or with friends. There is even increased evidence of children traveling without parents – a phenomenon unheard of a generation before.

The escalating rate of migration, in contexts of increasing impoverish-ment, landlessness and underemployment, the widespread mobility of females and males looking for jobs and incomes, has continued to dislocate the traditional gender divisions of labour and responsibilities in homes and farms. Now female labour burdens both on and off farms are often even greater than ever and women's autonomy often even more exaggerated than before.

The relationships and pathways of influence of labour migration on gender roles include effects upon the age and sex composition of populations and the erosion of kin and community sanctions on familial and sexual behaviour. Both of these types of changes bring people together in new contexts in which both innovation and deviance are possible and observed (C. Oppong and Wery 1994: 20). Evidence from studies on sexual behavior and networking, suggest that the relationships between increased human mobility, urbanization and sexual behavior are multiple. For example, an overall in-crease in the numbers of sexual partners over the lifetime is one observable outcome. In addition, new ideas of what constitutes 'acceptable patterns of sexual behavior' are apparent (ibid).

The implications and impetus for migration and the gendered and public health dimensions of such, are themes taken up in several of the essays in this volume. These themes – particularly the commodification of sex are as relevant today – in the context of the devastating HIV/AIDS epidemic as they first were in the colonial period – the time when syphilis and gonorrhea became problematic.

A significant consequence of periods of economic uncertainty is that they have led individuals to migrate away from rural Ghana to urban centers and neighboring countries or even further afield, as Amma Darko describes in *Beyond the Horizon*. This in turn has led to the dislocation of kin groups and the separation of individuals from their customary sources of support and traditional social control mechanisms. Increasing gender inequalities and power differences and exploitation of the weak are observed, as are breakdown of *post partum* sexual abstaining rules and child spacing rules and related taboos. This, leads to the need for responsible partners to continually reconsider sex and contraception and to renegotiate terms of engagement.

In many cases, the migration and spatial and social dislocation of populations is leading to the breakdown of traditional moralities and to cultural transformations old customs and rites in new guises with transformed meanings. There are frequent examples of rising fears of men about women's access to resources and freedom from male control. Meanwhile, escalating insecurity and anxiety at all levels is leading to public expressions of frustration, despair and anger.

THE CASE STUDIES

The case studies begin with an historical, macro-level exploration of mobility, sexuality and the spread of sexually transmitted diseases STD's (and latterly AIDS) in twentieth century southern Ghana. Akyeampong and Agyei-Mensah's chapter, *Itinerant Gold Mines*, firmly situates the history of STD's within a context of changing gender relations. It looks at the links between male and female sexuality, material accumulation and the history of STDs in twentieth century Ghana, building on earlier studies of the history of disease and medicine in colonial Ghana. As the authors note, the contemporary focus on HIV/AIDS has drawn attention to other sexually transmitted diseases, as HIV transmission in the region is mainly through heterosexual relations.

Significantly, people suffering from untreated STDs are more vulnerable to HIV infection. The authors, an historian and a medical geographer, draw on methods and insights from both disciplines in this essay in which they try to situate the history of STDs in Ghana in the context of the broader history of gender relations. They accordingly attempt an exploration of the culture and sexuality of the Akan, Ga-Adangme and Ewe peoples – and the 'political and moral economy' of sex. They consider the relevance of the cultural norms that form the basis of sexual relations. These include the marked segregation of conjugal role relationships, including financial arrangements and resource control already referred to. They go beyond the focus on commercial sex workers and single women and point to more complex cultural, social and economic factors which push women into seeking money for sex. Thus, they note pressures on mothers to provide for their children, resulting from the absence of responsible fathers and husbands and the long traditions of female trade, often involving travel already noted above. They set out to explore indigenous notions or understandings of travel, wealth and accumulation and the links between mobility of both women and men and the transmission of STDs and HIV. They challenge the commonly held belief that itinerant females were and are responsible for the spread of STD's (and AIDS) and advocate for a, 're-conceptualization of gender relations where mobility, sexuality and accumulation are concerned.' They sift historical evidence from earlier times to show that both urbanization and commercial sex work existed in pre-colonial times, noting how male discourse on the incidence of STDs in the colonial Gold Coast often blamed mobile women who went to towns to trade or who were financially self sufficient and refused to marry. But as they emphasize, medical records from the colonial period show that mobile men were also responsible. Thus, they conclude that it is the interaction between men eager to pay for sex and women willing to accommodate male needs in return for financial gain that creates the volatile situation that facilitates STDs. They accordingly underline the fact that we need to look beyond pro-stitution in our diagnosis of routes for the transmission of STDs. The colonial context was very influential in this regard. Labour migration was promoted on a massive scale. Law and order and infrastructure facilitated travel, while trade and employment opportunities attracted traders and migrant workers. As they noted, the ethic of accumulation for women and men was already present in the southern Ghanaian cultures. Meanwhile male biases in access to land, labour and credit pushed women further into trading and so they traveled in even greater numbers.

The gender irony is thus highlighted that in colonial and post-colonial towns, women in order to survive sometimes felt forced to exploit financially the very sexuality that rural men sought to control. A problem was that women lacked the educational and artisanal skills needed for salaried and wage labour. The services they could provide were domestic and sexual. Meanwhile, in the last quarter of the twentieth century, due to increasing adult male migration, more and more women were left providing for domestic groups, basically, their children and food poverty began to be documented especially, in such households.

Another important development they trace is the rapid growth of towns inhabited preponderantly by male labour migrants (miners and others), which became poles of attraction for women who sold sexual services. Thus they conclude that it was a combination of young men and women seeking to escape rural male dominance, plus wage employment opportunities and the possibility to indulge in sex outside marriage in the impersonal towns that facilitated the spread of STDs in the colonial Gold Coast. A result was that men accused women, especially traders of spreading STDs and women who did not marry were accused of being selfish and wicked. However, as they rightly stress, massive economic and demographic transformations were impacting both gender and generational relations and both syphilis and gonorrhoea were firmly embedded in the twentieth century political economy. Historical evidence tracing the evolution of these diseases to the pre-colonial era is presented, indicating the significance for their spread of towns, trade, economic developments and mobile labour. Venereal diseases were spread across the Gold Coast with the movement of migrant labourers along the expanded network of colonial roads and railways. Migrant labourers who traveled south to work in mines and farms spread the diseases in their families and communities on their return home. It was in the mid eighties with the onset of the spread of HIV/AIDS that interest in STDs was renewed. This chapter thus provides an important historical backcloth for situating the HIV/AIDS epidemic and the challenges it now poses, advocating the need to take into account the effects on gender roles of mobility and the desire to survive and accumulate. It underlines the necessity of understanding the political, economic, social and cultural forces at play in affecting sexual relations and the directions and speed of spread of sexually transmitted diseases.

The Eastern Region of Ghana – historically and today – is the region with the highest incidence of HIV in the country. It is also the region with the highest relative rates of female out-migration and in popular perception, the women of this region are reputed to be exceptionally beautiful. Meanwhile the Krobo peoples of this region maintain the most well known and 'enduring' initiation rites in Ghana. The rites known as *dipo* mark young girls' social 'transition into womanhood' and are an 'indispensable part of Krobo women's gender identity'. They therefore mark the beginning of a woman's sexual life. The relevance of the rites to contemporary Ghanaian life is hotly contested and much criticized – particularly in Christian circles – where the young ages and bare breasts of the initiates lead some to view the rites as providing a 'catalyst of teenage pregnancies, prostitution and further immoral behavior.' Accordingly, the title of chapter 2, '*A license to indulge in premature sexual activities?*' *Dipo and the image of Krobo women,* speaks to these concerns. The description of *dipo* initiation rites demonstrates the continuing strength of traditional norms and customary practices concerning the teaching of sex and gender roles and intimately affecting the growth of adolescents and their future adult life choices and life courses. The story Steegstra unfolds includes the fact that a consequence of underdevelopment, unemployment and out-migration of adult men in the Krobo area is that women too have joined the migration throng. In fact, many have gone to Abidjan, the capital of neighbouring Cote d'Ivoire, for some time the sub regional epicenter of both labour migration from surrounding countries and the AIDS epidemic. Abidjan is like those urban centres of an earlier era described in chapter one, in which a developing economy attracts single male migrant wage labourers, who are later followed by female migrants, who provide some of the domestic and sexual services required.

The initiation rites for Krobo girls, which are the subject of this chapter are celebrated each year for an estimated several thousand girls in Odumase and Somanya in the Eastern Region. Sex before undergoing the ceremony is a taboo which formerly resulted in being banned and becoming an outcast. Critics are concerned that the rites promote sexual promiscuity and contribute to the prevalence of AIDS. Others argue that *dipo* could contribute to prevent the spread of HIV and AIDS by integrating sexual education into the rites. It is claimed that the ceremonies have lost their function as girls even as young as two years have been initiated.

Steegstra's view is that an historical and dynamic approach is needed to understand dipo and that its meaning has always been changing in different contexts. Now she argues that it is especially linked to Krobo identity. Two questions she investigates are why *dipo* is so contested and what is its connection with a negative moral image of Krobo women. To answer these questions, she looks at the way colonial encounters with protestant missionaries of the Basel mission in particular have shaped the context within which *dipo* developed, indicating that the negative stereotypes of sexual immorality were reinforced during contacts with the Christian missionaries. She looks to the recent economic hardships suffered and the consequent mobility of labour to help understand the relatively high incidence of HIV/AIDS among Krobo women. The region used to be a booming agricultural production centre in the colonial times, but more recently, following loss of cash crops and land, the young have become doomed to unemployment and a meager existence on the fringes of underemployment.

The *dipo* ceremonies are vividly depicted (see Steegstra 2005). Since they are a precondition for sex, marriage and motherhood, one of their main themes is fertility, expressed in several of the rituals performed and associated symbols. Other themes are ritual cleanliness and belonging to Krobo society, symbolized by use of traditional artifacts, beads and foods. The rituals can only be performed in the home towns.

Steegstra examined Basel Mission reports from 1857 to 1917 which have many references to *dipo* which was seen by the missionaries as a major cause of immorality and a major obstacle to the Christian conversion of Krobo women. An aspect of *dipo* which the missionaries found objectionable was that *dipo* rites, not marriage were the prerequisite for sex and pregnancy. Children born before marriage belonged to the mother's father's patrilineage, whereas the missionaries considered such children illegitimate. As she notes, many missionaries passed on a very negative image of the Krobo, their heathen world and *dipo*. Subsequently, the Presbyterian church continued the same attitude to Krobo rituals. However attempts to ban *dipo* did not succeed but caused some profound changes in the ceremony and contributed to the negative moral image of Krobo women. Alongside the story of *dipo* is that of the economic fortunes of Krobo women and the pressures on them to migrate and work in the catering and hotel service sector, when the Akosombo dam was built, creating the Volta Lake for hydro electricity in the sixties and when land was inundated and thousands of people were displaced. When the construction workers left, women migrated to work in Accra, Kumasi and further afield abroad. From their hospitality work they built houses back home. Steegstra followed some of the women to Abidjan to see the kind of trade they were plying. Her conclusion is that among the Krobo, prostitution appears to have become more rampant during the 60s, 70s and early 80s mainly as a result of economic and demographic pressures. Meanwhile *dipo* rites have persisted even after more than 150 years of constant condemnation because they are deeply embedded in Krobo history and culture and remain an important marker of Krobo identity. She however notes that blaming these rituals for the spread of HIV/AIDS solves nothing.

The third chapter has some clear similarities in that it also deals with ancient rites concerned with transitions in gender status and new troubles resulting from cross border migration. It focuses on mounting sexual vulnerability in a south western location on route to Abidjan. It is about *Marital Morality and Sexual Vulnerability in Ellembelle Nzema Society* by Douglas Frimpong Nnuroh. It draws attention to potential linkages between the breakdown of traditional sexual moralities and related practices, beliefs and ritual sanctions ensuring chastity and the escalating HIV/AIDS incidence in the communities studied. Proximity to Abidjan, the AIDS epicenter in the sub region, is viewed as having serious health implications for the frequent cross border, female travelers. The author offers a detailed cultural case study, a problem oriented ethnography of changing conjugal sexual morality and the actions and conditions, which constitute a breach in the moral code. Sexual vulnerability and the sexual transmission of death are approached through discussions of pre-marital sexual relations, polygyny, adultery, migration and contraceptive choice. Culturally specific practices such as the ritual cleansing and sexual rituals that Ellembelle Nzema perform, to shed the state of ritual impurity occasioned by female adultery are described. The underdevelopment, poverty and consequent migration and break up of traditional institutions are seen as fuelling and facilitating the health crisis. Ironically, the people are depicted as being impoverished in the midst of abundant natural resources.

Traditional society from the past is painted as chaste and restrained, with no sex for girls before the performance of puberty rites and fidelity, at least for women, within marriage. Formerly, ritual purification was required by any cuckolded husband. Such practices have now decayed and as Nnuroh notes, migration and the mobility of people and urban life in larger communities with their characteristic anonymity has opened the floodgates for anomie, so that now, extra marital sexual activities go unnoticed, unchecked and unsanctioned. Meanwhile the rationality of certain beliefs has been called into question. Unemployed, dependent husbands appear helpless in the face of their wives' autonomous socializing activities. Educated wives challenge their husbands and some women traders are widely known to use sexual favours to gain economic advantage. The author accordingly claims that within the past decades, there has been a profound shift in sexual morality and behaviour, from a situation in which infractions of rules preserving female chastity and faithfulness were very publicly sanctioned, to more accommodating, if not lax sexual scenarios, which have their own repercussions for health and survival. And as he stresses, the idea that sexual promiscuity brings disease and possible death remains a salient societal motif. In the meantime, certain new risk factors as well as traditional beliefs and practices are viewed as facilitating the spread of STDs, including HIV. One is the traditional perception that sex between people who intend to marry is permissible. Another is the new lifting of the sexual restraints on the youth, who have much more freedom and lack social control in contrast with the past. In addition, sex has become something which can be bought and sold unlike the past, when according to Nnuroh, it was perceived as imbued with moral precepts and spiritual beliefs. Now youths can acquire money and pay for sex and faithful wives are at risk from the behaviour of philandering husbands. Monogamy does not guarantee sexual safety or reproductive health for either man or woman. Meanwhile the freer behaviour of mature formerly married women constitutes a risk for themselves, and any of their partners, as does the continuing practice of widow inheritance.

A key risk factor is the escalating mobility of women, who lack employment and economic security or kin or conjugal support and go to Abidjan to seek their fortunes. Women working in Abidjan are able to send money home to their dependent children- a great spur to risk prone travel. At the annual Kundum festival travelers return for the week long festivals. Hospital records of the escalating incidence of STDs and HIV tell the unfortunate outcomes.

In chapter 4, *Fat Money, Thin Body,* Irene Korkoi Odotei describes the lives of people in coastal fishing communities, their national and inter-national mobility, their marriages, family relations and potential vulnerabi-lity, due to the risk prone nature of some of the transient contexts in which they live and the altering roles they play. This case study highlights graphic-ally the widespread sexual risks encountered by people whose economic livelihoods entail perpetual mobility and the ways in which sexual relations have customarily been intimately interwoven with gendered divisions of labour and resources and reciprocity between females and males. Two decades ago, Hagan (1983) and Vercruijsse (1983) had shown among Effutu and Fanti fishermen and fishmongers how the family economy rests on the gender division of labour based on sex and conjugal cooperation, affected by latent or manifest conjugal conflict, – since only men go to sea and only women smoke, dry and sell fish.[18] Hagan had described the mobility of the Winneba fishmongers and the seasonality of fishing and seasonal separation of spouses linked to patterns of polygyny and divorce. The incidence of the last was shown to fluctuate with the fishing cycle. Meanwhile polygyny was a reaction to enforced conjugal separation. This chapter illustrates the individual strategies women and men adopt to survive and prosper, in this continually changing and insecure environment, characterized by international, chain migration of family members. Individuals have to continually adapt to new challenges of changing fishing methods and techniques; local environmental or political crises and familial ambitions and constraints. Women and men can become individually wealthy and express their ambitions in terms of new liaisons and more marriages and accumulation of offspring. However this mobile pursuit of fat money and reproductive success can lead unfortunately to reproductive disease and death in the era of HIV/AIDS.

Chapter 5, *Intimate Bargains: Sex Workers and Free Women Negotiate their Sexual Space* by Akosua Adomako Ampofo, relates the preceding discussions of vulnerability, migration, the 'transmission of death' and the, 'material bases of the relations that organize sexual behavior' to an examination of how sexual practice may be negotiated between women and their commercial and other sex partners. It uses a woman-centered perspective to explore the concept of 'safe sex' – especially condom use – and to analyze whether women feel 'entitled' to determine how sex is practiced, including activities generally considered deviant or abnormal in Ghana in the era of HIV/AIDS. The author notes that while examining sexual relations is a complex affair by the end of the field work and even before detailed analysis was carried out, she became aware that for many women the issues at stake were fairly simple. They had a financial need and believed that given their limited options, that need could best be met through transactional sex. She observes that while not every sexual contact of unmarried women in Ghana can be considered commercial, sexual intercourse tends to be regarded as something that is obtained by favours or by bargaining and that economic pressures provide the background for most sexual relationships from which material gain is expected. Consequently, Ghanaian women who bargain sex for material gain may find it difficult to propose sexual behaviour change and so for these women, she argues, the dilemma they face may be one of choosing between economic survival and unsafe sex. The common imbalance of power in the sexual relationship, as she remarks, makes it odd that safe sex messages aimed at changing sexual behaviour, have generally ignored the gender imbalance in which sexual relations are rooted. The study which she describes was carried out among three groups of Ghanaian women in the early nineties in Kumasi, Accra and Abidjan and was designed to look at reproductive and sexual knowledge, attitudes and beliefs and how they related to AIDS-preventive behaviour. Like the earlier authors, she notes how greater anonymity in these urban centres has enabled sexual relations to be less formalized and binding and subject to less scrutiny or interference from relatives or neighbours. She refers to the evidence that Ghanaian women have been commercial sex workers in Abidjan from as far back as the 1940s and that by the early nineties migration was recognized as an important correlate of HIV infection. Copious quotations are given of women's statements about sex (styles and aberrations), men, condoms and relationships, giving unusual and unique insights into women's sexual activities and gender roles.

The author's description of women's attempts to negotiate safe and meaningful sex for themselves and their partners concludes that sex workers seem more inclined to feel entitled to safe and traditional sex and less willing to compromise in these issues in their sexual relations with clients. Adomako's conclusion is that the implications of women's behaviours for their vulnerability and the continued spread of AIDS are grave. She emphasizes that so long as some women do not feel as entitled to safe sex, as they feel men are entitled to satisfying sex, the focus of AIDS education on persuading women to get their partners to use condoms is bound to fail. In the meantime, women need some kind of new method to protect them and keep them alive, giving great urgency to current trials in the region of new female controlled, potentially protective vaginal cream and the need for more widespread use of female as well as male condoms.

Explorations of the discussions and decisions regarding intimate relations between sexual partners are further extended and explored, mainly in the context of marriage, in the next chapter by John Anarfi, *Talking and Deciding about Sex and Contraception in Ashanti Towns*. This chapter presents and discusses both men and women talking about sex and sexuality, and the ways and means through which they initiate and talk about sex. As the author notes, ideally, a rational process of decision making about reproductive health issues and family size should involve communication between husbands and wives, but often little communication is reported. Yet knowledge about choice and communication is needed as a basis for the design of programmes to promote reproductive health, as is greater understanding of norms and practices, especially in cultural situations where in the past conjugal roles have been segregated, marital relationships relatively fragile and kin ties more close and enduring. His findings include the increasing fragility of marital bonds in the Ashanti communities studied and the continuing need to contain possible conflicts with matrikin and at the same time a persistent effect on behaviour of public approval and disapproval. Fears of female infidelity affect husbands' attitudes to contraceptive use and there is a disturbing communication barrier between parents and their adolescent children and indeed between the older and younger generations as a whole. In fact parents do not give their children any form of sex education, in a situation where the young consider their parent's ideas are outdated anyway. As the author notes both young and old remain in dire need of better up to date information, not to mention counseling, if they are to protect themselves and their partners and make better informed decisions affecting reproductive outcomes and health.The following chapter takes up this theme of adolescent ignorance and lack of guidance.

Chapter 7 by Doris Essah is entitled *School Children Learning about Sex and Love*. It is set in the Akan area, Akropong Akwapim to be precise. This chapter presents the daily life experiences, constraints and aspirations of Junior Secondary School pupils in a town where education for both boys and girls has been encouraged for over 150 years, and residents experience the influences of both urban and rural life. The account begins with the case of a fostered, pregnant school girl of eighteen, who has been prevented from attending classes but will be allowed to sit her examination. The young people's lives are characterized by limited access to books, information and advice on a topic they are very interested in – sex. Meanwhile they often express their adolescent emotions in love letters to each other and complain that adults will often not talk freely to them about maturation and reproduction. TV and films are major sources of information and influence. When a school girl gets pregnant, neither she nor her mother or guardian can go out freely. She can only do that either at dawn or dusk with head averted. While pregnant, she is punished but after birth there are celebrations. The children's testimonies showed their readiness to try false herbs or other more lethal remedies such as potions of ground bottles to cause abortions, or even to go to hospital to seek the same. Some teachers said there were not many recorded cases of pregnancy among the school children because pregnant girls cover up their state by wearing sweaters and saying they are ill till they cause an abortion. These findings from encounters with pupils and teachers in an area where schools have been established for a century and a half point to serious gaps in the sexual education of school children at the end of the nineties, which does not augur well for adolescent reproductive health at the turn of the millennium. The ready recourse to abortion as a solution to unwanted conception was subsequently confirmed by the results of the 2003 Ghana Demographic and Health Survey.

In Chapter 8, attention swings from the problems of the young to the experiences of the elderly. In *"It is a tiresome work": Love and Sex in the Life of an Elderly Kwahu Woman'*, Sjaak Van der Geest discusses intimate experiences of one single individual, an old Akan woman, a farmer and trader. She has lived and worked in several communities. She has had ten children, three marriages and, 'a lot of experience with men.' Through verbatim quotations – excerpts from her life history – we learn personal details about her life and her experiences of love and sex and the cross-cutting themes of strength, desire and beauty. The author notes the frequent material bases of intimate, heterosexual relationships. Once more we are reminded that sex and love were not traditionally expressed or discussed in public, making sexual education almost entirely the work of peers (possibly an important message for the design of contemporary reproductive health and sex education programs). Incidentally, Van der Geest reminds us that at least until very recently there was little information available in the public domain about Ghanaian sexual preferences and practices and that the information that existed was mainly confined to the norms or rules and taboos. There was little documentation of actual lived experience. Now as he notes, the emphasis is on sexual relations as risk factors for the transmission of HIV. His task is to look at the expressions of love and attraction which are normally hidden (other than perhaps in songs) and discussion of sex which might seem a taboo subject particularly among the elderly. In actual fact, in his research among the Kwahu (Akan) on old age, he found out that elderly men spoke enthusiastically about sex, while elderly women complained of lack of strength and publicly expressed their apparent disinterest. In fact the elderly are supposed to remain sexually restrained and disciplined in their desires. The community in which he worked is characterized by a high level of spatial mobility – trading to accumulate goods and wealth. When he interviewed her, Nana Dedaa, the subject of the chapter, was living in her home town. She discusses different types of love and liking, polygyny, co-wives, compensation for adultery, public comportment of couples (no kissing or show of affection in public), care of a spouse, the pleasure of sweethearts and lovers (interesting conversation and play); divorce, male irresponsibility among the youth, love potions etc. Van der Geest argues that the material basis of love is a repeated theme and that love is proven in the faithful daily provision of money and food and presents. Faithfulness is viewed more as a matter of persistent economic support than of sexual restriction. (Nana Dedaa clearly indicates that a husband or wife who cannot be sexually satisfied by their partner, for reasons of weakness, sickness or old age, should be allowed to go outside for satisfaction). Reciprocity is viewed as at the base of conjugal relations. Meanwhile, children and their upbringing are the main reason for marriage. She remains ambivalent about the excitement of love affairs in contrast to what might be a boring but devoted marital relationship. Meanwhile sex is seen as night work that an older woman may be too tired to undertake, if she has been working all day. Even a younger woman may want less of it than she gets, in view of her probably heavy daily workload!

In the remaining chapters, the themes shift from an explicit consideration of sex, sexuality and sexual relationships, to considerations of gendered identities and matters relating to 'womanhood' and 'manhood'. The chapters deal with perceptions, beliefs and representations and are often concerned with a society which – in the words of chapter 11 – is 'paralyzed by its own superstition.' Indeed, there is evidence from many quarters that superstitions and beliefs in supernatural forces such as witchcraft are escalating, as people daily face new problems, new anxieties, cultural traumas and dilemmas, often without the traditional sources of kin group support and security which they once enjoyed. Through an examination of popular fiction, songs, feature films and beliefs concerning unusual, supernatural phenomena the various authors below look at the perceived roles and ideas regarding the actions, resources, power and responsibilities of Ghanaian women and men in the past two decades and also how they appear to have been changing.

Thus, Chapter 9 by Susan Drucker Brown, *Mamprusi Witchcraft, Subversion and Changing Gender Relations*, deals with an escalating phenomenon in Ghana and the region, witchcraft beliefs and related practices, this time in the north, in the traditional kingdom of Mamprussi. The author is able to give historical depth to her account on the basis of field work spanning four decades of change. She indicates how alterations in traditional royal power and economic transformations and altering gender roles have been reflected in the changing theory and practice of witchcraft. Thus she documents changes in witchcraft beliefs and argues that these can be seen as a response to the increasing autonomy of women in the sexual division of labour and loss of control by Mamprussi men of the local economy. A changing balance of power is observed both between the central and local government and also between women and men in the political, economic and domestic domains. Significantly over time she notes a shift in the main population of witches' villages. At first, they mainly comprised women from other ethnic groups. Now they are mainly inhabited by Mamprussi women. She also observes a change in the way witches are caught and royal involvement in this enterprise, as well as changes in beliefs about what witches actually do. In recent times they are believed to change their victims into little helpless creatures (insects). Moreover, by the nineties, they were believed to be much more serious and pervasive than they were forty years before.

Significantly, women are more mobile and increasingly involved in trade. They are accordingly thought to have more opportunity to become involved in witchcraft activities and to make money by trading with the wealthier south. Meanwhile, at home, the demand for cash has escalated and men are losing their former monopolies of key assets, – education, transport and live-stock. In addition there is a loss of confidence observed in the power to counteract the witches. Drucker Brown concludes that Mamprussi witchcraft accusations can be seen as significant attempts to control the behaviour of women, who are viewed by men as increasingly difficult to control. Women are traditionally expected to be submissive and subservient to men and to senior women, but because of economic pressure they farm, travel and trade, in order to provide for their families. She sees their growing autonomy, paralleled by increasing male frustration and fear of witchcraft, as an indicator of the importance of the normally hidden female hierarchy. Belief in the increased frequency and virulence of witchcraft, as well as new ways of dealing with witches, are viewed not so much as mirroring a change in the nature of female power as a loss of control by Mamprusi men over their own economic and political environment. Men now need women's economic support. Women have the chance to be increasingly autonomous yet ideally, traditionally should be controlled by men. Meanwhile, Mamprusi men have always thought of women as potentially subversive. Drucker Brown argues that the fear of witchcraft has grown as men's dependence on women has increased. Accordingly, this essay provides rich and well documented evidence of economic and cultural changes in gender relations over a period of forty or more years and their social, psychological and political implications.

Ghanaian womanhood is the subject of Sutherland-Addy's chapter 10, *Fear Woman: The Image of Womanhood in Ghanaian Popular Performance Arts*. This essay explores the image of women in popular performance and argues that the saying 'fear woman' epitomizes and characterizes misogynis-tic, psychological and social tendencies. Using two forms of popular art, namely highlife songs and feature video films, she documents the different and often contradictory and ambiguous tendencies in the views of women and woman-hood. On the one hand, women are positively portrayed and revered for their reproductive capacities and maternal care, as being the source of life and sustenance, but on the other hand, there are more numerous portrayals of women painted as evil and as victims to be feared. Thus, she contrasts the praise poetry of Akan dirges, as recorded by J. H. Nketia, which reveals that women are frequently the subject of high-sounding classic praise, in which their roles are highlighted and given deep significance in public life. In contrast are the popular sayings and idiomatic expressions which intensify the impression that women are feeble minded and inconsiderate and want to gain easy access to wealth and status etc., after the men have toiled to achieve these. In fact she concentrates on the perpetuation and accentuation of the negative aspects of the feminine persona in two main performance genres, the first being highlife and the second, video films.

She notes that after viewing a considerable sample of Ghanaian video films, one is likely to come away with the same sense of overwhelming evil, malevolence and at best passive aquiescence to abuse associated with women. What is more, many plots make women victims of their own envy, greed and stubbornness as is found in the story telling tradition. It is instructive that most of the time the independent minded woman also pays dearly for her independence, for it is depicted as either a grievous misjudgement or fatal stubbornness.

Women who try to breach the bounds of their secure environment, by being adventurous or independent immediately face irreversible ruin. Women are also viewed as the embodiment of evil. As Sutherland-Addy concludes, viewing most of the video features as didactic moral narratives, womankind takes its place in the trinity of deadly traps: Drink, Money and Women. And as she ironically notes, this approach is absolutely in line with the popular view even promulgated from the pulpit, whereby men are counselled against the false allure of "*Nsa, sika, ne mmaa*", (Drink, money and women). (Yet females are the majority of church goers listening to such sermons!). Thus her chapter shows how film makers and highlife composers have exploited, amplified and entrenched the view that a woman is to be feared if one wishes to live long.

Chapter 11 *Pawns and Players*, explores the tragic fates that can befall

Ghanaian women, through an examination of the lives of three female protagonists in two of Amma Darko's novels. The authors of this chapter, Kari Dako, Helen Yita & Aloysius Denkabe, note at the outset that according to Amma Darko, it is hazardous, even dangerous to be a female in Ghana – you might end up as Mara in *Beyond the Horizon*; a physical and psychological wreck of a whore, addicted to drugs, owned by your pimp, or you may be declared a 'witch,' the fate of numerous older women.

They describe Amma Darko's feminism as unconscious in that it lacks a political edge and tends to dwell on the wider issue of the quality of social relations between women and men in contemporary society. They take her feminism to be cultural rather than political and see it as linked to her view of the Ghanaian, male as well as female – a sinister and cynical view related in her narratives. They describe how the life-stories of her female protagonists are told with little compassion or show of female solidarity. Her characters are allowed to speak for themselves, make their own choices or let themselves be manipulated into having decisions made for them. They see her work as cultural criticism of Ghanaian society.

Beyond the Horizon is the life story of Mara, who leaves the village and follows her husband to Germany, where he is bigamously married to a German woman. He forces Mara into prostitution to become her pimp and uses what she earns in the brothel to maintain his Ghanaian girlfriend in comfort and style. In the *Housemaid*, female characters and their stories are still central, but these are users of men, as well as victims of male exploitation. In her novels, as Ghanaians show no compassion for each other, so there are no constraints on them in their self-serving quest for wealth and power. The authors argue that Darko's female characters essentially use four specific survival strategies – fertility, sex, subservience and exploitation. Fertility as a tool is employed by almost every female in *The Housemaid*. Thus, Tika's mother, Sekyiwa, to get hold of a wealthy man to set her up in business, uses sex and fertility to trap him. She gets herself pregnant to strengthen her hold on him in order to exploit him. When she has achieved what she wants, she discards him. Efia is told by her grandmother to get pregnant in order to inherit Tika's wealth. In both novels, sex is used as a means of control. In *Beyond the Horizon*, the men use sex to manipulate their women. Mara supports Akobi, his girlfriend, Comfort and herself as a prostitute, thus Ghanaian men earn their living by sexually exploiting their women. In *The Housemaid* it is the women who control their men through sex. Sex is also a means to income in Germany and is a means of exchange in Ghana.

Significantly in Amma Darko's novels, schools appear irrelevant. The women do not invest in education neither for themselves nor for their children. Tika drops out of school and is rewarded with financial assistance from her mother to get started in business. Wealth is obviously more important than education for women, a fact which is supported by the evidence in the GDHS 2003, at least with regard to women's decision making power. Control of cash income counts and gives women power (Oppong 2005). Many higher educated women do not earn any income and so have to depend on men.

Kari Dako and colleagues argue that Amma Darko's writing reflects the angst in contemporary Ghanaian society – and that the themes she chooses echo the stories that we read daily in the Ghanaian press. For the headlines scream of "abandoned babies, brutalised and murdered women: wives, mothers, daughters, sisters, girlfriends; of ritual executions, of incest and rape, of sale of children; of child labour and of a general degeneration of society into one of oppression and violence".

The chapter sheds light on the mainly hidden, dark side of change – exploitation and abuse – in a globalizing world. Ultimately, the view of Ghanaian society presented here is a very pessimistic one, as are the portrayals of male-female relationships, based as they are on rampantly opportunistic, materialistic and consumerist tendencies.

Brigid Sackey's essay, chapter 12, *The Vanishing Sexual Organ Phenomenon*, examines a recurring series of apparently supernatural events, which swept through Ghana (and indeed West Africa) in early 1997. The episode involved extensive reports about the existence of people with special spiritual powers, who could apparently cause the disappearance, shrinking or stealing of the sexual organs of other persons, simply by touching any part of the victim's body. The mass hysteria and public lynchings that ensued are explored in the context of renewed evangelism, as well as the prevailing social, economic and religious stresses of the day. The phenomenon was most prevalent among men and Sackey concludes with a discussion of the power relationships between the sexes and their probable contribution to the superstitions surrounding the phenomenon.

Finally Phyllis Antwi and Yaa P. A. Oppong in, *Ghana's Attempts at Managing the AIDS Epidemic,* review the epidemiological evidence and analyze the changing, gendered and geographical patterns of the disease's spread. Initially women and rural dwellers were more at risk. However, recent trends indicate that the gaps between males and females and rural and urban population are narrowing. Yet policies aimed at reducing transmission and supporting the most vulnerable rarely incorporate social analyses and may perhaps inadvertently serve to perpetuate the perceived feminization of the epidemic.

End notes

1   On the apparent disruption of gender roles globally see for example the controversial view of Fukuyama (1999) and on the disruption of women's maternal roles in Ghana and elsewhere as witnessed by infant suffering and below optimal development see Oppong (1999; 2000; 2001; 2004a).

2   Roles are perceived as comprising a range of behavioural, attitudinal, legal and moral aspects and as having economic and political dimensions and spatial attributes. There are seven basic categories of gender roles adult women and men are likely to play in their social contexts. These include parental roles (mother /father), kin roles (sibling/ aunt, uncle et al.), domestic roles (in the household), occupational roles (paid and unpaid producing goods and earning income), community roles (as neighbour/citizen, political leader) and individual roles (as a self actualizing, leisure spending person). These roles have associated activities and conduct expected of them. They also have rights and prohibitions attributed to them and resources and opportunities which may be enjoyed, as well as influence and prestige they can command and power they may wield in different spheres. (see Oppong & Abu 1985).

3   For example for a brief overview of gender differences in aging in Sub Saharan Africa see Oppong (2004a).

4   See for example the seminal work of Boserup (1970) on the impact of development on women's occupational role in the region.

5   GSS (2004) provides an authoritative up to date summary of the state of the population and provides a basis for much of the recent factual information, especially demographic, presented at the beginning of the introduction.

6   Ghana was so named after the Soninke/Mande State bearing the same name.

7   See Appendix. p. 327

8   eg Fortes (1949 a & b; 1950) Tallensi and Akan; J. Goody (1954 & 1956) Lowiili and Lodagaa; E. Goody (1973) Gonja; Tait (1961) Konkomba; Field (1948, 1960) Akan and Ga; Nukunya (1969) Ewe.

9   On separate interests of Akan spouses see Oppong (1974, 1983); Abu (1983).

10 See for example the recent GDHS 2003.

11 The non cocoa crop sub sector includes cereals, roots and tubers and industrial crops, horticultural crops and other crops.

12 Crops make up nearly two thirds of agricultural GDP.

13 This involves slashing and burning forest and grassland and needs abundant land and low population density.

14 Canarajah et al. (1998) argued that the SAPs were "successful in raising living standards in the rural areas and other cities but not in Accra" and that the economic recovery program " has been judged to have been a remarkable success story".

15 Eg. Leith (1996:6) observed that by the early 1980s the country's educational and medical services functioned for all practical purposes in name only.

16 See the essays in Legon Research Review Supplement 16 (2004) Children at Risk in Ghana; Family Care under Review.

17 For descriptions of the kinds of complementarities common in the past see several of the essays in Female and Male in West Africa (ed.) C. Oppong (1983).

18 See also more recently Overa (2003) on the gendered exchange system and how gender ideologies vary considerably in fishing communities along the coast of Ghana and how for women's successful entrepreneurship a loyal and trustworthy relationship with a male partner is needed.

Bibliography

Abu K., 1983. The Separateness of Spouses: Conjugal Resources in an Ashanti Town. In Oppong (ed.), *Female and Male in West Africa*.

Adepoju A., 1983. Patterns of Migration by Sex. In Oppong C. (ed.), *Female and Male in West Africa*.

Adomako Ampofo A., 2001. The Sex Trade: Globalization and Issues of Survival in Sub Saharan Africa. *Research Review* 17.2 27-43.

Agyeman, D. K., J. B. Casterline, 2002. 'Social Organization and Reproductive Behavior in Southern Ghana' Policy Research Division. Working Paper No. 167. Population Council. New York.

Ardayfio Schaandorf E., 1993. Household Energy Supply and women's work in Ghana. In Momsen J. H. and Kinnaird V. (eds.), *Different Places, Different Voices: Gender and Development in Africa Asia and Latin America*. London: Routledge. Pp 15-29.

Asante-Darko N. and S. Van der Geest, 1983. Male Chauvinism: Men and women in Ghanaian High Life Songs. In Oppong C. (ed.), *Female and Male in West Africa*.

Avotri, J. A., V. Walters, 1999. 'You just look at our work and see if you have any freedom on earth': Ghanaian women's accounts of their work and their health. *Social Science and Medicine* 48 1123-1133.

Awumbila M., 1999. Fuelwood utilization and Conservation among Fish Processors on the Coastal Zone of Ghana. *Bull. Ghana Geog. Assoc.* no. 21.

Awumbila M. and J. H. Momsen, 1995. Gender and the Environment Women's time use as a measure of environmental change. *Global Environmental Change* Sep. 5 (4) 337-46.

Baden S., 1993. The Impact of Recession and Structural Adjustment on Women's Work in Developing Countries. *IDP Women. WP 19* International Labour Office, Geneva.

Bakker I. (ed.), 1994. *The Strategic Silence: Gender and Economic Policy.* Ottawa: Zed Press for North South Institute

Bequele A., 1980. Poverty, Inequality and Stagnation the Ghanaian experience. WEP_*Research Working Paper.* Geneva, ILO.

Blanc A. & C. B. Lloyd, 1990. Women's Childrearing Strategies in relation to fertility and Employment. In *Ghana Population Council Working Papers no. 16.* New York

Boserup E., 1970. *Women's Role in Development.* Allen and Unwin.

Brown, L. R., J. Kerr (eds.), 1997. *The Gender Dimensions of Economic Reforms in Ghana, Mali and Zambia.* Canada: The North-South Institute.

Brown, L. R., J. Kerr, 1997. Ghana: Structural Adjustment's Star Pupil?. In Brown, L. R., J. Kerr (eds.), *The Gender Dimensions of Economic Reforms in Ghana, Mali and Zambia.* Canada: The North-South Institute.

Caldwell J.C., 1969. *African Rural Urban Migration: The Movement to Ghana's Towns.* Canberra Australian National University.

Caldwell J. C. et al., 1989. The Social Context of AIDS in Sub Saharan Africa. *Population and Development Review* 15 (2) pp 185-233.

Canagarajah, S., D. Mazumdar, 1997. Employment, Labor Markets and Poverty in Ghana: A Study of Changes During Economic Decline and Recovery. *Policy Research Working Paper 1845.* The World Bank Africa Region.

Canagarajah S. and S. Thomas, 1997. Ghana's Labour market (1987-92). *Policy Research Working Paper.* World Bank.

Canagarajah, S., D. Mazumdar, X, Ye, 1998. The Structure and Determinants of Inequality and Poverty Reduction in Ghana, 1988-92. *Policy Research Working Paper.* The World Bank, Africa Region.

Chao, S. (ed.), 1999. Ghana: Gender Analysis and Policymaking for Development. *World Bank Discussion Paper. No. 403.*

Chernoff J.M., 2003. *Hustling is not Stealing: Stories of an African Bar Girl.* Chicago: University of Chicago Press.

Clark G., 2001. Gender and Profiteering: Ghana's Market Women as Devoted Mothers and 'Human Vampire Bats.' In Hodgson and McCurdy (eds.),

Collier P. and J.W. Gunning, 1999. The IMF's role in structural adjustment. *WPS/99-18 CSAE* Oxford.

Dalla Costa M. Dalla Costa G. (eds.), 1993. *Paying the Price: Women and the Politics of International Economic Strategy.* Zed Books.

Dinan C., 1983. Sugar Daddies and Gold Diggers: the White Collar Single Women in Accra. In Oppong C. (ed.), *Female and Male in West Africa.*

Fayorsey C., 2002. *Coping with Pregnancy: Experiences of Adolescents in Ga Mashi.* Accra, November.

Field M. J., 1948. *Akim Kotoku* Crown Agents for the Colonies.

Field M.J., 1960. *Search for security: an Ethno-Psychiatric Study of Rural Ghana.* London: Faber.

Fortes M. 1949a. *The Web of Kinship among the Tallensi.* London: Oxford University Press.

Fortes M 1949b. Time and Social Structure: an Ashanti case study. In M. Fortes (ed.) *Social Structure: Studies presented to A.R. Radcliffe Brown.* Oxford: Clarendon Press.

Fortes M., 1950. Kinship and Marriage among the Ashant. In A.R. Radcliffe Brown and D. Forde (eds.), *African Systems of Kinship and Marriage.* Oxford University Press.

Fortes M., 1971. *The Family: Bane or Blessing?* Open Lecture University of Ghana, Legon.

Fred-Mensah B. K., 2003. Looking up to Victims: Land Scarcity and Women's Roles in Food provisioning in the Ghana Togo Border Area. *Research Review .* Vol. *19. no 2.*

Fukuyama F., 1999. 'The Great Disruption': *Human Nature and Reconstitution of the Social Order.* Profile Books.

Ghana Statistical Service Accra and Macro (GSS),1999. Ghana Demographic and Health Survey 1998. Accra

Ghana Statistical Service (GSS) Noguchi Memorial Medical Institute (NMIMR), and ORC Macro 2004 *Ghana Demographic and Health Survey 2003* Maryland: GSS. NMIMR and ORC Macro.

Goody E., 1973. *Contexts of Kinship.* Cambridge University Press.

Goody J. R., 1954. *The Ethnology of the Northern Territories of the Gold Coast West of the White Volta.* London: Colonial Office.

Goody J.R., 1956. *The Social Organization of the Lowiili*. London.

Goody J., 1957. Anomie in Ashanti? *Africa vol. 27: 356-63*.

Goody J. (ed.), 1975. *Changing Social Structure in Ghana: Essays in the Contemporary Sociology of a New State and an Old Tradition*. London: International African Institute.

Hagan G., 1983. Marriage, Divorce and Polygyny in Winneba. In C. Oppong (ed.) *Female and Male in West Africa*.

Hodgson D. L. & S.A. McCurdy (eds.), 2001. *"Wicked" Women and the Reconfiguration of Gender in Africa*. Oxford: Currey.

Kunfaa E. Y. & T. Dogbe with H. J. MacKay and C. Marshall, 2002. Empty Pockets. In Narayan D. and P. Petesch (eds) *Voices of the Poor From Many Lands*. Oxford University Press and World Bank.

Kotey, N.A.D. Tsikata, 1998. Woman and Land Rights in Ghana. In Kuenyehia A. (ed.), *Women and Law in West Africa: Situational Analysis of some Key Issues Affecting Women*. Accra: Yamen.

Leith, J. C., 1996. 'Ghana: Structural Adjustment Experience.' *International Center for Economic Growth*, Country Studies. Number 13.

Lloyd, C., A. J. Gage-Brandon, 1993. Women's Roles in Maintaining Households: Family Welfare and Sexual Inequality in Ghana. *Population Studies*, 47: 115-131

Manuh T., 1994. Ghana: Women in the Public and Informal Sectors under the Economic Recovery Program. In Sparr (ed.)

Mikell, G., 1990. Women and Economic Development in Ghana: Fluctuating Fortunes. *Sage*, Vol. VII, No. 1: (24 – 27).

Newman, C., & S. Canagarajah, 2000. Gender, Poverty, and Nonfarm Employment in Ghana and Uganda. *Policy Research Working Paper # 2367*. World Bank

Nukunya G. K., 1969. *Kinship and Marriage among the Anlo Ewe*. London School of Economics Monographs on Social Anthropology no. 37. London: Athlone Press.

Ofori-Atta W., 1988. *Ghana: A Nation in Crisis*. Accra: Ghana Academy of Arts and Sciences.

Okali C., 1963. Kinship and Cocoa Farming. In Ghana in Oppong C. (ed.) *Female and Male in West Africa*.

Oppong C., 1973. *Growing up in Dagbon*. Ghana Publishing Corporation.

Oppong C., 1974. *Marriage among a Matrilineal Elite: A Family Study of Ghanaian Senior Civil Servants*. Cambridge Monographs in Social Anthropology No. 8, Cambridge University Press. Reprinted in 1983 as *Middle Class African Marriage*. George Allen and Unwin.

Oppong C. et al., 1975. 'Womanpower: Retrograde steps in Ghana'. In *African Studies Review*, December, Vol. XVIII, No. 3, pp. 71-84.

Oppong C., (ed.), 1983. *Female and Male in West Africa*. London: George Allen and Unwin.

Oppong C. (ed.), 1987. *Sex Roles Population and Development in West Africa*. London: Currey.

Oppong C., 1997. African Family Systems and Socio-Economic crisis. In Adepoju A. (ed.), *Family Population and Development in Africa*. Zed Press.

Oppong C., 1999. 'Infants' 'Entitlements and Babies' Capabilities: Explaining Infant Hunger. *Research Review* (Legon) vol. 15, no. 2.

Oppong C., 2000. Smiling Infants or Crying Babies. no. 2. In the *Occasional Research Paper Series*. Legon: I.A.S.

Oppong C., 2001. Globalization and the Disruption of Mother care in Sub Saharan Africa. *Research Review (Legon)Vol. 17 I*

Oppong C., 2004. Gendered Family Strategies and Responsibilities of Grandparents in Sub Saharan Africa.IAS *Occasional Research Papers Series 2000 Paper. 6* University of Ghana Legon, Accra.

Oppong C., 2004. Demographic Innovation and Nutritional Catastrophe: Change Lack of Change and Difference in Ghanaian Family Systems. In G. Thorborn (ed.) *African Families in Global Context*. Uppsala: Nordic Africa Institute.

Oppong C., 2005. Conjugal Resources, Power, Decision Making and Domestic Labour: Some Historical and Recent Evidence of Modernity from Ghanaian Families. *Occasional Research Paper No. 7* Institute of African Studies, Legon, Accra.

Oppong C. and Abu K., 1985. *A Handbook for Data Collection and Analysis on Seven Roles and Statuses of Women*. Geneva: ILO.

Oppong C. and Abu K., 1987. *Seven Roles of Women: Impacts of Education, Migration and Employment on Ghanaian Mothers*. Women, Work and Development series No. 13. Geneva: ILO.

.Oppong C. with A. Adepoju (eds.), 1994. *Gender, Work and Population in Sub Saharan Africa.*. London: Currey.

Oppong Y.P.A., 2002. *Moving Through and Passing on: Fulani Mobility Survival and Identity in Ghana*. New Brunswick USA:Transactions Publishers.

Oppong, C., and R. Wery, 1994. *Women's Roles and Demographic Change in Sub-Saharan Africa*. IUSSP Policy and Research Papers

Overo R., 2003. 'Gender Ideology and Manouvering Space for Female Fisheries Entrepreneurs Gender: Culture, Power and Resources.' *Research Review* (Legon) vol. 19. no. 2

Sparr P. (ed.), 1994. *Mortgaging Women's Lives: Feminist Critiques of Structural Adjustment.* Zed Books.

Steegstra M., 2005. *Dipo and the Politics of Culture.* Accra: Woeli Publishing Services.

Tait D,. 1961. *The Konkomba of Northern Ghana* London: Oxford University Press.

Teal F., 2000. Private Sector Wages and Poverty in Ghana 1988-1998 *WPS/2000-6 CSAE* Oxford.

Thorburn G., 2004. Prologue and Epilogue. In *Gendered Family Dynamics and Health: African Family Studies in a Globalizing World. Supplement 15 to the Research Review* (Legon)

Thorburn G. (ed.), 2004. *African Families in Global Context.* Nordisk Afrika Institut.

UNDP 1997. Ghana Human Development Report, Accra.

Vellenga D. D., 1983. 'Who is a Wife?' Legal Expressions of Heterosexual Conflicts in Ghana. In Oppong (ed.) *Female and Male in West Africa.*

Vercruijsse E., 1983. Fishmongers, Big Dealers and Fishermen: Cooperation and Conflict between the Sexes in Ghanaian Canoe Fishing. In Oppong C. (ed.), *Female and Male in West Africa.*

Ware H., 1983. Female and Male Life Cycles. In Oppong C. (ed.) *Female and Male in West Africa.*

World Bank 1999. Chao, S. (ed), Ghana: Gender Analysis and Policy Making for Development No. 145 Discussion Paper.

World Bank 2000 http://www.worldbank.org/afr/gh2.htm

World Bank 2002 *Countries: Ghana* http://www.worldbank.org

ITINERANT GOLD MINES? MOBILITY, SEXUALITY AND THE SPREAD OF GONORRHEA AND SYPHILIS IN TWENTIETH CENTURY GHANA

Emmanuel Akyeampong & Samuel Agyei-Mensah

This chapter examines the links between male and female mobility, sexuality, accumulation and the history of gonorrhea and syphilis in twentieth-century Ghana.[1] It builds on existing studies on the history of disease and bio-medicine in colonial Ghana (Patterson, 1981; Addae, 1996) and the more recent works on Sexually Transmitted Diseases (STDs) in contemporary Ghana (Pellow, 1994, 1999; Anarfi et al., 1997). The current medical focus on HIV/AIDS has drawn attention to other STDs, especially syphilis and gonorrhea, as HIV transmission in Africa is predominantly through hetero-sexual relations and untreated STD cases are more vulnerable to HIV infection.[2]

The chapter draws on the methods and insights of social history and medical geography. It situates the history of STDs in Ghana within the broader history of gender relations, examining the relevance of the cultural norms that underpin sexual relations, the existence of separate conjugal finances in marriage and male and female responsibilities in household structures and budgets. Recent studies of STDs in West African towns often focus on prostitutes and "single women", with the implicit assumption that single women facing economic hardships in towns would turn to commercial sex or strike opportunistic relations with financially endowed men (Anarfi et al., 1997; Pickering et al., 1992; Ison et al., 1992). This glosses over more complex cultural, social and economic factors, which push women into seeking remuneration for sex. In southern Ghanaian cultures for example, the cultural emphasis on the value of children and the absence of negative per-ceptions about illegitimacy make motherhood attractive even to single women. The absence of a male provider in this family context increases the pressure on women to earn money. Even in married homes, the maintenance of sepa-rate conjugal finances, and the allocation of household financial responsi-bilities to mothers and wives underpin a long tradition of market trading for southern Ghanaian women (Robertson, 1984; Clark, 1994; Greene, 1996). It is the combination of these cultural, social and economic factors, which saddle women with domestic financial responsibilities and make women in towns vulnerable to casual sex and the commercial sale of sex. This chapter explores indigenous notions or understandings of travel (including migration) and the accumulation of wealth, and the links between mobility, STDs and AIDS. It argues for a re-conceptualization of mobility, gender and sexuality, drawing attention to historical evidence that underscores the reality that men – and not just women – have become itinerant gold mines, and that female prostitution cannot become the single lens for explaining promiscuity and STDs in Ghana.[3] The next section of the chapter examines some of the cultural norms underpinning sexuality, using the Akan of southern Ghana as the major case study. In many African cultures, sexual intercourse is a spiritually charged act that is carefully regulated within marriage. A culturo-historical explanation is relevant to why and how women in southern Ghana managed to commercialize casual sex.

Culture and Sexuality in Southern Ghana

The Akan, Ga-Adangme and Ewe constitute the major ethnic groups in southern Ghana. They all belong to the Kwa linguistic group, and some cultural similarities facilitate a discussion of these three ethnic groups as a single group. The histories of these groups have also been intertwined from the pre-colonial era. But the cultures and histories of the Ga-Adangme, Ewe and Akan are not identical and caution must be exercised so as not to over-generalize. Though the Ga-Adangme and the Ewe are patrilineal, whereas as the Akan are matrilineal, patriarchy is common to all three groups and informs gender relations and sexuality. As Claude Meillassoux (1981) has argued, patriarchy revolves around the control of pubescent women. Moreover, Eugenia Herbert rightly points out that, "sexuality is too powerful a force, socially and cosmologically, to leave unregulated" (1993: 227). Culture or a people's world view influences their perceptions of sexuality. Political economy and power relations are crucial to understanding the history of sexuality in southern Ghana. Thus, the consumption of women is also an index of centralized political power. Hence, the Asantehene (king of Asante) could have up to 3333 wives, and no subject could have more wives than the king (McCaskie, 1981). It is not surprising that the state regulated adultery in pre-colonial Asante (Allman, 1996b; Akyeampong 1997). Control over stool lands and gold mines among the Akan promoted the accumulation of wealth among office holders to an extent unparalleled among the Ewe of southern Ghana, who lacked stool lands and mineral wealth. Patriarchy, wealth and political power facilitated the monopoly of women by male elders and chiefs with ambiguous implications for male-female relations, and relations between young men and their elders.

The first two social surveys conducted in urban Ghana, Sekondi-Takoradi (Busia, 1950) and Accra (Acquah, 1958), wrongly surmised that prostitution in these towns was a recent development and an urban phenomenon facilitated by the colonial political economy. Existing studies on prostitution in sub-Saharan Africa assume that urbanization promotes the anonymity considered necessary for prostitution, and that urbanization and rapid social change were themselves products of colonialism (White, 1990; Bujra, 1975; Little, 1973). Urbanization, industrialization and proletarianization thus provided the socio-economic setting for prostitution. There is some substance to these arguments, but they ignore the fact that urbanization preceded colonial rule, especially in West Africa, and that prostitutes existed in pre-colonial West Africa (Bosman, 1705).

More revealing of the cultural norms that underpinned sexual relations among the pre-colonial Akan, and the political and moral economy of sex, is the institution of "public women," whereby even a small village could corporately acquire female slaves to service the sexual needs of the young bachelors in the community (Jones, 1990; Akyeampong, 1997). Olfert Dapper (1668), Willem Bosman (1702), and Jean Godot (1704) have left vivid descriptions of these public women, detailing their recruitment, training, service and retirement in the small communities of Axim and Assini. These accounts are remarkably similar in detail despite the thirty-year gap between the descriptions of Dapper and Bosman and Godot (Akyeampong, 1997). Dapper and Bosman comment on public women (Abrakrees or Abelcre) in Axim, female slaves acquired by the chiefs and elders at the instigation of the young men. Older courtesans trained the female slaves in the deportment of their profession, and then they were initiated amidst great ceremony at the public market. The ceremony combined features of puberty, marriage, and priesthood rites, resolving the social and spiritual contradictions that marked the prescribed promiscuity of these public women (Akyeampong, 1977). These public women who were reserved for bachelors, could not demand any fees for their services outside the gifts given them by their clients, and even these token honoraria went to the king. Married men who visited these women were heavily fined. In Axim, public women enjoyed the freedom to take goods or food from homes or the market without fear of punishment (Dapper, 1668: 106; Bosman, 1705: 230). In Assini, the king increased their pensions when they were too old to work and they were allowed to live the rest of their lives in peace (Jones, 1990: 132)

It is instructive that Axim in the 1660s had a population that was probably not more than 500 inhabitants (Jones, 1990: 126, 137). It was patriarchy and polygyny that had created an artificial shortage of women and caused a serious imbalance in sex ratios. This situation could lead to a potential rupture in relations between elder men and young men, an eventuality averted through the institution of public women. Thus public women maintained the structures of gerontocracy and patriarchy, and enabled elder men to control the graduation of young men to adult status. This made young men sub-servient, as they needed the elders to assist them to marry and acquire land requisite for the status of an elder. What is striking here is that there was an explicit acknowledgement of the sexual needs of men without a concomitant recognition of a similar need for women. Female labor and sexuality were meant to be carefully controlled by men – fathers and then husbands – and directed towards production, reproduction or the satiation of male sexual needs.

Ignoring female sexual needs created the cultural perception that sex serviced only the needs of men. Hence, one puberty song among the Asante runs:

> *Osee yei, yee yei!*
> *Etwe Adwoa ei!*
> *Obi di wo, na*
> *Wamma wo ade a*
> *Ku no oo!*

> Rejoice! Rejoice!
> Vagina of Adwoa (name of girl born on Monday)
> If someone 'eats' you (has intercourse with you)
> And fails to reward you,
> Slay him (Sarpong, 1977: 24-25).

The injunction to "slay him" reflects the perceived spiritual powers of women, especially revealed in their awesome procreative abilities (Akyeampong and Obeng, 1995). The Asante refer to genitalia through euphemisms:

the vagina is alluded to as "treasure," *tano* (fetish), *or bosom keseε* ("great god").

Though sex was spiritually powerful and promiscuity dangerous, sexuality could be rewarded. Some women in towns would resort to prostitution, plumbing the cultural ethos that recognized men's sexual needs and acknowledged a woman's right to be rewarded for sex. The observance of the prerequisite rituals protected commercial sex workers from the spiritual ramifications of their hazardous occupation (Acquah, 1958: 74). Margaret Field encountered a Kumasi prostitute at a rural shrine in Brong Ahafo in 1956-7, who had come to seek the necessary spiritual protection for her profession.

As she was not married, approval was readily given to her enterprise. When I sought to know the general climate of opinion concerning this, I was told matter-of-factly, 'It is her work. When a man has to stay in a town like Kumasi one of the things he may need is a woman. Also travellers need somewhere to stay the night' (Field, 1960: 123).

Social recognition of these explicit male "needs" would expand the opportunities of female prostitution in colonial Gold Coast, and converge with an ethic of migrating in search of wealth.

Male-Female Mobility and Accumulation: Re-genderizing Itinerant Gold Mines

Exploiting sexuality for material gain has been associated with mobile women in the literature (Little, 1973; White, 1990; Naanen, 1991; Weiss, 1993). Male discourse on the incidence of STDs in the colonial Gold Coast often blamed mobile women, who frequented towns to "trade" or who were financially self-sufficient and refused to marry (Roberts, 1987; Allman, 1996). But medical records from the colonial period indicate that mobile men – porters, soldiers, sailors, migrant laborers, and traders – were equally responsible for the transmission of STDs in the Gold Coast (Patterson, 1981: 74-77). In contemporary sub-Saharan Africa, truck drivers have been identified as major transmitters of HIV/AIDS given their great mobility and lax attitudes during casual sex. We need to revise the perception that only females constitute "itinerant gold mines," and incorporate men into a broadened concept, examining the links between male-female migration, sexuality, and STD's. It is the interaction of men eager to pay for sex and women willing to accommodate male needs for financial gain, that creates the volatile situation that facilitates STDs. We need to look beyond prostitution in our diagnosis of routes for the transmission of STDs.

Colonial towns created by the colonial political economy – such as Nairobi, the Zambian Copperbelt, the Witwatersrand in South Africa, Sekondi-Takoradi, and Obuasi in Ghana – often exhibited imbalanced sex ratios, as colonial towns and the colonial economy were perceived as male domains. Old towns such as Accra and Kumasi did not exhibit such skewed sex ratios, as they did not owe their origins to colonial rule. It is at these nodal points in the colonial political economy that male and female migrants concentrated. Migration in search of wealth has ancient roots in West Africa. Importantly, as François Manchuelle (1996) reminds us, it was often the elites in traditional West African society that migrated in search of wealth to maintain their elite status back at home. Young aristocrats in Soninke society not eligible for office, for example, took to long-distance trade to acquire the means to maintain themselves in proper fashion (Manchuelle, 1996). Colonial rule expanded the horizons of labor migration. The abolition of slavery and pawning at the end of the nineteenth century and the beginning of the twentieth century enlarged the ranks of potential wage labor. Colonial law and order and colonial infrastructure facilitated travel. Commerce and employment opportunities offered by the colonial economy attracted traders and migrant workers.

Meanwhile, the ethic of accumulation is ingrained in the cultures of southern Ghana, and in the colonial era, commoners strove for the social mobility that had eluded them during the pre-colonial era. The *akonkofo* of early twentieth-century Kumasi, who formed the Kumasi Gentlemen's Club, represent an important example of entrepreneurial ability and social mobility (Arhin, 1986; McCaskie, 1983). Adam Jones (1995) and Emmanuel Akyeampong (2000) have highlighted how women in the Gold Coast also aspired to be "big women," women of wealth and social stature who conspicuously displayed their material riches. A Ga proverb states: *Enamɔ dzi efeemɔ* ("Capital is the backbone of all enterprises") (Ankra, 1966: 35). Other Ga proverbs underscore the importance of trade and wage labor in the accumulation of capital: *Kɛdzi okotsa ekwɔɔ nsu lɛ osliki duku kple-kée si* ("If your soft sponge does not travel beyond the seas, you will hardly see your silk headkerchief coming down"); and *kɛdzi otere moko dzatsu lɛ ohaa lɛ ehe tako* ("When you give a load to a carrier, you have to supply him with a pad commensurate to the size of the load"; that is a given contract must be matched by the fee) (Ankra, 1966: 48-49, 53). The acquisition of wealth by commoners in the nineteenth and twentieth centuries revised social gradations and the privileges of high birth. A Twi proverb highlights this shift in perception: *odehye nhyehye, na sika na ehyehye* ("Fame of being noble-born does not spread abroad, it is the fame of riches that spreads") (Rattray, 1916: 118). *Ohiani nni yonko* ("the poor man has no friend") underscores the loneliness of poverty (Rattray, 1916: 160).

Young men in the Gold Coast migrated to towns in search of wealth that would enable them to establish themselves as elders in rural communities. With the wealth from trade or wage-labor, they could acquire a wife or wives and land, and thus circumvent the control of male elders. The advent of cash crop farming also encouraged rural-rural migration in search of fertile land. The twentieth century has witnessed an increased tendency towards denying women access to productive resources such as land in both matrilineal and patrilineal societies (Nukunya, 1973; Benneh, 1971; Mikell, 1989; Greene, 1996). This has been partly a response to commercial agriculture and male domination of cash crops. Women also have restricted access to labor and credit facilities (Brown, 1996). One outcome has been to push more women into trading. Trading requires mobility, and female traders frequented towns and sometimes took up residence in towns.

Women who migrated to towns did so to escape rural poverty and/or patriarchal control in rural communities. For them migration was often an end in itself, and many did not intend to return to constrictive rural settings (Akyeampong, 1996: ch.3). The irony in gender relations in colonial and post-colonial towns is that women sometimes were forced to exploit financially the very sexuality rural men sought to control to survive in towns (Akyeampong, 1996b, 1997, 2000). Women lacked the educational and artisanal skills required in colonial wage-labor. However, towns spawned by the colonial political economy provided favorable conditions for female accumulation, as men outnumbered women in these towns. Women came to supply important domestic services to male migrants: cooked food, a place to sleep, and sex. The cultural value attached to childbearing encouraged single women to become mothers, even if it meant being a single parent. People were seen as "wealth," and a Twi proverb stresses that *wo wɔ nnipa, na wo wɔ adeɛ* ("If you have people, you have wealth"). The phenomenal expansion in rural-urban and international migration by adult men in twentieth-century Ghana increased the number of female-headed households in both rural and urban contexts. Studies in the last quarter of the twentieth century indicate food poverty was disproportionately high among female-headed households in Ghana, as female household heads struggled to meet subsistence needs in the face of restricted access to productive resources (Kyereme and Thorbecke, 1987; Brown, 1996). A recent study based on seven administrative regions in Ghana has underscored the rise in single-parent homes and female-headed households (Oware-Gyekye et al., 1996).

Women fared differently in "old" and "new" towns, new towns being those that emerged in the past century as a direct result of colonial economic activity. Obuasi's history is tied to that of the Ashanti Goldfields Corporation (AGC), established in 1897 to exploit Obuasi's gold resources. Railway construction began in 1898 from the tiny Ahanta fishing village of Sekondi to link interior mines with this natural harbor. The labor demands of mining and railway construction far exceeded local labor and migrant labor was recruited from other parts of the Gold Coast and neighboring colonies to resolve the labor difficulties. The migrant working class origins of towns such as Obuasi and Sekondi resulted in a predominantly male population. In the Gold Coast census of 1901, Sekondi had a male population of 3,469 and a female population of 626, a ratio of five to one.[4] This was in sharp contrast to the balanced sexual ratios of old, pre-colonial towns in the Gold Coast. In the 1891 census, Accra had an adult population of 6,467 men and 6,362 women, while Cape Coast had an adult population of 3,526 men and 3,603 women.[5] Kru and Ibo women were among the early female migrants to Sekondi. The Kru have a maritime tradition and Kru men were employed as canoemen and stevedores in surf ports along the Gold Coast. The first prostitutes in Sekondi were mostly Kru and Ibo women, but they were joined later by younger Nzima women and Fanti women from Cape Coast (Akyeampong, 2000: 226). The opening of a deep-water harbor at Takoradi in 1928 enhanced the cosmopolitan status of the twin towns of Sekondi-Takoradi. Prostitution had also become a feature of old towns such as Accra and Kumasi. In Accra, the headman of the Hausa community in Ussher Town was expressing his uneasiness in 1925 about the increase in prostitution among Hausa women.[6] In Kumasi, prostitutes had been settled in the Adum quarter with the permission of the Asantehene (Akyeampong, 1997: 164-66).

It was this combination of young men and women seeking to escape rural patriarchy and gerontocracy, the conducive conditions for migrant labor created by colonial economic activity and infrastructure, and the indulgence of sexuality in impersonal towns that facilitated the dissemination of STDs in the colonial Gold Coast. Disease became a central trope in the discourse of gender, as men in colonial Gold Coast accused women, especially acquisitive traders, of being conduits of gonorrhea and syphilis (Roberts, 1987; Allman, 1996). Women who opted out of marriage and thus deprived men of their labor and earning power were labeled as wicked and selfish (Allman, 1991). But as Megan Vaughan astutely observes:

> The real issue, of course was that with far-reaching changes taking place in economic relations, so enormous strains were placed on both gender and generational relations ... these complex changes were described in terms of degeneration, of uncontrolled sexuality and disease (Vaughan, 1991: 144).

As the next section will show, syphilis and gonorrhea were firmly rooted in the political economy of the twentieth century; identified with commercial, port, military and mining towns, associated with both mobile men and women and disseminated along trade and transport routes.

Syphillis and Gonorrhea in Twentieth-Century Ghana

Syphillis and gonorrhea existed in the Gold Coast before the colonial era (1874). Pieter de Marees writing in 1602 described the common ailments in coastal towns of the Gold Coast as "pox, the clap, gonorrhea, worms, headache and hot fevers" (de Marees, 1987 [1602]: 173). However, sexually transmitted diseases were not confined to the coast, the locus of European settlement and Atlantic trade. Dr. Tedlie, a medical doctor who accompanied Thomas Bowdich on a diplomatic mission to Kumasi in 1817, compiled one of the earliest medical accounts of diseases in the Gold Coast. Tedlie reports that on entering Asante several Asante suffering from the effects of venereal disease approached him for medication. In the list of diseases that he encountered in Asante, Tedlie listed several cases of syphilis, two cases of gonorrhea and three cases of stricture, possibly caused by venereal disease (Bowdich, 1966: 379). Tedlie noted that:

> Gonorrhoea is of rare occurrence, two cases came under my care, the patients had never used injections, they drank decoctions of leaves and bark, but could not tell me the plants they used ... The disease is allowed to take its course by the natives, as they are unacquainted with any method to stop it (Bowdich, 1966: 376).

Patterson observed that venereal diseases were well established in Ghana before the twentieth century, especially along the coast (Patterson, 1981: 75).[7]

The geographical distribution of gonorrhea and syphilis highlights the importance of towns, trade and other economic activities, colonial infrastructure and mobile labor in its dissemination. Between 1880 and 1907, medical officers reported on the devastation of syphillis and gonorrhea in the Keta District (Addae, 1996: 236). Keta had emerged as an important commercial entrepot in the second half of the nineteenth century and its surf port acted as the distributive and collection point for the regional economy (Akyeampong, 2001). Close to the south-eastern boundary of colonial Gold Coast and the district headquarters for the Keta-Ada District, Keta housed customs officials, a Hausa military force, and several government employees. It boasted of numerous merchants – European and West African. Its diverse labor force even included Kru canoemen. Considering the fact that several strangers in the Keta district considered their migration temporary, they were unaccompanied by their spouses or families. This was fertile ground for casual sex and venereal diseases.

Gonorrhea was also reported to be widespread in Kumasi before the First World War. Instructively, Dr. A. J. R. O'Brien, medical officer of health for Kumasi, reported a high incidence of gonorrhea in even villages outside Kumasi in 1914 (Addae, 1996: 236). This dovetails with Tedlie's observations on the commonness of venereal diseases in Asante. But a partial explanation for this increased prevalence of gonorrhea in Kumasi and its environs was the stationing of a military garrison in Kumasi. Soldiers, police and sailors due to their mobility and the fact that they are often unaccompanied by their wives have become major conduits of venereal diseases. Patterson comments that:

> Syphillis and gonorrhea were transmitted to new areas [in the Gold Coast] as soldiers, laborers, prostitutes, traders, and lorry drivers travelled to and from towns and about the countryside
> (Patterson, 1981: 76).

An international agreement on venereal diseases was signed at Brussels in 1924, designating or listing the clinics in various coastal towns where sailors could be treated free of charge for venereal diseases. In this international treaty, the connection between mobile single men and STDs was acknowledged across cultures. Accra was the designated site for the treatment of venereal diseases in the Gold Coast in the 1920s.[8]

Dr. C. E. Reindorf, after receiving special training in venereology in Britain in 1920, had opened a special venereal diseases clinic at the African Hospital in Accra. Reindorf's hospital enjoyed remarkable popularity because of his successful treatment of venereal diseases with Salvarsan and Neoarsenobisthmus. In 1922-23 the Medical Department launched a propaganda campaign against venereal diseases under the direction of Dr. Reindorf. The 1920s witnessed the development of medical statistics and high infant mortality at health centers in Accra was blamed – rightly or wrongly – on syphilis in African women.[9] The take-off in the cocoa and mining industries had heightened colonial concerns about labor in a colony with a small population, and these concerns certainly fed into the venereal diseases drive of the 1920s. Mass inoculation against yaws, related to syphilis and sometimes misdiagnosed as syphilis, from the 1920s assisted in arresting the spread of syphilis and by 1950, syphilis accounted for only ten per cent of venereal disease cases in the country. Indeed, yaws was included among the conditions to be treated at the first Venereal Diseases Clinic in Accra run by Dr. Reindorf as it was regarded by medical opinion "as a modified form of syphilis affecting primitive races" (Reindorf, 1954: 117). Figure 1 shows the number of venereal disease cases treated in the Gold Coast between 1902 and 1955. These statistics only relate to patients treated at government clinics or hospitals.

What is striking is the rise in gonorrhea cases as syphilis cases declined.[10] Gonorrhea cases peaked between 1940 and 1955 with the Second World War being a major contributing factor. In the mid-1940s, Gold Coast troops serving with the British had a fifty per cent venereal disease rate with gonorrhea being by far the most common infection (Willcox, 1956: 106; Pellow, 1994: 419). Indeed, the incidence of venereal diseases amongst African soldiers was considered a threat to the British war effort and was discussed at the eighth meeting of the West African War Council in 1943. Nigeria even legislated a "Bill for an Ordinance Relating to Venereal Disease" in 1943, making it an offence for anyone to conceal a venereal disease condition and not report to the medical officer of health for the area or a qualified medical practitioner.[11] In the Gold Coast, the port city of Takoradi was one of the military bases for the British war effort. Prostitution flourished in Sekondi-Takoradi in the 1940s, and "pilot boys" guided servicemen to prostitutes around the city for a small commission (Busia, 1950)

In 1945, Brigadier H. B. F. Dixon, Deputy Director of Medical Services to the West African Command, expressed concerns on an Accra Radio Program ("Army Calling") about the wider ramifications of the extremely high rate of venereal disease infections in the Royal West African Frontier Force.

> Venereal disease is a problem which will have to be tackled seriously in the peace but it is not only a military problem it is a civil one, too. It is no good Army doctors curing soldiers of venereal diseases if infected civilians do not obtain treatment also (*The Spectator Daily,* November 30, 1945).

The rise in reported cases between 1945 and 1955 may have substantiated Dixon's concerns. In 1949 a special venereal diseases clinic was established in Sekondi and local inhabitants came to refer to the hospital as the "seamen's clinic," as they were among the major patrons. The introduction of penicillin during the 1940s, and its effectiveness against gonorrhea, may also have contributed to the rise in reported cases, as patients may have been more willing to seek treatment.

Figure 1: Veneral Diseases Cases Treated (1902–1955)

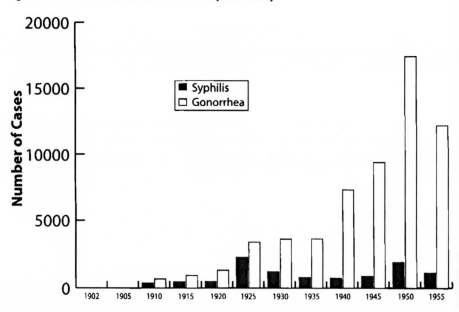

Source: Based on data from Patterson (1981)

The movement of migrant labor along the expanded network of colonial roads and railways spread venereal diseases across the Gold Coast. Northern migrants who came south to work at mines and on cocoa farms facilitated the spread of venereal diseases when they returned home. Addae argues that the Northern Territories of the Gold Coast were largely free from venereal diseases (especially syphilis) until the late 1920s, "when returning northerners having emigrated south in search of work, acquired the disease and spread it" (Addae, 1996: 239). Significantly, the early venereal disease cases in the north were found along motor roads, and it was referred to as "the Kumasi disease" in the north (Patterson, 1981: 76). The first patients were peddlers, drivers, and men who had traveled south to work on the railways, in mines and commercial towns. The demobilization of ex-servicemen after 1945 may have reinforced this pattern of mobility and venereal infection, as it cannot be ascertained that all venereal patients in the army had been successfully treated. The onset of secondary industrialization from the 1940s further strengthened rural-urban migration, placing more single men and women in towns (Peil, 1973).

Unfortunately, the venereal disease clinics were allowed to lapse after independence. In the 1950s there was no department responsible for venereal diseases. In the 1970s there were still no special clinics in Ghana for venereal diseases, and it was only with the onset of HIV/AIDS from the mid-1980s that there was renewed interest in other STDs. The medical examination of over one million Ghanaians repatriated from Nigeria in 1983-4 revealed that many were suffering from STDs. These were quarantined, and the Adabraka Polyclinic was established as a specialized STDs clinic to care for them. The clinic became dormant between 1989 and 1991, as there was no resident doctor (Pellow, 1994: 420). It was revived in the early 1990s as part of the Greater Accra Regional AIDS Control Program.

Conclusion

Studies of Sexually Transmitted Diseases, especially gonorrhea and syphilis, and HIV/AIDS in Ghana and West Africa highlight the connection between female prostitution and these diseases. Though this is a valid observation, this chapter expands the socio-cultural context of gender relations in twentieth-century Ghana and advocates the re-conceptualization of gender relations where mobility, sexuality, and accumulation are concerned. The growth in, and the increasing commoditization of, casual sex in contemporary Ghana require an in-depth historical analysis of these phenomena. The cultural norms that underpin gender relations and sexuality and the unequal gender access to resources make urban and rural women financially vulnerable and expose them to risky sexual behavior. The current HIV/AIDS crisis demands a thorough understanding of the political, economic, social and cultural forces at play in sexual relations and not a facile generalization that Ghanaians are extremely promiscuous. Travel in search of wealth has been a major factor in the spread of gonorrhea, syphilis, and HIV/AIDS. The nature of such migration is often not family-based. Individual migrants – male and female – thus create new social relations and networks in urban towns. Political economy is instrumental in shedding light on why towns become nodal points in the transmission of STDs. The comprehensive overview provided in this chapter is necessary for a deeper understanding of the socio-spatial context of gender relations, and the development of specific strategies to arrest the spread of STDs and HIV/AIDS in Ghana.

Endnotes

1   The discussion of venereal diseases in twentieth-century Ghana focuses on syphilis and gonorrhea as two of the most common forms of venereal diseases. There is also a longer history of recording medical statistics on syphilis and gonorrhea, though misdiagnosis of syphilis persisted into the 1920s and 1930s. Reported cases of syphilis and gonorrhea came largely from government clinics or hospitals in urban areas, from venereal disease clinics in Accra and Takoradi, and from African troops of the West African Command. These statistics should be taken as indicative of broad trends or patterns instead of an accurate reflection of actual incidence. An earlier version of this article was presented to the Medical Research Council in The Gambia (Fajara) on August 4, 2000, and the authors are grateful for the comments and suggestions of the well-informed audience.

2   Deborah Pellow (1994, 1999), in two important recent studies, places the aetiology of HIV/AIDS in contemporary Ghana within the broader context of the history of STDs from the late nineteenth-century. She highlights important continuities in the history of sexuality and the incidence of STDs and AIDS, but ignores the rich insights from the burgeoning field of Ghanaian social history (McCaskie, 1981; Allman, 1991, 1996a; Austen, 1994; Roberts, 1987; Akyeampong, 1996, 1997, 2000). The culturo-historical basis of her work is thus thin, and major generalizations on culture and the history of sexuality are drawn from the statistical evidence of a few surveys in the early 1970s, 1992, and 1993 (Pellow, 1999: 18).

3 The prefix in the title of this paper, "Itinerant Gold Mines," is derived from Naanen (1991), who examines the careers of Nigerian prostitutes in the Gold Coast between 1930 and 1950. "Gender" is a cultural construct, and the social discourse about gender is in reality about power relations and access to productive resources. Men seek to exclude women from certain political, economic, and social spheres based on arguments rooted in physical differences between male and female. These arguments acquire the

semblance of immutability, as they are rooted in unchangeable physical characteristics, obscuring the reality that gender is culturally constructed.

4 Gold Coast Colony, Census of the Population, 1901. National Archives of Ghana (NAG), Accra, ADM 5/2/2.

5 Gold Coast, Report on the Census of the Gold Coast Colony for the Year 1891. NAG, Accra, ADM 5/2/1.

6 Kadri English, Hausa tribal ruler, to District Commissioner of Accra, Ussher Town, May 13, 1925. NAG, Accra, ADM 11/1/922.

7 Gonorrhea is caused by the bacterium Neiseria gonorrhoeae. Syphilis is caused by a spirochete agent called Treponema pallidum, which is very closely related to the pathogen of yaws, Treponema pertenue. Victims of yaws acquired a partial immunity against syphilis because of the similarity in their causative organisms (Patterson, 1981: 75).

8 National Archives of Ghana, Accra, CSO 11/1/619.

9 National Archives of Ghana, Accra, ADM 5/2/5. Census Report for the Gold Coast Colony, 1921, 64.

10 In contrast, syphilis appeared to be on the rise in The Gambia and Northern Nigeria in the early 1950s. Sierra Leone revealed a trend similar to the Gold Coast (Willcox, 1956).

11 NAG, Accra, CSO 11/10/136.

Bibliography

Acquah, I., 1958. *Accra Survey*. London: University of London Press.

Addae, Stephen, 1996. *History of Western Medicine in Ghana* 1880-1960. Edinburgh: Durham Academic Press.

Akyeampong, E., 2001. *Between the Sea and the Lagoon: An Eco-Social History of the Anlo of Southeastern Ghana, c.1850 to Recent Times*. Oxford: James Currey.

Akyeampong, E., 1996. *Drink, Power and Cultural Change: A Social History of Alcohol in Ghana, c.1800 to Recent Times*. Portsmouth: Heinemann.

Akyeampong, E.,. 1997. Sexuality and Prostitution among the Akan of the Gold Coast c.1650-1950. *Past and Present*. 156: 144-173.

Akyeampong, E.,. 2000. '*Wo pe tam won pe ba*' (You like cloth but you don't want children): Urbanization, Individualism and Gender Relations in Colonial Ghana c.1900-39. In David M. Anderson and Richard Rathbone (ed.) *Africa's Urban Past*. Oxford: James Currey.

Akyeampong, E., and Pashington Obeng, 1995. Spirituality, Gender and Power in Asante History. *International Journal of African Historical Studies* 28, 3: 481-508.

Allman, Jean M., 1991. Of "Spinsters," "Concubines" and "Wicked Women": Reflections on Gender and Social Change in Asante. *Gender and History* 3, 2: 176-89.

Allman, Jean M., 1996a. Rounding up Spinsters: Gender Chaos and Unmarried Women in Colonial Asante. *Journal of African History* 37, 2: 195-214.

Allman, Jean M.,. 1996b. Adultery and the State in Asante: Reflections on Gender, Class and Power from 1800-1950. In John Hunwick and Nancy Lawler (eds.) , *The Cloth of Many Colored Silks: Papers on History and Society Ghanaian and Islamic in Honor of Ivor Wilks*. Evanston: Northwestern University Press.

Anarfi, J. K., E. N. Appiah and K. Awusabo-Asare, 1997. Livelihood and the risk of HIV/AIDS infection in Ghana: the case of female itinerant traders. *Health Transition Review* 7: 225-242.

Ankra, Nee-Adjabeng, E. A., 1966. *Agwaseŋ Wiemɔi Kɛ Abɛi Komɛi*. Accra: Bureau of Ghana Languages.

Arhin, Kwame, 1986. A Note on the Asante Akonkofo: A Non-Literate Sub-Elite, 1900-1930. *Africa* 56, 1: 25-31.

Austin, Gareth, 1994. Human Pawning in Asante, 1800-1950: Markets and Coercion, Gender and Cocoa. In Toyin Falola and Paul Lovejoy (eds.) *Pawnship in Africa: Debt Bondage in Historical Perspective*. Boulder: Westview Press.

Benneh, G., 1971. Land Tenure and Sabala Farming System in the Anlo Area of Ghana: A Case Study. *Research Review*. Legon 7, 2: 74-93.

Bosman, W., 1705. *A New and Accutate Discription of the Coast of Guinea*. London: J. Knapton..

Bowdich, T. E., 1966. *Mission from Cape Coast Castle to Ashantee*. London: Frank Cass. 3rd Edition.

Brown, C. K., 1996. Gender Roles and Household Allocation of Resources and Decision-Making in Ghana. In Elizabeth Ardayfio-Schandorf (ed) *The Changing Family in Ghana*. Accra: Ghana Universities Press.

Bujra, Janet, 1975. Women "Entrepreneurs" of Early Nairobi. *Canadian Journal of African Studies* 9.

Busia, K. A., 1950. *Report on the Social Survey of Sekondi-Takoradi*. Accra: Crown Agents.

Clark, Gracia, 1994. *Onions are my Husband: Survival and Accumulation by West African Market Women*. Chicago: University of Chicago Press.

Dapper, Olfert, 1676 *Naukeurige bescrijvinge der afrikaensche gewesten*. Amsterdam. 2nd Edition.

De Marees, Pieter, 1987. *Description and Historical Account of the Gold Kingdom of Guinea (1602)*. Trans. and (eds.), Albert van Dantzig and Adam Jones. Oxford: Oxford University Press.

Field, M. J., 1960. *Search for Security: An Ethno-Psychiatric Study of Rural Ghana*. Evanston: Northwestern University Press.

Greene, Sandra E., 1996. *Gender, Ethnicity and Social Change on the Upper Slave Coast: A History of the Anlo-Ewe*. Portsmouth: Heinemann.

Herbert, Eugenia, 1993. *Iron, Gender and Power: Rituals of Transformations in African Societies*. Bloomington: Indiana University Press.

Ison, C. A., J. Pepin, et al., 1992. The Dominance of a Multiresistant Strain of Neisseria gonorrhoeae among Prostitutes and STD Patients in the Gambia. *Genitourin Med* 68: 356-60.

Jones, Adam, 1990. Prostitution, Polyandrie oder Vergewaltigung? Zur Mehrdeutigkeit europäischer Quellen über die Küste Westafrikas zwischen 1660 und 1860. In Adam Jones (ed.), *Aussereuropäische Frauengeschichte: Probleme der Forschung*. Pfaffenweiler.

Jones, Adam,. 1995. Female Slave-Owners on the Gold Coast: Just a Matter of Money? In Stephen Palmié (ed.) *Slave Cultures and the Culture of Slavery*. Knoxville.

Kyereme, S. and E. Thorbecke, 1987. Food Poverty Profile and Decomposition Applied to Ghana. *World Development* 15, 9.

Little, Kenneth, 1973. *African Women in Towns*. Cambridge: Cambridge University Press.

Manchuelle, François, 1996. *Willing Migrants*. Oxford: James Currey.

McCaskie, T. C., 1981. State and Society, Marriage and Adultery: Some Considerations Towards a Social History of Pre-Colonial Asante. *Journal of African History* 22, 3: 477-94.

McCaskie, T. C., 1983. Accumulation, Wealth and Belief in Asante History: I To the Close of the Nineteenth Century. *Africa* 53, 1: 23-43.

Meillassoux, Claude, 1981. *Maidens, Meal and Money: Capitalism and the Domestic Economy*. Cambridge: Cambridge University Press.

Mikell, Gwendolyn, 1989. *Cocoa and Chaos in Ghana*. New York: Paragon House.

Naanen, Benedict, B. B., 1991. 'Itinerant Gold Mines': Prostitution in the Cross River Basin of Nigeria, *1930-1950' African Studies Review* 24.

Nukunya, G. K., 1973. Land Tenure, Inheritance, and Social Structure among the Anlo. *Universitas* 3, 1: 64-83.

Oware-Gyekye, L., et al., 1996. Family Law and Customary Practices for Child Maintenance and Inheritance in Ghana. In Elizabeth Ardayfio-Schandorf (ed.) *The Changing Family in Ghana*. Accra: Ghana Universities Press.

Patterson, David K., 1981. *Health in Colonial Africa: Disease, Medicine and Socio-Economic Change, 1900-1955*. Waltham: Crossroads Press.

Pellow, Deborah, 1994. STDs and AIDS in Ghana. *Genitourin* Med 70: 418-423.

Patterson, David K.,. 1999. Sex, Disease and Culture Change in Ghana. In Philip W. Setel, Milton Lewis, and Maryinez Lyons (eds.), *Histories of Sexually Transmitted Diseases and HIV/AIDS in Sub-Saharan Africa*. Westport: Greenwood Press.

Pickering, H., J. Todd, et al., 1992. Prostitutes and their Clients: A Gambian Survey. *Social Science and Medicine*. 34, 1: 75-88.

Rattray, R.S. 1916 *Ashanti Proverbs*. Oxford: Clarendon Press.

Reindorf, C. E., 1954. Influence of Fifty Years of Scientific Medicine on Beliefs and Customs in the Gold Coast. *West African Journal of Medicine* III, 3: 115-9.

Roberts, Penelope, 1987. 'The State and the Regulation of Marriage: Sefwi Wiawso (Ghana), 1900-1940.' In Haleh Afshah (ed.), *Women, State and Ideology: Studies from Africa and Asia*. London: Macmillan.

Robertson, Claire, 1984. *Sharing the Same Bowl: A Socioeconomic History of Women and Class in Accra, Ghana*. Ann Arbor: University of Michigan Press.

Sarpong, Peter., 1977. *Girls' Nubility Rites in Ashanti*. Tema: Ghana Publishing Corporation. .

Vaugan, Megan, 1991. *Curing Their Ills: Colonial Power and African Illness*. Stanford:Stanford University Press.

Weiss, Brad, 1993. 'Buying her Grave': Money, Movement and AIDS in Northwest Tanzania. *Africa* 63, 1.

White, Luise, 1990. *The Comforts of Home: Prostitution in Colonial Nairobi*. Chicago: University of Chicago Press.

Willcox, R. R., 1965. Prevalence of Venereal Diseases in British West Africa.*West African Medical Journal* V, 3: 103-11.

A "LICENSE TO INDULGE IN PREMARITAL SEXUAL ACTIVITIES"?
DIPO AND THE IMAGE OF KROBO WOMEN[1]

Marijke Steegstra

I happened to be passing through Odumase Krobo a week or so ago, and I was plain shocked to see a long queue of half naked girls in a dipo procession. (...) I was even more amazed to find out that the procession included an unusually large number of little girls, some even carried on their mother's backs. (...) What is all this mess about in the name of culture – but a licence to indulge in premarital sexual activities? (Kumah 1998).

The initiation rites for Krobo girls called *dipo* are annually celebrated for an estimated few thousand girls in and around the Krobo hometowns Odumase and Somanya in the Eastern Region of Ghana.[2] It is a taboo for these girls to have sexual relationships before *dipo*, and if they become pregnant before they are initiated, they will be banned from their family house and perceived as outcasts in their community. A girl has to have passed through *dipo* in order to be accepted for marriage and to be able to have a successful marriage, according to most Krobo people. As *dipo* is the prerequisite to be allowed to enter into sexual relationships, (and not marriage as such), those criticising *dipo*, like the writer in the comment from a Christian magazine (*The Watchman*), feel that this rule, combined with an initiation at a young age, promotes sexual promiscuity. They consequently think that it contributes to the prevalence of AIDS. Moreover, Krobo women, generally considered by Ghanaians to be beautiful, have a negative moral reputation among non-Krobo people in Ghana.

For a long time, the Eastern region, and the Krobo area in particular, was reported to be leading in AIDS cases in Ghana (e.g. Arbuckle n.d.; Decosas 1996; Hampton 1991; 'Agomanya leads in AIDS cases', www.Ghanaweb.com, 1 September 2002). According to estimates, the 2000 HIV prevalence rate in Ghana stood at 3.0%, while regional estimates revealed that HIV was lowest in the Northern Region (0.7%) and highest in 2000 in the Eastern Region (at a declining 7.8% rate) (Commission 2003: 5).[3] Hampton (1991), in a booklet about AIDS care and prevention in the Krobo area, has explicitly suggested that there is a connection between the cultural practice of *dipo* and the spread of HIV and AIDS. She proposes that the ceremony nowadays is purely symbolic, thereby joining the chorus of those who imply that in the past the *dipo* rites involved teaching of parenting and housework and are part of 'outmoded custom'. Because of the limited time and space within which the rites take place and the young age of many girls, she insinuates that the rites lead to sexual permissiveness, as girls may begin sexual activity after *dipo*. Because they are young, she writes, they either do not know about condoms or, due to their social position, would not be inclined to introduce them to their (often older) partners. Such an approach to *dipo*, as a functional ceremony, reasons that *dipo* contributes to AIDS (see also Afenyadu & Goparaju 2003), but such a reasoning also implies that *dipo* could contribute to *prevent* the spread of HIV and AIDS by integrating sexual education into the rites, as some writers and some NGO's suggest (e.g. Arbuckle n.d.; Schroeder & Danquah 2000 and the epilogue below).

The answers to the question whether there really is a link between *dipo* and the spread of HIV/AIDS is very hard to determine, as it would require a large scale comparative statistical study on sexual behaviour and relationships. Moreover, these questions presuppose that the *dipo* rites are 'puberty rites' and that the main purpose of *dipo* is to prevent promiscuity and premarital sex (e.g. Schroeder & Danquah 2000: 3). It also attributes the negative implications of *dipo* to changes from its 'original practice'. I argue that to understand the meaning of *dipo*, a historical and dynamic approach is needed. The meaning of *dipo* has indeed changed, but it has in fact always been changing in shifting contexts. The contemporary meaning of *dipo* is especially about the expression of a Krobo identity, as I will demonstrate.

The next important questions then to investigate are: why *dipo* is so much contested and what is the connection between *dipo* and the negative moral image of Krobo women? I will seek part of the answers in an analysis of the way colonial encounters with Protestant missionaries of the Basel Mission in particular, have shaped the context within which *dipo* developed. It will become clear that the negative stereotypes of the sexual morals of Krobo women have been reinforced in the interaction with Christian missionaries. I argue that in order to be able to understand why there is a relatively high percentage of HIV infected Krobo women, we need to pay attention to the specific local economic circumstances and be careful of judging cultural practices from moralizing and misinformed viewpoints. Therefore I will discuss this matter in the context of economic hardships and migrant mobility. After giving the necessary background information, I will first examine the contemporary performance and meaning of *dipo*, then I will discuss the impact of the Basel Mission's cultural policy and finally I will look at the relationship between Krobo migration and the spread of HIV/AIDS.

Economic Hardships

The major economic activity in the Eastern Region of Ghana today comprises agriculture (including hunting, forestry and fishing), in which over 54% of the labour force is employed, followed by 'wholesale and retail trade', with over 13%.[4] For many Ghanaians agriculture is a life raft to which they have clung, partly in order to survive the hardships of structural adjustment policies. However, the economy is extremely vulnerable to droughts, other natural disasters and international price fluctuations.[5] The Krobo district is a good example of a former centre of export crop production in decline.

In the past, the Krobo farmers were great palm oil producers (from ca. 1815), which caused them to expand their plantations further and further to the north. They also cultivated maize (from the second half of the 18th century) and later cocoa (from the late 1880s onwards). In the old days, at least until the 1940s and before the major economic decline, it was not uncommon for a father and/or family head to encourage his daughter, once she had passed her *dipo* initiation rites, to have children before she was married, or not to marry at all. The resulting *yo bi* then belonged to his patrilineage. In this way the daughters services were retained on his own farm and he had additional sons without expenses and obligations attached to marrying additional wives (Field 1941a:14). It ensured the future of the family and their wealth, as the children would provide a valuable labour force on the ever-expanding plantations. Population growth and consolidation of the family were thus partly fostered by the social institution of *dipo*, in addition to polygyny, especially after access to family labour became more important following the abolition of slavery in 1874.

Whereas the Krobo area was once considered the best agricultural district in the colonial era and received much attention from government agricultural services, with the decline of cocoa (partly due to the outbreak of 'swollen shoot' cocoa disease as well as WWII in the 1940s) the needs of the Krobo district have been forgotten. Amanor (1994) has described the weakening and ongoing marginalisation of Krobo farmers after the decline of cocoa. He notes the complex impacts of the crisis in cocoa production after the 1940s and the lack of new available land in Manya Krobo, on the social relationships of production and settlement patterns. At present the young are, more often than not, doomed to a life of unemployment and existence on the fringes of employment. Many people in Odumase are still involved in farming or (related) trading, but extended family labour no longer has any significant role as it had in the past. Men also work, for example, as drivers and mechanics, while men as well as women may work as artisans, hairdressers, dressmakers, or teachers. Most people share a piece of land, or are absentee owners of land in 'the village' in the up-country. Farming does not earn much cash, and wages in general are low.[6] Many women also trade. The creation of the Volta Lake for hydro-electricity in the 1960s contributed to the general economic decline, as many Krobo lost their land and livelihood, which is of particular relevance in the context of this chapter, and a point to which I will return later.

Christianity in Krobo Area

The Christianisation of the Krobo in Ghana began approximately 150 years ago with the arrival of Protestant missionaries of the Evangelical Missionary Society of Basel (*Evangelische Missionsgesellschaft zu Basel*) commonly known as the Basel Mission (BM).[7] The first encounter between the Krobo and a representative of the BM took place as early as 1836. More regular contacts occurred from 1857. Although Christianity took off slowly in the beginning, towards the end of the 19th century, mainly due to increasing interest in education on the part of the Krobo, the mission started to gain a strong foothold in Krobo society.

Nowadays most Krobo feel affiliated with a Christian church. Many Krobo are members of the successor of the Basel Mission Church, while others have joined former mission churches, of which the Catholic Church (established in Krobo in the 1940s) is the largest. The Basel Mission had a strong impact on Krobo society, as it held the Christian monopoly for a long time, founded many schools and is linked with the rise of the (Manya) Krobo paramount chiefs. In the meantime, especially since the early 1980s, Pentecostal or charismatic churches have become very popular in Ghana and in Krobo as well. They are divided into many small denominations. One thus cannot speak of a homogeneous group of Christians and it can be expected that opinions on Krobo cultural practices such as *dipo* will therefore differ. However, the missionary and colonial language has been so strong, that words such as 'pagan' and 'fetish' are still commonly used to refer to non-Christian practices, and to *dipo* in particular. All churches, with the exception of some of the African Independent Churches, strongly disapprove of their members' participation in *dipo* ceremonies.

The Performance of Dipo[8]

All girls in (patrilineal) Krobo today have to pass through the *dipo* rites, but there is no definite age set for it. In contrast to initiation rites for girls elsewhere, such as *bragoro* of the (matrilineal) Ashanti (Sarpong 1977), the *dipo* rites are not directly linked with the first menstruation. The girls may be anywhere from two to about eighteen years old, but the average age is about fourteen. (I shall come back to the age question later). *Dipo* is one of the life cycle rituals that constitute and gender a female Krobo person, and is mandatory for girls in order to become full members of Krobo society. Boys are circumcised when they are one week old, but there are no further rites attached to it. However, in the past Krobo men distinguished themselves from the Akan by being circumcised and therefore it was also an important marker of Krobo identity.

Dipo consists of annually performed, prescribed ceremonial events, for which girls are gathered together to be initiated in groups. Although maize has ousted millet since the second half of the 18th century, millet is still the central crop on the ritual agricultural calendar, around which revolve the annual ceremonies, performed by the local priests. The *dipo* rites are part of this annual cycle and millet plays a role in some of the *dipo* rituals. The rites are thus part of the cult of the goddess Nana Klowɛki, the most important Krobo deity. The Klowɛki priests determine the exact time for *dipo*, which is usually between February and May. A male priest can preside over the *dipo* rites, but the women perform the rituals. Most *dipo* priests will have two, three or sometimes even four subsequent groups in one season, which can add up to over a hundred girls per priest.[9]

When the parents, ideally the father, or another relative willing to take the responsibility, have saved enough money for the ceremony of a grown girl in the family, they inform the head of the family. Often her younger sisters and cousins will join the older girl out of convenience and especially to cut down the expenses. Girls from different families, but often from the same 'house' (paternal kin group) will join together to enact *dipo* in their hometown at a particular local priest's and/or priestess's house, who is usually from the same kin group.

The *dipo* rites last about ten days for one group, but can be shortened to one weekend.[10] Individual girls first go to the soothsayer and are purified. After this, some of the most important rites that take place under the priestess' supervision, consist of the shaving of the hair to mark a symbolic transition, several purification rites, such as a ritual bath in a stream and the sacrifice of a black goat (the usual sacrifice for the deity Nana Klowɛki) of which the blood is sprinkled on the girls' feet.[11] During the week of the ceremony, the girls are not allowed to drink tap water as it comes from the Volta, which is considered unclean, or eat food prepared out of fermented corn. Such food is considered 'foreign food' and therefore also as unclean and taboo.

The journey to the grove with the sacred stone (*tɛgbɛtɛ*) is the climax on a Sunday. Only the priestesses and the girls are allowed to enter the sacred grove. Each girl is seated thrice on the stone by a priestess. The secrecy surrounding the *tɛgbɛtɛ* contributes to its power, in addition to the belief that a concealed pregnancy will have serious consequences. In such a case misfortune will fall upon the family concerned. The girl herself may die and the family members may fall sick or die. They would also have to pay for the purification of the *tɛgbɛtɛ* and their house.[12] As an unclean person, the girl in question would not be allowed to eat or drink in her family house again for the rest of her life, that is, she is no longer a true member of her family. For the girls this fear has the psychological effect of making them take care not to become pregnant and remain virgins prior to *dipo*. Until the late 19th century, a girl who became pregnant before having passed the rites would be banished from the community forever. Her lover also had to pay a heavy fine. Often these unfortunate girls would marry into neighbouring communities. In earlier days, such girls might even be killed. Now such girls sometimes claim to be Christians, but because many initiands are fairly young, such banishments happen rarely these days.

After returning from the sacred grove, the girls' hair is completely shaved. Sometimes, however, parents pay additional money to the priests to prevent this, because they either do not want their school going girls to be shaved, or as Christians they want to hide the fact that *dipo* was performed for them. The girls are then given a conically shaped straw hat (*komi pee*) to wear. Only ritually clean people can wear this hat. Besides *dipo-yi*, only senior male priests are allowed to wear such a hat which is imbued with immense religious significance (cf. Quarcoopome 1991: 63).[13] The girls then show their dancing skills.

Finally on the following Monday morning, pictures are taken of the girls. These pictures with the particular 'priestly' dressing are the proof that they have passed through *dipo*. Some girls also later receive twelve small scars in clusters of three on the back of their hands. In the past these cuts formed the proof that dipo was performed. Literally they mean that a girl has gone through the "sweeping test".[14]

Singing and dancing are part of all the rites and at the final 'outdooring', the public coming out, the girls are expected to show their perfect dancing skills. The women sing *klama* songs. The girls are dressed in woven *kente* cloth or expensive wax print cloth and wear loads of precious glass beads. In the old days their fiancés would now come forward and marry them soon afterwards. Some old ladies told me this is what happened in their case in the 1930s and 40s. The *dipo-yi* move very gracefully and serenely in their beautiful dress and heavy, precious beads. The women spray them with perfumes, even spread their cloth for them on the floor, and excitedly dance around them. When it is not their turn to dance, the girls sit on the armchairs that are put outside for them, like queens on their thrones, and seem to feel like it. With their hips made big with beads and the headgear, even the smallest girls look like little women now.

Marking Krobo Identity

Rituals are multi-faceted and have many functions, both on the level of the individual and for groups or societies (Bowie 2000: 151-152). For individual girls going through these rituals, the *dipo* ceremony is a rite of passage that signifies a transition in life, a change in status and identity. As *dipo* as such is a precondition for motherhood and marriage, one of the main themes of *dipo* is fertility, which is expressed in several of the symbols and rituals performed. The *dipo* rituals are effective, as they depend on inherited, value-laden images that are driven, by repeated practice and performance, 'deeply into the bone' (Grimes 2000). People take great care to perform the rites correctly. Many of the rituals involved in the *dipo* performance are experienced as very efficacious, as really 'working'. Failure, for example, to pass the pregnancy test on the *tεgbεtε*, the sacred rock, can have disastrous consequences. In such cases the rituals have the ability to effect transformations. At the same time, the participants in the rites act very casually and these rites are performed in a relaxed atmosphere. The *dipo* performance also has the purpose of entertaining through dancing and singing. There is a lot of merriment and feasting during the rites. Simultaneously these actions evoke feelings and emotions related to deeper meanings. Even more important than the theme of fertility is the focus on ritual cleanliness and belonging.

Although some other Ga-Dangme speaking peoples perform similar rites, especially the much smaller groups of the Shai and the Osudoku, the *dipo* rites are associated with being Krobo. Furthermore, the fact that the rites are performed as part of the veneration of one of the indigenous and most senior deities, Nana Klowɛki, distinguishes Krobo *dipo* rites from initiation rites performed elsewhere among Dangme or other neighbouring people. Even though non-Krobo and also Krobo people might at times criticize the performance of *dipo*, associating it with "paganism" and "backward" traditions, the insistence of Krobo people on its continued performance conveys a sense of ethnic pride. Women enjoy participating in the rites and parents feel very proud of their daughters when they have passed through *dipo* as it distinguishes them from outsiders and they feel that *dipo* makes 'real Krobo women' of the girls, while Krobo families generally insist on partners who have passed through the rites for their men.

A number of aspects of *dipo* convey a relationship between *dipo* and an essential Krobo identity. First of all, *dipo* is a homecoming ritual. In the past, before 1892, every Krobo who wanted to perform *dipo* for their daughter, had to return from the farmlands to the hometowns on Krobo Mountain. Nowadays, *dipo* can only be performed in the hometowns in the plains (*dɔm*), and Krobo families return from all over the country and beyond for this event, in this way renewing family ties and observing their 'custom' (*kusumi*).

Secondly, it is believed that *dipo* makes one 'a real Krobo', that is to say, a pure person according to Krobo concepts. The *dipo* rites make the distinction between the ritually clean and the unclean, the initiated and the uninitiated. Through *dipo* a girl becomes pure and 'clean', like a boy becomes clean through circumcision. If a girl is found to be pregnant before she has passed through the rites, she is considered to be defiled, and extensive purification and pacification rites have to be performed to get rid of her pollution and dangers following her. Such a girl may harm the well-being of others, so she becomes an outcast in society. The strong taboo on a pregnancy before the rites shows the fear of rejection by the family in particular and Krobo society in general.

A third aspect that stresses the importance of *dipo* for Krobo identity during the performance of the *dipo* rites is the use of old, inalienable things and traditions that are regarded as authentically Krobo. For example, there is the emphasis on 'indigenous Krobo food' and well-water during the critical days of the rites. The use of 'indigenous' items such as natural sponges, clay pots, traditional grinding stones and traditional cosmetics is stressed. Glass beads and other typical decorations too are perceived as Krobo items. Whereas gold is of the greatest importance to the Asante, beads represent wealth in Krobo. Furthermore, the hair of the girls is shaved or groomed in an old, traditional Krobo style. Another element that used to identify a Krobo woman according to her ethnic origin were the scars that would remain a visible result of the twelve small tattoos put on her hand as proof of her *dipo*, and therefore of being a Krobo woman. The use of the Krobo language is emphasized and foreign languages are forbidden during *dipo*, and in particular in the shrine. The singing of *klama*, songs that are part of oral tradition, its specific lyrics and the typical dancing learned by the *dipo* girls also constitute an essential part of an atmosphere of 'ancient tradition'.

The use of old or 'real Krobo' features in *dipo* such as *klama* songs and beads and the strong relationship with the mythical figure of Klowɛki convey a 'given-ness' to *dipo*, which in turn contributes to a seemingly 'primordial' perception of Krobo ethnic identity. It is felt as something which is unchanged and authentic (cf. Renne 1995: 134). Many people stress that *dipo* is part of their 'custom' (*kusumi*). Being regarded as 'a real Krobo' implies a willing acceptance of this *kusumi*. The *dipo* rites are therefore effective means of defining individual and group identity, which means belonging to the family, the hometown and society as a whole.

All these ancestral items and aspects represent a sense of continuity and group unity in a material and cultural sense, despite the fact that certain features of *dipo* are changing and various intra-Krobo disputes persist, for example concerning chieftaincy affairs, the politics between Yilo and Manya Krobo districts and Christian points of view. Furthermore the question of young ages and changes in the duration of the rites is debated. *Dipo* is also criticised for assumed 'pagan', 'immoral' and 'backward' aspects of the rites. For example, some people claim that the goat used for the rites leads to immoral behaviour, because, as one pastor said to me, "the goat is a prostitute beast", and the girls would start behaving 'like a goat', that is, having sex at random.[15] This type of current perspective shows striking parallels with the 19th century Western missionaries' reasoning. Most changes in *dipo* performances are experienced in the context of Christianisation. Therefore delving into the history of the mission in Krobo society can contribute to a better understanding of the problems of today. Christianity has made *dipo* subject to dispute since the Basel missionaries arrived.

'A Swamp of Immorality': Basel Missionaries and *Dipo*

In the eyes of the Basel missionaries, conversion to Christianity in Africa meant the advancement of European 'civilisation' and 'enlightenment' (cf. Hefner 1993; cf. Van der Veer 1996). In this view, the only way to bring about conversion was for the new converts to abandon all contact with 'African traditional religion and culture' (cf. Kirby 1994: 208). In describing 'Krobo religion' the missionaries underplayed the importance of religious practices and emphasised 'belief' instead. In portraying Krobo culture and religion, the missionaries further created an antithesis with Christianity, whereby the darkness of 'Heathendom' was opposed to the light of Christianity. Some missionaries believed that the Africans belonged to the race of Ham and fell in consequence under the biblical 'curse' of Canaan. This line of thought also points to the Western linkage of skin colour and moral state (Braude 1997; Hastings 1994: 299-300), and the then current view of an analogy between race and gender degeneration (McClintock 1995). A very common means of describing the darkness of the 'heathen world' was therefore the depiction of the sexual immorality and degeneration of the 'heathen'. The following picture was composed in 'The Heathen Messenger' (*Der evangelische Hei-denbote*) in 1852 out of the descriptions of the Gold Coast by the missionary Johannes Zimmerman (to whom I will return below):

> Oh what a pitiful life is such a Negro life. And could a healthy moral life be able to unfold here? Where the soul has no living, holy and merciful God to hold on to, she has to perish in the abyss of sin. That is how it is with the Negro race. It is a swamp of immorality and wickedness into which the Negro peoples are immersed. The devil of animal lust in particular holds them captured, and not just men and women, young men and young women, but children between the age of six and eight suffer in these chains.[16] (Original in German, my translation)

Missionary reports assembled under the section 'Odumase' from the Krobo area are available from 1857, the year of the founding of a permanent mission post in Krobo-Odumase, until 1917, when missionaries of German nationality were forced to leave the Gold Coast as a result of World War I. In the many, very detailed descriptions, the large number of references to *dipo* may not be surprising.[17] Whereas polygyny and sexual behaviour were the grounds on which frequent decisions were made to prevent the baptism of applicants or exclude church members, *dipo* was seen as a major cause of immorality and the primary obstacle to the conversion of Krobo women. The characteristics of *dipo* served as exemplary proof of the necessary moral education of the 'heathen'.

The missionaries saw the exposure of the body of the *dipo* girls as evidence of their sensuality. However, girls who were not yet initiated, and therefore rather not yet allowed to enter into sexual relationships, could easily be recognised by their dress, a state of undress, according to the Basel missionaries, as the uppermost parts of their body was exposed. They would only wear a loin cloth wrapped around their hips, exposing the upper part of their body. It enabled social control, as in this way, the elderly women were able to detect a possible pregnancy. Girls going through *dipo* could also be distinguished easily by their particular way of dressing and hairstyle. In the initial stages the heads of girls would be shaved around the neck and the rest of their hair would be plaited. They would not wear any waist beads, but a simple string with a long, red loincloth, hanging down back and front, tied to it. Different stages indicating a girl's maturity before, during and after the rites were in this way clearly marked by her bodily adornment.

Although some of the missionaries were able to see that the *dipo* rites regulated sexual behaviour, to them the 'immoral' content of the rites dominated their negative opinion. The missionary Heck wrote for example in 1858:

> (...) secret sins avail, especially onanism. In general, this custom [*dipo*] consists of an enormous, sinful fleshliness – such an immoral life prevails among the black youth of both sexes on this [Krobo] Mountain, that my feelings do not permit me to describe it in more detail.[18] (Original in German, my translation)

Heck's reports and subsequent ones in later years, claim they cannot go into detail, because of the immorality of the rites. It is more likely, however, that the rites were a complete mystery to the missionaries. The mainly male missionaries hardly interacted with women, let alone with the secluded girls and priestesses on Krobo Mountain. The Basel Mission's regulations concerning contact between male missionaries and women made it difficult to approach girls. For example:

> In the outdoors, men walking near where native women might rest or bathe must always call out before approaching, in order to avoid unexpected contact with women who were by European standards less than fully clothed (Miller 1994: 55).

Any reference to sexuality was an abomination to the missionaries and confirmed their assumptions. However, girls were closely guided by priestesses and elderly women on the mountain. In case there was a fiancé, it usually meant that the girl had been promised for marriage by her father when she was still an infant.[19] A fiancé was allowed to visit his future wife from time to time when she was still 'under custom'. Sexual play between them was condoned, but full intercourse was strictly forbidden (Huber 1993: 98-100).

An aspect of *dipo* that comes to the fore again and again in the missionary descriptions, was the fact that *dipo*, not marriage, served as the prerequisite for girls to enter into sexual relationships and conceive. As I described earlier, if a Krobo woman was not yet married, any children she brought forth would belong to her father's patrilineage and not to her children's father. They would be called *yo bi* ('woman's child'). A father, lacking a large number of sons, in this way tried to maintain the strength of his family by not allowing his daughter to marry into another one. The missionaries considered children born out of wedlock as illegitimate children. However, to the Krobo these children were rather welcomed as an important labour force, and became full family members.

The first generation of Christian converts was given a hard time by other Krobo, as they challenged the customary laws of Krobo society. From some of the life histories collected by Odjidja (1977: 39 and 61), we can deduce that several converts became outcasts on the fringe of society and were often declared ritually dead by their families and symbolically buried. Many of the very early converts were on the margin of society anyway, as they were often (former) slaves or old women (cf. Hastings 1993: 112; Middleton 1983). One other important group of early converts and dropouts in Krobo society, were 'fallen *dipo* girls' who had become pregnant before passing through *dipo*. Christianity offered a way out for these girls. They were 'saved' from marginalisation by the missionaries. The Christian congregation in the outpost of the town Sra in particular consisted of several women who had become pregnant before performing *dipo* and therefore sought protection with the church. For these girls the mission provided an escape from the punishment of the priests. To the wider community, however, the mission was seen as an asylum for girls who had broken social mores by disobeying the priests and their elders. These women had lost all respect and status as adult marriageable women in their own society. Even though the missionaries strongly opposed *dipo*, they themselves recognised the 'bad influence' of 'fallen *dipo* girls' on the congregation, who had converted out of necessity. They blamed the bad state of the Sra congregation on the influence of these 'unchaste' women.

Many missionaries produced or simply replicated a very negative image of the Krobo, their 'heathen world' and *dipo*. The only true exception to this was the missionary Johannes Zimmermann (1825-1876). He wrote in 1866:

Young unmarried brothers have written many foolish things about this custom in the past. Girls are not 'temple harlots', nor are they 'devoted to the fetish', but they are, when they grow to maturity, gathered on the mountain and secluded until the wedding, that most of the time forms the end of the customs.[20] (Original in German, my translation)

Zimmermann seems to suggest that the fact that his missionary 'brothers' were young and not married explains their obsession with the sexuality of young girls. At the same time, Zimmermann was also convinced that *dipo* eventually had to be replaced by Christian education, because in his opinion too the practice led to immorality.[21]

Basel Mission Cultural Policy and its Consequences

The Basel missionaries created contradictions they were unable to resolve. On the one hand the missionaries identified the work among women as crucial to the success of Christianising the Krobo as a whole. On the other hand women were part of the problem of spreading Christianity, as they were not willing to dissociate themselves from *dipo*, which was a precondition for conversion. Whereas the Basel Mission wanted to turn Krobo women into good wives and mothers according to Christian standards, of course without letting them pass through *dipo*, matters of sexuality and reproduction were not limited to marriage according to the Krobo. Moreover, *dipo* was rather the precondition for pregnancy and marriage, because it was also linked to kinship ties, economic prosperity, the worship of Nana Klowɛki and the integrative aspect of the rituals that constructed Krobo identity. The costs of conversion were too high for Krobo women if it meant giving up *dipo*.

The Basel missionaries saw the education of girls as crucial, and as a replacement of 'the pagan way', that is, of *dipo*. However, despite the hopes and dreams of the missionaries concerning the education and conversion of Krobo girls, the progress was very slow for the remainder of the 19th-century, even after 1892 when the British colonial government put a ban on 'Krobo customs' (Steegstra 2004: Ch. 4). Even though from the early 20th century the situation as a whole started to improve slowly for the BM, the ban on *dipo* had some unforeseen effects. In the first years after the eviction from the Krobo Mountain, many girls were banished from their hometowns, because they became pregnant without going through any initiation.[22] Some of them may have ended up in prostitution. Instead of losing their power, as the missionaries expected, the priests rather continued to exert their influence. After a while all the necessary so-called 'fetish' rituals were performed again, in secret, but away from the Krobo Mountain and in a drastically shortened way. Instead of staying in seclusion on the Krobo Mountain up to one year, the girls now just had to pass through the essential rituals of *dipo* in the hometowns on the plains, which only lasted a few weeks. It also became a new practise among the Christian Krobo, to pass through *dipo* before being baptised. The subsequent younger ages of *dipo* girls can be seen as a strategy to cope simultaneously with traditional demands and Christianity.

After the Basel missionaries had left the Gold Coast as a result of the first World War, their successor, the Presbyterian Church and their Basel Mission trained representatives continued the same strict attitude towards Krobo traditions (see e.g. Odjidja 1973; Teyegaga 1985). The decrease of British suspicions of Krobo, the appreciating attitude of Konor Azu Mate Kole (reigning from 1939-1990) and the spread of new churches contributed to the renewed (public) celebration of Krobo ceremonies, *dipo* in particular, especially from the 1950s onwards. The churches in the Krobo area, however, still do not allow participation in *dipo*, nor have they succeeded or even tried to, institutionalise elements of *dipo* into church ceremonies such as confirmation, as has been recorded for cases in Southern Africa (see examples in Cox 1998). In spite of this I estimate that the vast majority of the women though mainly Christian have passed through the *dipo* rites (Steegstra 2004: 161). Conflicts over sexuality remain.

In sum, the Basel Mission's cultural policy and preoccupation with sexual morality had some paradoxical effects visible to this very day, as the ban on *dipo* did not result in its abolition, but caused some profound changes in the ceremony and contributed to the negative moral image of Krobo women (also see Steegstra 2002). In the next sections I will go into some of these changes and the continued contestation of *dipo*.

Age and Sexuality

One of the most common complaints about *dipo* these days is that people say that girls are initiated at a younger age than in the past, which is supposed to have undesired consequences. They are said to enter into sexual relationships at an early age, as this is allowed after *dipo*. A recent survey conducted in Kumasi, Accra and Agomanya in 2000, however, showed that in different communities in Ghana high portions of young people engage in sex at early ages (Commission 2003: 41-42). Apart from the distinction in rural/urban living conditions, no specific mention was made of cultural factors influencing these ages.

Many people feel that young ages at the time of initiation deviate from 'the original practice', and that it was different in former times. However, I found that the majority of the girls passing through the rites were around fourteen years old, which may not be so different from the past. It seems that most girls have their first period around this age. Only 27 out of 110 girls (24.5%) interviewed at the time of their initiation in 1999, were below eight years, while 60 out of these 110 girls (55%) were twelve years and older.[23]

Different people told me that they consider eight years or older an acceptable age for initiation, and pleaded for such an age limit.[24] It seems that from eight years onwards girls are considered to mature: they may start to menstruate and become sexually active, and comprehend what is happening. At the same time they therefore also enter 'the danger zone'. Hence Huber's explanation that girls are initiated below the age of eight because their parents are afraid of a pregnancy before the rites, (and the consequent punishment of expulsion) seems plausible (Huber 1993: 166). The parents want to be on the safe side.[25]

However, the supposed change in age for *dipo* initiands is not a recent change. Remarkably, the same minimum age was even already mentioned about 125 years ago, when missionary Weiss noticed in 1877 that not only mature girls went on Krobo Mountain, "but also girls of six or seven years old".[26] This mainly seems to have been a result of the increasing impact of missionary and colonial influence, as I described more elaborately elsewhere (Steegstra 2004). Interestingly, Huber (1993: 166), based on his research in the 1950s, considers the same age of 'seven or even less' to be deviating from 'the original practice'.

The fact that the ages of initiands are felt to be younger now than used to be the case is a matter of perception. A girl of fourteen may have appeared to be more mature in the past than today. In the past girls hardly attended school, (and many still do not).[27] When a girl's breasts began to grow she was considered to be maturing. After *dipo*, which was (and is) the main precondition for socially accepted pregnancy, girls were encouraged to have children early and even outside of legal marriage. At the same time, girls probably used to marry at a young age, as the ideal was to marry right after *dipo*. However, now that more girls attend school, the time gap between the onset of puberty and marriage has widened, as Oppong (1974: 4) already pointed out in 1974, while girls still often conceive early. 'Teenage pregnancy' is experienced as a dilemma now, partly in relation to the high number of female school dropouts, as pregnant girls are not allowed to attend school, partly because the hegemonic Christian morality places sexuality within marriage.

The reasons why some girls pass through the rites at a younger age than deemed desirable, are also of an economic nature and have to do with convenience. When investigating the earlier mentioned 110 initiands, only one girl of four years old was said to have come to her hometown (*dɔm*) without any older siblings or relatives to participate in *dipo*. I found that all other very young candidates had come along with one of their older sisters or cousins because it was time for the latter to be initiated. The younger ones had been added out of convenience.

Another important reason for parents to have their daughters initiated at a young age is the influence of Christianity. Huber does not say much about this subject. He only adds in a footnote that, apart from his already mentioned anxiety over a possible pregnancy before the rites, another reason for the young age of some *dipo* girls is that churches forbid *dipo* for their baptised members. Therefore parents let their daughters pass through *dipo* before baptism (Huber 1993: 166). This reason applies especially to the members of former mission churches and in particular to the Presbyterian Church, as it inherited this cultural policy from the Basel missionaries. Ironically, the same Christians who often complain about the young ages of the girls going through *dipo*, and regard it as proof that it is an 'outmoded custom', because they do not think that they learn much from it at such a young age, are therefore the ones who let their daughters be initiated at a young age.

Apart from influencing the ages of *dipo* girls, it may be (partly) due to Christianity and associated social changes that a number of rituals referring overtly to sexuality have rather disappeared from the ceremony and that the importance of *dipo* as a life cycle marker has decreased. Some early sources seem to confirm that during the seclusion time of girls on the mountain there was some kind of informal teaching, also about sexuality (Azu 1928:28-29).[28]

In former times, for example, an uninitiated girl could be distinguished from an initiated woman by the way she was dressed, as I mentioned earlier. One characteristic element was that she wore her wrapper below her naked breasts. The elder woman in the house could tell by watching the development of a girl's breast that she was coming of age. This would mark her readiness for the initiation rites into womanhood. In the past, massaging breasts to delay the onset of puberty was a common practice, which is called *nyo-kpami*. It is not directly related to *dipo* as such, but different people with whom I spoke made this connection, as it was seen a step on the road to maturity. It was an act that a mother would perform for her daughter, when she thought that the girl was becoming sexually mature too early. She would massage away the breasts of the girl with a stone. One informant thought it would delay the start of the menstrual cycle. Ashie's writings (n.d.: 43-44) confirm that the massaging would be done three times, with an interval of a few years. During this period a girl would be called a *smuggle*, he wrote, probably pidgin English for 'small girl'. When the breasts started growing, the girl was considered to have become old enough for *dipo*. Older women I spoke to specified their age by referring to their breasts. They might say for instance: 'I was a little grown, my breasts were just bulging out (when such and so happened).' When I asked older women at what age *dipo* was performed for them, they proudly said that they has big breasts when it was done for them.

Another example of the symbolic relation between *dipo* and sexual maturity was the marks on initiated women's bodies. Until recently, young women would have incised after *dipo* to prepare their bodies for adult sexuality and to mark them as Krobo women. Huber wrote that: "there is the conviction, dating from ancient times, that no Krobo girl can ever become a mature Krobo woman and a wife worthy of a Krobo man, unless she can show on her body and on her hand the visible marks of her initiation' (Huber 1993: 165). Today the 'sweeping marks' on the hands as a proof of passing the 'sweeping test' are still given to some girls. With a razor blade small cuts are incised, after which irritants are rubbed inside the wounds to encourage the build-up of the scar tissue. Most adult Krobo women can still be recognised by these marks. Some of the earlier educated and Christian girls did not receive any marks even in the past. A seventy-two year old woman told me: 'they didn't give me the marks the first time [around 1940]. I was a schoolgirl. None of the school girls did this'. She also said that her *dipo* was done 'secretly'. Most school girls in those days were Presbyterians. And to hide that they had been initiated, they did not receive these marks.

Apart from the marks on their hands, women used to receive scars around the waist (*aplamdɔ*), and on the belly (*yisi wombo*).[29] According to Tettey (1977: 6), *aplamdɔ* means 'marriage taboo marks', indicating that no man but the husband would be allowed to touch his wife's waist. Elderly women I met who were over seventy years old still had these marks, but also a befriended market woman I met who was in her forties showed the marks on her belly to me. The women, often chuckling, said that only their own husband was allowed to touch them there, so apparently they had erotic significance. One priestess said it showed a woman's capability of giving birth, another way of linking it with sexuality. Another old woman said that with these marks you can be recognised as a (ritually) cleansed person.

Krobo women and prostitution

Prostitution in the Krobo area and in Ghana in general is not something new. In his article on prostitution and the politics of sex in the Gold Coast from the seventeenth to the twentieth centuries, Akyeampong (1997) emphasises that prostitution on the Gold Coast in this time period was not a novel, urban phenomenon that would reflect the collapse of the traditional moral order with the advent of colonial capitalism. Prostitution had existed before. However, what *was* new about urban prostitution in the colonial Gold Coast, was its explicit connection to independent, material accumulation among women.

Europeans who mainly stayed in the coastal towns, were used to finding women there who exchanged casual sex for money. According to Akyampong (1997: 157):

> Although the colonial urban economy was essentially a male economy, the unwillingness of the colonial state and capital to provide for the social reproduction of their labour force, and the sexual imbalance in working-class towns, created economic opportunities for women in the interstices of the colonial system.

For newly arrived women the rendering of sexual services was an important initial strategy for subsistence: "The need for security and social networks encouraged prostitutes, often from the same ethnic group, to settle close together. This encouraged the construction of ethnic sexual stereotypes by other ethnic groups" (ibid. 1997: 158). Eriksen (1993: 155) explains that sexual stereotyping is related to ethnicity in many societies, as gender imagery is often used to describe ethnic groups as a whole. In such a practice gender can be used not only as a symbol of 'objective' cultural differences between ethnic groups, but also as an expression of myths and prejudices that can strengthen those differences (Santen & Schilder 1994: 133). Akyeampong mentions the preponderance of Krobo prostitutes in colonial and post-colonial Asante as an example, which encouraged the folk tradition that Okomfo Anokye, an indigenous priest instrumental in the founding of the Asante nation and state, had cursed Krobo women with prostitution (1997: 159). This story is well-known by non-Krobo people and different Ghanaians have told me a version before.[30]

Hence, prostitution was common on the Gold Coast and also among Krobo women long before Independence (1957). However, the creation of the Volta Lake for hydro-electricity in the 1960s had a profound impact on the number of Krobo women working in prostitution. Over twenty percent of the semi-deciduous forest area of Manya Krobo was inundated and about 80,000 inhabitants were displaced, many of whom were Krobo (Hart D. 1980). This contributed to the general economic decline in Krobo society. Consequently, there have been significant migrations to newer frontier farming areas and the urban sector within Ghana and other West African countries (such as La Côte d'Ivoire and Nigeria). Many women then first started to work as service workers in hotels and drinking spots that sprang up in the small towns of the area to serve construction workers working on the dam. According to Kofi (1986) and Decosas (1996: 5), from there it was only a small step into the business of prostitution. When the main force of construction workers left, the women took their business to Accra, Kumasi and then throughout West Africa. Their remittances became an important source of development capital in some towns in the Krobo region for a period of about twenty years:

There are more than thirty decent houses in the village [Kodjonya] including the house of the chief as well as three manufacturing businesses (soap and alcohol) owned by women working (in prostitution) abroad (Kofi 1986).

A relatively large community of Krobo people can still be found in Abidjan. The high migration rates, however, have created a new problem. They have shown a correspondence with high HIV prevalence rates, as many women working in prostitution in Abidjan return to their hometowns with the HIV virus. Especially in the initial stage of the AIDS epidemic in Ghana, (as noted in the epilogue below) there was a high percentage of infected women, which is attributed to return migration of female commercial sex workers. Initially the Eastern region therefore dominated as the focal point of HIV/-AIDS (Agyei-Mensah 2001). It was here that the first HIV cases were diagnosed in Ghana (Commission 2003: 9).[31] Decosas sees a relationship between the age structure among Krobo women living with HIV, the highest rate was among women aged 30-40 in a 1995 survey, and the fatherless daughters of the migrant construction workers who built the huge dam. He supposes these daughters of prostitutes followed their mothers into prostitution (Decosas 1996: 5).[32]

Different Krobo women living in Abidjan I talked to, have indeed been there since the 1970s or (early) 1980s.[33] Women at that time returning to Ghana with the much desired CFA (currency in Francophone countries), looking wealthy and glamorous, enticed other women to travel. This coincides with Tettey's findings from the 1970s. In his B.A. thesis, Tettey (1977) discusses some changes in the performance of *dipo*. He established that the gap between *dipo* and marriage has widened and looked for some of the causes. Some Krobo girls he came across said they preferred to stay single to get full time to engage in trading. According to Tettey, there were two reasons for this preference. First, girls felt that a marriage contracted immediately after *dipo* would make them too dependent on their husbands and restrict their freedom. As a second reason Tettey observed their taste for material things:

> Most of the girls admire things like sewing machines, electronic equipment like radios and record players, sweet-scenting cosmetics and assorted cloths brought by the local professional prostitutes from the neighbouring French-speaking countries. In fact the Krobo society is being deprived of its beautiful and marriageable girls largely as a result of the quest for "French goods". Even some married women have lent themselves to "the business" and many marriages have broken in recent years as a result. This is a problem facing the Yilo and Manya Krobo Traditional Councils and the earlier it is checked the better it will be (Tettey 1977: 26).

Young people of today are no longer very attracted to travel to Abidjan and running the risk of coming back sick and destitute. Those young people living there now, mostly either came along with their mothers or were born in Abidjan. Most of the Krobo migrants have little education. Many do not speak English, but they learned to speak French in Ivory Coast, (so that I conversed with them in both French and Krobo language). Now most of them are still poor, and do not have the money to go back and settle permanently in Ghana again. They live in poor circumstances in the slum areas of Abidjan. Many have fallen ill due to the work they do. Only a few openly admit that they 'sell their vagina', as they call it in Krobo. But in the evening time what many of the women here 'trade' becomes quite obvious from the way they sit in the doorsteps of their single-rooms, often wooden, houses, with make-up on their bleached faces and men approaching them.

As fewer Krobo women travel to such places as Abidjan to work in prostitution, the rate of AIDS cases seems to be dropping, and the Krobo area no longer leads in the number of cases in Ghana. The long presence of an AIDS clinic at St. Martin's hospital in Agomanya, which promotes awareness programmes, may have been an influencing factor. In recent years the Manya Krobo Queen Mothers Association has also become very active in the fight against HIV/AIDS, which may also have contributed to the apparently successful battle against the further spread of HIV/AIDS (see e.g. Palak 2003). However, the still relatively high percentage of HIV infected Krobo women seems to reflect the close connection between migrant mobility and the spread of HIV/AIDS, a connection noted elsewhere. For example Anarfi et al. (1971), in a study of women traders in Techiman and Yeji in the Brong Ahafo Region, found that women who travel long distances to different markets to purchase items for sale are at high risk of contracting HIV, as they become involved in multiple sexual relationships.

The Krobo people living in Abidjan maintain their relationships with their home in Ghana. For 'customs' many people regularly return to their hometown in Krobo. This ideally includes their own funeral. Many people try to go home when they are deathly ill, or their body is transported to Ghana for the funeral. It is still a taboo to mention AIDS as the cause of death, but it is a public secret that this is often the case for women returning from Abidjan. People also return to the hometowns for the *dipo* rites of their daughters. One man called Victor, for example, told me that he would perform *dipo* soon for his daughters, who were then seven and three years old, even though he himself had come to Abidjan with his mother as a very young boy. He said that if they did not pass through the rites, they would not be able to go to their family in Odumase or marry there. I also met several women in Abidjan who recognised me because they had met or seen me in Odumase or Somanya during the *dipo* celebrations of that same year just a month before. So even though these Krobo migrants stay in Abidjan, they continue to rely on their relatives in times of need and see themselves as Krobo people, and therefore maintain relationships with home by observing 'customs', including *dipo*.

Conclusion

In this chapter I tried to investigate why Krobo women are stereotyped as being promiscuous, and what the link is with *dipo*. I proposed that the Basel Mission's preoccupation with sexual morality caused some profound changes in the performance of *dipo* and reinforced negative stereotypes of Krobo women. The first written descriptions we have of *dipo* are from the Basel missionaries, the very people who wanted it to be abolished and who showed an obvious Western, Christian bias. Their view that sexuality should be situated within marriage is a Christian ideology and part of the Christian morality, which has been a point of tension with Krobo ideas of gender and morality from the beginning. However, even though *dipo* is the prerequisite to enter into sexual relationships, it is not to be expected that girls of less than eight years old will engage in such relationships immediately after they have been initiated. As I explained, the main aim of *dipo* is rather to make girls full members of their family and society. Moreover, the majority of the girls are older and the average still lies around fourteen. There is no proof that girls who have passed through *dipo* have sex at an earlier age than girls from other groups in Ghana.

Even though there may have been a longer history of a negative stereotype of Krobo women, the colonial impact, especially that of the Basel missionaries, has certainly reinforced this negative moral reputation of Krobo women, or even encouraged practices that are immoral from a Christian point of view. The missionaries' cultural politics resulted in undesired effects. It was quite paradoxical, for example, that they 'saved' unmarried pregnant women and hence made Christianity a way out for 'unchaste' women, who would normally have been banned from society. So whereas the Mission wanted to create 'Christian wives', the result was non-initiated women, unfit for marriage in Krobo eyes. And whereas they advocated strict Christian sexual morals, they actually supported illegitimate sexual relations and childbirth, in terms of Krobo perceptions. It is possible that in the past, Krobo women who were 'outcasts' were already engaged in prostitution outside the Krobo area. Now uninitiated 'Christian' women contributed to a negative image of Krobo women as 'loose'. The enforcement of 'proper dressing' contributed to such a message, for the initiated and therefore socially adult girls could no longer be distinguished from the uninitiated ones.

Mechanisms of cultural change cannot be studied in isolation from existing power inequalities. The colonial exercise of power over the Krobo was therefore not only expressed by the many negative views of the *dipo* practice by administrators and missionaries; it was also demonstrated by the fact that the Krobo to some extent internalized these negative meanings and that the Christian discourse became hegemonic. Discussing *dipo* can nowadays only be done through an idiom of conflict between 'tradition' and 'Christianity', thus within the limited discursive space laid out by the missionary and colonial discourse. This creates a constant field of tension with the actual practice of *dipo*, which for most Krobo is an entirely obvious phenomenon. The *dipo* rites are often talked about as the catalyst of 'immoral behaviour', teenage pregnancies and prostitution. Whereas the *dipo* rites are contested within Krobo society itself, other groups in Ghana often perceive Krobo women as promiscuous and they are known for supposed prostitution. The preoccupations of Basel missionaries with *dipo* as pagan and immoral have contributed to make women's sexuality emblematic of Krobo identity.

The idea therefore that sexual education about HIV/AIDS should be integrated into the *dipo* performance neglects the fact that former missions and Pentecostal churches, whose representatives are leading spokespersons in public debates, are so vehemently against people and that in their view *dipo* is linked with immorality. This idea also fails to understand the practice and meaning of *dipo*. It assumes that *dipo* used to be performed only to prevent premarital sex and that the ceremony now 'has lost its function'. This approach is based on an a-historical, static view of 'tradition', which supposes that *dipo* only recently changed and did not have a history before. However *dipo* is part of a living culture and the meanings of the rites have always been changing within shifting context. In addition, this is an Akan-biased approach assuming that *dipo* is similar to the Akan nubility or puberty rites (*bragoro*) (see Sarpong 1977). I prefer to classify *dipo* as an 'initiation' rather than as a 'puberty rite', as there is no link with the first menstruation, girls are initiated in groups and their ages may range from around two to about eighteen years.[34] If *dipo* was only about the life cycle of individual girls it is possible that the rite would have become less important long ago, as many girls are school going and the gap between *dipo* and marriage has widened. But the rites have persisted, even after 150 years of constant condemnation of the rite, because they are deeply embedded in Krobo history and culture. Today, they most of all are an important marker of Krobo identity.

Prostitution has probably always existed, but among the Krobo it seems to have become more rampant during the 1960s, 70s and early 80s, mainly correlating with economic circumstances. There is a close relationship between the resultant high population mobility, prostitution, and the spread of HIV/AIDS. There is no direct link between the spread of HIV/AIDS and *dipo*. For critics of *dipo*, it may be convenient to leave economic consequences of modernisation, such as resettlement, migration and poverty, out of the analysis of the problem of the spread of HIV/AIDS. However, blaming so-called 'backward rituals' will not solve anything. Therefore we should be wary of easy associations between cultural practices and the spread of HIV and AIDS.

Endnotes

1   I want to thank Birgit Meyer for her helpful comments on an earlier draft version of this chapter. This chapter is a result of my PhD project about the resilience of the *dipo* rites and the politics of culture in Ghana (Steegstra 2004). It is based on archival research and on anthropological fieldwork. I am grateful to Paul Jenkins and Veit Arlt for facilitating the historical research in the archives of the Basel Mission in 1997. The fieldwork was conducted in the Krobo area and partly in Abidjan from June 1998 to June 1999 and in June and July 2000. I want to thank all the Krobo women and men who shared their knowledge with me, especially Ju;liana Baidoo, Lalio Sahite and Manye Maku Tettey. The research would not have been possible without the financial assistance of the Netherlands Foundation for the Advancement of Tropical Research (WOTRO).

2   I conducted research in and around Krobo-Odumase, the capital of Manya Krobo, each with their own paramount chief (*konor*). The town itself has about 14,000 inhabitants, but is part of a conglomeration of towns of almost 45,000 people (see GSS 2002a: 32,38) The Krobo are the largest group among the patrilineal Dangme speaking people in what is today the Eastern Region of Ghana and they number about a quarter of a million people. Other Dangme-speaking peoples in the South of Ghana are the Shai, the Osudoku, and the coastal Ningo and Ada people. According to the latest census figures, the Ga-Dangme comprise 8.0% of the total population in Ghana, which makes them the fourth largest ethnic group. (GSS 2002c: table 4: 'Ethnic grouping of Ghanaians by birth by region').

3   In an interview with the director general of the Ghana AIDS Commssion, the rate was said to have come down to 7.5% for Manya Krobo in 2003, while Koforidua has shot up from 4.5% to 8.5% (Quist Arcton 2003). In recent years the Manya Krobo Queen

Mothers' Association has become very active in the fight against HIV/AIDS, not without success it seems (see e.g. Palak 2003).

4   Table 11: Industry of Economically Active Population by Region and Sex (GSS 2002c: 32).

5   Source: http://www.buitenlandsezaken.nl/ : 'countries and regions'.

6   However, the mostly subsistence-oriented farming reduces the cost of living and it is possible to sell some of the produce to cover school fees etc. High-profit farming is mostly centred on cash crops such as mango, banana or papaya, but the more easily exploited flat lands in the plains are expensive nowadays. Generally there is the wish to make fast money, which prevents people from making long-term investments that will yield higher profits over a longer period (much like their ancestors took up palm and cocoa farming). This is typical of the desperate economic situation in present day Ghana.

7   About the background of the priest missionaries of the Basel Mission, see, for example, Miller (1994) and Prodolliet (1987).

8   For a detailed description see Steegstra (2004).

9   There are said to be 38 *dipo* sacred 'stones' (*tɛgbɛtɛ*) in Manya Krobo, and about 24 in Yilo Krobo, each of which is supervised by a priest and each of which is used for some of the main rites by different 'houses' ('house' as a social unit, i.e. lineage) where *dipo* is performed.

10   All the essential rites can thus be performed in one weekend. There is a tendency towards a shortening of the rites in general. It cuts down the expenses, but also is one way for Christians to more easily cope with 'traditional' and Christian demands at the same time. In the past, after the main rites, a girl could remain on Krobo Mountain (the ritual centre until 1892) up to one year or more to be beautified, to be prepared for a future life as an adult woman and add to the prestige of the family before she married. The longer the relatives of a girl were able to afford her upkeep on Krobo Mountain before her final coming out ceremony, the greater their prestige.

11   Bringing a living animal in contact with a person and letting the blood flow over the person's feet and touching the feet with it, are characteristic details of purification rituals among the Dangme (see Huber 1958).

12   In case a girl violates the rule of chastity before *dipo* and becomes pregnant, the priest *Asaa* is the one who has to perform the necessary rites to drive the girl away from the town and cleanse the house.

13   This is because the palm fibre has ancestral associations. The same fibre (either *sɔni* or *komi*) is used at other moments during *dipo*. The fact that only ritually clean people are allowed to wear the hat, explains why the hats are worn after the *tɛgbɛtɛ*, when the girls have undergone the ultimate test and have come out as 'pure' Krobo women. Giving the hat to the *dipo* girls also symbolises the girls' engagement with Klowɛki in the manner of newly initiated priests (Coplan 1972: 28) The investiture with white calico, the killing of a black goat and the cleansing with its blood, the confinement with specific food prohibitions and the dressing up with beads, are also all features that the *dipo* ceremony has in common with the installation ceremony for a priest (Huber 1993: 189). Huber (1958: 168) states that: "Both before and during their puberty rites the girls are to a

certain extent regarded as 'spouses' or 'wives' of the gods, i.e., of the gods' guardians, the priests".

14   These cuts are still apparent on the hands of most adult women but it seems that it is not done these days. The photograph taken is the proof and is easier to hide than the visible marks on the hands which are considered "primitive" by church going people, who would not want others to know that *dipo* was performed for them.

15   Interview with pastor Samako, founder of the 'Christ City Church, Odumase, 7 October 1998.

16   *Der evangelische Heidenbote*, March 1852, No. 3, p. 19

17   Other examples are references to polygyny, adultery and fornication, and liquor consumption. For example, see Kanogo (1993), who describes the same attitude of missionaries towards cultural practices of the Kikuyu in Kenya.

18   BMA, D-1.9 Afrika 1858, Abokobi nr. 13, J. Heck, 25.5.1858, Abokobi, 'Reisebericht'; original in German, my translation.

19   Basel missionary reports show that in this way many strategic alliances were made between families. Although there was no physical coercion on the part of the parents in the choice of a marriage partner, the social and moral pressure was so strong that respectful children would have found it difficult to choose their own partner against the will of their parents.

20   BMA, D-1.18B Afrika 1866, Teil 2, Odumase, no. 3, J. Zimmermann, 06.06.1866, Odumase.

21   Johannes Zimmermann arrived on the Gold Coast in 1850. His exceptional position was partly due to his long stay in Africa, between 1850 and 1876, with only one leave to Europe in 1872. Many others did not survive long enough and died of tropical fevers. He also held a different position due to his marriage to a black woman, Catherine Mulgrave. Another decisive factor was his knowledge of the local languages. Zimmermann was a linguist and an ethnographer. His views grew milder over the years, and he increasingly became an insider in Krobo society. Zimmermann disagreed with the mission's view of a natural hierarchy, which scaled Africans in the lowest position and strongly discouraged socialising between Europeans and Africans in any form that suggested equality (Miller 1994: 132-133).

22   GNA / ADM 11/1115 (M.P. 4997 A /96?), J. N. Coy, D.C. Akuse, 14.07.1896, Akuse, 'Extract from a report from the District Commissioner Akuse to the Colonial Secretary dated 14th July 1896'.

23   I asked the age of 110 *dipo* candidates at the houses of seven different *dipo* priests. This age may not always be correct. In some cases it can be assumed that the girls did not know their exact age, as many people in Ghana do not know the precise date of birth. The largest number of girls (15) was found in the category of fourteen years old, eleven girls were fifteen and twelve girls said to be sixteen.

24   Paramount queen mother of Yilo Krobo, *Manyɛ* Nana Korlekwor Adjado III, is one of those people who plead for girls to be initiated at the age of eight and over. In an interview I had with her in July 2000, she explained that she had investigated the *dipo* rites in 1999. She established that there was dissatisfaction among her people about the young ages of many *dipo* initiates. She then proposed to the Traditional Council and

later in a meeting with Krobo priestesses to set an age limit for *dipo* with a minimum age of eight. In another interview I had with the old *wono* Asa in July 1994, he suggested the same. In a public speech, the *kono* of Manya Krobo, however, called for a restriction of the ages of girls going through *dipo* to fifteen years and higher (Doku 2000; GNA 2000).

25 However, Huber does not clarify why there would be a greater fear for a possible pregnancy at the time of his research, the 1950s, than before.

26 BMA D-1.29, Weiss, 18.2.1878, Odumase, 'Jahresbericht der Mädchenanstalt pro 1877 (als Beibericht zum Jahresbericht der Station Odumase)'.

27 The national literacy rate figures for 2000 were 45.7% for females, and 62.0% for males. For the Eastern Region these figures were 49.8% and 69.4% respectively. Census 2000, (GSS 2002c: 'Table 8: Selected Educational Characteristics of Population by Region and Sex'). The literacy rate of the northern regions is even lower than that of the southern regions in Ghana.

28 However later comparisons of (Basel mission educated) writers equating *dipo* with a western type of school, seem rather to be a Western projection. The first publication of Krobo history are written by members of the first generation of Krobo converts, eg. Noa Azu and Thomas Odonkor. These scholars were descendants of Odonkor Azu (1867), who is said to have been the first recognized paramount chief (*kono*) of Manya Krobo. He was the one who received the Basel missionaries warmly and through whose children's education they hoped to gain a strong foothold in Krobo society. Using them as sources of history one has to be aware that the authors were educated in mission schools, which causes a certain bias. By the very fact of introducing a written record, Christianity has therefore played an important role in shaping Krobo history and historiography.

29 Elsewhere the marks on the belly are called *fomi bo* (Schroeder & Danquah 2000: 5)

30 Usually the story goes that Okomfo Anokye once was travelling. When he stopped to take a bath in a stream a few Krobo women passing by were watching him from the bushes and made fun of him. When he noticed them, he became so angry that he cursed them and said that men would never leave them in peace.

31 Konotey-Ahulu's research showed that in February 1988 there were 30 diagnosed AIDS patients in the Krobo area, of which one was a male pimp, 28 patients were prostitutes, and one was the child of one of the sick patients (Konotey-Ahulu 1989).

32 However, he assumes that these women had no choice but to work in prostitution, as in a strictly patrilineal society they would not inherit anything. This is not true in Krobo society, where fatherless children (*yo bi*) belong to their mother's patrilineage and thus their maternal grandfather takes care of them and they inherit from him, as I explained earlier.

33 I visited Abidjan together with a female Krobo friend in May 1999.

34 Moreover the term 'puberty' or adolescence is problematic, as it is mainly an etic term which foregoes indigenous classification (cf. Roscoe 1995: 230).

Bibliography

Afenyadu, Dela, & Goparaju, Lakshmi, 2003. *Adolescent sexual and reproductive health behaviour in Dodowa, Ghana.* Washington: Cedpa.

Agyei-Mensah, Samuel, 2001. Twelve years of HIV/AIDS in Ghana: puzzles of interpretation. *Canadian Journal of African Studies, 35*(3), 441-472.

Akyeampong, Emmanuel Kwaku, 1997. Sexuality and prostitution among the Akan of the Gold Coast c. 1650-1950. *Past and Present. A Journal of Historical Studies, 156* (August), 144-173.

Amanor, Kojo Sebastian, 1994. *The new frontier: Farmer responses to land degradation: A West African study.* Geneva, London & New Jersey: UNRISD, Zed Books LTD.

Arbuckle, Anne N. (n.d.), *The condom crisis: An application of feminist legal theory to AIDS prevention in African women.* Retrieved 23-05, 2000, from the World Wide Web: www.law.indiana.edu/glsj/vol3/no2/arbuckle.html

Azu, Noa Akunor Aguae, 1928. Adangbe (Adangme) history – Concluded (arranged and translated by Enoch Azu). *The Gold Coast Review, IV*(1), 3-30.

Bowie, Fiona, 2000. *The Anthropology of Religion. An Introduction.* Oxford and Malden, Massachusetts: Blackwell Publishers.

Braude, Benjamin, 1997. The sons of Noah and the construction of ethnic and geographical identities in the medieval and early modern periods. *William and Mary Quarterly, 54*(1), 103-142.

Commission, The Measure project and the Ghana AIDS, 2003. *AIDS in Africa during the nineties: Ghana. A review and analysis of survey and research results.* Carolina Population Center: University of North Carolina at Chapel Hill.

Cox, James L. (ed.), 1998. *Rites of passage in contemporary Africa: Interaction between Christian and African traditional religions.* Cardiff: Cardiff Academic Press.

Decosas, Josef, 1996. AIDS and development – What is the link? *Development Express, 7*, 1-9.

Doku, Francis, 2000, June 29 – July 5. 'Krobo girls told: No more *Dipo* until age 15.' *Graphic Showbiz,* pp. 1, 8.

Eriksen, Thomas Hylland, 1993. *Ethnicity and Nationalism. Anthropological Perspectives.* London, East Haven: Pluto Press.

GNA. 2000, June 23. 'Manya Krobo to review cultural practices.' *Daily Graphic,* pp. 16-17.

Grimes, R. L., 2000. *Deeply into the Bone. Re-inventing Rites of Passage.* Berkeley: University of California Press.

GSS. 2002a. *2000 Population & Housing Census. Special report on 20 largest localities*: Ghana Statistical Services. Accra

GSS. 2002c . *2000 Population & housing census. Summary report of final results*: Ghana Statistical Services, Accra.

Hampton, Jamie, 1991. *Meeting AIDS with compassion. AIDS care and prevention in Agomanya, Ghana*. London, Nairobi, Colchester: ACTIOMAID, AMREF, World in Need.

Hart, D., 1980. *The Volta River project: A case study in politics and technology*. Edinburgh: University Press.

Hastings, Adrian, 1993. Were women a special case? In F. Bowie & D. Kirkwood & S. Ardener (eds.), *Women and missions: Past and present. anthropological and historical perceptions*. Providence, Oxford: Berg. Pp. 109-125.

Hastings, Adrian, 1994. *The church in Africa, 1450 – 1950*. Oxford: Clarendon Press.

Hefner, Robert W., 1993. Part one. Introduction. 'World building and the rationality of conversion.' In R. W. Hefner (ed.), *Conversion to Christianity. Historical and anthropological perspectives on a great transformation*. Berkeley, Los Angeles, Oxford: University of California Press. Pp. 3-44.

Huber, Hugo, 1958. Adangme purification and pacification rituals (West Africa). *Anthropos, 53*, 161-191.

Huber, Hugo, 1993. *The Krobo. Traditional social and religious life of a West African people*. Fribourg, Switzerland: University Press .

Kanogo, Tabitha, 1993. Mission impact on women in colonial Kenya. In F. Bowie & D. Kirkwood & S. Ardener (eds.), *Women and missions: Past and present. Anthropological and historical perceptions*. Providence, Oxford: Berg. Pp. 165-186.

Kirby, Jon P., 1994. Cultural change and religious conversion in West Africa. In T. D. Blakely & W. E. A. v. Beek & D. L. Thomson (eds.), *Religion in Africa: Experience and expression*. London: James Currey. Pp. 56-71

Kofi, A.R.T., 1986. *The siting of the Akosombo Dam as a cause of prostitution among Krobo girls at Kodjonya*. Sociology Department, University of Ghana, Legon.

Konotey-Ahulu, F.I.D, 1989. An African on AIDS in Africa. *The AIDS letter- Royal society of medicine, 11*, 1-3.

Kumah, Divine, 1998 May. Our girls on the Internet. Why are we feigning surprise? *The Watchman*.

McClintock, Anne, 1995. *Imperial leather. Race, gender, and sexuality in the colonial contest*. New York: London: Routledge.

Middleton, John, 1983. One hundred and fifty years of Christianity in a Ghanaian town. *Africa, 53*(3), 2-19.

Miller, Jon, 1994. *The social control of religious zeal. A study of organizational contradictions.* New Brunswick, New Jersey: Rutgers University Press.

Odjidja, E. M. L., 1973. *Mustard seed. The growth of the church in Kroboland.* Accra: Waterville Publishing House.

Odjidja, E. M. L., 1977. *Krobo Girls' School. Death and Resurrection.* Accra: Waterville Publishing House.

Odonkor, S.S., 1971. *The Rise of the Krobos (From an original Ga text by Thomas Harrison Odonkor).* Tema: Ghana Publishing Corporation.

Oppong, Christine, 1974. *Focus on cultural aspects of menstruation in Ghana. Paper for WHO.* Legon: Institute of African Studies, University of Ghana.

Palak, Thomas, 2003, November 21. 'Involving African chiefs. U of C researcher taking grassroots approach to fighting HIV/AIDS.' *On Campus weekly.*Cape Coast

Prodolliet, Simone, 1987. *Wider die Schamlosigkeit und das Elend der heidnischen Weiber. Die Basler Frauenmission und der Export des Europäischen Frauenideals in die Kolonien.* Zürich: Limmat Verlag Genossenschaft.

Renne, Elisha P., 1995. Becoming a Bunu Bride: Bunu Ethnic Identity and Traditional Marriage Dress. In J. B. Eicher (ed.), *Dress and Ethnicity* (pp. 117-138). Oxford, Herndon: Berg Publishers Limited.

Roscoe, Paul B., 1995. Conclusion. "Initiation' in cross-cultural perspective.' In N. C. Lutkehaus & P. B. Roscoe (eds.), *Gender rituals. Female initiation in Melanesia.* New York and London: Routledge. Pp. 219-238.

Santen, José van, & Schilder, Kees, 1994. Etniciteit en Gender: een verkenning in de Afrikanistiek. *Tijdschrift voor Vrouwenstudies, 15*(1), 123-137.

Sarpong, Peter K., 1977. *Girls' nubility rites in Ashanti.* Tema: Ghana Publishing Corporation.

Schroeder, Rose M, & Danquah, Samuel, 2000. Prevention of HIV/AIDS through traditional means: The cultural practice of *Dipo. Psych Discourse, 31*(10), 5-7.

Steegstra, Marijke, 2002. 'A Mighty Obstacle to the Gospel': Basel missionaries, Krobo Women and Conflicting Ideas of Gender and Sexuality. *Journal of Religion in Africa, 32*(2), 200-230.

Steegstra, Marijke, 2004. *Resilient rituals. Krobo initiation and the politics of culture in Ghana.* Münster: LITVerlag.

Streegstra, Marijike,. 2005. *Dipo and the Politics of Culture.* Woeli Publishing Services.

Tettey, Michael Teye, 1977. *The Dipo custom of the Krobo: Its history, practice, and significance.* Unpublished B.A thesis, Department for the Study of Religions, University of Ghana, Legon.

Teyegaga, B.D., 1985. *Dipo custom and the Christian faith.* Accra: Jupiter Printing Press LTD.

Van der Veer, Peter (ed.), 1996. *Conversion to modernities: The globalization of Christianity.* New York and London: Routledge.

MARITAL MORALITY AND SEXUAL VULNERABILITY IN ELLEMBELLE NZEMA SOCIETY[1]

Douglas Frimpong-Nnuroh

This chapter portrays the Ellembelle Nzema people in their socio-cultural milieu and the economic activities that propel their daily existence. It ultimately seeks to draw attention to linkages between the breakdown of traditional sexual moralities and related practices, beliefs and ritual sanctions ensuring chastity, and the escalating spread of HIV/AIDS in the communities. The Nzema people share a common boundary with the Republic of La Cote d'Ivoire on the Southwestern border of Ghana. This proximity to the capital, Abidjan, the epicentre of the HIV/AIDS epidemic in the sub region, has serious health implications for the frequent cross border travellers to and from Franzie, as the locals call the neighbouring country. There are push and pull factors that account for these migrations. Poverty, broken marriages and overburdening family commitments, as well as the perception that jobs and material wealth are available in Franzie are all cited. Female migration is circular in nature and since the migrant Ellembelle Nzema women frequently come home to renew their links with their families it puts the lovers, sexual partners and husbands of these migrant women at risk, at both ends of the migratory movement. In this regard, the Ghana HIV Sentinel Surveillance Report in 1999 gave some startling revelations about the health status of patients at Eikwe Hospital in Ellembelle Nzema, in particular the very high incidence of HIV.

As a background to this health catastrophe this chapter describes features of the local economy and changing livelihoods, as well as marriage and the customary sexual rights that are conferred on husband and wife when the suitor makes bride wealth payments. Marital morality is founded on the principle that what sustains life is good and what degrades life is evil, such that marital conduct should promote elements of reciprocity and harmony between spouses and also in-laws. The potential misfortune, occasioned by illicit sexual contact between husband and wife on the one hand and an adulterous wife and her lover on the other, is cleansed by the *Bisa Ezole* rituals. These rites, now almost defunct, are discussed in detail and their potential relevance to changing morality and sexual relationships, in an era of rapid spread of HIV/AIDS. Some evidence from a local hospital is presented and its implications analysed.

The Ellembelle Nzema people[2] live in the Nzema East District of the Western region of Ghana. They are the most centrally placed sub-group within the Nzema area, which lies within the tropical rainforest belt. Nzemaland is well watered and economic trees abound. The Ellembelle people are matrilineal; and like their neighbours the Akan, have a well-developed system of seven exogamous clans, each of which has associated dirges.[3] They explain the origins of matriclans and their progeny (Eboyi-Anza 1979: 40-50). There is also a well structured father-child tie or patrifiliation, which is the essential link between a sibling group and the kin of the parent who does not determine descent (cf. Fortes 1953:33).[4]

The traditional political organization of Ellembelle is centralized and pyramidal in structure. The paramount chief is at the apex and exercises absolute powers. The sub chief is his deputy at the town level and exercises delegated powers. The last in the relay of political patronage is the village head, who also enjoys devolved powers.[5] The Ellembelle perceive two worlds: the mundane physical world and a spiritual realm ruled by the deities. The Supreme Being is God, *Nyamenle,* meaning "owner of leaves". A notable malevolent deity is called *Manlamanlake,* a candescent entity, variously described as a hoary light that glows at night, especially during the early hours of the morning. This efflorescent mythical being is also believed to be a thigh of a human being lumbering along with a whitish hoary light. It taboos the sexual act. Therefore, it stalks and attacks men and women who engage in sex or immoral behaviour under cover of darkness. When they decide to pass over its place of abode without waiting for daybreak, *Manlamanlake* will expose them by making them ill. Habitual violators of the purity of *Manlamanlake* can be certain of instant death. Belief in this deity has clearly helped to promote chastity in the past. In recent times however, belief in this deity has dwindled but its potential malevolence is not in doubt, so people who know a likely abode of *Manlamanlake* would not dare desecrate it.

Economic Activities and Resources

The traditional occupations of the Ellembelle people are farming, fishing and gold smithing. The main staples in Ellembelle are cassava, rice and maize. The women make and sell a variety of traditional foods made from these staples.[6] Since 1945 the coconut industry has become synonymous with the economy of Nzema land. At the moment there exists a client-owner relationship between plantation owners and women who finance the maintenance of the farms in return for the nuts to produce coconut oil. Another industry that involves women as financiers, distributors and retailers is the distillation of the local gin called *kutuluku*. Pre-financing distillation camps involves huge capital outlays by local standards. The Abusa system ensures equitable allocation of a third part of the proceeds to each stakeholder. This way, the owner of the camp, the financier and distillers reap commensurate returns for their individual or collective efforts.

Gold, kaolin and silica abound in Ellembelle, but they are untapped in any appreciable quantities with the exception of kaolin. Ellembelle is the breadbasket of the Nzema East district, yet the Cape St. Paul Coconut Wilt Disease is systematically killing the livelihood of Ellembelle farmers, who cannot afford the improved variety of coconut seedlings from the Aiyinasi Oil Mills and Agricultural Station. The availability of electricity in Ellembelle since 1996 has helped to revive the Vegetable Oil Mills at Esiama (now Franza Industries), while Central Carbons Company Limited established at Esiama to use coconut shells to produce charcoal has since folded up. Industrialization and exploitation of the economic potential of the area has therefore been rather slow, leaving the people impoverished in the midst of abundant natural resources. Ellembelle has the majority of all educational institutions and five out of the eight public health institutions in the Nzema East District. Of the total 154 km of trunk roads, 94 km are in Ellembelle and 160km of feeder roads out of a total 294km are also in the district.

Marriage in Ellembelle

In the past, a number of customary beliefs and practices promoted and preserved female chastity at different life stages. For example until the performance of puberty or nubility rites, called *Aziziele*, an Ellembelle girl was restricted from having sex and within marriage there were practices to prevent promiscuity.[7]

Marriage is considered important in the religious, social, economic and political mainstream of the Ellembelle Nzema society. It creates room for the husband and wife who have agreed to cohabit to have children to perpetuate the lineage. Children born out of the union stabilize the marriage. Also children serve as insurance for their parents in future against old age, and want. Socially, marriage provides security for women against the outside world, and sexual harassment is minimized, because men know the serious consequences of seducing a married woman. An unmarried woman may be prone to proposals from all sorts of men, which could demean her social standing while there is ideally an aura of respect surrounding a married woman, which should automatically accord her certain immunities and privileges in the society.

Marriage also confers social maturity on a man who takes a wife and it is a basis for a successful adult life. It is expected that he can return home to good food and rely on his wife for chores to be performed. There is also ideally companionship, such that husband and wife are mutual keepers of each other. Wives are viewed as economic assets to their husbands, processing fish for sale or selling other wares of husbands who are artisans. Among the Ellembelle in particular and the Ghanaian society as a whole, marriage is an "unofficial" necessary qualification to high office.[8]

Customarily, the moment marriage occurs, the family of the bride has no further responsibility for her upkeep. It becomes the husband's responsibility and marriage confers mutual rights and responsibilities on spouses. It is also a sexual and economic union between husband and wife, which should ideally endure. Elopement of the suitor and the bride is alien to Nzema marriage. Beauty of character and respect for in-laws, including classificatory brothers and sisters of the spouse, are virtues expected of a bride. Meanwhile the children should all grow up in the father's compound, where sons who come of age put up their own rooms on their father's plot and live there. After marriage, sons should bring their wives to their father's home to live. As his own family expands, each son should be able to acquire his own plot.

One feature of matrilineal systems noted several decades ago was the many marital forms available (cf. Richards 1973:52ff). Today, only a few of the eighteen marriage types that existed in former times in Ellembelle have survived. Child betrothal is no longer practiced. Friendship is a relationship between a man and his regular sex partner, which later leads to marriage. During this period of non-married cohabitation, pregnancy should not result. If it does, the father alleges that, "you have broken my fence". This is in obvious reference to theft of the family's prerogative to marry off a daughter. Then there is concubinage in which a formal approach has been made with a bottle of gin to the girl's father declaring intent of marriage. The prospective suitor also undertakes to produce the girl by day or night on demand. Failure to complete the marriage requires that the woman be compensated. This is referred to as pushing the girl or putting her down gently. If the girl dies during such a relationship, the man would be called upon to perform all the traditional marriage rites before she is buried. Close kin marriages are carefully arranged to avoid any incestuous union. This type of marriage may be ideal (cf. Fortes 1992).[9] Other types obtain depending upon the status of the women.[10] Widow inheritance also occurs when a successor inherits the estate of his deceased brother or mother's brother and if the surviving wife consents, he may make a token payment to inherit her womanhood.

The three distinct stages in Ellembelle Nzema marriage are (i) search for the spouse[11] (ii) negotiations and transfer/exchange of matrimonial goods and (iii) consummation, accompanied by the traditional wedding. These stages flow one into the other and are aimed at establishing the legal, social and spiritual validity of the marital union between the man and woman and their families (cf. Agorsah 1997: 14).

The consummation is crowned with the traditional wedding ceremony called *atofoleliele,* in which the bride moves to her marital home with the bridal train on the nuptial night accompanied by her bride's maid. The payment of bride wealth confers on the husband claims to paternity of the wife's children and the right to her domestic services. The wife also has rights – including sexual satisfaction, so that if she has to share this with a co-wife not only must her consent be sought, but also she must be compensated by payment of cloth, cash and just demands on the husband.

In a matrilineal system, the father's rights over his children stand in contrast with the maternal uncle's possible control over his own sister's children. This has been referred to in the past as the matrilineal puzzle and the effect of this on Ellembelle marriage today is that many fathers, viewing children as demanding and costly and in view of their own often straightened circumstances, have reneged on their paternal responsibilities. In the meantime the mother's brother/sister's son relationship is often still important and tales of coconut plantations being bequeathed to nephews at the expense of children of the deceased continue to be told. Prior to the passage of PNDC L. 112 on Intestate Succession, a number of these inheritance cases were sent to court but till today this customary inheritance system is practiced in Ellembelle. However the pervasive ambiguity and possible conflict and room for irresponsibility that the system engenders means that many mothers and their children are left without the support they need from either husbands/fathers or brothers/uncles. To a large extent mothers have to fend for themselves, obviously a factor propelling many women to eventually migrate in search of employment and income of whatever kind.

Marital Morality

The Ellembelle believe that all living and non-living things are imbued with life traced to *Nyamenle*. The individual does not exist by himself, but lives in society with the spirit beings. In this vein, what sustains life is good and what degrades life is evil. The collective consciousness to reward or punish has both mystical and social dimensions. The rules about life are cosmic in origin and every moral breach has wider repercussions throughout the universe. Order is perceived in nature, which must not be disturbed. Rashness, intemperance, impatience, irascibility, greed etc. are all believed to precipitate calamity, injury or denial of cosmic rewards. Morality pervades the cosmology, the cultural norms and the expected behaviour of individuals who are integral parts of a close-knit community in which a person is never alone. Real human beings have to belong to the community. The solidarity of the group involves a feeling on the part of individuals that they are one people governed by a set of traditional norms that dictate rewards and punishments. Many proverbs are used in Ellembelle to illustrate moral values. Proverbs with moral precepts are often employed in actual situations.

The customary rules pertaining to sexual morality are clear and include pre-marital chastity for the youth, both girls and boys. Within marriage, sexual behaviour is equally restrictive and a married woman who is adulterous suffers social ridicule. This can affect her own children, especially daughters, who may be referred to derogatorily as anglers, who cast hooks to bait men. Men who keep multiple sexual partners for short durations are described as eaters of women. This is not a desirable sobriquet. Polygyny is permissible but should be played according to the rules laid down. Thirdly, the society recognizes the right of adults who are divorced, widowed, single or menopausal, to keep sexual partners. There is a certain level of permissiveness regarding sexual morality in this category of women, who may use sex to wield economic power. Women in such consenting liaisons are expected to respect the marriage of the women with whose husbands they cohabit. Above all, they should be self-respecting and not grant sexual access to people considered as socially immature.

Meanwhile, it is repugnant for a woman to suggest by word or deed that she is promiscuous, or has weak morals. It is also abnormal for an Ellembelle Nzema woman to go out and seek a man. If she does that, she is considered to be a *sanefele*, a cheap fish that could be bought at any price. However, women have their ways, which are known to men. Thus women must traditionally control their sexual impulses and expression of their love. A non-responsive wife in bed slows down a husband's libido, but a hyperactive wife may equally send wrong signals of sexual depravity.

Sex and Norms of Marital Conduct

Open reference to sexual organs or the sexual act in public is frowned upon. Elderly people, out of modesty, use euphemisms in reference to the genitalia in their public conversations. Incest, forcible seduction of a married woman or sex with a woman during her menses, all threaten life and are roundly condemned. Sexual immorality evokes emotional resentment and fear in men; the act will make the husband ill. Sexual connection with a woman during her menstrual period brings on a state of serious sexual impurity.

Marital infidelity in the past covered a broad definition that might capture actual penetration, or even unconscious adultery[12] and mere acts of familiarity calculated to lead to intercourse (see Busia 1968: 66ff, Ackah 1964, Pavanello 1998: Vellenga 1974: 52-54). Sexual immorality could also be extended to cover dreams, which are interpreted as manifestations of intention. Thus, having a dream of sexual intercourse with a married woman or man is taken as sexual reality. To give gifts to a married woman without the prior knowledge of her husband can be equated with seduction. The logic is that the woman by reciprocating the gesture may give sex to the gift giver. Significantly, the Ellembelle put religious overtones to adultery, as being responsible for a great number of god-sent diseases which can be stopped once the guilty intercourse ceases (Grottanelli 1998: 92).[13] To prevent it, a husband might place chastity spells on his wife so as to protect her against trespassers.[14] Sanctions are both social and ritual. In respect of the paramour, he brought opprobrium on his person, his lineage, his wife and office, if he were a ranking man in the society.

The marital code not only delineates acceptable sexual behaviour, defining conjugal behaviour and reciprocal expectations between partners, it also regulates in-law relationships and interactions, parenting and domestic responsibilities. The primary premise of this code is in respect of choice of marital and sexual partners. Under the code, abortion, which destroys life and upsets the aims of marriage, has no place.

Behaviour in marriage has to be learnt from early childhood, and like other patterns of behaviour, it is passed on from one generation to another and from parent to child (Dzobo 1975:11). A man was expected to be hardworking so that he could support his wife and children. If he could not maintain his wife and children by providing food, clothing and shelter, he was described as a useless person. An Nzema wife on her part should be proactive and supportive of her husband. A self-conceited wife will not survive her marriage; a good wife of necessity must keep confidential matters within the confines of marriage. The element of reciprocity in determining social relationships between in-laws and spouses is important.[15] An aggrieved wife is sure to deny sexual access to her husband by, "facing the wall," in protest. A wife with a low level of moral stability is believed likely to seek sexual congress with other men who would be prepared to provide for her needs. Bad marital behaviour includes a number of bedroom taboos and quarrels between husband and wife that disrupt their personal relationship.[16]

Bisa Ezole / Ritual of Cleansing

Bisa Ezole is a dramatic public event of ritual cleansing, performed in the past when marital sexual morality had been contravened. The two basic principles underlying the performance of bisa ezole are social justice and sexual discipline of couples in the discharge of conjugal roles.[17] The belief exists in Ellembelle that two things may bring about the performance of bisa. The first is fualelile, which means that couple have had sex while the woman was in her menses. The second is awuvolevale, which is seduction of a married woman by another man. The extra-marital affairs engaged in by the husband are not believed to physically affect the health of the wife. Yet, it is thought that the wife's sexual indiscretion can bring untold harm to her partner. In this regard, the cuckold could suffer various ailments ranging from imbecility, through lack of concentration or forgetfulness, to dribbling mouth, palsy and infirmity of mind and body. Gluttony and stuttering speech are other manifestations of bisa-related affliction.

A ritual specialist called bisamenle officiates during the rites of cleansing. The candidate for bisa is the bisasovo. He must not break his fast until the ritual meal is cooked. There are distinct stages involved in the cleansing ritual. The entire proceedings are preceded by the identification of bisa affliction and securing a ritual specialist who would consent to perform the rites for a fee. When he gathers the various ingredients, a date is fixed for the performance of the rites.

The cuckolded husband is stripped naked, save for his underpants and made to sit on the refuse dump. The specialist questions him on what he had seen that has necessitated the performance of the rites. This question is asked three times. An old broom is used to sweep the candidate's body three times. On each occasion, one broomstick is removed and planted on the refuse dump. The juices of certain leaves are squeezed on his eyeballs. The toe of a fowl is cut and the blood dropped on the tongue of the cuckold three times. The wife smears his body with pepper, medicine and spices ground into a paste. From there, he proceeds to the second stage of cleansing.

The medicine for purification is made of barks, roots, twigs and leaves of plants, which are pounded into powder and ground, on a stone by the wife. When the medicine is ready, the husband is dedicated to the gods to guarantee the success of the rituals. He is enjoined to be responsive, since absolute cooperation and good faith are crucial to his own cure. The essence of the purification is to fashion him anew to enable him to overcome his sick role and come back to normal life. He sits on the ground and carries an earthenware pot of medicine mixed with *doka,* raffia wine on his head.[18] He drinks much of the medicine while the ritual specialist daubs his body with some of the medicinal paste. Hot spices burn into his body, while some of the medicine is also spewed into his eyes, ostensibly to remove his *bisa*-affliction. The old broom is dipped in the medicinal drink and his body is smeared with it. Incantations accompany the cleansing.

Bisa dwu o!	Bisa come down oh!
Bisa dwu o!!	Bisa descend oh!!
Kodwo aye eli renya eva eha ye	Kodwo's wife has eaten a man and defiled him
Oti yeso Kodwo bisa o!	So we perform bisa for Kodwo oh!
Onye mendii	It does not make him inactive
Onye gyibilito	He should not be a moron
Onwu ezukoa onwu ye	When he sees money let him identify it
Oko eleka a owu eleka mo okoo	When travelling he should be focused on his journey
Onza onzi ongo eleka fofole	He should not miss his way to a different destination
Beso a ota o!	May the rites of purification hold!

The wife must produce her loincloth, which is made into a head pad to support the medicine pot so that it does not touch the ground.[19] When the husband finishes his rites of cleansing, all present are at liberty to drink some of the medicine. The participants stir the content of the pot with the broom and stoop to take mouthfuls of it. Another person also sweeps his entire body with the broom, which has been dipped in the medicine pot. The incantations that accompany the purification of the participants go like this.

Be nwo ede o!	May you be cleansed!
Be nwo ede o!	May you be purified!
Be nwo saanwo!	May you be sanctified!
Enye be gyigyilii o!	Do not make them imbeciles oh!

The participants partake in the purification as a form of indemnity from possible infidelity of their own wives, which may not be known to them. If a person had secretly slept with his wife during menstruation, this was the occasion to extricate him from any possible *bisa*-affliction in future, without attracting attention and shame to himself.

The ritual specialist cooks the *bisa* food on an open hearth made up of three big stones capable of supporting the cooking pot. The *bisa* chicken is sacrificed and its blood sprinkled on the hearth and on the firewood to neutralize any potential force in them. It is chopped into smaller pieces to be added to the chopped plantain and some of the *bisa* medicine. A bottle of palm oil is poured into the stew. After the meal is well cooked, the specialist names a price at which he sells it to other participants. It is the prerogative of the cuckold to taste first before the other participants eat. The meal is eaten at the ritual grounds with both hands, and should not under any circumstances be taken home.

The last rite of the *bisa* purification ceremony is fumigation. The entrails and feathers, of the chicken, some leaves and pepper, are put in the iron pot and roasted. The bones of the chicken eaten in the ritual meal are added and burnt. When the pepper and herbs begin to smoke, the wronged husband has to start his cleansing by fumigation. He is covered with cloth and blankets with the smoke underneath. The ritual specialist recites incantations aimed at exorcising the *bisa* spirit. When the medicine has burnt to soot the pot is removed from the fire and its contents ground into smooth powder. It is mixed with palm oil and divided to eat among all those who paid to parti-cipate in the ritual. The wronged husband after his cleansing is not expected to wash his body till the next day, to enable the medicine to enter his pores and remove any illness embedded therein.

Whenever differences in opinion between husband and wife affect the foundation of the marriage, it is always appropriate to bind the couple and remove the dirt that their disagreement occasioned before they cohabit again. Another ceremony, *Mokyea zo epele*, may not be a public ceremony, but nevertheless is one of the processes aimed at restoring the cuckold to his original position. This re-engagement ceremony is done to renew culinary commitment. The wife provides two fowls, left and right, which are slaughtered to wash the husband's soul. The blood of the immolated fowls is poured on the hearth, if the defilement was occasioned by the wife's sexual immorality. The defilement by extension also affected certain items within the domestic sphere that go to define the husband-wife bond. The belief is that by cleansing the hearth with the blood of the two fowls, the evil she precipitated on the hearth is diminished. Blood is thought to revivify the object on which it is poured.

Formerly, two effigies of a penis were made, one small and the other big. The wife would be forced by the participants to choose one. Whatever she chose had implications for her adulterous act. This has been discontinued due to the quarrels and fights that the practice brought about in the past. Formerly, the loincloth of the wife played a significant part in the ritual performance, but in recent times, a lot of women do not use such a garment.[20] This has taken some of the shine off the celebration of the rites. People asserted that whereas in the past the seducer was anonymous in the entire ritual performance, recently, some make attempts to change the course of things to cover their own misdeeds. Some paramours resort to psychic powers to cast spells of madness, drunkenness or even death on the cuckold so that the rites cannot be performed. The understanding is that, their own shame was intrinsic to the public performance of the rituals. Informants have cited non-performance in the rites by an adulterous wife and an incestuous father. This gave an indication that people cannot be compelled to participate in the rites, if they know that they are not put in any personal danger by their own refusal.

At the end of the rites, the ritual specialist proclaims the wronged husband cured of his *bisa* affliction and the candidate regains his spiritual, social, physical and mental capabilities. The *bisa ezole* rites are held to be curative of the cuckold's earlier state of malaise. This cure may be attributed to the collective potency of the herbs used in the ritual of cleansing. The *bisa ezole* ritual of cleansing is believed to be re-integrative and also restitutive, thereby guaranteeing the candidate's place in the society for him to contribute to its total development. The existence and continued performance of *bisa ezole* provides the rod for measuring adult morality. The performance of *bisa ezole* is also seen by ethno-jurists as a manifestation of justice as fairness. A just society protects the interest of its members, thus any man who seduces other people's wives loses his own self-respect before his fellow men. His action also brings shame to his own family, office or rank.

Social Change and the Bisa Ezole Ritual of Cleansing

With the passage of time and historical social changes this public ritual has decayed and been discontinued. Migration and mobility of people and urban life in larger communities with its characteristic anonymity has opened the floodgate for anomie. Most extra marital sexual activities now go unnoticed and unchecked, as compared to the rural setting and small, stable communities, where people know one another more closely. The rationality of certain beliefs, rituals and practices has also been questioned by informed logic. Educated women challenge their aggrieved husbands to seek divorce rather than subject themselves to dehumanising public rituals. Unemployed husbands, who depend solely on their working wives, also appear helpless when their wives have to attend business lunches and dinners. For purely economic reasons, some women traders in Ellembelle are widely known to use sexual favours to gain economic advantage. However, since their husbands do not appear to have suffered any ill health, the basis for *bisa ezole* rites has been further eroded. Furthermore knowledgeable people believe that no good practising Christian or Moslem would these days consent to go through the *bisa ezole* rituals of cleansing openly. Islam has its own code of punishing marital sexual infidelity. Thus the rites, as described above, accord ill with Islamic teaching.

Clearly, there has been a profound shift in sexual morality and behaviour in the past decades, from a situation in which infractions of rules preserving female chastity and faithfulness were very publicly sanctioned, to more accommodating, if not lax sexual scenarios, which have their own serious repercussions for health and survival. The idea that sexual promiscuity brings disease and possible death remains a salient motif.

Sex and the Transmission of Disease and Death

In Ellembelle, both certain new risk factors and traditional beliefs and practices may all facilitate the speed of spread of STD's including HIV. First is the traditional perception that sex among people who intend to marry is permissible. Then there is the new lifting of the sexual restraints on the youth, who have much more freedom and lack of social control now than in the past. Moreover sex has become a saleable and purchasable commodity, unlike in the past when it was imbued with moral precepts and spiritual beliefs. With the introduction of the money economy, youths are able to sell confectionery, serve as drivers-mates or weed coconut plantations, to acquire money. The money made through their own efforts can help them to buy any thing, including sex. The restrictive traditional norms on premarital sex no longer hold. Second, within marriage, monogamy does not guarantee sexual safety or reproductive health. Risk factors abound and a woman's marital faithfulness does not protect her.[21] Customary marriage remains potentially polygynous, and men are at liberty to cohabit with other women. Polycoital husbands, who are predisposed to unsafe sex, pose serious health risks to their wives and other partners. Meanwhile single, divorced or menopausal women who fend for themselves may be socially pardoned if they enter into consenting sexual liaisons with other men, yet such behaviour is increasingly risk prone. Sex in these categories of women may be for company or happiness or economic advantage. The men involved may be used in their occupations or for political leverage. This practice of traditional Ellembelle society constitutes one of the risk behaviours for reproductive health, as does the continuity of the traditional practice of widow inheritance.

At the same time, the increasing numbers and escalating mobility of people, in particular women searching for jobs and incomes to support themselves and their children, are raising the level of sexual risks they may encounter. The Nzema have strong cultural-historical links with the Republic of La Cote d'Ivoire, which they call Franzie, and in particular with the capital Abidjan only eighty-one kilometres away. This city remains the epicentre of HIV/AIDS in the sub-region, and an important focus for female commercial sex workers' activities, in view of the large numbers of unattached, migrant, male labourers in the city, from various countries in the region. Three categories of Ellembelle women migrate to Franzie. The first are Nzema women married to Ivorien men. The second move to settle with relatives and friends who have permanent abode in Franzie. The third category is women who face economic constraints back home and migrate to better their prospects (see

Anarfi 1993; Adomako 1991 on commercial sex workers). The factors that push women to migrate to Franzie include lack of local job opportunities; lack of basic skills to earn a decent living at home; poverty culminating in lack of access to working capital; spousal neglect that deepens economic crisis; single mothering and overburdening family commitments rather than kin support. It is known that women who can no longer solely provide food, clothing and shelter for themselves, their children and other dependants are able to send money to them when they travel to Franzie. Regarding pull factors, there is the general perception that personal effects, particularly wax prints are in abundance in Franzie. The sheer spirit of adventurism and the cultural links that binds the Nzema in the Republic of La Cote d'Ivoire to the Nzema of Ghana also acts as a spur for women to migrate. The last two categories of migrant women, who do not have one regular sex partner and involve themselves in risky behaviour, may become infected with STDs including HIV.

During the annual Kundum festival, a number of these sojourners return home to join in the convivial atmosphere. This week long cultural festival is celebrated from one Ellembelle town to another beginning from early August until late September when it is finally celebrated in the traditional capital. It is the one cultural event that has the potential of bringing all sons and daughters scattered abroad home for family reunion. During this festive occasion, some revellers renew their sexual liaisons with their fiancées, or make new lovers and sex partners. Health workers assert that new reported cases of STDs including HIV infections are at their peak in early October, the period immediately after the festival.

Until recently, female sojourners in Abidjan who returned home terminally ill to die were believed to be accursed.[22] In the past, knowledge of HIV/AIDS was scanty. However, considering the symptoms and the high prevalence level of HIV in La Cote d'Ivoire, it seems that those women who assign the "accursed reason" to their fate are indeed plagued by HIV and die of AIDS.

HIV/AIDS: Counselling and Surveillance

Two well-known Sexually Transmitted Diseases (STDs) in Ellembelle are *Sekpu* (gonorrhoea) and *Babaso* (syphilis). The Ghana HIV Sentinel Surveillance Report 1999 indicated that in the screening for syphilis in pregnant women, the highest prevalence of 1.8 percent was recorded at Eikwe in the western region. In the year 2000, there were 126 reported cases of STDs in the age group 15-45 for both males and females in all four public health institutions included in this study.[23] Out of the reported cases two thirds were female. Health workers believe that patients who frequently contract STDs are highly predisposed to contracting the Human Immune Virus (HIV), which causes AIDS. Patients who are treated for STD's are encouraged to take advantage of the counselling services on risk behaviour at the hospitals/-clinics. The thrust of the counselling is to educate people regarding the risk behaviour that leads to HIV/AIDS.[24]

Unfortunately, the most preferred Family Planning method available locally appeared to be injectable contraceptives, whereas condom use, which would offer protection from sexually transmitted disease, was very low. Off-the-counter sales records were also badly kept.[25] The injectables appear to provide an open sesame to transmission of STDs and HIV, because they only prevent pregnancy, but the condom is a protective shield against death and disease. Injectables were very popular as a family planning method, probably because of the uncooperative attitude of men to use of the condom. In fact, knowledge of and use of both male and female condom in Ellembelle appeared to be very low.[26]

The two broad categories of people on whom tests for HIV are conducted are blood donors and patients. The number of donors from 1996-2000 was 6,593. A cumulative total of 240 positive donors over the same period was recorded (3.6%). The number of clinic and hospital patients tested for HIV over the five-year period was 2,485, out of whom 1,157 tested positive. The overall cumulative percentage was 46.6. In year 2000, 561 patients were tested for HIV at Eikwe Hospital. Out of this number 269 were males of all ages, while females made up the remaining 292. 39% of males of all ages tested positive. 55% of females tested positive. 52.5% of the age range 20-39 years tested positive, and of these more than two thirds were female. These figures give sad and incontrovertible evidence of a very serious HIV/AIDS crisis, which is particularly prevalent among women.

Conclusion

This chapter on the Ellembelle Nzema of Western Ghana has examined norms and practices associated with Nzema traditional marriage and the sexual values and customs linked to chastity. The traditional sex regime was quite restrictive for both the married and unmarried. However, in the modern era, there seems to be evidence of a pervasive lack of chastity in the society, which may be linked to the speed of spread of Sexually Transmitted Diseases (STDs) including HIV /AIDS.

A large number of Nzema women who cross over the southwestern borders of Ghana stay in Abidjan. The risks these Abidjan sojourners are exposed to are many. This may account for suspected cases of HIV/AIDS related malaise in these returnees. Currently, this is explained away by sex workers who have sojourned in Abidjan as evidence of a curse. These terminally ill women travellers, who ultimately die, leave behind orphans, their parents and other dependants to rue for their death, especially since death cuts off their financial support and sustenance.

The failure to maintain traditional sexual norms and sanctions on the youth plus the emergence of the cash economy has allowed the youth to generate income out of their own labour and this has enabled them to enjoy early sexual experience in a situation in which sexual pleasure has become a commodity to be bought and sold. The lack of policing of traditional norms has contributed to juvenile promiscuity. The national average for first sexual experience is 17.3 years. In Ellembelle, children as young as 13 years are known to be sexually active.

Ellembelle marriage remains as always, potentially polygynous while at the same time the majority of men are estimated to have multiple sexual partners. In addition, traditional rites of widow inheritance and the general conviviality not to say, debauchery, associated with traditional festivals and the attendant risk behaviours have widespread and insidious health implications in the society. Not withstanding these risks, male condom use is low. The most preferred method of contraception dispensed, injectables, only prevents pregnancy, but does not afford protection against disease and death. Furthermore, knowledge and use of the female condom is virtually nonexistent in Ellembelle. These facts may help to explain the high prevalence of syphilis in pregnant women found at Eikwe Hospital.

Traditional morality in Ellembelle was targeted towards promoting the general good of society. Marital morality therefore, embraced acts and intended acts that promoted marital stability. Codes of marital conduct were meant to ensure harmonious co-existence between husband and wife. However, single, divorced or menopausal women were allowed a certain level of sexual independence. They could be in consenting sexual liaisons with men for economic, social, political or personal aggrandizement, practices that are clearly exaggerated at the present time.

In the past, the *bisa ezole* rituals of cleansing cuckolded husbands were aimed at enforcing sexual discipline among married women. They checked marital sexual infidelity. The rites were restitutive and restorative. However, social change has de-emphasised these rituals in contemporary times with the attendant effects on changing morality, as sanctions on promiscuous sexual relationship are relaxed, with consequent impacts on the spread of sexually transmitted disease and death.

Endnotes

1. This chapter covers similar ground to an earlier essay by the author which appeared in the *Research Review* (Legon) 2002, 18.1 and is based on an M. Phil. Thesis submitted to the Institute of African Studies, University of Ghana.

2. The Ellembelle are believed to be the autochthonous Nzema people found in the past between Sanzule and Elloinye. Now Ellembelle encompass the land from Sanwoma on the bank of river Ankobra to Atuabo. It is also the name of the second constituency in the Nzema East District. Ackah (1964) speculates that the Ellembelle got their name probably because of the white fufu they ate. Within Ellembelle are four other sub groups: Azanyevole, Akomuvole, Eletilevole and Azanevole also known as Ellembelle. It is believed that the Portuguese sighted Nzemaland on 9th February 1842, the feast day of St. Apollo and called the people and the region Apollonia. The Nzema resented the name and officially had their indigenous name Nzema around 1927.

   Three traditions explain the name Nzema. First is the adulterated Aowin / Sefwi phrase *Menze ma* literally translated "I don't know". *Menze ma* was gradually corrupted with the syncopation of the first two letters *m* and *e* to become Nzema thereby losing its original meaning. Second is the pejorative Sefwi word *Nzenlema* meaning "those who passed by". The corrupted name now refers to the people and their language. The third, *Nzisan* means an agglomeration of tribes, a mixture or medley of tribes and the name Nzema thus suggests that they settled at their present home from different locations and formed one chain. These traditions are aetiological and used to explain the origins of a name that has moved out of its original moorings to present day acclaim.

3. These seven *abusua* matriclans are: *Alonwoba, Nvavile, Adahonle, Asamangama, Ezohile, Azanwule* and *Ndweafoo*. Second, each *abusua* has totem(s), taboo(s) and props, which depict their group identity and social standing in the community. At social or religious functions, such as funerals, arbitrations, pouring of libation, enstoolment of a chief etc. the staff, *abusua kpoma* is borne aloft by the *abusua* linguist or spokes person.

4. The five patrifilial groups in Nzema are *Abelanwo, Esonwo, Anyiado, Obele* and *Amu*. The origins of these patrifilial groups are believed to throw some light on their nature. *Abelanwo* is derived from *bela* to circle or surround, and this alludes to executioners. *Esonwo* is from *yezo wo* to welcome therefore, *esonwo* people are welcomed everywhere they go. *Anyaado* means one who is much respected and also loved. *Obele* alludes to *akole bele* the mother hen that is a good parent. *Amu* also means one who does not talk much but is a good orator.

5. The *Odikro* had no direct contact with the paramount chief, neither was he represented

on his traditional council. Therefore, they could not immediately by-pass the sub-chief to present their petitions to *Awulae*. It becomes crystal clear that within the chiefdom, the sub-chiefs exercise delegated powers, while power and authority devolves on the *Odikro*, who as an anchorman in the relay of political patronage is responsible for governance at the village and hamlet level.

6. Some of these staples are *fonvom*, which is kenkey made by pounding the boiled corn dough in a mortar. *Akyeke* is a coarse-grained cassava meal that is steamed over a watertight utensil. *Atuku/mkpokpole* is also a cassava meal processed like *akyeke* except that it the grains become compact when it is well cooked. *Abodaso*, *tokuma* and *awule bolo* or rice cakes are other traditional Nzema foods. Women learn how they are prepared and sell them on the markets to generate income.

7. The well known practice is the *bisa ezole* ritual cleansing which is discussed elsewhere in this chapter. However, if a married woman can affirm that she has had extra marital affairs with twelve men, the usual expression used is that *yedia menya* meaning she has counted men and the cuckolded husband cannot claim adultery fees. Such a woman was ridiculed during the annual Kundum festival by singers called *atwenekwasimma*. To be stigmatised in any particular year was socially demeaning for the adulterous wife and her immediate and extended family.

8. The general argument is that if a man cannot manage a home with a single wife, then he cannot manage the affairs of the larger society when entrusted with higher or political office of national character.

9. This is often referred to as *suanu agyale* meaning home or arranged marriage. It is the cross cousin marriage where a man can conveniently marry the daughter of his mother's brother. Even though he belongs to the same matrikin as his mother's brother, his mother's brother's daughter belongs to her mother's clan so marriage between the two cousins was permissible. The merit and demerit of this type of marriage is beyond the scope of this chapter.

10. In the distant past, various marriage types existed such as *asiyele*, child betrothal, *guadi* or *anzonebole agyale*, where a lover seduces a bride before her main suitor could conclude the final rites of marriage. *Kisame*, means lean on me and refers to concubinage.

11. It was the duty of the male to woo a woman and this process involved a long and thorough search to ascertain if marriage between a suitor and a bride did not break the rules of incest or whether the bride was respectful and could bear children. Obviously, a lazy man cannot be given a wife in Ellembelle; neither will a family knowingly marry off their daughter to a kleptomaniac or a man who dabbles in evil medicine or has bad antecedents.

12. Unconscious adultery is an imaginary sexual offence that can be precipitated by a lovesick married woman to get a man who has spurned her favours into trouble. Instances of this in the past involved a woman applying urine an admired male left on a wall into her vagina and going ahead to confess to adultery. A trial by ordeal established that indeed water from the man's body had indeed entered the woman's vagina. Other more visible expressions of this is when a man shaves off the pubic hairs of a married woman, removes her loin-cloth, plays with her buttocks, beads or other more intimate parts of the body. It has been established also that if a man beats up a married woman, the husband in righteous anger can demand adultery fees.

13. The Nzema people believe that when a married woman sleeps with another man and sleeps also with her own husband, the offending semen of the seducer will make the husband ill. The gods punished such infractions on the part of men who knowingly seduce other people's wives.

14. The chastity spell is a charm that husbands impose on their wives with a view to protecting them from being violated by other lecherous men. This operates by coded principles and the women on whom the spell has been cast may not even be aware of such a charm. The most common in Ellembelle is called *babaso epele*. A man who sleeps with a woman under such a spell passes blood with excruciating pains in the genitals and waist. Other variants are that one cannot sustain an erection to penetrate a woman put under such a spell or alternatively the seducer's penis is perpetually erect and painful. This is reversible by the spell owner but only after the person has confessed his crime of seducing a married woman and paying adultery fees asked by the aggrieved husband.

15. A husband or wife ingratiates himself or herself with in-laws by sending them gifts occasionally. The gifts must be properly weighted especially in the case of wives. To send too little is bad and disrespectful, not to send gifts at all means that one is mean and greedy and to send too much is an indication that she was wallowing in abundance and opulence. A husband who does not send gifts to his in-laws is sure to do so at least on festive occasions and engage his father-in-law in manly talk over drinks.

16. People think that petty domestic fights that do not get settled but occur frequently may be associated with bedroom "politics," that is too much or too little sexual intercourse. These and other intimate bedroom wrangling should not be discussed in the open. The man or woman who pours out such intimate bedroom occurrences in the open cuts a sorry picture of himself or herself.

17. The rituals are both restitutive and curative and come in handy when in the discharge of conjugal roles the established norms of decency and propriety are breached.

18. This is the white fluid that comes from the raffia or piassava palm. It has low alcohol content and as a beverage, it has a long stimulating effect on drinkers who take a lot of the stuff. Because it is mild in alcoholic content mixing it with medicine for the *bisa ezole* rituals is to be preferred to the more powerful *kutuluku*.

19. According to the ritual specialist the pot for the *bisa ezole* rites should not touch the bare ground otherwise the life of the candidate for *bisa* would be jeopardised. It rests on the *siale*, loincloth of the wife of the *bisa* candidate and the aphorism is that the older the *siale*, the better. In Ellembelle society, it is believed that the *siale* on its own has innate power that can overpower charms and amulets when they come into contact with *siale*. A woman who strikes her husband with her *siale* has done an abominable thing.

20. The *siale* is a woman's most prized undergarment that protects her vagina. It is only husbands and men who have been given special dispensation who can touch it let alone remove it. Therefore if it was brought in public and hoisted as a flag and made a mockery item, then it was a big shame on the owner. The paradox here is that with the context of *bisa ezole* cleansing, men can hold the *siale* and wipe their bodies with it without fearing any repercussions possibly because the *bisa* medicine immobilises the power in *siale*.

21. Men engage in high-risk behaviours by philandering. Their wives risk having sexually

transmitted infections from them even though they remain in stable relationships with their husbands.

22. Believed to be suffering from the wrath of a river deity, most of these Abidjan sojourners are emaciated, have frequent stools, shingles and oral thrush and in some other cases hair loss. It becomes easy to sympathise and also accept the gravity of their predicament when a curse is blamed for the terminally ill condition.

23. The health institutions mentioned here are: St Martin de Porres Catholic Hospital, Eikwe, Aiyinasi Health Centre, Esiama-Nkroful Health Centre and Asasetre Clinic.

24. Avoidance of sexual promiscuity and practice of unsafe sex are the thrust of these counselling sessions. Those who have tested positive for the virus that causes AIDS are also advised not to reinfect themselves by engaging in unsafe sex.

25. The stigma associated with the use of condoms is the greatest disincentive for their use even though they are known to protect against pregnancy and death. People find it difficult to buy them off the counter.

26. In societies where condom culture has not caught on very well with the people, women are known to refuse sex with a condom because they feel humiliated by the implied offence. A married woman who possesses condoms without the husband's knowledge exposes herself to the accusation of marital infidelity.

Bibliography

Ackah, J.Y., 1964. *Kaku Ackah and the Split of Nzema*. Unpublished MA thesis. Institute of African Studies, Legon

Adomako, A., 1991. *Marginalised Women and AIDS in Ghana*. Unpublished manuscript.

Agorsah, K., 1997. *Marry Me in Africa*. Newark: Black Arrow Publishers.

Anarfi, J.K., 1993. Sexuality, migration and AIDS in Ghana. In *Sexual Networking and AIDS in West Africa Health Transition Review. Vol.3 Supplementary Issue* Pp.45-67.

Asare Opoku, 1978. *West African Traditional Religion*. Accra: Far Eastern Publishers.

Beattie, J., 1964. *Other Cultures Aims, Methods and Achievements of Social Anthropology*. London: Cohen and West.

Busia, K. A., 1968. *The position of the Chief in the Modern Political System of Ashanti*. London: Frank Cass and Company Ltd.

Christensen, H.T., 1963. A cross- cultural comparism of Attitudes Towards Marital Infidelity. In Mogey (ed.), *Family and Marriage*. Leiden: E.J. Brill.

Danquah, J.B., 1928. *The Akan Doctrine of God*. London: Lutterworth.

Dolphyne, F., 1988. The Volta Comoe Languages. In Kropp Dakubu M.E. (ed), *The Language of Ghana*. London: Kegan Paul. Pp. 50-57

Dzobo, N.K., 1975. *African Marriage: Right or Wrong.* Tema: Ghana Publishing Corporation.

Eboyi-Ansa F.K., 1979. *Benlea Maamela.* Accra, Bureau of Ghana Languages.

Fortes, M., 1953. The Structure of Unilineal Descent Groups. *American Anthropologists* Vol.55.

Fortes, M., 1962. *Marriage in Tribal Societies.* Cambridge: Cambridge University Press.

Frimpong-Nnuroh D., 2002. Conjugal Morality and Sexual Vulnerability: The Ellembelle Case. *Research Review* (Legon) NS 18.1 pp. 27-32.

Grottanelli, L., 1969. Gods and Morality in Nzema Polytheism. In Pavanello M. (ed.), *An Italian Tribute to Ghana.* Pisa, Universita Deli Studi Di Pisa.

Gyekye, K., 1987. *An Essay of African Philosophical Thought the Akan Conceptual Scheme.* Philadelphia: Temple University Press.

Kwaw, S., 1990. *Mande Ye Elomboe.* Unpublished manuscript.

Manuh, T., 1995. Changes in Marriage and funeral Exchanges in Asante: A case study from Kona Afigya-Kwabre. In Guyer (ed.) *Money Matter.* Portsmouth: Heinemann. Pp.188-201

Ministry of Health 1999. *HIV Sentinel and Surveillance Report.* Ghana.

Muller, J.C., 1978. On Bride wealth and Meaning among the Rukuba, Plateau State Nigeria. *Africa* 48 (2).

Nukunya, G., 1992. *Tradition and change in Ghana.* Accra: Ghana Universities Press.

Oppong, C., 1995. A high price to pay: for education subsistence or a place in the job market. In *Health Transition Review. Supplement to Vol.5* pp.35-57.

Parkin D & Nyamwaya D. (eds.), 1987. *Transformations of African Marriage.* Manchester University Press.

Richards, A., 1950. Some Types of Family Structure Amongst the Central Bantu In Radcliffe-Brown and Forde, D. (eds.), *African Systems of Kinship and Marriage.* London: International African Institute.

Vellenga, D.D., 1974. *Changing Sex roles and social tensions in Ghana: the law as measure and mediator of family conflict.* Unpublished Ph.D. thesis.

Vellenga, D.D., 1971. Attempts to change the Marriage Laws in Ghana and the Ivory Coast. In Foster G. and Zolberg A. (eds.) *Ghana and the Ivory Coast: Perspectives on Modernization.* Chicago: University of Chicago Press.

Warren, D., 1986. *The Akan of Ghana: A Survey of ethnographic literature.* Accra: Pointer Press.

'FAT MONEY, THIN BODY'
BETWEEN VULNERABILITY AND SURVIVAL
IN THE ERA OF HIV/AIDS:
THE CASE OF MIGRANT CANOE FISHERMEN
AND FISHMONGERS IN GHANA

Irene K. Odotei

Some of the first cases of HIV/AIDS reported in Ghana in the eighties and early nineties included women working as commercial sex workers who had returned from La Cote d'Ivoire. This gave the initial impression that AIDS is a disease brought from outside especially by prostitutes. From a low figure of 42 in 1989 the figures have kept on growing as the disease spreads over the whole country. The 2003 HIV sentinel report of Ghana gives the prevalence rate as 3.6%, up from 2.3% in 2000. In 2002, it was projected that by 2004, 365,000 people would be living with HIV and about 200,000 children would be orphaned because of AIDS in the country. This situation poses a great challenge, in the light of the fact that whereas a number of countries, such as Senegal and Uganda, have made significant progress in stalling and reducing HIV prevalence in their respective countries, Ghana's figures keep steadily rising (J. R. Oppong and S. Adjei-Mensah 2004). Moreover, in addition to an uneven geographic spread, surveillance data and studies conducted give ample evidence pointing to the fact that infection is particularly high among people of particular occupational groups, especially mobile occupations such as trading and driving. Furthermore among other factors, the crisis of HIV/-AIDS seems to have spread rapidly, as a result of changes in lifestyles and the disruption, dislocation and disintegration of families, especially husbands and wives. Yet this is an era when many people everywhere have been forced to adopt mobile, economic strategies for survival, in times of major transitions, due to increasing loss of natural resources; the monetization of economies; rampant individualism, and the spiralling costs of living in an age of widespread impoverishment. The quest for survival has caused people in Ghana, as in many other parts of the world, to take various risk prone strategies to alleviate their economic hardships and to cope with such economic downturns and political instabilities. The kind of strategy adopted may be common to a collection of people with a certain common identity, such as people in similar occupations or living in the same geographical area or of the same ethnicity. In Ghana for instance, many young females from the three northern regions have resorted to migrating to the southern part of the country (mainly Accra and Kumasi) to work as porters, *(kayayoo)* as an economic strategy to alleviate their hardships.

Many studies looking at occupations at high risk of HIV/AIDS infection have focused on occupations such as commercial sex workers, long distance truck drivers, itinerant traders and food vendors, mine workers and the military (e.g. Anarfi (1995); J. R. Oppong and Agyei-Mensah (2004); Caldwell C.J. et al. (1993) & Barnett T. and Blaike (1992)). Not much attention however has been given to fisher folk, both females and males, who by virtue of high mobility and other attributes are also extremely vulnerable. This chapter looks at a section of the artisanal marine fishing industry in Ghana that adopted a new technology as a result of migration and was able to spread the use of the technology in Ghana and other West African Countries and acquire material goods and wealth in the process.

These men and women live as transnationals, undaunted by national boundaries. They are highly mobile and widely dispersed, contributing immensely to both rural and urban development not only in their own country Ghana, but also in other West African countries, where they carry on their operations. They produce, process and distribute fish, a valued protein commodity that is highly prized for sustaining life. But embedded in their clearly gendered mode of operations, mobile culture and risk prone life style are dangers that may lead inevitably to death through HIV/AIDS infection. Their method of fishing is called *Awam sea* or *La gas* fishing.

The Artisanal Marine Fishing Industry of Ghana

Fish, fresh, smoked and salted, constitutes the bulk of animal protein in the diet of the Ghanaian (Odotei 2002a). The artisanal, marine fishing industry that produces most of this fish is a major economic activity along the coast of Ghana, stretching for over five hundred kilometres. It provides employment for an estimated one hundred thousand or more fishermen working in close collaboration with female fishmongers and supported by canoe carvers, fuel dealers, mechanics, firewood sellers, food vendors, traders and other allied occupational groups (ibid). Some of these men and women also have personal histories of movement between inland fisheries and inland markets, taking along with them their skills, produce and possibly communicable diseases.

Perhaps a word about the history of the artisanal marine fishing industry would be in order at this point. This is a traditional occupation that predates the arrival of the Europeans in Ghana in the closing decades of the 15th Century. European writers were impressed by the organization of the industry, its associated activities and its coordination in the coastal communities and marketing inland communities (Pereira, A. 1518; Dapper O. 1670; Muller W. J. 1673; Tilleman, E. 1697; Bosman W. 1704, Rask J. 1754; Barbot, J. 1732). The numerous features of the industry and the communities, relevant to the subject matter of this paper, include the manufacture of fishing canoes and gear; the training and socialization of children by parents for participation in the industry and the gender-specific nature of activities and responsibilities, including fish preservation and marketing, financial management and leadership. In addition there was and still remains a significant religious dimension and belief system, with rules and regulations for controlling and managing the fishery resources and migration of fishermen along the coast. The presence of the Europeans along the Guinea Coast enhanced the industry as its products fed the many captives and displaced persons who were transported to the coast as slaves and detained until it was possible to be later transported across the Atlantic Ocean to the Americas (Odotei 2002a). As the coast lacked natural harbours, fishermen were also hired by the Europeans to transport goods in their canoes to and from ships that had to be anchored some distance away from the shore. These opportunities provided by the European presence accelerated migration, especially of Fante fishermen, who were acknowledged experts. These fishermen known as 'Mina Fishers' migrated along the coast of the Gold Coast to neighbouring states as far away as the modern Republic of Benin. Barbot, a seventeenth century European observer stated that :

> The Mina blacks drive a great trade along the Gold Coast and Wida [Ouidah] by sea and are the fittest and experienced men to manage and paddle the canoes over the bars and breakings which render this coast, and that of Wida [Ouidah] perilous so that it is toilsome to land either men, goods or provisions (Barbot p. 155).

Over the centuries the industry has absorbed new gear and methods of fishing, which have affected not only the development of the industry, but also the men and women who participate in it, their communities and the country in general. Of all the innovations, the introduction of the outboard motor had the most phenomenal impact. It led to faster operations, bigger canoes, bigger and multi-mesh size nets, larger crews, bigger catches, and new processing equipment and techniques (Seini, 1977). It led to the generation of wealth, which attracted non-fishermen to invest in the fishing industry. It also affected the demographic characteristics of the industry. Fishing, which was considered an occupation for illiterates started attracting a few people with at least basic formal education or even higher (Odotei 2002a). The industry also became increasingly dependent on political stability, national economic policies and international markets for its operations, especially, as dependence on imported fuel and fishing inputs grew. In case of unmet needs and expectations in their own country, the men and women of the industry have had to look elsewhere for their requirements. In the 1970s and 1980s, Ghana went through a long period of economic downturn and political instability that increased the volume of international migration of the fishermen and women of the artisanal, marine fishing industry.

Migration of Fishermen and Fishmongers

Migration is an integral phenomenon in the artisanal marine fishing industry. Fishermen have always followed the seasonal pattern of upwelling, which produces abundant catch of herring (*sardinella aurita*) at specific periods along the coast. In addition to these seasonal migrations, there are other types of mobility which can be classified as semi-permanent or permanent. Fishermen migrate with the intention of spending a few seasons or years to achieve an objective, such as building a home, acquiring fishing gear or capital for investment (Odotei 2002b). As they meet obstacles and struggle to achieve their goals they may ultimately spend more years than they had planned, with no urgency to return to their hometown. They may end up leaving these migrant posts from time to time to fish seasonally in other waters. Such fishermen became transnationals shuttling between their home country, Ghana, and their transit homes, which could be in Benin, Togo, La Cote d'Ivoire or Nigeria and their seasonal post (Odotei 2002c).

Over the decades, Ghanaian fishermen have acquired a great reputation for skill and expertise in fishing as they migrate to other West African countries and affect the industries there. All three coastal ethnic groups, the Fante, Ga-Dangme and Ewe can be identified at specific locations on the West African Coast, from the Gambia to Gabon, specializing in specific methods of fishing. For example, the Fante are noted for purse seine fishing; the Ga-Dangme for hook and line, and the Ewe for Beach Seine fishing (Atti-Mama 1991; Overa 1998).

Ghanaian migrants in La Cote d'Ivoire, Togo and Benin gave the following causes for international migrations:

- Economic conditions at home exert pressure at certain times for migration to another country to make a better life.
- The extended family may require investment and expansion of the fishing business for the upkeep of members
- National policies, such as the ban on the sale of some types of net (e.g. anchovy nets), encourage migration.
- Ecology – sea erosion or the danger of the beaches to nets, canoes and human beings caused by rocks and wreckage of industrial and semi-industrial-fishing boats may prompt movement to safer beaches.
- The desire to escape from social obligations that require expenditure considered irksome by the fishermen makes people flee.
- Dislike of traditional taboos, such as those which forbid fishing on certain days, may make people want to go away.
- Incentives, such as subsidized fuel given by La Cote d'Ivoire government to fishermen or the willingness of foreign companies to give outboard (machine) motors on credit to Ghanaians, may make fishermen want to migrate.
- Strong foreign currency such as the CFA is attractive, particularly at times when the local Cedi is weak. When converted, strong currency fattens the purse and enhances purchasing power, investments and reinvestment potential.

The successes of initial migration and settlements in host communities tend to lead to chain migrations in which wives, children, lineage members, friends or other members of fishing communities and neighbouring towns or other fishing communities in the country and other occupational groups, join the migration. Ghanaian fishing migrants tend to reside in host countries according to ethnic groups providing initial support for kinsmen, community and ethnic members in a chain migration. Indeed, towns and villages in Ghana are linked up to migrant communities in other West African towns. For example, Immuna can be linked to Akpakpa Dodome in Cotonou, Komenda to Grand Bassam, Elmina, New Ningo, Kedzi to Vridi I, II, III and Port Bouet in Cote d'Ivoire.

The contribution of migrants to host communities is remarkable. For example, in La Cote d'Ivoire Ghanaian migrant fishermen control more than

90% of the production and in Benin and Togo about 50% of the artisanal marine fisheries (Atti-Mama 1991; Odotei 2002c). Migrants also contribute to the economy by their consumption and purchase of products sold by the host countries. For their home communities, migrants send or take home income they have earned from fishing for the upkeep of their families and other obligations or personal projects such as building a house and investing in fishing or other businesses. A visit to fishing communities, such as Komenda, Immuna and New Ningo reveals signs of affluence. Mud houses associated with fishing communities have given way to brick houses. Furthermore, the communities show signs of development and modernisation through the provision of pipeborne water, electricity and other amenities.

Technology transfer and diffusion of fishing skills is a major benefit of migration. In Benin and Togo, the local people confirmed that they acquired their fishing skills and technology from Ghanaian migrants (Odotei 2002c). In La Cote d'Ivoire, a Ghanaian migrant, a mechanic from New Ningo, observed the long distance hook and line method from Senegalese migrant fishermen there. Their method entails staying at sea for three to five days preserving the catch with ice. He returned home, adopted the technique and brought in fishermen from his hometown to Abidjan. He was so successful that in a chain migration, the New Ningo fishermen were able to oust the Senegalese fishermen and take the lead position in this method of fishing, *Awam Sea* or *La gas* fishing (Odotei 2002d).

La gas fishing revolutionalised hook and line fishing in Ghana. High quality fish such as the sea bream was now available from other fishing grounds in the course of the year. This fish is used as food for the gods and could only be fished after a ritual ban and opening of the season during the Ga-Dangme annual *Homowo* and *Kple* festival. From La Cote d'Ivoire, New Ningo *La gas* fishermen spread their technology and skill to other towns, including Tema, Elmina, Sekondi/Takoradi in Ghana, Lome in Togo, Cotonou in Benin, Lagos in Nigeria and recently, Conakry in Guinea.

La gas fishing brought wealth to New Ningo. Fat monies were acquired, but the mobile pursuit of wealth unfortunately rendered them vulnerable to HIV/AIDS, which in the long run produced emaciated, thin bodies associated with the final stages of the disease. The selected examples presented below illustrate the vulnerability of the men and women, who in their pursuit of wealth are exposed to life styles, backed by cultural practices regarding sex and gender which may put them at heightened risk.

Fishing Operations and Wealth

La Gas fishermen operate either on a trip-by-trip basis, sharing proceeds after every trip, weekly or monthly as they do back home or based on a Company System. In the company system, fishermen are contracted to work for a period, usually one or two years. At the end of the period, accounts are rendered and each fisherman receives his share of the proceeds. During the contract period, the company is responsible for accommodation and feeding of the fishermen. They also receive some pocket money and can ask for small loans in times of crisis. The wife of the boat owner and captain (*bosun*) and two or three women, usually wives of hard working members of the crew, are included in the company. The rest of the crew may either bring their wives on their own or hook up with other women. Their preference is to leave their wives behind and risk hooking up. They think it is cheaper and easier.

> If you have your wife and children around you when you are working, it is not good for your economy. In the morning they say one of the children is ill. In the morning they ask, what are we going to eat? The little money you have, you settle and spend all. By the time you have to come back you do not even have money for transport back home for you and your wife. (interview with an elderly *La gas* boat owner)

In addition to fishermen who are members of crews in Abidjan, there are independent or freelance fishermen, who fill in vacancies or assist other fishermen as labourers. Outboard motor mechanics, carpenters, clerks and 'hustlers' also provide support services to the *La Gas* fishermen. From their earnings, augmented by loans from family, lineage, community members, friends, strangers or canoe owners, or in partnership with any of these, hard-working and efficient fishermen and artisans are able to start their business as canoe owners. Examples are, a fisherman who owned a canoe in partnership with his sister and another fisherman who at age twenty-two owned two canoes. An outstanding success story (cited in Odotei 2002b) is that of a 54-year-old fisherman, Jacob, who rose to be the chief fisherman of the Ghanaian community in La Cote d'Ivoire. He owned fifteen canoes, eleven operating in La Cote d'Ivoire, and four in Ghana. He also owned cattle, four commercial trucks, a pick-up and a Mercedes Benz car. He has built a three-storey 35-bedroom house with two 'boys quarters' of 18 rooms each in his hometown, New Ningo. Being illiterate and shuttling between Ghana and La

Cote d'Ivoire, he has employed a private secretary to keep his records and manage his business in La Cote d'Ivoire. He even used his personal money and resources to fight what he considered a social crime, that is, the luring of young girls from Ghana into prostitution in Abidjan, on the deceptive promise that they would be employed as shop assistants.

Women interviewed fall into four categories. These include married women, who are members of their husband's company; non-company members married to fishermen and other occupational groups; unmarried, separated, divorced and widowed women, independent of male control and lastly young adolescent women in bonded service to other women. The nature of post-harvest operations and fish marketing of the catch of the *La Gas* fishermen is such that women cannot do what they are used to doing back home in Ghana as sellers and processors of their husbands' catch, on which they get commission and make profit (Hagan 1983). One of the outstanding features of the artisanal marine fishing industry in Ghana is the separation of sex roles, or gender segregation. Men fish and women take care of post harvest operations. Marriage (and sexual relationships) are intricately woven into business relationships and business relationships can easily turn into conjugal relationships (see Vercruijsse 1983; Hagan 1983; Odotei 1991). On migration, this relationship between male and female partners is sometimes jeopardized, depending on the type of fishing and the conditions in the host community. For example, in Abidjan the catch of *La gas* fishermen is sold by public auction at the harbour. Women therefore have to renegotiate their activities, rights and responsibilities. Wives who are incorporated into the fishing company cook and wash clothes for the men. They are sometimes given a generous quantity of fish for cooking, some of which they sell. At the end of the contract period, the wives together are given the equivalent of one man's share. Thus, women are able to turn into paid employment the free domestic and conjugal services they render to their husbands at home in their own communities (Bortei-Doku 1991). The wives also act as chandlers for the company, providing the crew with engine oil and provisions for their fishing trip. While the men are at sea for days fishing, these wives use their free time to do their own business such as the sale of cooked food. Some of these women eventually purchase their own boats and recruit fishermen to work for them. Success is however not limited to women married to boat owners and company fishermen or even married women in general. Kinship and other relationships coupled with diligence and business acumen also produce wealth for the women (Odotei 2002b).

Among the fishmongers are those who become very successful and prosperous. An example is the case of Mamle, a young woman (cited in Odotei 2002b) who dropped out of school due to teenage pregnancy and was living with her child and grandmother, surviving on commission earned out of peddling bread in New Ningo. She came to Abidjan on the invitation of her sister, and was given a little capital which enabled her to sell cosmetics. She augmented this with earnings from a small-scale savings scheme *(susu)*, which she initiated. After a market survey and advertisement, she started selling fried *tsofi* (turkey tails) to *kenkey* sellers, moving from one crate to eighteen crates per weekend alone. In her own words,

> Money was just multiplying in my hand. It was wonderful I could not believe it. I made at least 100% profit on each crate of *tsofi* (turkey tails).

Eventually she started selling maize and making *kenkey* herself with the assistance of bonded servants she brought from Ghana. Through her entrepreneurial skills she became a dynamic partner to the fishermen by assisting them to overcome some of the challenges encountered by the *La Gas* fishermen in La Cote d'Ivoire. The story of her schemes and successes are better told in her own words:

> In the Ivory Coast, where we live, foreigners, including Ghanaians are not permitted to dispose of fresh fish on their own. Harbour authorities, who are government officials, are the only people who can do so, but for every trade there must be a way out. I devised some means of acquiring fresh fish at the fishing harbour. Through this our Ghanaian fishermen also manage to dispose of their fish subtly to other women counterparts. This is the way it went.

> First, I acted as a 'supplier' for Ghanaian fishing boats. The boats' crews commissioned me to buy provisions for them on credit. Other women did this before I went. But when I went, I became so popular with most fishermen that I was virtually the only one who bought for many boats. Sometimes they would agree on CFA 2,000-5,000… But you know women, we have our own way of going to all lengths to get the last franc. You have to pinch the men somehow to get what you want. For instance, I could buy something for CFA 3,000 and tell them

that I bought it for CFA 5,000, which is the price that they would have bought it for, if they had gone to the market themselves. It's pathetic the way the men are cheated. Hence they must connive with us to alleviate that problem. When we (women) go to the harbour, the fishermen excuse the harbour authorities that their wives have come for fish for domestic use. They smuggle a few crates and distribute them to us. We sell this fish in the vicinity, take the money home and share with the fishermen.

Mamle also acted as money lender to the fishermen who paid for their loans in fish "bit by bit". She contrived another way of making money by hiring out plastic buckets to the fishermen for scooping their fish from the canoes. These buckets were paid for in fish and the proceeds shared with the fishermen.

This successful fishmonger/businesswoman went further to own a boat in partnership with her brother. She got into the export business – exporting cosmetics and cloth from La Cote d'Ivoire to Ghana. With her earnings she built a house in her hometown. As a security measure for crisis management she joined an association called *Tsuishitoo ji kunimyeli* meaning 'patience is victory' or *Oshika Nti* which means, "your money is growing fat or thick,' to which she made monthly contributions. She was able to get CFA 40,000 from the association when she lost her mother and when she gave birth she received CFA 75,000, an aluminum head pan of soap, a bowl of cosmetics, a crate of minerals and a carton of beer for outdooring her baby.

In contrast to Mamle is a group of other independent women who left home due to unfortunate circumstances and 'bad marriages'. They form work groups of three or four women based on kinship or friendship. These women have inadequate capital, which they obtain through loans. They are barely able to purchase good quality fish, which is their preference, from the harbour. They most often resort to smoking surplus fish, which Fante women are not able to smoke from their husbands' catch and left over herring from the baits of the *La Gas* fishermen. They do not even own ovens and therefore have to smoke their fish in hired ovens belonging to male fish smokers from Burkina Faso or other northern states. They feel marginalized and discriminated against by the other members of their own community who come from New Ningo and are doing better than they are.

Another group of women are young girls, given in bonded service to other female relations or friends who have migrated to Abidjan. They provide labour in labour intensive enterprises, such as the making of *kenkey* and other cooked food, which they peddle, traveling long distances. They are bonded to work for two years, during which they are provided food and accommodation, but receive no pay. After the bondage they receive ten to twelve half pieces of wax-print cloth (*dumas*), that is, between sixty to seventy-two yards of cloth. They live under constant threat of repatriation without the agreed items.

From the above it is clear that migration to La Cote d'Ivoire offers hope and opportunities for individuals to acquire wealth (Fat Monies). Although not all succeed in this endeavour, they are at least able to earn enough to purchase consumable items valued in their home communities and to display these when they go home. The *La Gas* fishermen and fishmongers, their home communities, and Ghana in general have gained tremendously from this enterprise. New Ningo for example is a rural community that has done very well in self-help projects. Mud houses have been replaced with brick houses; schools, pipe-borne water, electricity, a good road and a hotel are visible signs of rural development. In recognition of the role of *La gas* fishing and its contribution to the development of New Ningo, Mr. Jonathan Nartey, the initiator of *La gas* fishing, was voted as the assemblyman in the first District Assembly Elections. Wealth from Abidjan however is fraught with danger, for HIV/AIDS has been identified as the leading cause of adult death in Abidjan (de Cock et al. 1991) and Abidjan has been identified as a major destination for many Ghanaian women migrants (Anarfi 1990), especially those engaged in commercial sex. Besides women who have stayed in Abidjan were among the first group of AIDS victims in Ghana.

"Fat Money" and development not withstanding, migrants, wealthy and poor, are vulnerable to the HIV/AIDS pandemic and all those they come into contact with are at risk. Wealth, poverty, the worldview, belief systems, culture, customs, lifestyles and environment are contributory factors to this risk. For example, a group of young men working and living under harsh conditions, that is, spending their nights on the open sea in open canoes and when on land living together in crowded hired compounds, are bound to look for women to provide the necessary sexual comforts.

In a discussion with an experienced *La gas* fisherman and leader in New Ningo, the issue was addressed. He stated that fishermen have a way of solving their sexual problems. They seek the services of prostitutes. He himself has availed himself of their services at Korle Wokon, when he was a young apprentice in Accra. He asserted that you do not need to be away from your wife before you use the services of a prostitute.

If your wife is with you and you will do it, you will do it.

There is also a culturally endorsed open door – polygyny, which allows men to have multiple sexual partners. In the fishing industry, polygyny has a certain economic and social value. Men like to have as many children as possible to work in their canoes. It also gives status. This they believe can better be achieved through polygyny.

We can boast or take pride in this town of the number of children we have. If a man has fourteen children, then others who have few children are not co-equals with him. So because of this boasting, one can marry about five wives. This one will give birth to three, another will give birth to four and another five etc. so people marry many women as they desire.

The practice of polygyny has become more widespread and on the increase through migration. A married man who leaves his wife behind or travels with just one or two easily acquires more wives on migration. Men with money and access to fishing resources are the worst culprits. For example, at age twenty-two, an owner of two canoes was found to already have four wives and nine children.

Jacob, the wealthy boat owner and leader described earlier stated:

I used to have nine wives but I have divorced one because she was non-cooperative. I wish I could have a dozen wives so that I could have more children, because the nature of my work calls for it. In fact, I would have had a dozen wives by now but unfortunately some were barren for about three years and I had to send them away because I married them for children. My youngest wife is eighteen and pregnant. My sons handle my canoes well because they know that they will inherit them from me. (Odotei 2002b: 49-52)

Jacob has twenty-eight children.

Polygyny therefore has an economic and cultural value that transcends multiplicity of sexual partners. It gives respect and honour to a man and ensures many children. Five of the wives of Jacob were acquired while on migration to La Cote d'Ivoire. Some of his wives live in Ghana and he spends time shuttling between Ghana and La Cote d'Ivoire.

Some of the wives acquired during migration have been married before and they could have had any number of sexual partners before getting married to him. Since a man has the cultural right to acquire more wives, he can easily, while sampling the women, get AIDS and bring in the virus to affect not only his many wives, concubines and girlfriends but also the children born in such relationships.

The various groups of women are also subject to the same vulnerability as the men. A wife had this to say:

> Men here have the tendency to have affairs with many women because they think they have enough money which can enable them handle the needs of the women they go after. As a wife I can tell my husband if I find him in such situation that I am not happy with it. If he decides to stop then I am lucky. (Odotei 2002b: 110)

Decision-making on sex, under such circumstances, is in the hands of the men.

> I decide on who sleeps with me at one time. If I want a particular woman always at the expense of another, the latter has to find out why. (Odotei 2002b p.50)

This means that a wife who is starved sexually by her husband may decide to remain faithful, but what about the ones who cannot wait for the time that their husbands may decide to have sex with them?

The case of Mamle, the successful, female businesswoman/fishmonger and her category is no better. After working in La Cote d'Ivoire for some years, she got married to what she termed a 'good husband', who is a seaman with two wives. This is how she describes her 'good catch':

> It is through traveling that I have got such a "good husband". The man with whom I had my first child didn't marry me. It was just a teenage pregnancy. I had that child without formal marriage. When I came to the Ivory Coast, I met my husband, a seaman who came home to marry me formally. He had two wives at first but I'm the only wife he has now. (Odotei 2002b: 93)

Ousting the two co-wives did not mean that the husband would not have other sexual partners. Being a seaman gives ample opportunities for multiple sexual partners. Aware of this, Mamle has to invest time, energy and resources to maintain her relationship:

> Since my husband does not reside in the Ivory Coast to work, I do sponsor his visits to me in the Ivory Coast and shop for him to return home. When I don't see my husband for about 3 months, i.e. if he tells me he will come but he delays, I have to come home to find out what is wrong. When he goes to sea, I plan my going home to coincide with his return.(Odotei 2002b: 91)

The impression given here is that if Mamle does not monitor the schedule of the seaman husband, he may stay in his hometown in Ghana, perhaps, with another woman, whilst Mamle is waiting for him in Abidjan.

Just like Mamle the wealthy businesswoman, the group of single women who struggle to make a living are also at risk. These are women who look down on commercial sex workers and take pride in the fact that they are hard working 'decent women'. In fact, they get upset when people mistake them for 'prostitutes'. Most of them, divorced from bad marriages at home, are still on the look out for new husbands. The lament: "Madam, do you think a woman like me should not have a husband" (Odotei 2002b: 102), is very eloquent and signifies frustration at not having found a husband yet.

The life style of these women offers opportunities for sexual relationship with men.

> We normally go to drinking bars. After ordering for drinks, we listen to music or dance. Some Ivorian women join us in dancing but others despise us and call us names... When a relative of an Ivorian dies, because they do not know how to organize funerals they solicit our help in order to make the ceremony a success. (Odotei 2002b: 107)

In Ghana, a successful funeral means a huge crowd, dancing, eating and probably starting up relationships between men and women. There is a popular joke among women that it is when you go to a funeral that you find a husband. It is even said that women practise how to weep seductively before they attend funerals. Funerals bring people of varied backgrounds from different places to the location of the funeral. Making a good catch by both men and women is common practice. For these women HIV/AIDS can be found lurking at funeral grounds, drinking bars and other places while they are looking for good husbands.

The adolescent female is a victim of promiscuity while on migration in Abidjan. Those in bonded service are particularly vulnerable. Bonded to a mistress in a labour intensive work and walking long distances to peddle her cooked food, she needs to take short rests, preferably, at her boyfriend's. Threats from her mistress to send her home with nothing may aggravate her situation. In the words of one mistress:

> Sometimes, I threaten them when they misbehave. For instance, when reports reach me that they visit their boyfriends, especially while they are on their peddling rounds. I threaten to dispatch them to their parents without anything except lorry fare. Some of them could turn arrogant, you know. Despite everything, they get scared of being dispatched home without acquiring anything. (Odotei 2002b: 90-91)

Under such circumstances, the bonded servant may depend on gifts from her boyfriends as a security measure and coping strategy. In such cases, sexual favours assume a critical economic role and thus increase vulnerability to AIDS. The more boyfriends she has, the faster she can accumulate the material requirements that will enable her to go home with 'something'. In the course of their amorous encounters, pregnancy sometimes ensues and these adolescents join the pool of women who provide sexual services to the men as wives, concubines or 'freelance' sexual partners. Single women claim that marriages contracted during migration are very brittle. The men do not take the relationship seriously in the absence of family backing. The vulnerability of these men and women is exacerbated by the fact that there is a large population of Ghanaian female commercial sex workers in Abidjan. As a sizable number are Ga-Dangme women, belonging to the same ethnic group, the men avail themselves of their services, networking between the various categories of women.

While the potential vulnerability of all these groups is evident, AIDS was not observed at the time of the original research in Abidjan in 1989. It was too early in the history of the disease. In Abidjan, migrants were usually sent back home for treatment when they became seriously sick. Meanwhile the women say they have no confidence in Ivorian doctors and prefer to go home for difficult pregnancies, childbirth and serious illnesses. Further probing revealed that migrants think that medical expenses in Cote d'Ivoire are exorbitant. One "can build a Hall and Chamber" with the cost of treatment there. For evidence of HIV/AIDS, research was extended more recently to New Ningo.

From Perception To Reality

At New Ningo, interviews with the elders, ex-migrants and boat owners revealed the sad prevalence of HIV/AIDS. They said that when HIV/AIDS first appeared in the community, it was interpreted as a curse placed on individuals as a result of conflict, quarrels or deception. This is in consonance with the worldview and belief system of the people. Fisher folks are said to be very outspoken and rough. Getting into conflict is therefore quite common. Remembering threatening words indiscreetly spoken by someone is therefore not difficult for any person who has a lingering sickness that cannot easily be diagnosed or cured. The elders said that they received public information on HIV/AIDS for the first time in 1993. Even with this, people continued to treat it as a curse and resorted to traditional healers and spiritualists for a cure. As is the practice among fisher folks, they start with self-medication, then visit a drug store, before seeing a medical doctor. Unfortunately New Ningo has no clinic so sick people have to visit the one in Prampram or the hospital at Battor, Tema or Korle Bu, thus escalating the problem.

Death through AIDS is considered a disgrace because of its association with prostitution and promiscuity. There is a tendency for such deaths to be hushed up by the family or explained away as a curse, as stated earlier. However now with the introduction of support for AIDS victims and their children, families are coming out with information that will entitle them to receive assistance for the care of the sick and orphans. Hopefully, this will give a clearer picture of the AIDS pandemic in the community and facilitate prevention strategies.

One man noted that as a protective measure some of the men try to use a condom only to be rebuffed by the women who consider it an insult and an implicit suspicion by the men that the female partner may have contracted AIDS through immoral living. A cynical attitude has also developed.

> People are saying that death existed before AIDS came into the world. So AIDS cannot stop death. They cannot allow AIDS to prevent them from having sex. If you will die, you will die.

Through migration and wealth, New Ningo, a rural community, is acquiring the characteristics of an urban community. Marriage and family values are being undermined. The traditional system, which lays emphasis on consensus building and agreement by both families before a marriage is contracted, is increasingly under threat.

Young people become sexually active at a very early age. Left in the care of grandparents, when parents go on migration, the youth get out of control.

> A young man may attend a party, concert, bar or go to watch a video. There he may meet a girl and both of them get attracted to each other. They begin 'to play together' and pregnancy ensues. (Odotei 2002: 82)

The youth are not the only ones affected by disruptions to family life. Men have resorted to disregarding their obligations of supporting their wives and children. This has led to women looking for partners in the absence of their husbands in their quest for survival.

It is not unusual for a married woman in a polygynous marriage, whose husband is in Cotonou, to decide to go to Abidjan and leave her children in the care of her mother. The elders lamented on the moral decadence that has engulfed the family.

> Right now there are some people who have gone and left their wives and do not send them anything. They take other women and enjoy with them at bars. Meanwhile their wives are here and they must give them something and they are not doing so. So by the time you return, she also gets another man and 'turns around' with him. If you point to her, she will say it is not her fault since you were not sending her any money. So you see, many times you leave your wife and you don't think of her, by the time you come she too has changed.

In a patrilineal society where the paternity of children is critical to establishing legitimacy and membership of the lineage, the only fear these women have is pregnancy with another man in the absence of their husbands. It is the ground for stigmatization for both the mother and the child. There is therefore an increase in the use of contraceptives, which in turn gives the women a feeling of security.

It appears that some women do not even have to wait for their husbands' absence before engaging in extra marital relationship. They feel cheated by the men. An elder of the community stated,

There is a base called 'Com Cee'. Over there, it is assumed that no one has a wife or husband. Yes, we live together. Sometimes when you see a woman and take her to 'Com Cee' you might even meet your wife already there with someone else.

The statement ends on an ominous note:

It will get to a time that there will be nothing like a wife. Marriage will no longer exist.

As the people of New Ningo meet in their hometown from all their migrant communities in Ghana and other West African countries to celebrate annual traditional festivals and funerals, sexual inhibitions may drop and create health problems for New Ningo, Ghana and their host communities and countries after their return.

It has been stated earlier that migration of fishermen is caused by socioeconomic factors, political upheavals, natural disasters and traumas in the migrant communities and the hope and possibilities of overcoming the challenges for personal advancement. When Ghana was experiencing economic difficulties in the 1970s and 80s, La Cote d'Ivoire offered Ghanaians and other West African nationals a stable political climate, liberal economy and strong currency among other advantages. With the threat of instability as a result of political upheaval in La Cote d'Ivoire, some *La gas* fishermen have moved away to experiment in new fishing grounds. Five canoes with crews of 16 men each went to Conakry in Guinea and stayed for two years fishing. They went without their wives which means they were dependent on local women as sexual partners. They were very focused on their work. They came back with a lot of money, "Fat Money", more money than those who went to Abidjan. More canoes are planning for the next trip. Of the eighty who went, several have already died of AIDS at New Ningo. These victims could have carried the AIDS virus with them from Ghana or Cote d'Ivoire to Conakry, where they have transmitted them to local or other migrant women.

Did they take the virus to Conakry? Where did they carry it from, Ghana or La Cote d'Ivoire? And what did they bring from Conakry?

The endeavours of the fishermen and fishmongers of New Ningo and their plight have policy implications, which in an indigenous Ga-Dangme philosophical expression translates as "somebody's concern is somebody's concern" (*moko he sane moko he sane ni*).

Policy Implications

The recent political turmoil and its consequences in the sub region have proved that populations continue to be displaced and seek refuge in other countries. Their problem then becomes their neighbour's problem. Examples are the case of Liberian, Sierra Leonean and Ivorian refugees in other countries. Fishermen's migration is only one stream of population movements that has marked and continues to characterize the history of West Africa. The streams have a tendency to intermingle, move in unison, branch off or change direction.

Viewed in its totality, fishermen's migration and their vulnerability to AIDS should be given an integrated approach by governments of the sub region. While regional integration is being considered on the macro-level, there is an informal micro-level of integration by men and women, who have developed coping strategies living as transnationals. Their vulnerability and the spread of HIV/AIDS should be a matter of concern not only to their countries of origin and the donors that operate there but should be given an integrated, multi-national and multi-donor approach. Ghana cannot implement a successful anti-AIDS policy without linking up with the other countries which have become supplementary homes to her nationals. In the meantime, the work of international, non-governmental agencies such as World Vision is crucial in promoting peer education and counseling activities at the local level and helping communities to help themselves. For, in a globalizing period of massive out migration of health staff, people have to take their own survival and health into their own hands and find new ways to protect themselves and those yet unborn.

Bibliography

Anarfi, J. K., 1995. 'Sexuality, Migration and AIDS in Ghana.' In *Health Transition Review* .Vol. 3, Supplementary Issue.

Anarfi, J. K., 1995. *Female Migration and Prostitution in West Africa-The Case of Ghanaian women in Cote D'Ivoire.* GTZ Regional AIDS Programme for West and Central Africa, Accra, Studies in Sexual Health No. 1

Anarfi, J. K.,1995. Sexual Networking in Selected Communities in Ghana and the Sexual Behavior of Ghanaian Female Migrants in Abidjan, Cote d'Ivoire. In Dyson, T. (ed.), *Sexual Behavior and Networking: Anthropological and Socio-Cultural Studies in the Studies on the Transmission of HIV./* IUSSP

Anarfi, J. K., 1995. *Female Migration and Prostitution in West Africa. The Case of Ghanaian Women in Cote d'Ivoire.* GTZ Regional AIDS Programme for West and Central Africa.

Atti-Mama, C., 1991. *Fishermen's Migrations in Togo and Benin in Fishermen's Migrations in West Africa.* IDAF/WP/36.

Atobrah D., 2004. *Children Orphaned by AIDS in Ghana, the Case of AIDS Orphans in Manya Krobo.* Unpublished M. Phil. Thesis.

Barbot, J., 1732. Description of the Coast of North and South Guinea. In A Churchill, *Collection of Voyages and Travels.* London 1917, Volume V.

Barnett T. and Blaike P., 1992. *AIDS in Africa: Its Present and Future Impact.* London: Belhaven Press.

Bortei-Doku, E., 1991. *Migrations in Artisanal Marine Fisheries Among Ga-Adangbe Fishermen and Women in Ghana, Fishermen's Migration in West Africa* IDAF/WP/36.

Bosman W., 1704. *A New and Accurate Description of the Coast of Guinea.* London (Utrecht).

Caldwell C. J. et al., 1993. African families and AIDS: context, reactions and potential interventions. In Orubuyole et al. (eds.), *Sexual Networking and AIDS in Sub-Saharan Africa: Behavioral Research and the Social Context.* Canberra.

Dapper, O., 1670. *Unbstandliche und eigentliche Beschreibung von Africa.* Amsterdam.

Davis, O., 1967. *West Africa before the Europeans.* London: Methuen and Co. Ltd.

De Cock, K.M., B. Barrere, L. Diaby et al., 1991. AIDS – 'The leading cause of adult death in the West African City of Abidjan, Ivory Coast.' *Science 247.*

Delaunay, K., 1991. *Artisanal Maritime Fisheries In Cote d'Ivoire, Fishermen's Migrations in West Africa.* IDAF/WP/36

Haakonsen, J. M., 1988. 'Socio-economic Aspects of Ghana's Canoe Fisheries.' In *Recent Development of the Artisanal Fisheries in Ghana.* IDAF/WP/21.

Hagan, G. P., 1983. 'Marriage, Divorce and Polygyny in Winneba.' In Oppong, C. (ed.), *Female and Male in West Africa.* London: George Allen and Unwin Limited.

Hill, P., 1963-64. Pan-African Fishermen. *West Africa.* Volume 47 and 48.

Irvine, F.R., 1947. *The Fishes and Fisheries of the Gold Coast.* London: Crown Agents.

Johnson, F. R., 1941. *The Prisons Department Fisheries Scheme, Gold Coast.* Report dated 18th October 1941. Accra.

Lawson, R. M. and Kwei E., 1974. *African Entrepreneurship and Economic Growth: A Case Study of the Fishing Industry of Ghana.* Accra: Ghana Universities Press. Maraes, P., 1602. *Description and Historical Account of The Gold Kingdom of Guinea,* translated by A. Van Dantzig and Adam Jones. Oxford University Press, 1987.

Muller, W. J., 1673. *Die Afrikanische auf der guineischen Gold Coast Gelegene Landschaft Fetu* (Hamburg), translated by Adam Jones in German sources for West African History1599-1669, Wiesbaden 1983.

Nukunya, G.K., The Anlo-Ewe and Full-Time Maritime Fishing Another View. *Maritime Anthropological Studies.* Vol.2 no.2

Odotei, I., 1991. *Migration of Fante Fishermen, Fishermen's Migrations in West Africa 1991.* IDAF/WP/36.

Odotei, I., 1991. *Migration of Ghanaian Women in the Canoe Fishing Industry, Fishermen's Migrations in West Africa.* IDAF/WP/36.

Odotei, I., 2002a. 'The Artisanal Marine Fishing Industry in Ghana', *A Historical Overview.* Legon, Institute of African Studies, University of Ghana.

Odotei, I., 2002b. *'There Is Money In The Sea', Ghanaian migrant fishermen and women in the Ivory Coast.* Accra: Royal Gold Publishers.

Odotei, I.,2002c. *"Sea Power, Money Power", Ghanaian Migrant Fishermen and women in the Republic of Benin.* Accra: Royal Gold Publishers.

Odotei, I., 2002d. *Migration, Fishing and Development: A Case Study of Ningo.* Accra: Royal Gold Publishers.

Oppong J. R. and Agyei-Mensah S., 2004. HIV/AIDS in West Africa: The Case of Senegal, Ghana and Nigeria. In Kalipeni E., Craddock S. et al (eds.), *HIV & AIDS in Africa, Beyond Epidiology.* Blackwell Publishing Ltd.

Overa, R., 1992. *Fish Mammies: The Role of Women in the Artisanal Fisheries of Ghana.* Master thesis, Department of Geography. Bergen: University of Bergen.

Overa, R., 1992. Wives and traders. Women's Careers in Ghanaian Canoe Fisheries. *Maritime Anthropological Studies,* 6(1/2): 110-135.

Overa, R., 1995a. Gender and Entrepreneurship in Ghanaian Canoe Fisheries: the Case of the Fante Fishing Town Moree. In Bivand, R. and Stokke, K. (eds.) *Investigating the Local: Structure, Place, Agency, Series B: Monographs from Department of Geography,* No. 1. Bergen.

Overa, R., 1998. *Partners and Competitors: Gendered Entrepreneurship in Ghanaian Canoe Fisheries.* Bergen: Universityof Bergen.

Overa, R., 2003. 'Gender Ideology and Maneuvering space for female fisheries entrepreneurs.' *Research Review.* Vol. 19 Issue 2. Institute of African Studies, Legon-Ghana.

Pereira, P., 1518. *Esmeraldo de Situ Orbis,* London : The Hakluyt Society. 1937.

Rask. J., 1754. *En Kort og Sandfaerdig Reise – Beskrivelse til og fra Guinea.* Trondhjem.

Romer, F. L., 1760. Tilforladelig Efterretning om Kysten Guinea. Copenhagen.

Seini, A., 1977. *Economics of Operation of Outboard Motors in Ghana's Canoe Fisheries.* (Unpublished M.A. Thesis). Faculty of Agriculture, University of Ghana.

Tilleman, E., 1697. *En liden enfolding Beretning om det Landskab Guinea.* Kobenhavn.

Vercruijsse, E., 1983. 'Fishmongers, Big Dealers and Fishermen: Co-operation and conflict between the sexes in Ghana Canoe Fishing.' In C. Oppong, (ed.) *Female and Male in West Africa.* London: George Allen and Unwin Limited.

CONFIRMED PRESENCE OF GHANAIAN FISHERMEN OUTSIDE GHANA (1986-87)

COUNTRY	LOCATION(S)	ETHNIC GROUP(S)	OBSERVATIONS
Mauritania	Nouadhibou	Fante	A few "left over" fishermen working as crew on Mauritanian canoes
Gambia	Brufut ("Ghana town")	undetermined	Not really fishermen but rather Ghanaian men and women engaged in drying of fish to be exported to Ghana
Guinea	Conakry	Ga-Dangme, Fante	Ghanaians are "drifting" back after long absence
Sierra Leone	Goderich (near Freetown) probably elsewhere as well	Fante, Ewe	Ghanaians expelled in 1967. A few are coming back now.
Liberia	Monrovia, Robertsport, Greenville, Harper	Fante, Ewe	Responsible for at least 90 percent of Liberia's Artisanal catches.
Côte D'Ivoire	Abidjan, San Pedro, Cassandra, Grand Bereby, Tabou and almost all other fishing villages along the coast	Fante, Ga Dangme, Ewe	Responsible for nearly all the Artisanal catches (marine) in Côte D'Ivoire
Togo	Lome port only except some Ewe beach seiners scattered along the coast	Fante, Ga Dangme, Ewe	The tendency in the last few years is for Artisanal fishermen, including Ghanaians, to base their activities in Lome port.
Benin	Cotonou port mainly, but also in scattered villages along the coast	Fante, Ga Dangme, Ewe	Same tendency in Ghana towards Cotonou port.
Nigeria	Lagos	Ga Dangme, possibly Fante	Migrant fishermen were affected by expulsion of 2 million Ghanaians from Nigeria in the early 1980's but they seem to be drifting back now.

INTIMATE BARGAINS:
SEX WORKERS AND FREE WOMEN NEGOTIATE
THEIR SEXUAL SPACE

Akosua Adomako Ampofo

Well, if a condom is supposed to protect you from having male sperm enter your body, why do you have to take the same sperm into your stomach? Or your stomach is not part of your body? – Adobea, age 32.

The above was the response of a sex worker in Accra to the question whether she performed oral sex for her clients. Recently made aware of the risks of "unprotected sex" for HIV-infection, she laughed at the question, appalled at the prospect.

The past decade has produced several studies on HIV-risk related behavior and prevention efforts have sought to educate women, especially, about their risk for HIV-infection.[1] Nonetheless, there are indications that many women still engage in "risky" or "unprotected"[2] sex, and that the number of AIDS cases among women continues to rise (Adomako Ampofo 1998a; Campbell 1995). Across Africa, we know that while many women may be willing to use condoms, their male partners may refuse to do so. Nonetheless, HIV-prevention education has continued to be dichotomized, targeting women and men separately, and stressing the importance of using a condom. However, this approach relies on women's skills in persuading men to cooperate in condom use and "safe sex",[3] a strategy which Campbell (1995) argues is a return to the dependence of the 1950s, where a woman's only option, if the man is unwilling, is to end the relationship. Further, many women may erroneously believe their partners to be monogamous and thus may not consider themselves to be at-risk. Additionally, there has been little discussion of issues such as oral and anal sex in the African context. Perhaps this is so because of an assumption that these types of sex acts do not feature among African people. By ignoring these specific sex acts, oral and anal sex have escaped the "safe sex" influence. And thus the emphasis on condom use in peno-vaginal sex has remained the focus of much of AIDS education directed at women. In this chapter, I examine the efforts of a number of Ghanaian women in negotiating for "safe sex", including condom use and the practice of oral/anal sex. I also examine the extent to which the women feel justified in negotiating for this safety.[4]

The study from which the data for this chapter are taken set out to examine the nature of sexual relationships and sexual behavior among a sample of single ("free") women and (commercial) sex workers.[5] At the time of the study in the early nineties, I was primarily interested in understanding the material basis of the relations that organize sexual behavior in Ghana today, and how this was related to HIV-prevention strategies among the women, especially condom-use. Sex workers were chosen for two important reasons. First the AIDS literature on Africa at the time had a propensity to associate the spread of AIDS in Africa with prostitution, migrant work, and single urban residence (see Akande and Ross 1994; Hunt 1989; Nsanze 1990; Schoepf 1988). Furthermore the very nature of their work puts sex workers at risk in both quantitative and qualitative terms. Quantitative in that the more partners they have the greater their chances of contracting sexually trans-mitted diseases (STDs) including AIDS; qualitative, because their work may require them to engage in specific types of sexual acts, which are more likely to enhance HIV- transmission, such as those which cause tears or lacerations in the skin, or genital mucosa.[6] If condom use is not strictly adhered to, the risk factor increases. Low-income single women were selected to reflect the situation of women who, while not engaged in "commercial" sex work, might be dependent on sexual exchange for economic survival (Ankomah and Ford 1993). They also presented an interesting alternative group in that presum-ably they had fewer partners, considered themselves less at risk, and therefore were less likely to practice "safe sex". [7]

While examining sexual relations is a complex affair,[8] by the end of the field work, and even before detailed analysis was carried out, it became evident that for many women the issues at stake are fairly simple. They have a financial need, and they believe that given their limited options that need can best be met through transactional sex (Adomako Ampofo 1994). As one woman succinctly put it, "my cocoa is between my legs".[9] In earlier analysis I have examined how "safer sex" practices are related to health beliefs and how the potency of (sexual health) knowledge is socially defined through asymmetrical gender relations (Adomako Ampofo 1998a, b). By assessing women's risk behavior as separate from the behavior of men, the AIDS discourse, and subsequent prevention strategies, have failed to acknowledge gender power differences (Campbell 1995; Adomako Ampofo 1998b). These differences are sharpened when we compare "commercial" and "non-commercial" sexual relations, as well as the sexual practices of sex workers with (paying) clients and boyfriends (Adomako Ampofo 1998b).

In this chapter, I examine how sexual practices, especially "safe sex", are negotiated between the women and their partners in the face of conflicting interests,[10] and whether women felt *entitled* to determine how sex should be practiced. I believe that the situations must surely differ, depending on whether a woman is more directly selling a service (and can decide when, how and to whom to offer that service) or engaging in an expected activity with a regular partner. In the current analysis, I explore the forms of two-party negotiations women employ in their sexual encounters, if any; how they arrive at compromise, if at all; and whether the "compromise" arrived at is efficient and satisfactory for them. I also examine women's sense of entitlement regarding "safe sex" and in what ways particular issues arise for different groups of women. Hopefully, the discussion of the data will provoke further debate on the culture of sex, as well as a re-examination of HIV-prevention education.

The rest of the chapter is set out in the following format. The section that follows is devoted to a discussion of what I perceive to be the different options regarding negotiating positions available to the women in this study. Included in this section is a brief review of how gendered power may affect women's negotiation options, and how this, in turn, relates to the traditional approach regarding HIV-prevention education. The third section indicates the locations and population which are the focus of study. The fourth section discusses my findings. In the final section, I present concluding comments and suggestions for policy and future research.

In looking at the outcomes of sexual encounters in the face of initially conflicting goals, two possible scenarios present themselves. In the first, both parties ultimately gain (a win-win situation); in the second a gain by one party is at the expense of the other party (a win-lose situation, Kersten and Noronha 1996). This translates into two negotiating positions. Negotiation is the process whereby parties confer, haggle or bargain to achieve their desired outcomes. On the one hand is the position of compromise, where both parties redefine their goals, and seek alternative outcomes that are still mutually acceptable (win-win). For example, a woman unwilling to perform oral sex, out of fears of infection, or distaste about touching a penis with her mouth, might ultimately agree to do so, if her partner wears a condom. The second position can become a highly antagonistic negotiation (potentially both walk away from the negotiations) where neither partner is willing to compromise. An example of the latter situation is where a sex worker insists on condom-use (her gain) with a client who feels this will hinder his sexual satisfaction (his loss). However, if one partner compromises or is forced to give in to the other partner, while the other holds to his/her position, this leads to a win-lose situation. For example, if the sex worker were to agree to, or be forced into a sex act without the use of a condom, the client's sexual satisfaction (his gain) would be against her will, and at the expense of the possibility of her contracting a disease (her loss). In other words, where the parties are in strict opposition and only one is willing/or is coerced to modify her/his goals, there can be no joint gains.

Negotiation is a process which has its own attributes, such as time, effort, communication and monetary requirements (Kersten and Noronha 1996). For a woman to have to spend time convincing a client or partner can be costly, especially for "commercial" sex workers, in terms of potential client loss. Sexual exchange underscores the importance of options as bases of power in social exchanges and the way these are negotiated. For most women, their experiences of sexual encounters are grounded in questions of gender rela-tions and power. Indeed, the hierarchies of power and money, and the organi-zation of social and sexual networks, all affect sexual conduct at the indivi-dual level (Fowlkes 1996). Engels emphasized the role of economic relations in shaping sexual norms and traditions (Tucker 1978). Rather than arguing that sexual behavior is a construct of cultural symbols and ideological assumptions, he related these to socio-economic relations. Biological sex is considered as static and the social construction of gender is separated and considered to respond to changes in economic relations.

Where the economic situation generally leads to women's dependence on men,[11] it is less likely that a woman will oppose an unsatisfactory sexual encounter. Building on a feminist model of power, Lennon and Rosenfeld (1994) posit that those who are trapped in a situation with few alternatives need to maintain a sense of cognitive consistency between what they think and what they do. In this case, women who rely on the financial rewards of sex work, or women who are dependent on boyfriends' contributions, will be less likely to view themselves as entitled to the outcomes they desire or prefer. The higher their relative income and the greater their alternatives, the more likely women will be to define the forms their sexual relationships take according to their own health goals (and physical/emotional satisfaction). The perspective employed by Lennon and Rosenfeld (1994) further suggests that the resources and options available to an individual influence their expectations and willingness to negotiate for a "win" situation for him or herself. A feminist model of power incorporates a gendered analysis of power relations that analyses how women's own notions of a win or lose situation are internalized and these themselves become barriers to, or aid women's exercise of power (Rowlands 1998). This can result in a vicious cycle where a financially dependent woman feels indebted to her male provider, and thus feels that he is entitled to dominate decisions, including those in the sexual domain.

Women may be willing to forego opposition to outcomes, even where these are in conflict with their own utility, due to their economic dependence. At the same time, where (men's) financial contributions count more than (women's) provision of sexual services, men may also have more power to enforce their own goals. In other words, men have more to offer (or more to threaten to withdraw) and are thus better able to induce women to perform such behaviors as they desire (Thibaut and Kelley 1959). This dependence is further related to the extent to which the more powerful individual can get those same needs satisfied elsewhere. In other words, if an individual wants or needs certain things that a second individual possesses and is willing to give to the first individual, then that first individual is dependent on the second (who possesses these things) in proportion to the strength of those desires or needs. Thus if a woman's boyfriend or client feels that he can find an alternative sexual partner, more than the woman believes that she can find an alternative source of income, the woman is more likely to take a position of compromise than one of opposition in negotiating sexual practices.

While not every sexual contact of unmarried women in Ghana can be considered "commercial", sexual intercourse tends to be regarded as something that is obtained by favor or by bargaining (Ankomah and Ford 1993). Furthermore, economic pressures provide the background for most sexual relationships from which material gain is expected (Adomako Ampofo 1995; Ankomah and Ford 1993; Anarfi and Fayorsey 1995; Assimeng 1981).[12] If women are of the view that they do men a favor by agreeing to have sex with them, and the men, in return believe they must support the women materially (Ankomah and Ford 1993), then contrary to Engels' assertion, sex also takes on ideological assumptions. Although women can make themselves available to be selected by men, in contemporary Ghana they still rarely take the initiative in propositioning a man (except in some forms of sex work) which can give men the upper hand in sexual exchange negotiations. Condoms are more frequently used to avoid pregnancy (a use men may agree to) than to prevent disease (a use men may disagree with). This is reflected in Ankomah and Ford's (1995) study, where none of their sexually-active respondents was using condoms as a protection against HIV infection although virtually all the respondents considered condoms an effective form of protection — and yet 20 percent used a condom during their last sexual encounter to prevent pregnancy.

In terms of "safer sex", where patriarchal ideologies give men considerable power in the sexual realm (Adomako Ampofo 1998b; Dodoo 1998; Dodoo and Adomako Ampofo 2001; Worth 1989), Ghanaian women who bargain sex for material gains may find it difficult to propose sexual behavior changes. For these women, the dilemma they face may be one of choosing between economic survival and "unsafe" sex.

HIV-Prevention Education and Behavior Change: Women, Men, or Women and Men?

In the face of women's disadvantages in society generally, and in the sexual domain specifically, it is surprising that "safe sex" Information-Education and Communication (IEC) messages aimed at changing sexual behavior have generally taken a standard approach, without considering the gendered landscape that sexual relations are grounded in.[13] The Global AIDS prevention strategy, until the mid 1990s, the time when this study was carried out, had two foci vis-à-vis changing behavior and hence promoting safer sex: (1) promoting condom use, and (2) exhorting people to reduce the numbers of their sexual partners, better still, to "stick to one partner".[14] Implicit in these messages are two assumptions, (1) that people have personal control over their sexual health and (2) that they make "rational" choices (Adomako Ampofo 1998b; Campbell 1995; Nutbeam et al. 1991). These assumptions are problematic for a number of reasons, the first of which should be obvious from the foregoing discussion. While one would wish that all individuals, especially females, have control over their sexual health, this is not the case in reality (Adomako Ampofo 2000, 1998 a, b; Campbell 1995; Heise and Elias 1995; Richardson 1990). As discussed, in situations where women's partner choices are predicated on financial considerations, their ability to negotiate for so-called "safer sex" may be limited. Furthermore, women can only influence and not control the use of condoms; hence, their protection is largely dependent on their abilities of negotiation and influence, often with an unwilling partner (Heise and Elias 1995). Several studies have shown that sex workers have more leverage than women in the general population when it comes to negotiating condom use (Heise and Elias 1995). However, while this may be true of sexual encounters with clients, what is often ignored is the extent to which this affects their relationships with their regular partners. Moreover, clients themselves are not always compliant.

Since the advent of AIDS, public health strategies have focused on how to reduce women's (sexual health) risks. They have often treated women's behavior as separate from that of men, without acknowledging gender power differences (Campbell 1995; Richardson 1990; Ulin 1992). Or they have focused on empowering women to negotiate for "safe sex", thereby implicitly placing the responsibility for "safe sex" on them (World Bank 1990). Yet studies have shown that men report more lifetime sexual partners than women do (Carael et al. 1990). Further, women may be unaware of their partner's sexual behavior outside their particular relationship – that is they may be unaware of the gamut of men's past or present behavior (Adomako Ampofo 2000, 1998b; Campbell 1995). However, in complying with exhortations to "stick to one partner" women may have the mistaken belief that they will be safe from HIV (Heise and Elias 1995).[15]

The second assumption, that people make "rational choices", is based on the premise that individuals evaluate the level of threat associated with a disease and their own level of risk, and then assess the costs and benefits to them of taking the required action. The limitations of this approach, when it comes to assessing sexual behavior, is that while engaging in "safe sex" can be viewed as a preventive strategy, as far as becoming HIV-infected is concerned, these strategies are not one-time or occasional inconveniences. Rather, they require a commitment that stretches to cover each potential and possible sexual encounter. For a woman, this means that upon entering each new relationship she needs to raise issues such as condom use and types of sexual acts, and that within existing relationships this remains a continuous process. However, what may be "rational" at one point in a relationship does not necessarily hold true throughout the relationship, or upon entering a new one. This is especially so with the question of condoms, since they are frequently associated with infidelity (Heise and Elias 1995). By raising such issues, a woman implies that either she is not monogamous or free from disease, or that she suspects her partner is not. These are hardly issues most people are willing, or able, to confront at the start of a relationship. Furthermore, condoms can no longer be insisted on when a couple begins to consider having a child. Finally, attempts to intervene in "high-risk" behavior are frequently based solely on Western categories of relationships (eg. marriage = monogamy), and medical perspectives, an approach which is bound to be inadequate among people who still place immense faith in traditional health systems (Adomako Ampofo 1998a, b; Fowlkes 1996).[16]

Roamers, High Class, Seaters and Free Women

This discussion is based on a larger study carried out among two groups of Ghanaian women ("commercial" sex workers and women who engage in "non-commercial" sex) between September 1992 and July 1994, to determine reproductive and sexual knowledge, attitudes, and beliefs, and how this related to AIDS-preventive behavior.[17] Sex workers were classified into three groups: and *Roamers, High Class and Seaters* as follows. *Roamers* refers to women who, as their name suggests, "roam" from place to place in search of clients. Such places include hotels and nightclubs, lorry stations, secluded street corners, and social functions, such as funerals and parties. They generally go with the client to an inexpensive hotel, patronized predominantly by sex workers and their clients; only rarely will a woman go to a client's home.[18] Some are only part-time sex workers and may be apprentices, students, traders, or have some source of income outside commercial sex work. *Roamers* usually cater to clients from lower socio-economic groups, hence their charges tend to be lower than for the other categories of sex workers. This is especially true for younger girls. Two levels of service are offered, "short time", which refers to a quick sexual exchange, and enables a woman to have several clients a day, and "full night" which is when a client spends the night and expects more than a sexual encounter, for instance domestic services.[19]

High Class sex workers refer to those women who generally dress in a sophisticated manner and are more likely to have wealthy and/or expatriate clients. Although they may also "roam" around hotels and social functions, these tend to be "up-market" places, which do not generally acknowledge that "commercial sex" takes place on the premises. Like the *Roamers, High Class* workers also go to hotel rooms, though in their case the hotels are usually more "respectable" establishments not necessarily known for entertaining sex workers. They occasionally go to a client's home but, like Roamers, are reluctant to do so unless the client wants a longer term relationship (as is often the case with expatriates). Unlike *Roamers* and *Seaters*, *High Class* usually have only one client a day/night, usually "full night". They sometimes spend a weekend or longer with a client. High Class do not always have fixed charges, sometimes preferring to leave the question of payment to the judgment of the client, convinced that if they give good service they will be fairly compensated, often in foreign exchange or in kind with clothes or jewellery.

Seaters are most easily identifiable as sex workers because they have a fixed place from which they operate — their homes. Traditionally knows as *Tuutuu,*[20] I refer to them here as Seaters because, unlike Roamers and High Class who may actively solicit, they can be seen, sitting on low chairs in front of their homes waiting for clients. Seaters live together in small districts and form close social communities.[21] They tend to be middle-aged women who are divorced, widowed, or "retired" from marriage, and usually cater to older clients. *Seaters* generally cater for "short time"; "full night" being discouraged.

The women who engage in "non-commercial" sex in this study are unmarried. Most are in a sexual relationship. They were selected from certain particular sectors and included sales girls, typists, clerks, hairdressing assistants, seamstresses' apprentices and petty traders. These particular professions were (non-randomly) chosen because I was primarily interested in women from lower socio-economic groups or with low incomes.[22] For ease of discussion, hereafter I refer to women engaged in "non-commercial" sex as "free-women", to distinguish them from women engaging in sex for pay.[23]

The study was carried out among Ghanaian sex workers in three cities, Accra and Kumasi and Abidjan. "Free women" were only selected in Accra and Kumasi, which have both had old, established sites of settled sex workers (*Seaters*). Meanwhile their commercial basis has seen the emergence of other kinds of less formal sex work in recent years. Greater anonymity and loosening of social controls has also enabled sexual relations in these urban centers to be less formalised and binding, and subject to less scrutiny and interference from kith and kin. In the case of Abidjan there is evidence that Ghanaian women have been sex workers from as far back as the late 1940s (Kouassi 1986) and migration was considered an important correlate of HIV-infection at the time of the study (GACP 1994). More recent work suggests that among migrant males in Abidjan Ghanaian women are the most common source of sexual contact and the ones most frequently referred to in terms of commercial sex (Painter 1992).

All the "free women" had some education, mainly secondary and post-secondary. Although a few sex workers had some secondary education, gene-rally their highest level of education attained was primary. More than a quarter had never been to school. *Seaters* were the women with the least education.

Among the 46 "free women" only just over a third were fully self-supporting. Their level of financial dependence on others is important, as it has implications for the extent to which they were able to negotiate within their sexual relationships. The majority (twenty-seven women) were financi-ally dependent on family members and boyfriends and a further 3 were totally financially dependent on partners.[24] Hardly any have *never* had any paid occupation. Ghanaian women have a tradition of being industrious and independent income earners, generally in the "informal sector". More than half of the sex workers were traders before entering commercial sex work; the rest were farmers or in service occupations. However, at the time of the study, only one in ten had any source of income other than sex work. All of these were involved in petty trading or the service industry.

The women studied form a culturally very heterogeneous group. Among the sex workers, the single largest ethnic group is matrilineal Akan (47% reflecting their proportion of the whole Ghanaian population) followed by Krobo (21% – who are considerably over represented), Ewe (11%), Ga-Adangme (8%), and others (13%). Almost two thirds of the "free women" were Akan, Ga 15 percent, Ewe 11 percent, and all others 9 percent.

Since the intention was to select single women, it is no coincidence that more than four out of five "free women" were under the age of 25. Among sex workers, the majority were under 35 years old. However, important diffe-rences emerge among the categories. *Roamers* were mainly in their early twenties. *High Class* women were mainly in their mid to late twenties and *Seaters* were mainly in their late thirties to early forties. *Seaters* were older because traditionally, they were divorced or widowed women and the presi-dent of the association of *Seaters* in Ghana explained that single, and espe-cially childless women, are not allowed to join their ranks.

The majority in each category claimed to be orthodox Christians. The rest were Muslims or practiced a form of traditional African religion. Indeed the latter is often practised even by professing Christians in times of crisis such as illness, or for protection from perceived evil forces.

Most "free" women" had a regular boyfriend, with three of these relation-ships being non-sexual. Nearly a quarter indicated that their boyfriends had other partners and more than half of these were married men. Very few sex

workers were customarily married[25] or in a consensual union. Those customarily married lived apart from their husbands and had virtually no contact
with them. Less than half of sex workers had regular boyfriends.

Negotiating the Sex Act

Women's sense of entitlement regarding acceptable sex is framed within a
context of their feelings about the sex act itself, which are sometimes ambivalent. Most women see sex as an inevitable part of a relationship with a man
and feel obliged to have sex with their boyfriends and partners when, and
how, the men want them to, even if they themselves feel disinclined. Hajia,[26]
a 23-year-old "free woman", explained it thus,

> with me, I don't treat it (sex) as anything really special. . . the way
> people talk about it, to be sincere with you, I don't feel that way...I
> prefer the romance...it is my partner who is really enjoying sex, not me.

Janiv, aged 25, also a "free woman", said that the sex act "bored" her, and
that after the act she did not feel like going near a man. Other "free women"
believed that sex should be wanted by both partners and that no woman
should feel obliged to have sex with a man. Said 23-year-old Doris,

> If you have a boyfriend and are sleeping with him I am sure you can
> tell him you don't want it, but if you accept it, and are going to
> complain it's up to you.

Caro, aged 19, insisted that no woman should have sex with a man unless
she wants to:

> If you have a boyfriend and you realize that he is doing something you
> don't like, chasing women up and down, you have the right to break up
> the relationship, because I for instance I haven't started my life yet for a
> man to get me any disease which will lead to my death. If you are not
> interested you can't, the man cannot force you to his house and have sex
> with you...It is the men who carry (sic) the AIDS. A woman can stay for
> 100 years without sex but the men they (sic) travel and all they think
> about is girls.

Caro pointed out that in the AIDS-era, an unfaithful partner is a dangerous one to have, ultimately leading to a choice between the man and death. She also raised an important perspective, the belief that women may be able to live without sex (hence resist men).

Among sex workers on the other hand, and in contrast to sex with clients, women said that sex with boyfriends is something that "belongs" in the relationship, and therefore whether they enjoy it or not is immaterial. The sex act with a boyfriend is the context within which sex workers often feel reassured, needed, and possibly loved. Women need these relationships and will rarely negotiate when, where, or how the sex act should take place. Though like "free women" they may often have sex with boyfriends when what they really want is some tenderness and affection, it is difficult to ascribe these as "win-lose" situations, since little effort is even made to negotiate alternative arrangements.

Sex with clients, on the other hand, is a business transaction. Women often felt disgusted and were keen to end the sex act as soon as possible. Said one woman,

> *How can I enjoy it? With a stranger? I don't have any feelings at all, I am just there!*

For most customers, the condition for payment is ejaculation, while for sex workers the concern is about time spent. They feel entitled to payment whether the client has ejaculated or not. Women said that they sometimes interrupt a prolonged sex act and demand payment for their time. The customer refuses to pay because he has not yet had an orgasm, blaming his delay on the use of the condom, which the woman insisted on.

Women demanding payment from troublesome customers frequently lodge complaints surrounding this type of conflict at police stations in Abidjan. Twenty-four year old Harriet, a *High-class*, narrated one such experience she had with a client who was, according to her, taking too long to climax. She tried to appeal to a sense of fairness by asking if he would want to be treated the way he treated her:

> *I got bored and intentionally started quarrelling with him but I had by then not taken my money (the man had taken in some alcohol). The man went to clean himself and when he came back he told me that if I didn't allow him to take me again for him to have an orgasm he*

wouldn't (sic) pay the money. So I told him that the way he wants to treat me, if it's done to him he won't like it and — so I won't allow it, he should give my money to me.

Harriet needed money for her transport back home so she agreed to give the client another chance, but he still did not ejaculate and so she got up, explaining;.

I then made up my mind to pull his penis but before I could attempt to do so all I saw was that he gave me a hard slap in the face so I sank my teeth into his flesh and started scratching and biting him. But the more I bit and scratched him, the more he hit me and so the screams and crying brought the other (hotel) guests and watchman running . . .

Eventually Harriet and her client ended up at the police station where one of the officers succeeded in getting twice the original charge from the client on behalf of Harriet. Her story showed the extent to which sex workers may be willing to negotiate for a "win" situation with clients while they may not negotiate at all with boyfriends.

Condom Use

The use of condoms as a prophylaxis, but also as a contraceptive, is the most important negotiated aspect of the sex act.[27] Because they are frequently seen as interfering with male satisfaction and performance, the use of condoms can be problematic for women as well as men. If wearing a condom delays a man's attainment of orgasm, or hinders this altogether, it affects his sense of manhood and can introduce conflict into the relationship, something no woman wants, whether sex worker or "free" woman. Whether there is conflict or not, a client's failure to gain, or delay in attaining orgasm reduces the total number of clients a woman can receive. As Harriet's situation above illustrates, it can even result in non-payment. Fewer than half used condoms all the time. Frequency was lowest among "free women" (one in five *always* used condoms), and highest among *Seaters* (nearly two out of three *always* used condoms). Among those sex workers who said they never used condoms, the majority were to be found in Abidjan.

Sex workers who expressed their determination to negotiate for a "win" situation regarding condom use generally framed this in terms of their survival. According to Yaa, a 40-year-old *Roamer*, the condom allows her to stay alive and take care of her children:

> *My sister it is true that poverty is a curse... with these diseases and my coming here, at least seeing my children every day, don't I like it? But as it is, just because of someone's 1000 (Cedis*[28]*) or something I'll die and leave them at an early age! Sister is that fair? As for me I think that the condom helps us a lot.*

Fifty-six-year-old Afua, a *Seater* who also insisted she always used a condom with her clients, was asked by the interviewer if she would accept to have sex without a condom if the client increased the price.

> *I: So if somebody wants to pay ¢5000 so that he doesn't use the condom?*
> *R: Where will that person get the ¢5000? If that person gives me all that money what will he eat himself?*
> *I: So if the person says he will pay some more money because he doesn't feel like having sex with a condom, what would you do?*
> *R: He should go to his wife. When there was nothing like AIDS it was "free", there was nothing like the use of condoms, now that we have the disease everyone has to use the condom.*

Patricia, a 35-year-old *Seater* confirmed the high rate of condom use among *Seaters* in Accra. She believed that it was not likely that any client would find a woman who would agree to have sex without a condom, since the sex workers belong to associations and the (new) code of conduct includes the use of condoms. Each group of sex workers in a locality has a "queen mother," who is like a mother, school prefect, and counsellor rolled into one. They collect dues, provide a shoulder to cry on, organise social affairs, such as trips to the funeral of a colleague's family member, and, recently, work with health officials to educate the women. Sex workers take antagonistic positions towards women who do not live by the code of conduct and the "queen mother" has the power to banish them from the community. Condom use among *Seaters* in Kumasi was also high because of the social control provided by belonging to an association. They have also had regular educational sessions. Fifty-year-old Akosua explained:

I didn't use it initially, I started just about two weeks ago when I returned for the last time. I was told on my arrival that everybody was supposed to use the condom so if I wanted to continue with the work then I should use it.

Seaters in Accra and Kumasi seemed to have internalised the fact that AIDS is real, has no cure, and kills. They are committed to their own protection, that of their clients, and, in some cases, a few of them even mentioned the fact that these men have wives and it would be unfair for them to contract an STD. A field worker with the AIDS Control Programme (ACP) in Ghana confirmed that as a result of regular educational sessions with the *Seaters*, condom use among them is high. He told the story of a woman who was accused by her colleagues of agreeing to receive a client another sex worker had turned away, because he did not want to use a condom. She was given a strong warning by the queen mother, and the ACP took the opportunity on that occasion to reinforce its messages.

A few women are so vigilant that they even insist on the use of two condoms. Sometimes, a condom can burst, 29 year old Stella, a High-class explained, and so possible infection is protected against by studying the type of penis the man has, "if it's a soft p enis you use one (condom), if the penis is too hard you use two."

Sex workers in Abidjan were much less likely to take an antagonistic position regarding condom use than their counterparts in Ghana. Frequently, clients are judged on the basis of outward appearance. If they look healthy they are not considered as a possible source of infection. The same is true if the man is considered to be a "good man", or a woman "just likes him". In most instances, it is the offer of more money that tips the scales in favour of a compromise not to use a condom. One 34-year-old woman, Doris, who admitted that she did not use condoms with all her clients, explained, as if this should be self-evident to the interviewer, that some men do not like it. Sex workers in Abidjan said they do not insist on condoms because they feel that men, whether paying clients or boyfriends, are entitled to their satisfaction and if condoms obstruct this, then they have to be dispensed with. Perhaps, this attitude was pervasive because women in Abidjan were the most likely to experience difficulty finding alternative partners — whether boyfriends or clients.

Some sex workers also used condoms during sexual encounters with regular partners. These women conceded that their boyfriends might have other girlfriends and that these women might be sex workers too:

> *It's possible he doesn't know the work the girl does, like me, coming here at night without his knowledge. Or it could be the girl has another boyfriend somewhere who may also be quite promiscuous. So by all means when he comes I have to make sure that I use the condom. You can't sit and deceive yourself that with a boyfriend you are safe and so you won't use the condom. [Comfort, 23, High-class].*

Adiza a 32-year-old *Roamer* was committed to her own protection which she felt she deserved and she demanded that her boyfriend use a condom. She explained,

> *you know, when a man becomes my boyfriend, because I don't know you, I don't allow you to use me by heart (any how).*

According to her, "unsafe" sex is tantamount to taking advantage of her, or, as she put it, "using her".

However, not all women negotiated condom use with boyfriends from positions of strength. Usually they found it difficult to insist on its use and were inclined to compromise their wishes. This was especially true for new users who, though they considered condoms beneficial, sometimes found them as uncomfortable as men did. Among sex workers, this is not difficult to imagine, since when a woman is not aroused, as sex workers rarely are with clients, they have dry vaginas. Use of a condom under such circumstance causes friction, which is worsened by prolonged and frequent intercourse.

Whereas sex workers view condoms mainly as prophylaxes, "free women" viewed them mainly as a contraceptive. Thus, few insisted on their use for the purpose of practicing "safe" sex, and condom use among them was correspondingly low. If a boyfriend is married, then preventing a pregnancy becomes even more important. Twenty-one year-old Yvonne said she had an ex-boyfriend who was married, and would not marry her. Neither she nor her boyfriend wanted a pregnancy, so though she would have preferred to use a condom for each sex act (as a prophylaxis), she agreed to its use only when she was "not safe" (as a contraceptive) because her boyfriend did not like condoms. Many partners rejected the condom outright and some women narrated stories about partners who beat them when they insisted on using it. In these cases, it appears that the woman's attempt to introduce a condom is interpreted as an indication of her own infidelity which then precipitates the beating. Generally "free women" do not insist on condom use even when they know that their partners are not always faithful to them. Thus, they end up in a "win-lose" situation. Their ability to negotiate for a "win" is affected by fears that such an attempt will jeopardise the relationship thereby losing the financial support that comes with it. Comfort explained:

He was a womanizer already when I met him so really I need to be patient until the time that he will perform the marital rights.

Because women like Comfort are concerned about losing a provider, they take a totally non-oppositional stance. Insisting on "safe sex" would jeopardize Comfort's position as a potential wife.

Even when women feel sufficiently entitled to "safe sex", they often compromise after having been in a relationship for a while. This is because, condom use as a prophylaxis is difficult to sustain. Twenty-four year old Dorcas' situation typifies this. She wholeheartedly recommended the use of condoms for preventing unwanted pregnancies as well as for protecting against sexually-transmitted diseases. However, although she has used condoms right from the onset in some of her past relationships, the more usual situation she described is as follows:

No, the last one, I had a relationship with I studied the man for sometime [before stopping condom use]. I know even that one is risky because if somebody has HIV it may not be apparent for the first few months. [...] I make sure at least I start with using condoms.

Dorcas was not using condoms with her current partner because she believed him to be faithful to her, adding, "I told myself, no, this man couldn't have it (AIDS)". This was despite the fact that she was aware that, "if somebody has HIV it may not be apparent for the first few months." The most important factor, nonetheless, remained *the man's* (un)willingness to use a condom.

I think, I don't know, I don't know, it happens alright; sometimes you may even have the condom and the man will say, the man might not be the one who likes using condom, and the two of you might be in the mood at that time, and you just say, OK, no problem. At that time everything goes away from your mind, you just say OK, no problem, but you know that you stand (sic) at a risk. But with this, the relationship in which I am now I didn't start with condoms, I told myself, no, the man couldn't have had it (AIDS). When you even mention this thing (using condoms) the man will become furious, you don't know what this will generate, and you can't start the relationship using condoms till it ends, I don't know. You start a relationship using condoms, and maybe you will like to marry the person, do you continue using this condom forever? No. I don't know how to go about it. [author's emphasis]

Dorcas put her finger at the heart of the dilemma surrounding negotiating condom use. If it is used as a prophylactic does one use it forever? How can one sustain a supposedly mutually faithful relationship this way if the man does not enjoy sex with a condom? Most "free women" believed that a level of familiarity with their boyfriends removed the need, indeed the right, to insist on condom use. Barbara, after accepting the risks involved in "unprotected sex", said that she did not use the condom "because I know my man". Bernice, after accepting that condoms have their usefulness in relationships where one cannot be sure of the partner's monogamy, also said she was not likely to use the condom because she knew her partner and felt safe. However, Dorcas cited above concluded with advice for women:

Women should [insist on the condom] – because mostly in this our African society, married women don't go about having sex with men a lot, it's the men who go about having sex with young ladies – so you can have short talks with your partner now and then, you know, telling him about your fears about AIDS and how you wouldn't like him to go about having sex with young ladies, because that can bring AIDS into the family.

Straight Sex or "Styles"?

My own contention is that sex should be a mutually pleasurable activity and that no one should be compelled to engage in acts they consider distasteful or unpleasant — that begs the question regarding sex as work. Nonetheless, in this section I attempt to examine the extent to which women, including sex workers, are able to negotiate specific activities. The whole drama surrounding the relationship between former US president Bill Clinton and White house staffer Monica Lewinsky highlights the fact that the idea of a "sexual relationship" means different things to different people. The issue of what is involved in the sex act itself is also extremely important for any discussion of "safe sex". IEC efforts tend to focus on peno-vaginal intercourse to the neglect of other forms of sexual activity, that are as "risky" (if not more so) when performed without using a condom. The very silence on the topic of oral, or peno-rectal sex, itself can create the impression that these acts are less risky.

Most sex workers are usually able to negotiate with clients what they will and will not engage in. They are paid for "straight" sex, no frills and that's what they are willing to provide. As 31-year-old Amalia, a *High Class* puts it,

> *some people like being (sic) romanced, (but) normally I will not allow any man to touch me, its straight sex or nothing else.*

Said another,

> *we cannot allow them to have sex with us as they would want to do with their wives or girlfriends.*

Only rarely will a sex worker undress completely for a client, and then only at an extra cost. Many have learnt from experience that anything other than "straight" sex can unnecessarily prolong the encounter, or introduce a degree of familiarity that can compromise the client-sex worker relationship. In some cases the conflict that these "styles" engender can lead to abusive situations.

> *Ei, he started squeezing and biting me and did not take his time at all. There was a time he even put his hand inside me and started using his hand. That was what I complained about and he beat me. He didn't even pay me in the end so I had to use my money to go to the hospital the next day...because I became sick after that for some days. Styles? Ei then he'll go! I don't even know how to do those styles and I am not prepared to learn now at my age [Adobea 32, Roamer].*

In Adobea's case, willingness to give in to a client's preferences had immediate painful consequences as he sought to extend his perceived rights.

However, boyfriends can be just as problematic and sex workers try to be as resolute with them as they are with clients. Adobea once had a boyfriend who tried to get her to engage in oral sex. She was willing to compromise for the sake of the relationship, but says

> I tried it once but found it too painful, so I never allowed it again. [emphasis mine].

Sex workers are generally in control with their clients and the format for the sex act is as follows: the woman (and client) remove their underwear, the man is permitted to touch her intimately with his penis. As soon as he achieves an erection she places the condom on the client, the sex act takes place, he pays (if he has not paid beforehand) and leaves. On rare occasions, sex workers may develop some romantic feelings or attraction for a client and permit petting of the breast and oral or anal sex. This can lead to a more regular relationship and increase the price the client is willing to pay. However, generally, oral and anal sex are considered aberrations. Feelings about anal sex are well captured by 42-year-old Esther, a *Seater*, who says,

> Ei! I feel if I go, excuse me, to the toilet, I can't even ease myself how much more go and stick this in my anus – I can't.

Ghansah made comparisons between sex workers of her generation in the "good old days", and the young girls working today who have, according to her, literally brought the profession into disrepute by their indulgence in these types of sex acts.

> Now it's only dirty work they are doing here in Abidjan. There are women who are penetrated from behind. First, ours was the best, we called it 'life', now they call theirs 'life' but the work is not as vibrant. As I sit here I know what they do in Abidjan and if I get somebody from Ghana, a 'big' man who can clear all these girls, I would like it, because of what they are doing. [50, High Class].

Ghansah complained that the allegedly huge amounts of money received from oral sex are merely wasted on marijuana and other drugs. Although only one sex worker admitted to ever having consented to anal sex to avoid a beating from a boyfriend, nearly a third admit to having performed oral sex or had it performed on them. Nevertheless almost all the respondents considered the practice of both anal and oral sex distasteful, shameful, and even taboo. Many women, especially older sex workers considered both practices as modern/Western aberrations and would either try to negotiate a "win" position for themselves or forego the sexual encounter. More importantly, oral and anal sex have been associated with disease transmission, even before AIDS education came along, and are considered more dangerous to sexual health even than non-condom use in peno-vaginal sex. Emphasising her oppositional stance to oral sex Stella, an Accra *High Class* described a situation with a client:

> *Three days ago I meet (sic) one man at Circle, the man ask (sic) that he want to take me short time, I say 'okay'. We talk finish and he ask me whether I could do everything. I say everything like what and what. He say that I will [deleted by author – reference to oral sex] ... I say I [deleted] you with this my mout?, I eat with my mouth! You [deleted] me through my vagina not my mouth! Then I say sorry, I won't do that, he (sic) say okay. He went away. [29, High Class].*

Stella was unwilling to earn extra money to perform oral sex. She would, however, allow a client to perform oral sex on her if he wished. Asked whether she ever engaged in oral sex with her boyfriend, she says,

> *even if you marry me and you are my husband, not at all! I cannot put my mouth on your penis!*

Among some sex workers in the Abidjan sample, or with foreign (white) clients, women sometimes made exceptions and permitted some foreplay or "unusual" forms of sexual activity. This was because of the more obscure nature of these clients' requests- sometimes only to hold a woman, which women sometimes felt compelled to oblige in order to retain clients. One 19-year-old says "that is part of our work". However, while sex workers are able to negotiate for a "win" in the form of sexual practice with clients, they are not generally quite as successful with boyfriends. Said 44-year old Adwoa, a *Roamer,*

> *he is my man, so if he means to hold any part of my body, I will allow him... but for a stranger I will not allow that.*

"Free" women experienced the same feelings of a lack of entitlement with their boyfriends. Ayeshetu, an apparent exception, described what some "free women" experience:

> *My friends complain that their boyfriends when they have sex with him he will like to have sex with you lets say in an hour he will like to have sex with you twice or thrice before you sleep, but I never met any man like that before. I am not very strong so if I meet someone who likes having sex several times in an evening, or someone who asks for styles and things like that, then we will be on our way to putting a stop to our relationship.*

The bottom line is that there is a perceived financial trade-off to accepting or rejecting sexual "styles". The more willing a woman is to acquiesce to her partner's wishes, the better she believes her bargaining power for material rewards to be. On the other hand, *because* of this dependency, women feel un-justified in refusing their boyfriends' wishes in any case. Ayeshetu explained that some women are actually scared by these "styles". It is unclear whether Ayeshetu's friend's fear was for her physical safety or whether she wondered about the boyfriend's mental health. However, what is clear is that this friend felt she had no right to bargain because of her financial dependence.

> *Okay, at times a lot of my friends complain about it (styles); I even have a sister called Mama who has her own boyfriend. She tells me that if she is to open her mouth to tell her boyfriend that she needs clothes or something the boy will buy it for her... [but] because the way the boy flirts with her she is always scared of the boy...*

Conclusions

This chapter has examined women's attempts at negotiating safe and meaningful sex for themselves and their partners. While it is impossible to generalize from the data, one can say that sex workers seem more inclined to feel entitled to "safe" and "traditional" sex and less willing to compromise on these issues in their sexual relations with clients. When it comes to sexual relations with boyfriends, even where they are not dependent on the latter financially, they are less antagonistic about achieving personal satisfaction.

The same, of course, is true for "free women". While both groups of women may have emotional ties with their boyfriends, sex workers tend to need the emotional support more, while "free women" generally need the financial support more. In any case, for both groups of women this dependency affects their feelings of entitlement, and women tend to see it as their responsibility to ensure their partners' sexual satisfaction. In other words, women exchange the right to negotiate for a "win" in terms of preferred sexual practice with boyfriends in exchange for emotional or financial support.

The implications of these behaviors for women's vulnerability and the continued spread of AIDS are grave. So long as some women do not feel as entitled to "safe" sex as they [and their partners] feel men are entitled to "satisfying" sex, the focus of AIDS education on persuading women to get their partners to use condoms, is bound to fail. It is crucial that we acknowledge gender power differentials if we are to make any headway in changing behavior. This chapter has shown that relying on women to "negotiate" sexual practices has limited success, especially among non-sex workers. For them the ability to negotiate for "safer" sex is limited, ironically, but not surprisingly, more so if the man is not monogamous. Married men are especially jealous of their partners having other affairs.

For sex workers, the "power" to negotiate "safer" sex, especially among the *Roamers* in Accra and Kumasi, is not an easily available option. This is because their extremely disadvantaged position makes it almost necessary for them to consider clients without using condoms — either because they might lose the client otherwise, or because he may offer a higher price for non-condom use. While Seaters are most likely to take an antagonistic, no-compromise negotiating position, high-risk behaviour cannot be clearly assigned to any particular group, cutting across educational, and ethnic lines. However, because Seaters are in associations which have strict codes of conduct, social control for appropriate behaviour, in this case condom use, can be enforced since non-compliance brings sanctions. Some educated "free women" posses enough knowledge to create a sense of entitlement about "safe" sex, yet they lack the willingness or ability to negotiate alternative behavior on the part of their partners. Further, and very importantly, some Ghanaians, contrary to popular discourse, do engage in more "obscure" sexual practices such as peno-rectal and oral sex. Konotey-Ahulu (1989) argues that the rectum has not been "designed" to accommodate an erect penis hence penetration can cause severe lacerations. The lining of the mouth is also extremely tender and if a virus is present in either the mouth, penis or vagina, it is more easily transmitted into the blood stream. While a man may wear a condom during oral sex, the female condom does not protect the outer female sexual organs. In any case the female condom was only recently launched in Ghana,[29] and anecdotal evidence suggests it is not accessible to most women. Programs need to recognize that women's problem is not merely lack of knowledge, but in some cases, perceptions of powerlessness. As Haleh Afshar notes, while questions of politics, resource allocation and power remain paramount, feminist discourse on the empowerment of women recognizes the need to shift away from grand paradigms and panaceas to the "specifities and differentiated needs of differing groups in different places" (Afshar 1998:1). However, we need to be clear about what we mean by empowerment. Is it about access to, and control over, resources? Is it about the ability to make choices for a "win" outcome? If we see it as a process much like negotiation and not as something that an external agent "does" for, or bestows upon a woman (Rowlands 1998), then the whole framework of AIDS-education, which seeks to empower women, might take a different approach. While empowerment should be seen as a dynamic process, contrary to some feminist arguments (see for example Rowlands 1998) I believe that we should still seek particular sets of results, otherwise we risk constantly being in the process of empowerment while never becoming empowered. It does not matter that women's empowerment may not necessarily mean loss of power for men so long as men believe it does. After all, if a woman succeeds in getting a man to use a condom it should not mean that he has "lost". However, it is important that the man also views this as a "win" situation for himself.

Clearly, the emphasis of AIDS IEC needs to shift to placing an equal responsibility on men. One option is to begin targeting men as (individual) *men* rather than (incidentally) as half of a couple. If we have learnt anything useful for sexual negotiation from family planning research, it should be that men and women's attitudes to contraception differ and that programs directed specifically at motivating men have been influential in lowering men's fertility desires and increasing their responsibility in family planning decision making (Piotrow et al. 1993). Focusing on men does not mean women should not be targeted. However, men should be made to feel responsible and gender stereotypes avoided. For example, one advertisement on Ivorian television has a woman reminding her partner as he leaves the house not to forget his "prudence" (condom brand). While this may encourage condom use by suggesting that even wives advocate husbands' use them, it also reinforces the notion that men *will* have additional partners and is not helpful in promoting monogamy as a method of preventing HIV infection.

Several programs have had some success by associating their condom with sports and masculinity (Adomako Ampofo 1994; Campbell 1995) and such efforts should be promoted. However, there is a need for independent research to find out the effects of such programs on gender relations, whether they make men more "responsible" about sexual health while reinforcing their control, or whether they lead to greater gender equity. We also need to carry out more general evaluative assessments of the effects of the content of sexual-behavior change campaign information for gender stereotyping. Men also need to be given the same reproductive counseling currently being offered to women (Campbell 1995), such as that on the possibility of inter-uterine infection from mother to baby. Campbell (1995) goes so far as to recommend that programs should target women with "alternative gender roles" designed to empower them. While women can "learn" about alter-native roles, at the same time what is needed in order to live these roles is a shift in men's position towards mutual responsibility in sexual relations.

Finally, sexual behaviors reflect the interface of the biological and the social, hence, effective intervention strategies depend on understanding not only *what* people do sexually, but also why, and the circumstances under which particular behaviors take place (Fowlkes 1996). This includes seeking to understand what goes into gender identities. Studies from South Africa, for example, suggest that male identities are threatened when a woman suggests that a condom be used. Work by Wilton (1997) suggests that a man's very (male) identity – masculinity – is threatened by condom (use). She argues that when the sugges-tion for use comes from a woman this essentially means that the woman is defining the terms of the sexual encounter. Further, a man may interpret this to mean his having to "deprioritise" his own sexual pleasure in favour of his partner's. She also argues that by instituting condom use (an act which requires a pause in the sexual encounter), a man has to control his sexual urge – which is a contradiction since by definition, male sexuality is uncontrollable. These are aspects of male identity and masculinity that need to be explored further. We need to know about, and analyze, the extent of opposition, especially among men, to condom use. This might be helpful in designing couple communication strategies to reduce this opposition. As one "free" woman suggested, communication can facilitate a reduction of (male) opposition, and a movement to a win-win situation.

While we work on gender relations, women's "empowerment" and men's redefinition of sexual goals, perhaps it is not inappropriate here to plead for more options in terms of cheap, easy-to-use, female methods, which women can control. While this may be a "band aid", covering deeper problems of inequities, as Heise and Elias justifiably argue (1995), without this band-aid some women would bleed to death before long-term strategies take effect.

Endnotes

1   Adomako Ampofo (1995; 1998a, b); Akande and Ross (1994); Ankomah and Ford (1993); Dodoo and Adomako Ampofo (2001); Nsanze (1990) and Campbell (1995).

2   While the term usually refers to engaging in ("unsafe") sex without the use of a condom, a meaning I also employ here, it should be noted that women could also be exposed to other dangers, such as undesirable sexual practices, intimate violence, etc. For this reason I opt to parenthesize the expressions "safe/unsafe" or "unprotected" sex throughout this chapter.

3   Women sometimes interrupt a prolonged sex act and demand payment for their time. The customer refuses to pay because he has not yet had an orgasm, blaming his delay on the use of the condom which the woman insisted on.

4   The research for this paper was supported by a research grant from the WHO Special Programme of Research, Development, and Research Training in Human Reproduction. I am also grateful to the African Gender Institute, University of Cape Town, for providing a three-month Visiting-Associateship which afforded me the "space" and resources for much of the thinking and writing that went into this chapter. Finally, I wish to express my most heartfelt gratitude to the women in Accra, Kumasi and Abidjan who agreed to be interviewed about intimate details of their lives.

5   Sex workers have objected to the term "commercial' in defining the work they do, arguing that all work is "commercial". While this assertion is debatable – for example housekeeping is usually non-commercial work — I parenthesize the term to show that even supposedly "non-commercial" sexual exchanges may be so only in terms of imposed definitions.

6   Such practices might include frequency, vigor and duration of coitus, and also whether the vagina has been sufficiently lubricated. Furthermore, even though a male having sex with a female is considered as a heterosexual activity, some clients request/insist on peno-rectal ("'homosexual') sex which can be even more traumatic for the anus, causing tears and cuts in the anus and thereby increasing the risk of HIV transmission.

7   A view which was confirmed (Adomako Ampofo 1994, 1998a)

8   See Adomako Ampofo (1994, 1997) for a detailed discussion of questions of validity.

9   Reference to one of Ghana's major export earners, cocoa.

10 Thanks to Iqbal Shah (WHO) for fuelling this curiosity.

11 Elsewhere I have discussed how the changing economic situation in Ghana has led to a reduction in women's income-earning options and the relationship of this to sexual exchange (see Adomako Ampofo 1995, 1998a).

12 For as many as 67 per cent of the respondents in Ankomah and Ford's study, for example, immediate material gain was the primary focus of the relationship, and they saw nothing wrong in terminating one relationship for a materially more rewarding one. Nonetheless, their data do not demonstrate an association between what women expected (materially) and what they actually received.

13 Perhaps this is not so surprising when one considers that for decades population information and research took a female-focus approach as if women took reproductive and sexual decisions on their own. [For some early exceptions see Dodoo 1993; Ezeh 1993].

14 A third focus involves treating concurrent STDs in populations at risk of HIV. The emphasis on an "at risk" group is itself problematic in that it shifts responsibility for changed behavior to particular groups in the population.

15 In one study in Rwanda, 24 percent of women who thought they were in mutually monogamous relationships were HIV positive, and even among the two-thirds who had only one life-time partner, 21 percent were infected (Allen et al. 1991).

16 Elsewhere I provide an account of the context of health beliefs and health care in Ghana and discuss its relationship to HIV/AIDS (Adomako Ampofo 1999).

17 A few clients of sex workers, and some opinion leaders and medical workers were also interviewed but are not discussed here.

18 Although both High class and Roamers do go to a client's home, most decline because of the risks involved, such as not being paid, being beaten or robbed, or suddenly being confronted by an angry wife or girlfriend. Women prefer to use hotel premises, and if they move to an unfamiliar one they will either ask a friend to accompany them or leave word about where they are going.

19 Another important distinction between the two is that with "short time" a client is only permitted one orgasm, while with "full night" several are allowed.

20 A name, I learned, that emerged from the rate of two shillings and tuppence that they charged during the colonial era.

21 In Ghana the women share public bath and toilet facilities and cook in little groups in the compounds behind their homes. In Abidjan, between 11- 20 women live in separate rented rooms in apartments. They also share toilet and bath facilities, however, very little cooking is done, cooked food mostly being bought from street vendors. While they wait for clients they can be found leaning on their balconies or sitting around in the ground floor courtyards of their buildings.

22 I am in no way suggesting that women in these professions are more or less likely to be engaged in certain types of sexual relationships. They included 8 (17%) apprentices, 11 (24%) students, 3 (7%) seamstresses, 3 (7%) secretaries, 10 (22%) typists/clerks, 2 (4%) sales girls, 1 (2%) trader, and 8 (17%) unemployed.

23 The final sample included 46 "free women" and 139 sex workers (50 *High class*, 39 *Roamers* and 50 *Seaters*)

24 For a detailed description of the sampling method see Adomako Ampofo (1999). Included is one woman whose financial support came from another woman with whom she had occasional sexual encounters. She did not acknowledge this as a lesbian

relationship and seemed somewhat surprised at the suggestion, as she had had boyfriends in the past. However, she had never had sexual intercourse with any of her boyfriends.

25 Ghana operates under a dual legal system which includes both customary law and jurisprudence inherited from, and developed since colonialism. Couples can be married under customary law, the ordinance, or both, with the former preceding the latter.

26 All names have been changed.

27 Whether women feel condoms are necessary or effective as a prophylaxis depends on a number of factors (see Adomako Ampofo 1998a, b). Briefly stated, these are (1) whether a woman believes AIDS is a result of natural or supernatural causes; (2) whether she believes AIDS has a cure; and (3) whether a woman believes she can determine a person's HIV-status from his (her) appearance.

28 At the time this was equivalent to approximately US$1.50.

29 The female condom was launched in Ghana in May 2000, several years after the study period. In any case it is not as widely available. Further, while a male condom costs a few 100 cedis, the female condom sells for 10 times that amount in pharmacies. Even though the female condom is reusable, the high cost would surely be a disincentive for many women.

Bibliography

Adomako Ampofo, Akosua, 1994. *Report of an Exploratory Study into the Sexual Behaviour of Ghanaian Sex workerss with their Clients and Partners, and 'Free Women' and their Partners.* Accra: IAS/WHO.

Adomako Ampofo, Akosua, 1995. Women and AIDS in Ghana: " I Control My Body (or do I)?", Ghanaian Sex Workers And Susceptibility To STDs, Especially AIDS. In *Women's Position and Demographic Change in Sub-Saharan Africa.* Edited by P. Makwina-Adebusoye and A. Jensen. Liege:Ordina Editions. 233-251.

Adomako Ampofo, Akosua, 1997. Costs and Rewards – Exchange in Relationships, Experiences Of Some Ghanaian Women. In *Transforming Female Identities.* Edited by Eva Evers Rosander. Uppsala: Nordiska Afrikainstitutet. 177-196.

Adomako Ampofo, Akosua, 1999. Nice guys, Condoms and Other forms of STD Protection; Sex Workers and AIDS protection in West Africa. In Becker, Charles Dozon J. P., Obbo C. et Touré M. (eds.), *Vivre et Penser le Sida en Afrique / Experiencing and Understanding AIDS in Africa.* Paris: Codesria, IRD, Karthala, PNLS: index, 561-590 /559-588.

Adomako Ampofo, Akosua, 1998b. Framing Knowledge, Forming Behaviour; African Women's AIDS-Protection Strategies. *African Journal of Reproductive Health* 2 (2).

Adomako Ampofo, Akosua, 2000. *"Who is the Driver and who is the 'Mate'?; Gender Orientations and Household Decision Making in Ghana.* Paper presented at the Annual Meetings of the African Studies Association; 16- 19 November 16, 2000. Nashville, Tennessee.

Akande, Adebowale and Michael W. Ross, 1994. Fears of AIDS in Nigerian Students: Dimensions of the Fear of AIDS scale (FAIDSS) in West Africa, *Social Science and Medicine.* Vol. 38: 339-342.

Allen, S. et al., 1991. Human Immunodeficiency Virus Infection in Urban Rwanda: Demographic and Behavioral Correlates in a Representative Sample of Childbearing Women, *JAMA* 226: 1657.

Anarfi, John K. and Clara K. Fayorsey, 1995. "The Male Protagonists in the 'Commercialisation' of Aspects of Female Life Cycle in Ghana." A Paper prepared for the Seminar on *Fertility and the Male Life Cycle in the Era of Fertility Decline*, Zacatecas, Mexico, 13-16 November.

Ankomah, A. and Ford N., 1993. *Pre-marital Sexual Behaviour and its Implications for HIV Prevention in Ghana.* Institute of Population Studies, Univ. of Exeter.

Assimeng, Max, 1981. *Social Structure of Ghana.* Accra-Tema: Ghana Publishing Corp.

Campbell, Carole A., 1990. Women and AIDS. *Social Science and Medicine* 30: 407.

Campbell, Carole A., 1995. Male Gender Roles and Sexuality: Implications for Women's AIDS Risk and Prevention. *Social Science and Medicine* 41(2): 197-210.

Carael, M. et al. nd, Research on Sexual Behavior that Transmits HIV: the GPA/WHO Collaborative survey – Preliminary findings. In Dyson T.(ed.), *Sexual behavior Networking: Anthropological and Socio-Cultural Studies in the Transmission of HIV.* Liege: editions Dervaux-Ordina. 65-87.

Centers for Disease Control, Operational Research Section, 1992. *What we have Learned from the AIDS Community Demonstration Projects.* 15 June.

Dodoo, F. N., 1993. A Couple Analysis of Micro-Level Supply/Demand Factors In Fertility Regulation, *Population Research and Policy Review.* 12:93-101.

————— 1998. Men Matter: Additive and Interactive Gender Preferences, and Reproductive Behavior in Kenya. *Demography.* 35: 229-242.

Dodoo, F. N. and A. Adomako Ampofo, 2001. AIDS-Related Knowledge and Behavior among Married Kenyan Men: A Behavioral Paradox? *Journal of Health and Human Services Administration.* 24(2): 197-231

Emerson, Richard. M., 1962. Power-Dependence Relations. *American Sociological Review* 27: 32-41.

Ehrhardt. A. A., 1992. Trends in Sexual Behavior and the HIV Pandemic. Editorial. *American Journal of Public Health.* 82: 1459.

Ezeh, Alex C., 1993. The Influence of Spouses Over Each Other's Contraceptive Attitudes in Ghana. *Studies in Family Planning.* 24(3): 163-174.

Fowlkes, Martha R., 1996. Review of Conceiving Sexuality: Approaches to Sex Research in a Postmodern World edited by Richard G. Parker and John H. Gagnon. *Contemporary Sociology.* 25(3): 376-378.

Haleh, Afshar., 1998. Introduction: Women and Empowerment – Some Illustrative Studies. In Haleh,Afshar (ed), *Women's Empowerment; Illustrations from the Third World.* Houndsmills: Macmillan Press. 11-34.

Heise, Lori L. and Christopher Elias, 1995. Transforming AIDS Prevention to meet Women's Needs: A Focus on Developing Countries. *Social Science and Medicine.* 40(7): 931-943.

Hunt, Charles, 1989. Migration, Labor and Sexually Transmitted Disease: AIDS in Africa. *Journal of Health and Social Behavior* 30: 353-373.

Kersten, Gregory E. and Sunil, Noronha, J., 1996. *Rational Agents, Contract and Inefficient Compromises.* Centre for Computer Assisted Management, Carelton University. Ottawa: ON.

Konotey-Ahulu, F.I.D., 1989. *What is AIDS?.* London: Tetteh-A'Domeno Co.

Kouassi. G., 1986. *La Prostitution en Afrique, un Cas.* Abidjan: Les Nouvelles Editions Africaines.

Lennon, Mary Clare, and Rosenfeld, Sarah, 1994. Relative Fairness and the Division of Housework: The Importance of Options. *American Journal of Sociology.* 2: 506-531.

Nsanze, H. et al., 1990. The Association of Genital Ulcer Disease and HIV Infection at a Dermatology Clinic in Uganda. *Journal of Acquired Immune Deficiency Syndrome.* 3: 1-4.

Painter, Thomas, 1992. *Migrations and AIDS in West Africa, a Study of Migrants from Niger and Mali to Cote d'Ivoire: Socio-economic Context, Features of their Sexual Comportment, and Implications for AIDS prevention initiatives.* New York: CARE.

Piotrow et al., 1993. Changing Men's Attitudes and Behavior: the Zimbabwe Male Motivation Project. *Studies in Family Planning* 23(6): 365-375.

Richardson, D., 1990. AIDS Education and Women: Sexual and Reproductive Issues. In *AIDS: Individual, Cultural and Policy Dimensions.* Edited by P. Aggleton, P. Davies and G. Hart. London: Falmer Press. 169-179.

Rowlands, Jo., 1998. A Word of the Times, but what does it mean? Empowerment in the Discourse and Practice of Development. In Haleh Afshar (ed.), *Women's Empowerment; Illustrations from the Third World.* Houndsmills: Macmillan Press. 11-34.

Schoepf, B.G., 1988. AIDS and the economic crisis in Central Africa. *Canadian Journal of African Studies*. 62: 625-644.

Thibaut, J. and Kelley, L.H., 1959. *The Social Psychology of Groups*. New York: John Wiley and Sons.

Tucker, Robert C., 1978. *The Marx-Engels Reader*. Second Edition. Edited by Robert C. Tucker. New York: W.W. Norton and Co.

Ulin, P.R., 1992. African Women and AIDS: Negotiating Behavioral Change. *Social Science and Medicine*. 34: 63.

Worth, D., 1989. Sexual Decision-Making and AIDS: Why Condom Promotion among Vulnerable Women is likely to fail. *Studies in Family Planning*. 20: 297.

World Bank, 1990. Investigating Health, *World Development Report*. Washington: The World Bank.

TALKING AND DECIDING ABOUT SEX AND CONTRACEPTION IN ASHANTI TOWNS

John K. Anarfi

This chapter looks at perceptions of marriage and sex among men and women in several Ashanti towns and examines their statements on how they negotiate and discuss sex and their relationships. It attempts to fill a gap in studies which in the past have focused on birth planning and birth spacing and contraceptive use and ultimately fertility, especially among women of child bearing age. It focuses instead on couple interactions and decision making. In the past, studies on family planning often focused on women, ignoring their partners' roles and the interaction between the sexes in shaping fertility behaviour. However, more attention has been given in the past two decades to studying contraceptive use and demographic innovation among men (eg. Mbizvo and Adamchak, 1991; Oppong, C. 1987).[1] This development became necessary because globally, husbands' desires have been found to have important effects on a couple's fertility.[2] In a situation where ancestral customs give men rights over women's procreative powers, the husband's approval may often be a precondition for a woman to use family planning. Husbands' disapproval has often been cited as one of the reasons for non-use of contraceptives in many regions of the world.

Ideally, a rational process of decision-making about reproductive health issues and family size should involve communication between husbands and wives. But many studies have reported a low level of communication between spouses about family size and family planning and women with low levels of contraceptive use have also reported little communication with their husbands (eg. Muhawenimcha, 1988).[3] To be able to design and develop effective programs to promote reproductive health and reproductive choices, therefore, it has become increasingly necessary to understand more about the socio-cultural norms and practices, which either promote or act as barriers to adoption of services or acceptance of advice.

Here in Ghana as elsewhere in Africa, relatively little information on the role men play in family planning is available. Similarly, few studies have explored the relative influence of the sexes on couples' reproductive behaviour. Given the very low use of modern contraceptives in Ghana (about 13%), such studies would be particularly useful. It is also of interest to observe how women among the matrilineal Akan have translated their much-talked about customary autonomy into behaviours that allow them to take control over their sexuality and, for that matter, their fertility. It has been observed in the past that couples in Ghana often pursue separate interests within single-sex groups, and interactions between husbands and wives are relatively limited (Bleek, 1976; Gaisie, 1969; Verdon, 1983). For example, couples rarely pool their economic resources (Abu 1983). In the words of Wolf Bleek (1976:143), this practice, "reflects the dominant view of marriage, namely that a husband and wife are not one, but two". It is therefore particularly important to explore the attitudes of both men and women and to understand the role of each in decisions about sexuality and family planning. It is also important to hear the views of the general society, and to determine whether or not they make a significant impact on decision-making on these issues.[4]

Marriage

Marriage is central to reproductive health and fertility issues. Although all sexually active females are at risk of becoming pregnant and/or contracting a sexually transmitted disease, those in marital unions may be most at risk. And women who enter into marriage quite early tend to have more births, just as societies in which marriage is more or less universal are likely to have higher fertility levels. In the Ashanti communities studied, marriage was found to be an important institution, which should be accorded much respect, mainly because it confers respect upon the people who enter into it. Significantly, wives are protected from disrespectful behaviour from other men. As one married woman noted,

If you are of age and you do not marry, you lose your self-respect.

Another added:

It is important for people to see that you have a husband and that will prevent people from proposing to you just anyhow.

Another reason given for the importance of marriage was that it helps people to lead a stable life and thereby bring about peace and stability in the whole nation. Said one woman:

If you have a wife and children and you are all living together you will realise that nothing worries you in life.

Another woman took it further:

I think when you marry, bad behaviours like gossiping, attending night clubs or even improper sexual relationships are put to a stop because it is then that you have to think together with your husband on how best to raise your children for them to become good citizens to the state. When everyone is living peacefully with the husband, to me it brings a wholesome peace to the nation because all forms of bad habits and behaviours are stopped.

People also found the mutual support married couples enjoy in marriage to be another positive aspect of the relationship. They mentioned in particular the support a married person gets from the spouse in time of sickness. Above all, procreation emerged as the main objective for people to enter into marriage, which ideally creates the congenial atmosphere within which children grow to become responsible adults. Such children then serve as old age economic and social security for the parents. However, the fear was expressed that due to westernization and economic hardships in particular, marriages are becoming increasingly unstable and young people are finding it difficult to contract new marriages. One married woman lamented:

In fact, there are some people who want to get married, but times are hard these days, and even trying to get money to do this, is not easy to come by. This situation is making the men unable to marry, so you see them hopping from one woman to another.

Sexuality

Sex is a very sensitive topic and even in everyday life not much is said about it. Yet it is central to family planning and reproductive health matters, so an attempt was made to find the place of sexuality in male-female relationships.

Everybody agreed that sex is very important in the relationship between males and females especially in marriage. Males were even more emphatic about this, adding that the absence of it can bring about divorce in marriage. For example one man noted:

> *That is what brings about quarrels in marriage. If you are going to sleep and you are in shorts, or in the case of the woman, if you are not in your period, not sick and say you won't have sex with your husband, it will bring about dissolution of marriage.*

People related the place of sex in male-female relationship to the need to procreate. In that respect, the general feeling was that sexual intercourse must always end with penetration otherwise it will amount to unfinished business. This feeling was expressed by both males and females, old and young. The male youth were more blunt about it and one young man emphasised,

> *I think that if you take a woman and you only kiss each other, then you have done nothing because the feelings that the woman should get is not all that she will get and even you the man will not get all your feelings.*

On whether kissing and fondling could be considered as sex if the partners get their feelings, another added:

> *There is no way that can happen. Also in the night you can both fondle each other but that is not sex. Sex only happens when you use your penis.*

In matters of sexuality, women are perceived as playing a passive role in many societies in Africa including in Ghana. A woman who plays an active role in the negotiation for, and the act of, sex is traditionally considered to be spoilt and this view persisted in the study communities. All the groups who discussed the matter stated that customarily, women should not take the initiative in demands for sex. However, the general feeling was that there was nothing wrong for a married woman to do that to her husband. The wives admitted that they actually do it in their marital homes. The youth generally shared similar views, that the usual thing is for males to take the initiative but there was nothing wrong for females to do the same when they are in the mood.

The women mentioned a number of techniques they commonly use to attract or distract the attention of their partners.

As for me, on the days that I don't want that, when I go to bed I wear my underwear securely. But when I need it by the time he comes home I'll be in bed naked and he'll know what I want. If he sleeps earlier than me I will lie on top of him and wake him up. Sometimes I can even call him and ask why are you sleeping? so that he will know.

Others reported using more subtle techniques to get their way.

When you wake up and you feel it and the man is asleep or even gone out you can call him back to the room and start holding and touching him.

You can tell him that he should not keep too long at work because you would want to sleep with him that day. After bathing you can put on some powder and wear your night gown and be roaming about in the room whilst he is there and he can sense something then.

Commercial Sex Workers in Obuasi were more outright about the approaches they use;

What I think is that if I am with my husband and you haven't called me for a long time and I feel for it, after we've taken our bath and we are about to sleep, I will ask him what is wrong with him and that if I need something can't he see.

said one. Another added:

As for me I won't use my mouth to say it. I will put my legs on him and start caressing him, and fondle him and kiss him ...If he does not respond, I won't understand. In that case I will force him to do it.

Asked what she would do to force him, the same woman said:

I will ask him exactly what I have done to him. I will ask him if he is doing that to me because I have wronged him in some way or doesn't

he see when I need something, or does he expect me to call him before
he does anything because such things can spoil marriage.

Male views tended to be more ambivalent, on the one hand feeling that either the male or the female has the right to initiate sex and on the other confirming the societal expectation that men should initiate sex.

Both of us can initiate sex; sometimes it is the man because he has
control over the woman. Because it is you the man whose power comes
when you hold the woman's breast.

Another added:

It is all because of overly respect that makes us think it is. You see, the
woman is so shy of the man and it has even become an accepted norm.
And when it happens you will say the woman is spoilt, thus, the man
will perceive the woman as loving sex too much. But there is nothing
wrong with it when the woman initiates sex.

Males' disapproval of a woman initiating sex was based on societal expectations and also some hidden anxieties. There was the general feeling that a woman who calls for sex too often from her partner is a whore. In the words of one man

the women who go after men so much are really prostitutes.

Men expressed their fears in the following words:

If a woman does that often, it is real promiscuity. Such a woman if her
husband travels for about two years and leaves her behind, she can't
wait for him

Generally the men confirmed what the women said they did to attract their partners when they wanted to have sex with them. The men do not always verbally call for a "match". Like the women they also use signs some times. Said one man:

As for me, when I want to play the match, the cloth that we both use to cover ourselves, by the time you come to the bedroom, I would have folded the cloth and placed it at your sleeping place, then you can know.

Similar messages could be relayed,

from the way you will be sitting in the room, from the way you converse. That is, if the conversation swings to that area so she will know you have those intentions welling on in you.

Contrary to the supposedly domineering position of men over women in sexual matters painted in the literature, there appeared to be a lot of accommodation in male-female relationship in the study communities. It appears that the men do not force their wives too much if they make approaches and they refuse mainly on the grounds of health and when the woman is in her period. There was evidence of mutual understanding, trust and respect for each other's condition and feelings. For example one man commented:

Your wife is not your slave so just as sometimes she will feel for you but you will not be in the mood, similarly she can also say because of this or that please or she can say she is tired, so let us make it tomorrow at dawn.

There was the general consensus that men achieve orgasm more often than women. However, a woman conceded that on a good day women can have about two or three orgasms before the men have theirs. Another sign of mutual understanding and respect is the fact that each partner makes the effort to ensure that the other is satisfied in the sexual act. However, it appeared that in most cases if the other partner, particularly the woman, does not express her feelings no attempt is made to bring her to her climax. The women confessed that often they do not achieve orgasm because most of them are unable to demand further effort from their male partners.

Talking Together

For any community based intervention programmes to be effective there is the need to understand the existing norms and practices that may either enhance or hinder communication. In the case of Family Planning programmes, communication between men and women in general and between spouses is very important. Also important are inter-generational communication linkages. Studies have indicated very little communication between parents and their children on sexual issues.

There were mixed reactions in this study regarding the existence of possible traditional norms restricting communication between men and women. There appeared to be different norms regulating communication between couples according to whether they were married or not. Between a married person and an unmarried person for example, everybody said society does not approve free open communication, especially if the people involved are of the opposite sex. Sex in particular was considered as a very sensitive topic and should be avoided. One man noted:

If someone is not my wife, I cannot discuss sex issues with her; it is not acceptable. Even the husband can sue me.

In fact there is a traditional injunction which authorises a man who thinks another man has talked to his wife in an indecent manner to sue for what is known as *ayefade*. This is usually in the form of a penalty which is paid in cash and/or kind. Hotels, drinking bars and obscure or secluded places are seen as the most unacceptable for a man to talk to a woman who is not his wife. A husband can usually sue for *ayefade* if he sees a man with his wife in what he considers to be an unacceptable place.

The discriminatory aspect of the *ayefade* injunction did not escape some of the participants. One man was quick to remark:

When we look at our customs, the men are cheating on the women because, me I have the right to go out. I can even go to some women's room and play with them, and do a whole lot of things. But woe unto my wife when I get to hear she was sitting on a different man's bed or in his room in a bad manner. So it is not every place that you can sit with someone whom you are not married to.

Women expressed concern about public opinion and what a woman can say or do with a man. They noted that gossip restricts the interaction between females and males.

It would have been better if men and women could talk as they wish. But there are bad people amongst us, and human beings normally think evil for their fellow human. It could happen that as we sit here now, I could come and talk some things over with you which could be in our interest, while you mean nothing to me, but someone somewhere will gossip about us.

The married men blending Christianity with Akan tradition seemed to endorse male supremacy in marriage, while apparently advocating mutual respect. They stressed the need for the wife to be submissive to the husband. One man said:

In our tradition what I see is that all the time the man is higher than the woman. As the man knows that he provides the 'chop' money and looks after the children, we normally override the women. But the woman has to know that the man is big and should give him respect and we the men normally see them as children before our eyes.

The men felt that if there is submission on the part of the women, husbands overlook their wrongs if they should commit them. However, there was evidence that men are steering away from this traditional hard-line. They attributed the change to Christianity making reference to the biblical injunction, "do unto others what you want others to do unto you". The increasing economic empowerment of women is also easing the way.

That's what I was saying that in these times that we're in, even the financial matters, you both have to be aware of it. The way things are now, it's become like you've become one. It's not like in the past where only the men look after the women: everything they take money from the men. Right now the woman brings some and the man also brings some.

It appears men in the community have prepared their minds for the change and are actually working towards egalitarianism. It has been observed that in the matrilineal system to which the study communities belong, women are known to maintain a stronger alliance with their matrilineage than with their marital families. Among the Akan, a bridegroom is reminded that all fortunes of the bride should be brought to her matrikin and all misfortunes to the husband. This age old injunction was challenged by one husband thus:

There is a difference now between marriage in the past and marriage nowadays because at first it was the man that we know did everything and gives chop money, but now it's like one helps and that one also helps. Normally in the past, when one enters marriage she's told that if you incur any debts it is for the man but when you get money bring it home. I know this thing still exists now but it doesn't work well anymore.

Some of the married women commented on the new closer relationship between married couples in these words:

That's why I am saying that we the young people of today, when we marry we play with our husbands but my parents for example don't do that. We do everything together. [A woman at Adamso].

I for example when my husband comes home and I am pounding fufu, he will come and help me. If he comes and I am busy he doesn't mind going to the market for something and coming to cook. [Another woman at Adamso].

On whether there were restrictions on the topics that a married couple can discuss, the unanimous view was that there was no restriction. But certain topics were considered too sensitive to be discussed. The men felt that they should not discuss their jobs with their wives. This is related to the fact that joint savings between couples is almost unknown in traditional Ashanti marriages. In the same vein, the men felt that issues concerning their extended families (matrikin) must not be discussed with their wives. One of the men commented:

No, maybe things concerning you the man's job, you shouldn't discuss it with the woman and the woman too when she goes to the market, what happens there is not that important. But when it comes to things concerning your lives and how you can ensure that your life will prosper, then you have to discuss it together. Let's say if I tell you that I want to do something for my mother, you can change my mind so that I'll think that what I meant to do is not good while I know that I'll feel better if I do that for my mother. So some things like that I can't discuss it with her.

It is not a common practice for a married couple to decide jointly on the number of children they should have. The few who take a joint decision are likely to be educated. For the generality of the people, they have the children if and when they come. One man commented:

What I know is that most people don't think like that. Those of us who think like that are only few. In the past all that they cared about was here are Kwaku and Kwabena my children, just like that. Even now it is the same. There are some who don't care that don't have money and just go on giving birth just like that. So those of us who plan this, I think, are not too many.

Nevertheless, the people cherished, and actually expressed the desire to have few children in view of the harsh economic conditions prevalent in the country. This view was expressed by one wife in the following words:

...in these present days life is not easy; even with Christmas approaching the least money you would spend will be about ø100.000 if you have two kids. So you plan the number of children to give birth to and that will give you the opportunity to cater for them all."

In the absence of a joint decision on the number of children a married couple should have, the general consensus was that the man's decision should stand. This position was premised on the grounds that it is the man who bears the responsibility of catering for the number of children. While there was agreement among the males on this issue, among the females there were disagreements and/or inconsistencies. It appears the women's concern was based on the observation that men generally do not care about the number of children to have. The apparent confusion among the women was probably more an expression of frustration about a situation which they appear to have the greater control over, but lack the power to decide. In the words of one woman,

the woman has a say but her power doesn't really work.

The powerlessness of women on family planning issues emerged strongly when all groups were asked to express their views about the situation where a woman goes for family planning without the husband's knowledge and approval. The unanimous decision was that it was wrong for a woman to practice family planning without her husband's approval. The men gave reasons for opposing a unilateral decision by a wife.

> *My reason for saying that is, whilst going for the protection and she runs into any problems, who are the family members going to question? They will come and question me since I am the husband. Furthermore, this woman may be seeing another man apart from her husband.* [A married man at Akrokerri].

The men viewed such an action so seriously that they felt it should be brought before a family arbitration if it should happen. There was evidence that some women who did that in the study area paid the ultimate price for it. One of the men shared his experience:

> *Oh me, my wife has even done it. In fact, it was after she had done it that she came to tell me. I was deeply worried and I have even divorced her.*

There was also evidence that the men really favour family planning and perhaps would support it if things are done properly. The same man who commented above added:

> *When my wife did that, because we did not have to give birth again, I liked it but then what worried me was why she went ahead to do that without letting me know.*

Everybody felt that the prevention of pregnancy and diseases in a relationship between sexual partners should be the responsibility of the man. In the words of some of the women,

> *I think it is the man because when the man contracts the disease, he can easily pass it on to you* (i.e. the woman).

The women felt that way,

> *because you* (i.e. the woman) *are married you can't go anywhere. It is the man who can be going out, so it is still the man's duty.*

An important question was what kind of relationship exists between parents and their children, and for that matter, between the older and the younger generations. Specifically, we wanted to find out whether they interact freely or not and what kind of sex education the parents give to their children if they do give any at all. The observation was that there appears to be a barrier between parents and their children such that they cannot discuss such issues easily. People said that this has been the situation traditionally but children appeared to be more obedient and respectful in the past than now. One man summed it up in the following words:

> *In the past, they* (i.e. the children) *couldn't come to us but we the elders could call them and talk to them. Even nowadays that's how it is. In the past, if your son wanted to marry from a particular family you could tell him that you don't want him to marry from there and you could do the same with your daughter. But today it is not so. He/she just goes in for what he/she wants.*

If children want to discuss sensitive issues with their parents they have to pass it through a respectable elderly person.

There appeared to be some antagonism between older women and young adult girls in the communities. When asked to comment on the kind of relationship between older women and adolescent girls, one woman remarked:

> *It is very distant, because the youth of today are in fact, .. some are very disrespectful. So if you want to be free with them, they can talk to you just any how.*

The youth generally confirmed their lack of respect for the elderly in the communities. In the words of one girl:

> *Today we the children who have come we don't respect. We don't listen to our parents but in the past, the children were humble. Now we don't have humility. We have become too proud.*

Some of the youth blamed the situation on modernisation which seems to have outpaced the older generation. They therefore, see whatever their parents say or do as obsolete.

One effect of the gap between the older and younger generations in the communities is that very little passes on from the former to the latter by way of sex education. In the words of an elderly man,

"Right now everyone has his/her own ideas as to what to do. You can't go and tell someone that he/she should do this or that.

So parents do not give their children sex education in the strict sense of the word. The best some parents, mainly mothers, do is to warn their daughters against unwanted pregnancy. What to do to prevent such a pregnancy is often not taught the children. Fathers are particularly passive about the education of their children on sexuality. The churches are now recognised as the major source of imparting some "sex education" to the adolescents in the communities. But we should expect the churches to give moral education rather than sex education as we know it to be. The youth, therefore, depend on whatever they see and hear from the television and the radio and what they hear from friends. Sessions with fieldworkers of some Non-governmental Organisations (NGOs) and other health workers are increasingly becoming popular among the communities. A general observation was that, children of today, particularly the girls, have lost a lot from the descent into disuse of such traditional practices as puberty rites, which used to equip the initiates with some useful advice on sex and home management.

In the absence of any formal sex education, certain entrenched norms and values seem to have a powerful influence on the youth's sexual behaviour. Marriage is still held in high esteem in the communities. Every girl looks forward to a successful marriage in the future and would not want to do anything to jeopardise this. One young woman observed:

Some women take too many men when they are of age and there are some men too who don't like it if you have too much space in you. Maybe you have slept with many men and your vagina becomes too big.

Young girls dread the prospect of pre-marital pregnancy. For such a girl:

Her life becomes bad. She doesn't get respect. Also because she is not married and is pregnant, she won't get money to go to the hospital.

Even if the man responsible gives her money,

she may be shy to go to the same hospital with grown ups who are married.

Such girls are likely to encounter difficulty finding a good husband. It was observed that such girls often go through a lot of hardship and they and their children become a burden on their parents. Older people dreaded such a situation and condemned it in no uncertain terms.

Conclusions

In the several Ashanti communities studied, marriage appears to be held in very high esteem. The importance which the communities attach to marriage includes the respect and stability conferred, the mutual support, the context for child rearing and the contribution through offspring to old age security. Procreation is still perceived as the main objective. However marriages are not very stable in the communities studied. In fact marital instability has become more common in recent times due to economic hardships. One result is serial polygyny as marriages break and new ones are contracted by people in previous unions.

The central role played by sex in male-female relationships was clear. Men stated the position more strongly, emphasising that the absence of sex in the marital relation could, and actually does bring about divorce. The importance of sex in the marital relationship was further linked to the need to procreate. This, and the feeling among the people that only penetrative sex can be regarded as sexual intercourse in the true sense of the word, have important implications for the promotion of reproductive health and family planning programs in the communities.

The traditional expectation that women should play a passive role in the initiation of, and participation in the sex act, was re-echoed by the members of the communities. They conceded, however, the fact that women can, and do initiate the demand for sex particularly in marriage, often through the use of body language. Men expressed certain anxieties about women who call for sex, fearing that such women cannot remain faithful when their husbands are away. Although it came out that both men and women experience orgasm during sexual intercourse, men tend to achieve theirs more often than women. While both parties make the effort to bring each other to the climax, women do not seem to have their way quite as often as they feel embarrassed to urge the men on.

The fact that the women cannot determine when to have sex, as well as the fact that they cannot compel their male partners to bring them to the climax, put them in an awkward position in the sexual relationship. The situation makes it difficult for them to refuse the advances of their male partners, since they would not know when the next chance would come, and the anticipation that they would attain their climax in this act. Fortunately, there appeared to be some amount of accommodation in the male-female relationship with both partners having mutual respect for each other. Such mutual respect must be taken a step further to include the consideration of each other's feelings.

Regarding inter-personal communication, there are no hard and fast rules restricting communication between the sexes. Society, however, expects a certain amount of decorum when men are dealing with married women. Sexuality is generally regarded as a sensitive issue and it is avoided as much as possible in open conversation. Certain traditional sanctions regarding sexual offences tend to be discriminatory against women. For that reason, the husband's approval is necessary if married women are to be involved in pro-grammes at which sexual matters are discussed.

Public opinion seems to be strong against people whose sexual behaviour appears improper in the eyes of the public. For that reason, people strive to present a positive image to the public. This watchdog role of the public could be capitalised upon to shape a positive image for protection and promotion of reproductive health.

Citing cultural and religious norms to support their point, people endorsed male supremacy over females especially in marriage. However, there was evidence that men are steering away from the traditional hardline. Increas-ingly, the relationship between married couples is becoming closer. This is happening at a time when married women are increasingly contributing sub-stantially to family finances. This seems to confirm the view that economic empowerment may go a long way to improve their decision making stand on reproductive health issues.

Suspicions about the intrusion of matrikin into the affairs of married couples are prominent in the minds of people, particularly women. For that reason, men would want to keep whatever they are doing for the matrilineage secret from their wives. By extension, perceived interference of matrikin could influence the decision of a couple on reproductive health and birth planning matters.

Most married couples do not take a joint decision on the number of child-ren they want to have. That notwithstanding, there was evidence that the people have the desire to limit the size of their families in the face of the prevailing harsh economic conditions. In the absence of joint decisions on the number of children to have, the general view was that the man's decision should stand. The women, however, appeared frustrated by the fact that although they produce the children, they lack the power to decide whether or not to have them. Both males and females alike felt that it was wrong for a woman to use contraceptives without the approval of her husband. The major reason for men's disapproval of their wives' use of contraceptives is the fear that it will give them the licence to become involved in extramarital sexual relationships. The fear of unplanned pregnancy has been a major constraint on the sexual activities of African women both within and outside marriage. Indeed sexual abstinence has been the main traditional birth control/spacing method in most African societies. Studies in West Africa have observed that traditionally the African woman is available for sex for only one-third of her reproductive life span. The remaining two-thirds were spent in sexual abstinence mainly after birth, which could last as long as 24 months or in some societies till the last child was walking.

While the source of a pregnancy as a result of a wife's infidelity may not be ascertained immediately, sometimes the resulting issue could betray the culprit. There is also the belief that the pregnancy resulting from a woman's secret extra-marital affairs often results in difficult labour which could sometimes be fatal. The use of contraceptives removes this fear by preventing pregnancy.

Wives are concerned about their husbands' infidelity and the possibility of their being infected with sexually transmitted diseases (including HIV/AIDS) as a result. This concern stems from the fact that culturally men have the right to have more than one sexual partner, while women are restricted to only one at a time. For that reason, women feel that the responsibility for preventing diseases in a sexual relationship rests solely with men. It would appear that faithfulness in conjugal relationships should be made a central issue in family planning and reproductive health programmes.

Another disturbing observation is the existence of communication barrier between parents and their adolescent children and between the older and younger generations as a whole. Parents do not give their children any form of sex education. The older generation think that the youth of today are disrespectful and would not listen to advice. But the real issue is whether the older generation know the right kind of information with which to educate the youth. This point is confirmed by the observation of the youth that their parents' ideas are outdated. There may therefore, be the need to equip both old and young with more suitable current information.

Endnotes

1   Several studies have found significant divergences in men's and women's reports about contraceptive use, attitudes towards family planning, and fertility preferences and intentions (Coombs and Chang, 1981; Koenig, Simmons and Misra, 1984; Mitra et al., 1985).

2   One school of thought argues that in Africa, men often make the couple's decisions about fertility limitation (Dow, et al., 1986; Khalifa, 1988; Piotrow, et al., 1992). Another has suggested that women themselves take the initiative to limit their fertility without the involvement, and sometimes without the knowledge, of their husbands (Akinkugbe, et al., 1983).

3   Studies in Nigeria and Mali have found that decision making processes between spouses are positively associated with contraceptive use (Oni and McCarthy, 1991; Van de Walle and Maiga, 1991). Based on these findings, Salway (1994) has proposed that a model that assumes joint decision-making is probably not suitable for Africa. This is because family relations involve both congruence and conflict (Sen, 1989), and benefits and costs of childbearing and childrearing are not distributed equally between men and women (Kabir, 1985).

4   The study was part of a bigger project which sought to address some of the reproductive health needs of the inhabitants of the Adansi West District in the Ashanti Region of Ghana. The final goal was to contribute to the household and health security by empowering people to achieve their reproductive intentions and reproductive health. One of the initial activities was a baseline survey to establish indicators as well as provide insights into the psycho-social behaviour of the population studied to facilitate the effective implementation of the project. Towards this end, a baseline survey was conducted in the district from 25th November to 18th December 1999. The survey focused mainly on the family planning aspect of the project. The survey involved questionnaire interviews and focus group discussions (FGD). This paper is based on the focus group discussions only.

The purpose of the FGD was to collect qualitative information on issues which require detailed socio-cultural explanations. Quite often conventional survey questionnaires are unable to capture some of these finer details particularly when the issues involved are sensitive. The objective of the FGD, therefore, was to gather information on:

* The existence of concerns regarding sexual and gender interaction

* Informal communication channels and barriers to communication among partner and with women: and

* The role of social and marital conflicts in promoting reproductive health risks.

FGD Organisation

The focus group discussions were organised on the basis of sex and age. Sessions were held for married couples and unmarried youth respectively. A separate session was organised for Commercial Sex Workers in Obuasi. The others were held in Akrokerri, Fomena, and Adamso in the Amponyasi sub-district. A total of 26 sessions were planned but in the end 16 sessions were accomplished, five each in Akrokerri, Fomena and Adamso and one in Obuasi. The break down of the sessions according to groupings were as follows:

Male youth	3
Female youth	4
Adult Married Males	3
Adult Married Females	2
Mixed Married Couples	3
Commercial Sex Workers	1
Total	16

Obuasi is a mining town and largely urban. The other towns could be described as semi-urban with rural outlook. All the FGDs were recorded on tape and were later transcribed. The information was then analysed using the NUD.IST software for qualitative data analysis.

Bibliography

Abu K., 1983. The separateness of spouses: Conjugal resources in an Ashanti Town. In Oppong C. (ed.), *Female and Male in West Africa*. London: George Allen and Unwin.

Akinkugbe, O. et al., 1983. Does the responsibility for family planning rest primarily with the woman? *Planners Forum Magazine*, 1:12-13.

Bleek, W., 1976. *Sexual Relationships and Birth Control in Ghana: A Case Study of a Rural Town*. Vitgave, Netherlands: University of Amsterdam.

Coombs, L. C. and Chang, M. C., 1981. Do husbands and wives agree? Fertility attitudes and later behaviour. *Population and Environment*, 4:109-127.

Dow, T. et al., 1986. Characteristics of new contraceptive acceptors in Zimbabwe. *Studies in Family Planning*, 17:107-113.

Gaisie, S. K., 1969. *Dynamics of Population Growth in Ghana*. Accra: University of Ghana.

Kabir, N., 1985. Do women gain from high fertility?. In H. Afshar (ed.), *Women, Work and Ideology in the Third World*. London and New York: Tavistock Publications.

Khalifa, M. A., 1988. Attitudes of urban Sudanese men toward family planning. *Studies in Family Planning*, 19:236-243.

Koenig, M. A., Simmons, G. B. and Misra, B. D., 1984. Husband and Wife inconsistencies in contraceptive responses. *Population Studies*, 38:281-298.

Mbizvo, M. T. and Adamchak, D. J., 1991. Family Planning Knowledge, Attitudes and Practices of men in Zimbabwe. *Studies in Family Planning*, 22:31-38.

Mitra, S. N. et al., 1985. *Measuring contraceptive prevalence: Responses from husbands and wives in Bangladesh.* Paper presented at the annual meeting of the Population Association of America, Boston.

Muhawenimcha, A., 1983. L'homme dans les programmes de planification familiale. *Famille, Santé, Development.* Dec. 13, pp. 35-38.

Oni, G. A. and McCarthy, J., 1991. Family Planning knowledge, attitudes and practices of males in Ilorin, Nigeria. *International Family Planning Perspectives,* 17:84-90.

Oppong, C., 1987. Responsible Fatherhood and Birth Planning. In Oppong C. (ed.) *Sex Roles Population and Development in West Africa.* London: Currey Publishers.

Piotrow, et al., 1992. Changing attitudes and behaviour: The Zimbabwe Male Motivation Project. *Studies in Family Planning,* 23:365-375.

Salway, S., 1994. How attitudes toward family planning and discussion between wives and husbands affect contraceptive use in Ghana. *International Family Planning Perspectives.* Vol. 20, Number 2, June.

Sen, A., 1989. Cooperation, Inequality and the Family, in G. McNicoll and Cain, M. (eds.), *Rural Development and Population: Institutions and Policy, Supplement to Population and Development Review.* Vol. 15.

Van de Walle, F. and Maiga, M., 1991. Family Planning in Bamako, Mali. *International Family Planning Perspectives,* 17:84-90.

Verdon, M.,. 1983. *The Abutia Ewe of West Africa: A Chiefdom that Never Was...* Berlin, Germany: Moulton Publishers.

SCHOOL CHILDREN LEARNING ABOUT SEX AND LOVE

Doris Essah

Joanna is 18 years old and in Form Three. Six months ago she was found to be pregnant and so suspended from school. She granted an interview at her family house, where she is staying for the final months of pregnancy.

Joanna's parents farm in a village near Koforidua, the capital city of the Eastern Region. Just like her siblings who are in school, she has been sent to live with a relative in town so that she can receive a "good education". Her mother's sister, with whom she was living in Akropong paid her school fees on time, takes care of her and meets any added financial problem she has, and then collects the money from her parents. Joanna, however, confides directly in her mother about her emotional problems. She leaves out sexual issues because she believes her mother would not agree with her decisions. She rather tells her closest friend, Sally, who will not tell on her.

Joanna attained menarche at 14, but first learnt about sex at 16 when a friend lent her a novel entitled **I Can't Stop Loving You**. So, in Form One she willingly entered into her first and only sexual relationship with a boy in a nearby Senior Secondary School. To date, Joanna does not know the implications of her menstrual cycle or 'safe period'. Several factors also stop her from using contraception. She feels it is her partner's duty to do so, she doesn't know how to get protection although she knows where it is sold, and in fact, she feels embarrassed to try. Two years on, Joanna has experienced her first pregnancy. Worried, she sought to induce an abortion at the Mampong Hospital, but was told that it was too dangerous because the foetus was too advanced. She is also afraid of using other methods of abortion she knows, such as drinking '*akpeteshie*' (local liquor) with Hacks toffees, or causing an enema with a solution of water and smoothly ground bottles.

Things rarely worried Joanna – not even her aunt's complaints about the frequent visits of her (female) friends. Now she worries constantly, about the consequences of her pregnancy. It has halted her social life, but hopefully, it has not curbed her academic potential. She no longer indulges her hobbies of watching films, and attending Red Cross meetings and those of the Junior Youth department of the Presbyterian Church. Fortunately as a final year pupil despite being sanctioned from attending classes she can join her mates in school to write the national Basic Education Certificate Examinations in August – in barely two months' time. However, Joanna has no urge to learn. She likes school a lot, but she cannot concentrate on her books and she has not got a teacher. Yet she is positive that she will do well. In her last report, a year ago, she was placed 14 out of 76 pupils. Her parents would like her to continue to the Senior Secondary School. She even prefers to continue to a training college to become a caterer "because there is a lot of money in it".

Young boys' and girls' socio-cultural experiences in their homes, schools and communities influence their knowledge, skills and values, especially concerning the age at which they initiate sexual relationships. Too often, early sex results in complications of sexually transmitted diseases, unwanted pregnancies, abortions or early parenthood and curtailment of educational and therefore (job) aspirations – as pregnant girls are made to drop out of school. An important intervening factor is adolescents' access to information, education and communication on Family Life Education, which guides them to postpone initiation of sexual relationships and use scientifically proven contraceptive methods when they choose to be sexually active. With such issues in mind this chapter looks at the gender role attitudes that appear to shape the daily life experiences, constraints and aspirations of Junior Secondary School pupils in Akropong.[1]

Akropong

A small town on a mountain ridge of the Eastern Region of Ghana, Akropong enjoys a blend of cultures, traditional and modern. It is the capital of the Akwapim State, and the administrative capital of the Akwapim North District. The Akwapim people are described as affable and respectful, and their climate is conducive for people from temperate regions. The Basel Missionaries settled in Akropong in the early nineteenth century and spread Christianity and its principles. They discouraged traditional socialisation through secular dances, songs and rites (as at puberty for girls) and set up more conservative forms of socialisation, through church services and confirmation into the adult congregation. Schools were built for boys and girls up to the teacher training level. School children could earn pocket money and provide funds for the schools by craft work such as plaiting and selling straw hats and mats. They focused on practical subjects and acquired skills in professions such as carpentry, masonry, crafts, agriculture and clerical work, to meet the demand of the expanding Ghanaian economy, and in particular, the boom in cocoa production in the latter half of the nineteenth century. The two World Wars however affected the management of Christianity and schools in Akropong, and the swollen shoot disease of cocoa in the 1940s destroyed the town's economy. It caused many adults to earn their livelihood in other towns, while their children continued to acquire primary education in the home town.

Current Situation

Today, young boys and girls aspire to a limited number of stereotyped professions that neither match what they study nor follow their parents' occupations. Boys want to be doctors or engineers, while girls want to be teachers or doctors. There was no indication that pupils would have the long-term economic support required to meet the many years of formal education and school expenses entailed by such high professional aspirations. Meanwhile many children did not even know the details of their own fathers' education, living more often with mothers than fathers.

Indeed, economic deprivation was already the lot of many, as a third of pupils' school fees were paid late. Parents paid the fees themselves, or pupils who lived with their parents during the vacations were handed the money when school reopened; or the money was entrusted to the care of their guardians. For a number of the children were staying with guardians in the town.

Pupils' educational aspirations are likely to be curtailed when parents do not send money for their children's upkeep, (In particular when they do not even stay together during holidays); or when guardians misappropriate the money for their own needs, with a view to paying the fees later.[2] In one grandmother's opinion, many guardians are not educated well enough to value the education that a fostered child would receive (also GNCC, 1997). Junior Secondary School children who pay their fees late may have been doing so since primary school. Each year such pupils are forcefully sent home during class hours. Class work is likely to be affected and disrupted, and they may be stigmatised with poverty, to the extent that they may dread going to school (see Akuffo, 1987). Additional economic difficulties such as paying for stationery and meals may influence them to settle for jobs that require fewer years of formal education (GNCC, 1997).

Out of School Activities

Children's main activities out of school include recreation, attending to household chores and studying. They study the prescribed texts and class assignments to augment what they are taught in class. Pupils are particularly challenged to excel at the junior secondary school level because their internal examination results form a fraction of the final nationally held examination results (the Basic Education Certificate Examination). Boys had more time to study than girls did, yet they were more dissatisfied with the amount they had. Most pupils, however, spend much of their out of school time tackling one household chore after another. More girls than boys begin doing these chores immediately after school. Often, girls sweep, go to the market, cook and wash dishes and both boys and girls launder clothes. Akropong is on a ridge so water pipes do not often flow. Households place barrels under eaves to collect frequent rains, and thus, save most children the task of going to fetch water from commercial tanks in people's houses. Weeds flourish in the compounds and gardens and boys usually uproot them. Parents may be content that their daughters are occupied with chores so they would not have the opportunity to give in to negative peer pressure, societal influences, or their own sexuality.

Recreational activities are potentially important channels for Information, Education and Communication (IEC) about Family Life, Reproductive Health and Sex education. Many non-governmental organisations, including the Red Cross Society and the Planned Parenthood Association of Ghana use football, snakes and ladders, pick and act and films to help develop adolescents. On their own, boys often play football, and girls *ampe*.[3] As girls grow into adolescence they play *ampe* less and less. They come out of their individual homes to socialise late in the day, a time not conducive to jumping and making noise. Often dusk fell soon after pupils started playing and as the neighbourhood became dark, peers sat upon the ledges of various houses. At Akropong the weather turns so cold in the evenings that it is remarkable that pupils are willing to stay out in the cold.[4]

During an interaction with boys aged 13-15, the weather that was warm and sunny thirty minutes earlier turned cold and windy by 4:30pm. We were sitting in a circle under a big mango tree. It was chilly. I saw a couple of boys crouch to avoid it, so I said:

Moderator: *Oh you're feeling cold eh? I will soon finish.*

Henry: *Oh it doesn't matter.*

Peter: *Even if we are cold, what we are discussing has made us hot.*

They all laughed. I constantly felt that they grouped as we were doing then and discussed such issues about their sexual maturation, which is a novelty at puberty. There was no tension. They were often amused and did not seem shy or embarrassed, even when nothing funny or sensitive was being discussed. The words they used were not remarkable, and the explanations they gave were clear. They seemed to play a game in which people compete and brag about what they know. For example, they competed to say the methods that people use to cause abortion. I had to let them keep quiet and then indicate the person who would speak next. There was a loud silence however when I asked about their own sexual experience and whether they discuss their sexual problems with friends. By not bragging even about imaginary sexual experiences, they were unlike boys in a study in Tanzania who make up stories about having sexual experiences with girls in order to look good before peers (Mziray et al., 1998). Pupils rather tease boys and girls who play together. While boys said they did not have a major problem, girls said that as adolescents, they worry about this reaction of other people to their friendship with boys. As a girl in Form Two complained:

Ama: *Madam, when you are playing with a boy, and you are not thinking of anything then the girls and boys start teasing you, and saying you are doing things you have not thought about.*

Girls had to be encouraged to express their opinions about any topic being discussed. They did not brag, and seniority (Form) was respected. They assumed that they are expected to be quiet and wait for their turn, or be asked to speak.

The Planned Parenthood Association of Ghana has a project using trained peers to facilitate development of responses to adolescents' sexual and reproductive health needs. But parents and pupils, however, view peers as a negative influence and source of worry for pupils. Parents often chastised pupils about the number of friends that visited them at home. Parents felt that friends make pupils so playful that they do not concentrate on their house-chores and homework. They make pupils stay out so late in the night that they wake up late. Bad peers encourage others to take up their bad habits and behaviour. The headmaster of Salem JSS, who had just been transferred from Adu Krom, a neighbouring town, said that the pupils' behaviour that amazed him most had to do with the sheer number of love letters he was seizing from pupils. The letters came from the primary schools, other junior secondary schools, senior secondary schools, the only teacher training college and even from within his school. Children in basic level schools in adjacent towns expressed their romantic thoughts orally, but to the headmaster two centuries of formal education in Akropong influences the way pupils express their feelings in Akropong. These love letters buttress parents' fears that when their children are not at home, peers influence them negatively.

Both boys and girls felt that girls are more influenced by peer pressure, that conversation between peers about sex led them to dwell on it, and that curiosity led to adventure. Yet, pupils do not think that they depend on their friends as a source of information on their own sexual and reproductive health. Only a couple of girls and boys said that they learnt about sex from their friends, and that when they have sexual problems they talk to friends. As one girl stated, "Now after you have told her, you don't know who she will reveal your conversation to." When some boys were asked whom they confide in about their sexual problems, there was a long spell of silence. A boy then responded with an incomplete statement: "Well, maybe if you have a grandmother at home, or someone who is older than you..." Their silent reaction was rather unusual for the discussion. So I continued probing, again, I asked whether they do not converse about it with friends. They responded in the negative, explaining that:

Adams: *These days the friends who have come, when you tell them about your problems then they go and tell their friends.*
Henry: *He will tease you ...*
Obeng: *He will let it spread.*
Larry: *He can even go and tell a teacher.*
Henry: *Another thing that happens is that if one of us has a girlfriend and they know that he doesn't do anything with them the boys will tell the one: "You're not good enough. You're not good enough. You have got a girlfriend but you can't do anything" ...*

These pupils do talk about sex, but they consciously do not focus such conversations on themselves. Perhaps they will confide more in friends as they grow older, and as they face common problems, which may shock them into seeking the aid of friends in like situations. Nabila and Fayorsey (1995) found that adolescents, most of whom are sexually experienced, get information on sexual matters from friends.

Social Clubs

More than two-thirds of pupils who took part in the survey belonged to at least one of the various social organisations such as the Red Cross, Wild Life, Scripture Union and other church groups. Clubs were also the second most frequent source of information for pupils who had knowledge about sex – one pupil had learnt from the YWCA, but the rest from the PPAG. Yet discussions proved that with the exception of the PPAG, clubs that operate in the JSS do not address sex and romance. The YWCA stationed at Akropong, for example, does not deal directly with school pupils, but equips dropout girls with vocational skills. The Planned Parenthood Association of Ghana has been doing a lot to help adolescents in Akropong and the Akwapem North District. In 1984, it collaborated with teachers who were concerned about the state of reproductive health and teenage pregnancy on the Akwapim Ridge to set up offices and train people. In 1991 it began the Family Life Education (FLE) Clubs in most schools especially in Akropong. The PPAG's activities are, however, widespread and not targeted at junior secondary school children in particular. Teachers who volunteer also tend to be either overloaded with other duties, are nurturing their own young children, or away from Akropong for further studies. Conversation with teachers in one school further indicated why they are not eager to have the club in the school. Their reason is that:

Madam Bernice: *(About five years ago,) the man who used to lead the school children started befriending them. They also started befriending each other. Any time they had meetings you would see the club members in pairs.*

There was no way of verifying the teachers' statements, since the male teacher they referred to was on transfer, and all of the pupils who belonged to the club had completed the school. These teachers' views however had a common link with parents' fears, that giving children sex education corrupts them. During focus group discussions, only one girl gave accurate responses to questions on sexually transmitted diseases, so I asked her for the source of her knowledge. She said that she belonged to her primary school's FLE club which was no longer functioning. Further enquiries in the school revealed that the teacher had to stop because pupils' parents protested that their children were too young to have sex education.

The result is that at least between 1998 and 2000 (the duration of this study) Family Life Education meetings did not take place in any of the schools studied. Pupils who belong to these clubs could not get sex education from the club. The PPAG however visited some schools and organised football matches, during which time they discussed Family Life Education with those pupils who were present, and answered pupils' questions. No girl in this study said that she went to PPAG's youth centre. However, some boys who were not satisfied with the limited contact with the PPAG in school trekked to the PPAG's counselling and youth centre at Abiriw, the next town from Akropong. Many went to use the library, while some went there to join, others to listen to facilitators on sexual relationships and how to avoid pregnancies. Pupils had confidence that these two needs would be met there because there was a known procedure for acquiring the books and the information on healthy sexuality.

Henry: *Okay if you want to read it there they do not collect money but if you want to take it home you pay five hundred (cedis) and they will give you a card. You will send it to your teacher to fill it.*

Moderator: *Peter,* when you went for information about how to avoid pregnancy did you go to a particular person to tell you or...

Peter: *No they often teach it (Sex Education) there*

Moderator: *Okay, so you went, sat-in and listened* (Peter nods his head, assenting).

Pupils, however, felt that the PPAG would not meet their demands for contraceptive methods. One girl said that friends who are sexually active could not buy contraceptives from the centre because it sells only to people aged 18 and above. However, as one official said:

Lisa: *We do not have an age limit for people who can buy contraceptives. Adolescents who are sexually active can buy contraceptives here. It is they (pupils) who do not come to the centre to buy contraceptives ... Maybe the friends who said so went to one of the chemists ... I have heard cases where people send their young brothers and sisters, a child of about seven years to buy the contraceptives, and the chemist refuses to sell it. Maybe that is what they are referring to.*

The chemists said that the pupils do not buy contraceptives from them. Students who buy contraceptives are usually from the Senior Secondary Schools and the Presbyterian Teacher Training College.

School

Pupils start learning about sexual matters from age five, and by age 10 more boys know about sex than girls and almost all know by 13. They obtain knowledge mainly from the classrooms, clubs, homes and friends. Most girls and the majority of the boys in the study said they learn about sex education in school, from the "Life Skills" course, but they complained that the course had been removed from the syllabus. Apparently the council on education found that too many courses were offered at the Junior Secondary School level, so that certain courses including Life Skills are no longer studied. Relevant topics that were included in these courses are to be merged into a new course, the Population Family Life Education (POP/FLE) ancillary course. An official of the Curriculum Research Development Division of the Ministry of Education said that Life Skills is actually still a part of pupils' syllabus, but as in the case of Physical Education in the previous educational system, Life Skills is not examinable. Therefore, many schools have not made time for it on the timetable. Yet the topic on reproductive health was very interesting for pupils, so that they still refer to it. Pupils usually read the chapters in their textbooks, even when these chapters are not being treated immediately as a subject in class. However, they are brought out only during the scheduled time for the course. This means that the present lack of place for ancillary courses on the timetable, and limited access to relevant books will seriously reduce pupils' exposure.

For the current courses that are still being studied teachers chronologically follow the chapters in the textbooks, so that often sex education is taught towards the end of Form Three. In fact, boys in the discussion group did not think of the classroom as their first source of sex education. They exclaimed and laughed at the first boy who mentioned school as his source of knowledge, so that the boy had to defend himself. In fact some teachers choose to educate pupils about the implications of their burgeoning sexuality.

Girls knew that a broad scope of issues fall within sex education, so that they readily talked about the rapid physiological developments, including menstruation and issuing of sperms that occur at puberty, and the consequent need for good hygiene in adolescence. The classroom however could not have been their source of knowledge on sex, pregnancies and sexually transmitted diseases, since they were less articulate about their knowledge on these topics.

Gender attitudes influenced the information pupils went looking for, outside the prescribed courses. Once two boys asked me why I had let them (boys) answer questions that concern girls. They said that matters such as menstruation, puberty rites and abortion only concern girls. Other boys nearby laughed and seemed to agree with these boys. If this is the attitude of both sexes, then it would signify that except for curiosity, pupils would show more knowledge and pay more attention to what they think or realise affects them directly.

Menstruation and the menstrual cycle

Girls complained that adults are not prepared to talk to them about menstruation. Abena narrated the story of 12-year-old Pokua, who saw a woman washing her pants and a rag soiled with blood at the stream. Pokua asked her mother if the woman was hurt, and why there was so much blood. Her mother got angry, and told her to "shut up" and not "be a bad girl". The next day, at school, Pokua felt uneasy and so went to the toilet. She saw blood in her pants. She became scared that because she was a bad girl the previous day, "the woman's disease had attacked her".

Another girl said:

> Agnes: *Our teacher said that a few women can menstruate in their palms, they do not bleed, but their palms become red when it is time to menstruate.*

Many people, pupils and adults believe this. Again, girls often linked menstruation with initiation of sexual activity and parenthood:

> Anita: *Some people would not have reached the time to have their period, but they allow males to hold them, so that they start early.*
>
> Oforiwaa: *They said when you menstruate you can give birth as mothers do. As for that if you sleep with a male it does not matter, but if you have not started menstruating and you do so, it is bad.*

Moderator: *Why is it bad?*
Ama: *You will have **beriberi*** (others laugh, meaning that it is not true)
Oparebea: *You will have AIDS or Gono* (all laugh).

We all laugh, but it is obvious that girls don't know why it is wrong to have sex before they begin menstruating. It is simply a cultural taboo. Another girl, Ama linked this idea of menstruation with pregnancy and perhaps the cultural pressure to have children. She commented to a friend that:

Ama: *When I see the blood, my heart burns* (beats fast).... *I am afraid that when I am ready to marry I won't get children. That is why some people* (those not in school) *get pregnant. So that this worry will be done with.*

Boys also said:

Kofi: *Some girls sleep with too many men.*
Adams: *Some may not have slept with a boy before, so blood flows out, it is the blood that is in the eggs. After it breaks and the blood flows out, the girl is no longer afraid and she can give birth.*

Pupils have not gained their knowledge from anybody who teaches sex education. They had not been taught about the menstrual cycle or its relevance. Only one-tenth of pupils knew the time during the menstrual cycle that a female is most likely to conceive – during ovulation or the 'unsafe period'. Interestingly most of these pupils were boys.

Most pupils knew that sex causes pregnancy. Girls begin menstruating from the age of ten years onwards and boys begin spermarche from 13 years. By fourteen years 17 per cent of girls had attained menarche. Just about 12 per cent of boys had attained spermarche. They did so at ages 15 and 16. About one in five girls said that they had performed puberty rites. However none of these pupils said that they had learnt about sex issues from these rites. Adults said that puberty rites do not take place in Akropong, but pupils said that when girls attain menarche, they are given a meal of *oto* (mashed yam with palm oil) and boiled eggs, then they are advised that the blood indicates that they are now capable of having children, so that they should be very careful about the company they move with. They should not initiate sexual intercourse until they are capable of parenting.

The Media

Television and radio programmes designed for adolescents and programmes that use the local languages are an important, subtle source of information on sexuality and reproduction. Pupils hardly mentioned the media first as their source of reproductive health knowledge, and the boy who did so had to defend himself by arguing that he first learnt about reproductive health issues on "Concert Party", broadcast by Ghana Television. Boys in the gathering burst into laughter. The concert party is a local drama in which characters wear fancy clothes with strange white make up on the face and body. They joke, sing popular songs often adapting the lyrics, and dance (Bame, 1985). When the boy narrated the play, almost all the others helped to recall the story line. They had watched it too. Girls linked their sexuality with "The Growing Child" a programme for adolescents, sponsored by the PPAG and shown on TV3. After this, pupils more frequently explained a point by referring to another programme they had heard or watched in the media, such as *Odo ne Asomdwe* (Love and Peace) that has a popular hostess, Maame Dokono on Choice FM, and "Mmaa Nkomo" (Women's Conversation) on Ghana Television (GTV).

Knowledge of Sexually Transmitted Diseases

All junior secondary school pupils can mention at least one sexually transmitted disease. Boys had variations in knowledge while girls showed extremes in their knowledge. The latter either had good knowledge about a disease, or could give no response at all. Most pupils know that AIDS is a sexually transmitted disease, while only one out of every two pupils could mention gonorrhoea. (Yet gonorrhoea has a local name, *babaso* that is used in several languages and has been known in Ghana much longer than has AIDS.) This means that pupils were familiar with diseases that they hear talked about. They generally had a sparse knowledge of the causes of sexually transmitted diseases. More girls than boys stated that people can become infected with AIDS through sexual intercourse, syringes, infected blood and/or that an infected pregnant female could pass on the disease to her unborn baby. However, one-fifth of the pupils thought, wrongly, that mosquito bites or evil spirit attacks cause AIDS, while others did not know HIV, and that it leads to AIDS. Some pupils also knew that a rash appears around the genitals of a person with gonorrhoea, that the male passed painful urine, and that people had discharges. They also knew that a person with gonorrhoea experiences a fever, but some thought that malaria causes both the fever and the gonorrhoea.

One-third of pupils knew that using hospital prescribed drugs could cure some sexually transmitted diseases. Others felt that clinical drugs and herbs could help to prolong life. Yet, a large minority of boys could not state whether AIDS has a cure. It is not clear what depth of knowledge pupils have about this looming disease, as they enter the modal age at which AIDS is infecting most Ghanaians. Is it that these boys do not believe that AIDS still has no cure? The study ended without finding plausible answers.

Pupils had little knowledge of contraceptive methods, except the condom. Few thought of abstinence as compared to use of condoms. Girls also knew traditional methods (whose efficacy has not been proven) such as having an enema with herbs, which pupils could not identify, before and/or after intercourse.

Adolescent Reproductive Behaviour

While most boys want to wait until they are older before initiating sexual intercourse, girls (and two thirds of boys) want to wait until they are married. They expect to marry, generally, between 23 and 30 years. Their responses support the 1998 GDHS findings that there is a noticeable trend towards later marriage. Other pupils said that they are not emotionally ready, or they just would not like to be sexually active. So except for young people becoming sexually active out of coercion (Adomako Ampofo, 1993), or to meet their economic needs (Akuffo, 1987; Adomako Ampofo, 1993; Ankomah and Ford, 1993), provision of incentives such as adequate family life education, adequate access to school or vocational training, and adequate economic resources would encourage young people to postpone initiation of sexual activity.

A pupil said he had received information on sex from his pastor and boys laughed at him. Intermittently, churches have talks on the need for young people to lead upright lives, and so not to fornicate. Although adolescent sexuality is discussed during classes organised for young people attending confirmation classes, no pupils had begun to take such sessions.

Christianity strongly influences the reactions of residents of Akropong to the consequences of premarital sex. When an unmarried girl becomes pregnant neither she nor her mother can freely go outside their house. Each of them leaves home early, at dawn, and returns late, with head pointing towards the ground. I had to go from one family member's house to another, looking for Joanna, a pregnant schoolgirl. The people in each house commented that she never went out, so she was definitely in one of the other homes. Two young men offered to send me to the girl's house, one commented to the other that in fact, for a long time he had not seen the girl, but if her aunt said that she was in a particular house, then she must be there. Then the other responded, "Oh the girl is still in Akropong." He shrugged and said the girl's situation is taking the usual course. When a pupil takes a young boyfriend, they are seen together in the evenings, on the streets of Akropong. Therefore, people notice almost immediately, and when a couple stop seeing each other, they can find out the cause and whether they are both still in town.

Perhaps, this is the way the Akropong society punishes the girl and her family, and demonstrates to others that premarital pregnancy is a moral and social cancer. Yet, when the pregnant schoolgirl gives birth, community members join the young mother to celebrate the birth and naming ceremony of her child, as they do for other births and naming ceremonies. A poor, unmarried girl who completes school may be inclined to get pregnant, so that at least her presence and achievement in childbearing would be celebrated.

Daily life experiences teach pupils to follow their self-interest to negotiate for a wealthy and/or a healthy life when they begin initiating intercourse. Both boys and girls said that financial reasons, together with curiosity and naughtiness cause early adolescent sexual experience, and pregnancy. It is notable that boys said they faced financial problems much more often than girls did. When they have financial problems boys would more readily ask their fathers, or both parents, while more girls ask both parents, or their fathers. Hardly any boy said he asked his mother for funds, although for girls mothers were the third most frequent source of support. Boys would rather ask their grandparents, pray or ask an aunt. Pupils said they ask these particular people for aid, either because they are their confidants, or because as children pupils are generally expected to do so. Rarely did pupils, especially boys, indicate that the person could afford to meet their needs. As they grow older, adolescents' financial needs are likely to mount. Already, boys stated that girls accept men's proposals and even chase men for financial reward. They are stating the normal, culturally acknowledged pattern for young females to meet their needs – by taking older men (Dinan, 1983, Akuffo, 1987, Nabila and Fayorsey, 1995). Neither boys nor girls mentioned the less known and hardly documented pattern of boys taking older women (as recorded by Nabila and Fayorsey, 1995).

Financial constraints rather proved to deter some boys from beginning a sexual relationship. Boys who have girlfriends are expected to provide girls with some gifts, sometimes on a daily basis and this deters some pupils from initiating a sexual relationship. When asked for their opinion about a JSS boy impregnating a girl, one boy remarked to a friend:

> Adams: *I should go and impregnate a girl then give her the ¢500*
> *daily chop money* (snack) *my father gives me? Then when*
> *I am hungry, I use my mouth to hit a stone!*

Probably, boys who begin a relationship would expect to experience sexual activity.

> Henry: *If a person is in school and wants to misbehave with a girl,*
> *then he must use a condom.*
> Moderator: *Why?*
> Henry: *So that she does not get pregnant.*
> Moderator: *Is that the only reason?*
> Henry: *So that the boy does not get infected.*

Sexually Active Adolescents

Five boys and six girls aged between 14 and 16 years had initiated sexual intercourse – starting from the age of ten. All the boys had had only one partner, but girls' partners ranged from one person to five. (The last girl reported she was gang raped by boys she thought of as her friends.) They had various living arrangements, participated in church activities, and said that they loved school, and performed well in class. Boys, however, seemed to have more financial worries. They also did not have an in-depth knowledge of sex and family life education – only one girl and two boys knew about ovulation, and only three males and two females had ever used a method of contraception. They said that they always used contraceptives, yet contradicted themselves by stating that they sometimes did not think of using, or felt it was their partners' responsibility. Only one girl used the pill. Two girls felt too embarrassed to try to obtain a condom, while two others did not think of contraception at all. In the absence of sex education this lack of a common attitude for initiating sexual activity confirms views on the varied ways through which young people initiate or are pressurised to begin sexual intercourse (as found in Nabila and Fayorsey, 1995, 1997; Ankomah and Ford, 1993; Akuffo, 1987; Vellenga, 1969).

Some of these sexually experienced adolescents said that they had used herbs or saccharine to effect abortions, but they did not face any apparent negative consequence. They all lacked the counselling necessary to help them tackle their reproductive health need for condoms to avoid experiencing sexually transmitted diseases, pregnancies and the possibility of dropping out of school, which Joanna was facing.

Joanna would not talk much, but she communicated that fear gripped her when she first found out that she was pregnant. She did not want to be dismissed from school, so she sought to abort her pregnancy at the nearest hospital, at Mampong. However the doctor told her that the pregnancy was too far advanced and inducing an abortion for her was illegal. The only local method she knew was a concoction of *akpeteshie* (a local gin) and smoothly ground bottles, but she was afraid to drink it to self-induce an abortion. So, Joanna kept the pregnancy, and the school dismissed her. Fortunately, as a final year pupil who had registered for the national exams, she would be able to graduate with her mates. What comes out clearly is that Joanna has always had financial support from her family, but she lacks Sex Education. She gleaned information from romantic love stories and her friend, and became pregnant. There is no indication that she has now gained knowledge on how to protect herself from such complications. In fact, the pregnancy made her lose emotional support from her boyfriend, foster family and friends.

Differences in the consequences of a pregnancy for girls and boys reflect the gender dynamics of societies. Boys are rarely reprimanded. The myth is that they are dismissed or caned, but no pupil knew of any male who had received such punishment before. The general attitude is that: "Whichever way you look at it, the situation has already occurred so the boy should be advised never to repeat his mistake." Schoolgirls who got pregnant were viewed by pupils in a totally different light – they were mainly responsible for the pregnancy.

Oforiwaa: *Some girls want the baby so they like the pregnancy.*

Anita: *Some girls like being with boys so when they get pregnant and they don't want the pregnancy, they throw it away* (abort foetus).

Girls: (Method) *She can grind bottles ... And pour it in water or beer.*

Oforiwaa: *Some also use Guinness and sugar.*

Oparebea: *They drink a certain small tablet sold at the drugstore.*

Ama: *Some use **aborototo** ...*(they point at the fences of nearby houses – **Jatropha Curcas**). *When its inner seed or its ground leaves are inserted into their vagina, the baby comes out as blood.*

Agnes: *Some also go to the hospital so that a certain thing will be inserted into their stomach, and all the liquid with the baby will be pulled out. Some doctors do it, but others say they won't do it.*

Boys had additional views on what a girl who finds out that she is pregnant can do.

Amponsah: *She can visit a fetish priest and the fetish priest can de-stroy the foetus or make it vanish.*

Moderator: *What kind of medicine is she given?*

Kofi: *Poison!*

Amponsah: *Oh no. Why poison? She will die.*

Obeng: *She can also perform enema using 'nansa yi woho aye fe'* (a local drug used to cure yaws and skin rash)

Amponsah: *And Key soap.* (with water as an enema)

Peter: *Or a drink such as coke with a lot of sugar added.*

Kofi: *And also leaves that are rubbed, then the juice is squeezed out.*(They don't know the specific leaves)

Pupils were prepared to go through all measures in order to avoid becoming a parent at a time they think is too early, and so inconvenient. Boys more than girls seem to be socialised or to socialise themselves to avoid becoming parents of unwanted pregnancies. At least one boy was visiting the PPAG centre to find out how a sexually active boy can avoid impregnating a girl, while other boys could give a step-order description of how a condom should be worn. Most pupils know (and would go for) *ad hoc* local "curative" measures that they refuse to think of as poisonous and fatal rather than preventive measures. Some teachers said that there are not many recorded cases of pregnancy among school children because the pregnant girls cover up their state by wearing sweaters and saying that they are ill till they self-induce abortions. Knowledge of the essentials of reproductive health could cushion pupils, help them stick to their reasons, and achieve other aspirations (PIP, 1995),

Conclusion

This chapter has looked at the early gendered behaviours, attitudes, aspirations and constraints that subtly affect the development of young schoolgirls and boys in Akropong. Both girls and boys demand that they be better equipped with needed family life education.

Endnotes

1   This chapter is based on the author's M.Phil. thesis presented to the Institute of African Studies, University of Ghana. The research, conducted in 1999, involved a survey of one hundred pupils (45 boys and 55 girls aged 11-19 years) and two focus group discussions with 16 pupils (eight boys and eight girls aged 12-15 years). It also involved interaction with members of the community.

2   A headmaster said that for example, some female guardians are noted for using the money to "cut a funeral cloth". They often use the money meant for school fees to buy and sew cloth that has been chosen as the uniform to be worn at an oncoming funeral or celebration.

3   A local game which involves two people clapping, jumping and throwing a leg with the aim of outwitting the other jumper

4   An adult even attributed the cold weather and the fact that adolescents stay out in it as the cause of adolescent sexual activity.

Bibliography

Adomako, A., 1991. *Attitudes And Practices Regarding Pre-Marital Sex Among Adolescents in Ghana.* Institute of African Studies, University of Ghana.

Akuffo, F. O., 1987. Teenage Pregnancies and School Drop-Outs: The Relevance of Family Life Education and Vocational Training to Girls' Employment Opportunities. In Oppong, C. (ed.), *Sex Roles, Population and Development in West Africa.* London: James Currey. Pp. 154-164.

Alan Guttmacher Institute, 1998. *Into A New World: Young Women's Sexual and Reproductive Lives.* New York.

Ampofo, D.A., 1970. 330 Cases of Abortion Treated at Korle-Bu Hospital: The

Epidemiological and Medical Characteristics. In Konotey Ahulu (ed.), *The Ghana Medical Journal.* Accra-Ghana. Pp.156-157.

Anarfi, J.K., 1990. "Sexual Networking in some Selected Societies of Ghana and the Sexual /Behaviours of Ghanaian Female Migrants in Abidjan, Cote d'Ivoire." Paper presented at the IUSSP Seminar on Anthropological Studies Relevant to the Sexual Transmission of HIV. Sondeborg, Denmark.

Ankomah, A. & Ford, N., 1993. *Premarital sexual behaviour and its implications for HIV prevention in Ghana.* Institute of Population Studies, University of Exeter, UK. Occasional Paper NO.22.

Bame, K.N., 1985. *Come to Laugh: African traditional theatre in Ghana.* New York: Lilian Barber Press, Inc.

Blanc A.K. & Way A.A., 1998. Sexual Behaviour and contraceptive knowledge and Use among Adolescents in Developing Countries. *Studies in Family Planning.* 29, 2:106-116.

Bongaarts, J. & Cohen, B., 1998. Introduction and Overview. *Studies in Family Planning.* 29, 2:99-105

Brokensha, D., 1966. *Social Change in Larteh.* Ghana. Oxford: Claredon Press.

Brokensha, D., 1972. *Akwapim Handbook.* Accra: Ghana Publishing Corporation.

Caldwell, P.J. & B. & I. Pieris, 1998. The Construction of Adolescence in a Changing World: Implications of sexuality, Reproduction and Marriage. *Studies in Family Planning.* 29, 2:137-153.

Center for Population Options, 1992a. *Adolescents and Unsafe Abortion in Developing Countries: A Preventable Tragedy.* Washington, DC.: The Center for Population Options.

Center for Population Options, 1992b. *Adolescents Fertility in Sub-Saharan Africa. Strategies for a new Generation.* Washington, DC.: The Center for Population Options.

Demographic and Health Surveys, 1992. *Adolescent women in Sub-Saharan Africa: A chart book on marriage and childbearing.* International Programs Population Reference Bureau, (Washington, D.C.)

Dinan, C., 1983. Sugar Daddies and Gold-diggers: the white-collar single woman in Accra. In Oppong, C. (ed.), *Female and Male in West Africa.* London: George Allen and Unwin. Pp. 344-366.

Essah D., 2002. Family Life Education needs of School Children: a study in Akwapim Akropong. *Research Review.* (Legon) . 18.1 43-50.

Gage-Brandon, A.J. Meekers, D., 1992. "Sexual Activity Before Marriage in Sub-Saharan Africa." Paper presented at the 1992 Annual Meeting of Population

Association of America, Session of Sexual Behaviour Before Marriage, Denver, Colorado.

Geronimus, A.T. Korenman, S., 1990. *The Socioeconomic Consequences of Teen Childbearing Reconsidered.* Research Reports, Population Studies Center, University of Michigan.

Ghana Education Service, 1989. *Social Studies for Junior Secondary Schools.* Pupil's Books 1-3. Adwinsa Publications.

Ghana Statistical Service [GSS] & Macro International Inc. [MI], 1994. *Ghana Demographic and Health Survey 1993.* Calverton, Maryland: GSS & MI.

Ghana Statistical Service [GSS] & Macro International Inc. [MI], 1999. *Ghana Demographic and Health Survey 1998.* Calverton, Maryland: GSS & MI.

Government of Ghana, 1994. *National Population Policy, Revised Edition.* Accra, Ghana: Population Council.

Government of Ghana, 1996. *Adolescent Reproductive Health Policy.* National Population Council.

Gyepi-Garbrah, Nichols, D.J. B. Kpedekpo, G.M., 1985. *Adolescent Fertility in Sub-Saharan Africa: An Overview.* Boston: Pathfinder Fund: 51

Mensch, B. S. Bruce, J. & Greene, M. E., 1998. *The Unchartered Passage: Girls' Adolescence in the Developed World.* The Population Council, New York, USA.

Ministry of Education, 1987. *Ghana Science Series.* JSS Pupil's Books 1-3. Accra: Sedco Publishing Ltd.

Ministry of Education, 1989. *English for Junior Secondary Schools.* Pupil's Books 1-3. Accra: Afram Publications.

Mziray, J.C., 1998. Boys' Views on Sexuality, Girls and Pregnancies. In Rwebangira, M.K. & Liljestrom (ed.), *Haraka, Haraka . . . Look before you leap. Youth at the Crossroads of Custom and Modernity.* Nordiska Afrikainstitutet, Stokhom.

Nabila, J.S. & Fayorsey, C., 1995. Adolescent Fertility and Reproductive Health in Ghana. In Ardayfio-Schandorf, E. (ed.), *The Changing Family in Ghana.* Proceedings of the National Research Conference held at the Golden Tulip Hotel, Accra, Ghana from 25th-27th January, 1995. Accra: Ghana University Press.

Nabila, J.S. Fayorsey, C. & Pappoe, M., 1997. *Youth and Reproductive Health in Africa Assessment of Adolescent Reproductive Health Needs in Ghana.* Legon: Media Design.

National Research Council, 1998. *Critical Perspectives on Schooling and Fertility in the Developing World.* Washington, D.C: National Academy Press.

Population Impact Project, 1995. *Adolescent Fertility and Reproductive Health in*

Ghana. Population Impact Project. Department of Geography and Resource Development, University of Ghana.

Vallenga, D.D., 1969. *The Dilemma for Young People Today*. Legon, University of Ghana, (unpublished).

Yeboah, K., 1998. *Social Support and Pregnancy in Adolescence: A Study of Teenage Mothers to be in Cape Coast*, Ghana. A Doctor of Philosophy Thesis submitted to Brown University. (Unpublished).

Yeboah, Y., 1993. "Equal Opportunities for Women: The Implication of Adolescent Pregnancy and Childbirth in sub-Saharan Africa for ILO Policies and programmes." Working papers of the World Employment Programme, International Labour Organisation POP/WP.186.

"IT IS A TIRESOME WORK"
LOVE AND SEX IN THE LIFE OF AN ELDERLY KWAHU WOMAN
To the memory of Nana Mary Yaa Dedaa

Sjaak van der Geest[1]

Love and sex are not topics to be easily discussed in Kwahu-Tafo, the town where Nana Mary Dedaa lived most of her life and where I carried out anthropological research. Love between men and women is seldom shown in public. It is only some young people who have the courage to walk hand- in-hand with their sweetheart lover. Kissing in public is "not done". The middle-aged and elderly even seem to dissuade any kind of mutual affection. If demonstrating love is inappropriate, talking about sex is a taboo. Only "bad people" speak about it. Mill and Anarfi (2002: 334) quote people as saying that "...openly discussing sexuality in schools and other public settings would be viewed as a violation of traditional values and culture." Parents, according to the same authors, feel uncomfortable talking about the topic of sex with their children and do not give them instructions on sex. (See also Anarfi and Essah above). Here too, the taboo prevails. Sexual "education" is almost entirely the "task" of peers (Bleek 1976). Sexual desires and practices are secrets that one may share with a special friend who will not divulge them to anyone. It would be "shameful" if others were to find out about one's sexual habits. Parents also do not give their children instructions on sex. Here too, the taboo prevails.

Sex, by consequence, is not only silenced in daily life, it is also silent in research and publishing. Very little information is available on how people in Ghana view sex and what their preferences and practices are. The scarce information that exists is mostly on rules. Virtually no research has been carried out on the *experience* of sexual desire and practice.[2] That holds true for Akan society but also seems to apply far more widely in Africa as is borne out by two overviews (Standing & Kisekka 1989, Savage & Tchombe 1994). It is only in the context of HIV/AIDS that sex is now increasingly being explored, not in its own right as a source of pleasure or as an expression of an emotional relationship, but as a risk factor.[3] HIV-related sex research limits itself mainly to some technical details and to the question of how condom use can be promoted. It does not deal with affection and sexual attraction desire.

If expressions of love and sexual attraction are kept hidden in Ghanaian society at large, how much more will this be the case for the older generation.[4] The middle-aged and elderly even seem to reject any kind of mutual affection. Indeed sexual desire and activity are widely regarded as incompatible with old age, if not morally, certainly aesthetically. Sexual intercourse between elderly people is considered embarrassing. That idea is found in scientific publications, popular writing and literary work. It seems an almost universal, super-cultural "fact" that a "normal" elderly person is not or should not be interested in sex; and should certainly not *show* his/her interest nor speak about it. The more surprising and refreshing, therefore, were the two conversations about love and sex we had with an elderly woman in Kwahu, Nana Dedaa. She spoke freely about intimate experiences in her life up to her old age. Her style could be characterised as both wise/resigned and slightly "coquettish".

The conversation with Nana Dedaa took place in the context of a much wider research project on social and cultural aspects of growing old in a rural Akan Kwahu community.[5] Topics explored included the concept of "old", the status of *opanyin*, respect and reciprocity, blessing and cursing, various types of care-giving, wisdom and *bayie* ("witchcraft"); the role of money in gaining respect, the importance of building a house and the rendering of post-mortem care in funerals.[6] Towards the end of the fieldwork, sex presented itself as a possible topic, in spite of the taboos surrounding it.

It started one day with a group discussion of about fifteen middle-aged and elderly women who were remarkably open about (their disinterest in) sex. But the break-through came in the afternoon of that same day when I visited an elder in a nearby town. The man was involved in a lively discussion with three friends. I joined the conversation and we talked about the different stages in a person's life, about funerals and various other topics. Then the discussion turned to sex. To my surprise the old men took a keen interest in the topic and seemed to enjoy it. It was indeed a break-through and several subsequent meetings with elderly people were devoted to the same issue. Strength and respect presented themselves as key concepts during those conversations.

Many elderly – and not so old – women complained of lack of strength and said they would rather not have sex anymore.[7] Men, however, rejected the women's objection to sex; women did not need strength, they said, "they only had to lie down." It was rather the men who needed strength to "do the job". The link with respect was ambiguous, particularly for men. An *opanyin* (elder) is someone who should be married and, therefore, is supposed to be – at least moderately – sexually active. An elderly man's sexual activity and interest should, however, be orderly and restrained. He should not behave like a young man, that is "chase women". Too much sex would be harmful to him and shorten his life (Van der Geest 2001).

The general fieldwork mainly consisted of conversations with about thirty-five elderly people plus a few relatives or household members. Some of these conversations were lengthy, others short and casual. I met frequently with some elderly people, with others, only a few times. Additional information and understanding was acquired through participant observation, short visits to the elderly and in discussions with young people about the elderly. Finally, I conducted some research in various schools in Kwahu-Tafo and its surrounding towns involving questionnaires, incomplete sentence tests and drawings of an elderly person.

There is nothing very special about Kwahu-Tafo. It is an "ordinary" rural town on the Kwahu Plateau near Nkawkaw, in the Eastern Region. Due to its altitude, (about 700 meters) it has at least for me – a more pleasant climate than most other, more lowly rural towns in the south of the country. Trading and a high degree of mobility are typical of the inhabitants of Kwahu-Tafo, as it is for all other Kwahu towns. In nearby towns such as Obo, Abetifi, Pepease, Obomeng and Bepong, one finds impressive buildings put up by successful inhabitants as proof of their achievements in life, usually trading and cocoa farming. Kwahu-Tafo is less blessed with such large and beautiful houses. The town looks impoverished. Many of the houses are dilapidated and the streets are in bad condition. The town has electricity but only a minority of the population can afford it. Piped water is available but many taps have been closed because there is no one to supervise their use and collect the small payments. Wells remain the main source of water for most people.

For people of Nana Dedaa's generation, men as well as women, a somewhat common life cycle was to grow up in Kwahu-Tafo, then to travel and trade in Accra or another commercial centre anywhere in the country and finally to return to Kwahu-Tafo to settle as a farmer (cf. Bartle 1977).

Nana Mary Dedaa says she was born in Kwahu-Tafo, on a day that somebody's sheep gave birth to a being half sheep, half man. She does not know the date. She went with her father to Kukurantumi and returned to Kwahu-

Tafo after her father's death. She then went to stay with her mother who was farming in the village of Asubone, now covered by the Volta Lake. She was betrothed to a man in Asubone and two years later, after she had begun menstruating, the man performed the customs of marriage. They had five children together. After her husband died, she married a policeman at Aboam and had five children with him as well. Their marriage ended in divorce. She married and divorced again. From her stories, we detected that she has had a lot of experience with men, apart from her three marriages.

During our conversation she was staying in Kwahu-Tafo but because her family house had collapsed she had been given a room in another house. Nana Dedaa, who had been a farmer all her life, was still very active, selling things, doing chores in the house and visiting friends and relatives, but she had stopped farming. In 1999 she paid a visit to her son in Nkawkaw where she fell sick and died. Her body was brought to Kwahu-Tafo and buried there.

First Conversation: Love

On the 26th September 1996, I paid a visit to Nana Dedaa, a lively and very open elderly lady, with Obeng Boamah, my friend, assistant and key informant. Apparently she enjoyed our interest in her life history and her views on various topics related to old age. She surprised us with her directness and her ability to talk plainly – both with humour and regret about intimate details of her life. In total, we had four long conversations with her. The first one on that day in September was mainly about love, the second one was on building a house, the third one – to be presented later – focused on sex and the last one – fittingly – dealt with death.

After a brief discussion on her life history, in which she related that she was sent to the North to a priest healer to join her husband, Obeng Boamah (OB) and I (S) asked her (MD) opinion about love (ɔdɔ). The following conversation ensued.

MD   *It is good to love. You are staying with somebody. You love him and he also shows love for you. If you love me and I love you, we become one. If somebody hates you if you talk, it annoys him and he starts quarrelling with you. That is not good. But the one who loves, even when you offend him, does not take it seriously. When he offends you, you also don't mind, that is love. When he cooks, he gives you some food to eat. When you cook, you also give him something to eat. That is love....*

Love is being kind. When you meet your brother and he gets money, he gives you some of it. Then you know that he loves you. When I have money, I also give him some. We become one. That is love. But if you have money and you don't give me part of the amount, that is not love.

S   *Ask her to explain the differences in love between wife and husband, parent and child, grandparent and grandchild.*

OB   *We have different types of love. Love between husband and wife, parent and children. So we shall deal with them one after the other. What is the sort of love that exists between a mother and her child?*

MD   *When I gave birth to my children, I sent them to school. Some of them did not go. It was only one of them who attended school. So he is the one who cares for me. When he gets two thousand cedis* (then about US$ 1.50), *he sends it to me. That is love. He cares for me, so I like him very much. Those I cared for, do not care for me, yet I do not hate them. I pray for them. One of them has come back home sick. I have not rejected him, I care for him, I always pray that he recovers. He even attends the Catholic Church.... If you have cared for a child, he also cares for you, the parent. That means he loves you and you also love him/her. But the one who scolds you, does not love you and you also don't love him. When this happens, the only thing you can do is to pray to God that he will change so that you become one.*

S   *There is a saying that "When your mother dies, your family is finished". Why is it that a mother loves her own child more than the child of someone else?*

MD   *The reason why she loves her own child most is, that it is her own blood that brought the child to life. It is God who put the seed into her womb for months. When the child is born she feeds it with her breast. So it is her blood that brings him up and so if the child grows, it is his responsibility to care for his/her mother. When he is young, it is the mother who directs the child: You should not go here or there because of these reasons. Listen to my advice. If you take my advice, all will be well with you.*

OB   *It is through the blood of both the father and the mother that the child is produced. Does the father have the same love for his child as the mother?*

MD   *Yes, it is through the man that a woman becomes pregnant by the grace of God. So if the man cares for the child, the child will also grow and love the father. Some of the men do not care for their children. They don't love their children while some do. Some men join their wives and care for their children. Some men shirk responsibilities and the burden goes to rest only on the mother. He will not take care of the child's education.*

OB *Does a child love his mother more than his father?*

MD *If the father takes good care of his child, the child will love the father but if he does not, he will love the mother most.*

OB *What do you know about love between men and women?*

MD *When you marry a woman, you become one with her. You love her, she also loves you. You see to it that she does not become hungry. There are some who marry but later become enemies. Others marry and love everything of you, even excuse me, your sex organ. He loves your clothes, your body and your sex. That is love and the two of you become free. There are some who become angry and insult you if you talk to them. You may even be surprised at being insulted that way. When you are hungry he will not give money to cook yet if you cook, he will eat. That person does not marry you with love.*

OB *What will a woman do to show her love for her husband?*

MD *She does not let the husband go hungry. Even if the man does not have money, she will cook and give him some of the food to eat. I remember one day in my life, my husband was not there. When he came, I had prepared food for him. He asked how I had managed to get money and I told him I had my own money. When my husband ran short of money, I used my own money to cook.*

OB *What is the difference between love today and love in the past? The way you used to love people and how people love one another nowadays?*

MD *During our days we showed real love. We stayed with our husbands alone but the present women leave their husbands and go after other men. This is the practice of present women. In our youthful days, we were not doing that. Our husbands could leave us for over a year yet we never followed other men. But some of these children can't abstain for a week. We really loved our husbands.*

OB *You told us before that when you married you were a child. In your days parents chose marriages for their children. How did men take wives their parents had picked for them? Was there real love?*

MD *There was love, especially for the beautiful ones. Some refused to take ugly wives. In our days, it could happen that somebody staying in Accra or Europe would request his parents to arrange a marriage for him. At that time they used to examine certain things, for example, if there was any illness; if she had a good character and was hardworking. The man would then be invited to come and marry her. Then the father performed the customary rites. But sometimes he refused to marry the woman his parents had chosen.*

OB   *In the olden days, it was the parents who chose wives for their children but now it is the men and women themselves who meet and decide, take their decision. Which of these types of marriage lasts longer?*

MD   *That of today does not last. Even when a man is with the wife, the woman leaves the husband and goes to visit another man. In our days, it was not like that. If the husband had anything against you, you had to stay until he sent you to your father. When you go they will ask "Did she steal your things?". When you marry, you marry. You are made to swear the oath, Kwasi Atia Mfia, which says that when the woman gets any good thing, for example, wealth, she sends it to her parents. When she runs into debt, it is the man who pays for it.*

S   *What is the difference between "Medɔ wo' (I love you) and "Mepɛ wo" (I like you)?*

MD   *When someone tells you he likes you that is not very good because '"I like you'" does not last. The like vanishes but when one loves someone, it lasts forever. For example, when there is dry season, the leaves are dry. It is when it rains that the weeds begin to grow. As for love, it is always there...*

OB   *Who is happier, a man who has only one wife or one who has two or three wives?*

MD   *In the olden days a man had several reasons for marrying more than one wife. He might get one woman who was good in washing and tidying up the house. Another woman might be very good in cooking and the other might be good in "sleeping". These were some of the reasons why some of them married many wives. Sex was very important. Some liked it very much.*

S   *So a man who has married three women, can he share his love equally, among the three wives?*

MD   *Please, when a man marries three women he has three tongues. Wherever he goes, he goes to tell sweet stories to make the woman believe that he loves her most. He would also go to the others and tell similar sweet stories to make them believe that he loves each of them most.*

S   *So he is playing a game. What about the women?*

OB   *How do the "rivals" (co-wives, akorafɔɔ) stay?*

MD   *He will not let them know.*

OB   *Once he has performed the rites, would they not know that he has other wives?*

MD   *Some of the men who have money may decide to marry as many wives as they want. The rich man may tell the wives who don't agree that they can leave. One of the women may detect that the man loves the other two more than her. She may decide to ask for a divorce. Another woman may stay in spite of the maltreatment because she has children with him. She will continue to endure all hardships and stay like that until death separates them.*

S   *Why is it that a man can marry two wives but a woman can't marry two husbands?*

MD   *That is how God made it: that a woman should get one husband. A woman can marry a second husband only after she has divorced. A man on the other hand can marry as many women as he likes.*

S   *Why is it so?*

MD   *It is God who made it so. When a woman visits any other man the husband has every right to divorce the woman. The man who has got money can marry four, five or even more women. If a woman visits another man and the man gets to know it, he will have to be compensated by the other man.*

OB   *Is there any special reason why a man can marry as many as he likes while a woman cannot do so?*

MD   *God did not create it that way. God took one rib of a man to create a woman. So man is made the head of the family. Men control women. Women do not control men. Sometimes a man can take another woman. When the woman learns of it, he compensates the woman and they continue their marriage. Some women do not accept the compensation but rather go and fight the other woman. That is not a good habit. The mother of that man did not bring him up for you alone. He has the right to marry as many as he likes. Any of the women who behaves well stays as a wife while those who cannot cope go away or divorce.*

S   *In my country, men and women sometimes show their love in public. They can kiss, hold hands and embrace each other in the street. Why do you not show love in public?*

MD   *Our custom does not teach us that. Your custom is different. If you hold the hand of somebody's wife, the husband has every right to collect compensation money from you.*

OB No, he means when you are walking about with your own wife.

MD That is not our custom. We feel shy to do so..

S Why do you feel shy? Is it a sin?

MD No. It is not, but your custom is different. You may see a man holding the hand of his wife but kissing the wife in public is not good. It is not good. It is shameful. God did not create us like that in this country.

OB If you can kiss your wife in the room why can't you kiss her in public?

MD It is different in the room. You may have sex in the room and during the course of it, you may do it, but not in public. It is shameful. If you are staying with your wife in the house, do you have to kiss her in public? Your custom is not good. Ours is very good. It is because we have to respect each other. It is in bars and hotels that some people may do so while drinking but you can't do it in public. So that practice is never good.

S What is the difference between marriage according to customary rites and mere friendship which is not officially known to the parents?

MD Please, there may be people who love their friends more than their wives, but friendship does not last. Marriage, on the other hand, lasts. It is your wife who usually cares for you. When you are sick, she is there. When you are dying, she is there.

OB We want to know whether there is more enjoyment in marriage or in friendship (mpenafa).

MD Really there is more enjoyment in friendship.

OB What makes that more enjoyable?

MD It is because you may not like what your wife will do you may not like but you will like whatever your lover (mpena) does. I have had lovers some years ago and really there is enjoyment in it. Your lover gives you better treatment. However, she does so with fear. She fears your wife may start a fight with her when the affair becomes known. However, if there is no quarrel then you will feel happy. There is always interesting conversation. In marriage you may not converse so nicely. The man may not have much time for the wife. Instead of appearing nicely, before going to bed, he goes to drink. But when going to visit his girlfriend, he will not drink before sleeping. He goes with clear eyes and converses a lot. Sweet conversation, but it does not last long. Eventually you have to go back to your wife.

S   *When you get a lover, you get emotional feelings. Does it remain until the end or does it diminish as years pass by?*

MD   *When you love somebody you may love him to the end. You may also love somebody and getting to the middle of it, the love is lost. My first husband, for instance, I loved him and it was death that separated us. He loved me as I loved him. He used to give me a clothes every six months, during the Christmas and in the middle of the year.*

OB   *Did you love him because he provided your needs?*

MD   *No, not only that. I rather believe that it was the work of God. Just after he had declared his love to me, I also began to love him. God blessed it. When he died, I felt miserable.*

S   *Is there any difference between the love men have for women and the love women have for men?*

MD   *Yes, there is a difference. Men usually do not give their love to one woman. They visit other women. They may compare the character of the new friend with that of the old one and decide to stay with the latter. There are some women who are called "bediiwaa". They come only to consume. They come to demand whereas other women are prepared to stay even if the man is poor.*

OB   *We want to know the difference between the love a man has for a woman and the love a woman has for a man.*

MD   *They may love one another equally. He may have a good character and the woman also may have a good mind. Their love will be one. When they are like that, they don't divorce.*

OB   *You said earlier on that men do not love one woman. They may jump from one woman to another and now you are saying their love is the same. How do you explain that?*

MD   *Yes, I told you earlier on that some men marry three wives. The love of today's youth is different from what we were doing. In our time, we respected each other. A lot of these young women visit other men when the husband fails to provide them with their needs. But if that man takes proper care of them, they may remain faithful.*

OB   *So are you telling us that just as the man can't stay with one woman, a woman can't stay with one man?*

MD   *Yes, that is it. A pregnant woman who gets to know that the man who made her pregnant is incapable of taking care of her, may even give the baby in the womb to another man. She will drive the man away denying that he was the one who put her in the family way. Some men also detect that the women are not stable and they refuse to accept the pregnancy of their girlfriends. That is the character of the present generation.... Some men drive their girlfriends away when they become pregnant. The girls attempt to abort the child and meet their death.*

OB   But what do you say about a man's love for a woman?

MD   *Yes, you men are very wicked. You are sometimes not honest. Today's youth have different ideas. A lot of young men put a woman in the family way and refuse to take care of her.*

S   We have heard that there is "konya" (juju, magic) for marriage. What do you know about that?

MD   *Yes, in our time when a woman refused to accept a love proposal, the man could use that magic. He made it in a pomade form, and rubbed it on his head and face. As soon as the woman saw the face of the man, she developed love for him. The girl disliked him perhaps, yet when he rubbed the medicine on his face, the woman developed love for him. There was another type called "sokosare". In applying that magic, the man will mention the name of the girl and press it. Wherever she might be, she will have to go to where he is. That was what some men were doing. When this happened, a woman developed extra love for the man, which could even lead to marriage.*

OB   Does the power in the juju not end abruptly?

MD   *Yes, sometimes the power was lost in the middle of the marriage so that the woman decided to leave the man.*

OB   What were some of the causes which made couples divorce?

MD   *A reason could be that the man failed to take good care of the woman, for example, if he did not give her clothes. Some women preferred going naked without a husband to having a husband and going naked anyway.*

OB   Why did some women ask for a divorce?

MD   *It might be because the women were not good. They perhaps refused to help their husbands to do their jobs. Perhaps she did not go to farm with the man or refused to wash his clothes. Those were some of the causes. Some women were lazy, some men too were lazy. They would not go to farm. Some divorced simply because they had lost their love for the other.*

OB   Are there other reasons for divorce? For example, childbirth?

MD   *Yes, that is correct. When the two do not get issues, it sometimes causes divorce. The fault could come from any of the two. They may separate and try to have children with someone else.*

If there is a constant theme in this conversation, it is the material basis of love. Beauty counts, certainly to the men, but it is material support which is decisive. Love is proved in the faithful daily provision of money and food and in the thoughtfulness of giving presents. Mill and Anarfi (2002) describe how this traditional value still holds among young people today. Young women take lovers who give them money, food, cloth and other gifts. Love relationships may shade into strategies for economic survival or take on a more commercial character (cf. Bleek 1976; Dinan 1983).

In the case of Nana Dedaa, faithfulness is indeed more a matter of continued material support than of sexual restriction. It is not the material goods in themselves, however, which show and feed love, it is their capacity to be a token of the attitude of the other, which makes them valuable. However small the support may be, it is valued in the light of the other's ability. Where the material signs of love disappear, the other partner is likely to leave unless another pressing matter – usually children – continues to bind him/her. Reciprocity is the oil of any love relationship. That also applies to the love between parents and children, as Nana Dedaa explained several times.

Children are indeed the *raison d'être* of marriage. Nana Dedaa does not say much about it, it is too obvious to mention it. But when we asked her explicitly about it, her answer was clear. Finally, she is ambivalent about extra marital love. On the one hand, she extols marital fidelity, using her own first marriage as an example. On the other hand, she acknowledges that things in marriage may become boring and that there is more excitement in a love affair.

Second Conversation: Sex

On the 4th October 1996, I invited Nana Dedaa to the house of a good friend of mine, Monica Amoako, a single woman who, after several marriages, did not hide the fact that, for her, sex was something of the past. Her frankness about sexual experience made her an ideal person to reassure the old lady in speaking freely about sex in her own life. We felt, however, that the topic was too delicate to discuss outside where others undoubtedly would come to listen to the conversation and perhaps join it, so we retreated into Monica's room. I asked most of the questions, which were sometimes repeated and clarified by Monica (Mon). These repetitions have not been recorded in the transcription. The conversation started on sex at old age but soon widened to sexual experiences throughout her life time.

S   Some people say that only the young have a desire for sex. What is your opinion?

MD When I was young I used to indulge in it but I have stopped.

S   Would you not sleep with your husband now if you had one?

MD I would do so but not regularly. Now I don't have one but I stopped sleeping with my husband quite a long time before he died because he was weak.

S   So if you had a husband at this age, would you show your love for to him by sleeping with him?

MD I would do so occasionally. If he had the strength and desire to do it regularly, I would respond. I would allow him to go to another woman. I would explain to him that whenever I had the strength for it, I would let him know.

S   You talk about strength. Does a woman need it? I think it is rather the man who needs strength.

MD It is a tiresome work for a woman because the man is strong. When I was young, I was able to do it twice in a night but now I am old and don't have a man. I have been living with a dependent son for the past eight years, I could have got a man if I had wished and had sex with him at least once a week or once a month. Anyway now I am old and I can't do it any more. (Matwa mu) I have passed the stage.

S   If you have a husband, and his sex becomes weak, can't you help him in another way to make him feel satisfied?

MD My husband who died was in that situation and he did not allow me to sleep in the night. He always made an attempt to do it but it was impossible. Throughout the night he could worry me till the next morning begging me to let him try again (Wo deɛ, ma menhwɛ sɛ ɛbɛyɛ dɛn a). He would be saying: "Oh let me try, oh let me try", till day break. (Wo deɛ, ma menhwɛ, wo deɛ, ma menhwɛ, saa na adeɛ akye). In fact, it was annoying.

S   If not because he was overdoing it, wouldn't you have enjoyed it?

MD No. I always asked him to stop it because it was useless. He was only keeping me from sleep.

S   What did he do?

MD He always wanted real sex by penetration but he couldn't because the thing was soft (Ɔpɛ sɛ ɔhwɛ sɛ ɛbɛkɔ anaa, nanso adeɛ no ayɛ mmerɛ).

S   Wouldn't you have liked it if he had used another method, for example, using his fingers?

MD   *I have always disliked such things since I was young. I am not used to such things because I didn't practise it. I loved my first husband very much and was able to play with him but he died and after that I never played with other men in bed again. In fact, I loved my first husband. I was able to play with him before we did anything (Na yɛedi agoruɔ ansa na sɛ yɛbɛyɛ biribi a yɛayɛ). I stopped doing such things when he died.*

S   *Is there nothing you can do to help a man you love but who can't sleep* [have sex] *with you?*

MD   *You can play with him and have conversation until you become sleepy. Then you ask him for permission to sleep. When you play throughout the night, you get pain in your eyes the next day. My first husband didn't have that problem but the second one could not understand that he was not able to do it. If you asked him to get some medicine, he complained that I disgraced him. Because of all this I divorced him. He was jealous and suspicious about my movements and was always thinking that I had another man. I was afraid that he might do me some harm.*

S   *Can a man who is impotent (ne kɔte awu) but still loves his wife, permit her to go to another man?*

MD   *Some men do it but not my husband. Some men who are impotent permit their wives to go out and have pleasure with other men. All they need is that you come back, bath and sleep with them to indulge in playful acts (di agorɔw). But my husband would not permit such a thing.*

S   *Does the desire for sex go down in old age and does it go down earlier in men or in women?*

MD   *The desire stays longer in women than in men (ɛmaa deɛ yɛn ho nyoduwo ntɛm). I don't like it now but if I had a husband, it would be possible for me to do it.*

S   *Has the desire in you gone due to old age or it is because you don't have a husband?*

MD   *It is because of waist problems that I don't have desire for it. Do you notice how I walk ? It is due to waist problems. Otherwise I would still do it...*

S   *When did you notice that your desire for men was going down?*

MD   *I noticed it after the waist sickness started.*

S   *How many years now ?*

MD   *About ten years ago.*

S   *Some people in my country claim that the desire for men in some women increases when they grow older. What do you think about it?*

MD   *It has reached the sweetest point (Eyi na ahyɛi ato ɔdɛ). That is what people say. If you have a husband, you can do it, but not always. Some people like it and they do it until they are very old. Even when they are old and without a husband, they look for a man. Some old women try to look young to attract men and succeed in doing so until they die. They won't have children any more so they pretend to be young through their dress and take men just for the joy of it....*

S   *If you love your man and he becomes impotent, what would you do?*

MD   *I will explain to him that I love him and that his condition bothers me so we should find a solution to it. If he understands he may allow you to have another man secretly to satisfy your desire.*

S   *Is it possible to like without love or to love without like?*

MD   *A person may like someone and have a desire to have sex with the person because of appearance. That is not love. A person also can love someone but because of appearance may not like to have sex with that one. Anyway, some manage to maintain their love despite the ugly appearance of their partner.*

S   *Some say sex in old age is good, others say it is not good. What do you think is true?*

MD   *If it is possible for you to do it but you abstain from it, you may fall ill.*

S   *There are some children who prevent their old fathers from marrying again after the death of their mother. Why?*

MD   *It is jealousy. They feel jealous of another woman joining them in their father's house. Let me tell you something. Some time ago, I came and stayed in this town for three years while my husband was not here and a certain man proposed love to me. When I told him that I had a husband, he advised me to go back to him, or divorce him so that I could have another man. If not, I will fall sick. I was then very strong and able to work. I could look after myself and did not need the assistance of a man, financially or otherwise. So I didn't take the advice. I stayed for five years without a man and then I fell sick. I was all the time feeling dizzy and weak. It was only after I had gone to my husband, that I became better. By then I had not yet stopped menstruating. So if you are fit to sleep with a man and you abstain from it, you can fall sick (Se wonyaree na sɛ wo gyae ɔbarima nna a, ɛbɛbɔ wo yareɛ). But if your time has passed and you refuse to do it, it won't worry you too much.*

S   *Is it good if an old woman marries a young man? For example if Ababio (Patrick, one of my assistants) married you?*

MD   I am older than he is so he will become old in a short time (ɔbɛyɛ akwakora ntɛm).

S   So it is not good for a young man to marry an old lady?

MD   No, it will make him old in a short time. What will come out of him and flow to the woman will be good for her but it will make him old in a short time.

S   What about if a young woman marries an old man?

MD   It is the same. The water from the old man is not good so it will make the girl old. It will make her ugly and sick.

S   If the juice of the old man will make the girl old, why can't the juice of the young woman make the old man young?

MD   A young woman can't bring a change in an old man. If the old man is weak he will continue to be weak.

S   Do you think the desire in an old man who is weak will become strong when he sleeps with a young woman?

MD   It can make him a bit strong (Ebɛtumi ayɛ no kakra).

S   Can an old person keep the qualities which made him attractive when he was young?

MD   You can never keep them. The skin would by all means develop wrinkles (Wo honam bɛyɛ ntwutwo-ntwutwo).... As you grow older, the beauty diminishes.

S   Can't a person keep a kind of beauty even in old age?

MD   Some people look beautiful to the end (Ebi wɔ hɔ a wɔnsɛɛ kosi se wɔbɛwu).

Mon. What I have observed is that farmers who do very hard work without proper nutrition and medical care grow old and are not nice-looking when they reach old age. But those who have money and are able to eat good food and have proper medical care keep some beauty in their old age.

S   To me, it seems an old tree looks more beautiful than a young one. Am I not correct?

MD   Some are nice but others develop humps.

S   In what sense are some beautiful?

MD   Some are nice but others bend and develop humps on them, which make them useless for building.

S   Let us go back to the tree. What is more beautiful a young tree or an old tree?

MD   A young tree is more beautiful.

S   Can an old person look beautiful?
MD   Yes, some old people look beautiful.
S   What makes them look beautiful?
MD   They keep themselves neat (Wɔdi wɔn ho ni).
S   Is it due to money?
MD   Yes, if I have money to buy clothes and if I bathe and wear clothes I will by all means look beautiful.
S   A lot of things can determine beauty, even how a person talks.
MD   It is true, during funerals, I sing playful songs which make people admire me and they come around me and we joke and laugh.
S   What about dancing, does it show beauty?
MD   Yes, there is beauty in dancing. When you are dancing, someone can say: "Oh, this woman is old but look how beautifully she is dancing."

Five things struck me in this conversation. The first was Nana Dedaa's emphasis on strength as a condition for sex. Of course, love is a first condition but without strength, sex is not possible. The man's strength is mainly thought of in genital terms. Sex is indeed an overwhelmingly genital affair. If the potency disappears, sex becomes "useless", that is, impossible. She still vividly remembers her second husband's useless attempts – till daybreak – to have sex with her. It was not only he who lacked the strength, she too become tired of it and finally divorced him. The strength a woman needs for sex has a wider connotation. First of all she has to respond to the strength of her partner. More important, however, is that when she grows older she spends all of her strength on work and needs the night to rest. Sex becomes a "tiresome work". In a conversation with a group of women one of them said:

If you are married and your husband is someone who likes to have sex with you every day, it may weaken your body and make you lose your beauty. Because having sex is hard work. If a day's work on the farm and at home is followed by sex every night, it will not be good for the body.

Interestingly, studies on the heavy workload of women in Ghana never mention the "tiresome work of sex."[10] Avotri and Walters (1999) remark that reproductive health problems did not figure prominently in the interviews they held with 75 women in the Volta Region, but sex is totally ignored. The authors quote several women who sum up the many tasks they have to do from early morning to late at night when they finally go to bed. No one hints at the fact that even then they may still not find rest. The taboo reigns.

A second observation is that "strength" can become a convenient euphemism for desire. "'No strength'" (*mienni ahɔɔden*) shades into "'no interest'" (*me kɔn nnɔ*). When I asked another old lady whether elderly men had more interest in sex than elderly women, she answered: "Yes, men have more strength", as if strength and interest were one and the same thing. A similar view was expressed by a man who emphasised that a woman never lacked the strength to sleep with a man "Their thing", he said and laughed, "does not spoil, it only grows old. But with a man it can spoil". So, when a woman said that she had no strength, it simply meant that she did not have the desire, he said.

A third striking conclusion from Nana Dedaa's conversation, as already mentioned, is her exclusively genital view on sex. "Playing" did not attract her, although she admitted that she did it in her youthful days. Although we did not go into details, she made it clear that she firmly disliked any other form of sex. Other conversations during our research suggested that most people, women as well as men, shared that view.

The fourth important point I want to draw attention to is Nana Dedaa's ambivalence towards sex in old age. At certain moments she seems to reject it and provides her own life as an example; at other moments she indicates she would still be interested in it, be it less frequently than before. It is her circumstances, no partner and sharing her room with a handicapped son that prevent her from having sex in her old age.

The final topic that raised my interest and which will take us back to the first, was her concept of beauty. Growing old, in her view, meant losing beauty and attractiveness. That held for people but also for trees. Wrinkles, whether on a human face or in the bark of a tree implied loss of beauty. Her definition of beautiful included smooth, young, tender, neat. Loss of beauty was usually linked to hard work. Those who grow old in years may succeed in retaining some of their beauty if they do not have to work so much. If they have money to buy good food, medicines to keep their skin smooth and fancy clothes, they will stay young. As some other conversations bore out, having only a few children and not being forced to do hard work – two prerogatives of the well-to-do – also helped to retain youthful beauty. One middle-aged woman remarked:

Before it can be said of a person that she is beautiful, strong or healthy, she must be a bit well off. If you have these qualities but you have no money to maintain them, you will soon be like an old lady. But it is different if your husband does his work, if he helps you look after the children and yourself so that the children grow up and are well off. They will be remitting you money and sending you delicious food, clothes, etc. Then you may never grow old and even if you become old, you can still maintain your beauty, and stay young and healthy because of your high standard of living.

Monica spontaneously joined in the conversation at this point. The common saying *sika yɛ abrantes* (money is a young man, that is when one has money, one looks young, handsome and strong) could be extended to *sika yɛ ababaawa* (money is a young lady).

Love and Sex in Old Age

Dedaa's account contains two trends in marital life which I found to be common during my conversations and observations with all elderly people I encountered during my fieldwork. The first, but least prominent, is the marriage which lasts a lifetime and is only dissolved by death. Nana Dedaa's first marriage represents that trend. It was a good marriage in the sense that both partners continued to support one another throughout their lives.

The second, more common, trend was that a marriage dissolves in old age as the woman does not see the "'use'" of continuing it. The reason, usually, is that she feels that her husband has little to offer her any more and that she is not bound to him because he has failed to give her substantial (material) support during his active life. Marriages survive or end on the basis of reciprocity. Where a husband has failed to invest in his relationship with his wife and children, the wife does not feel obliged to stay with him and to care for him at old age. It is more attractive to her to leave him and either return to her *abusua fie* (family house) or to stay with one of her children. Love, as we have seen, is measured in material terms. Old age is the time for drawing up accounts and taking things into one's hand. The slogan that Cattell quoted from elderly Kenyan women suits the attitude of Nana Dedaa: "Praise the Lord and say no to man" (Cattell 1992).

As far as sex in old age is concerned, Nana Dedaa's views largely conform with what has been published about this topic on Northern societies. On the one hand, they report a general decline of interest in sex among elderly people. On the other hand, they notice that sexual desires continue to be felt throughout the life course and that their apparent reduction is as much a social and cultural as a biological matter. The phenomenon that the younger generation disapproves of continued sexual activity among the elderly and that the latter tend to comply with that disapproval, seems nearly universal. It was also found among other elderly people in Nana Dedaa's community (see Van der Geest 2001).

That ambivalence towards sex in old age, self-censorship and loss of desire ("strength") on the one hand, and continued interest on the other, showed itself in Nana Dedaa's disarming personal account.

End Notes

1   The research was carried out with the help of many people. I am particularly grateful to Monica Amoako and Anthony Obeng Boamah who accompanied me during my visits to Mary Dedaa.

2   Two earlier collections with contributions on Ghanaian women (Oppong ed.1983 &, 1987) keep silent on the topic of sexuality. An extensive bibliography on Ghanaian women (Ardayfio-Schandorf & Kwafo-Akoto 1990) with 754 annotations has only three references to "sexual behaviour". Two exceptions, studies that do contain some description and discussion of sexual practice in Ghana, are Kaye (1962) and Bleek (1976).

3   See for example: Vance (1991), Anarfi (1993), Awusabo-Asare et al. (1993), Ankomah (1998), Mill & Anarfi 2002.

4   Apt's (1996) study of elderly Ghanaians does not contain any reference to the topic of sex.

5   The research was carried out with the help of many people. Most prominent was the assistance given by my Ghanaian co-researchers Kwame Fosu, Samuel Sarkodie, Patrick Atuobi, and Anthony Obeng Boamah. Benjamin Boadu and Yaw Darko Ansah typed most of the research material. I am further indebted to Monica Amoako, Martin Asamoah, Abena Ansah, *Abusua Panyin* Daniel Osei Yeboah, Marek Dabrowski and Grzegorz Kubowicz for various kinds of help. I dedicate this essay to the memory of Mary Yaa Dedaa. May she rest in peace after all her hard work!

6   *Opanyin* ('elder') is someone past middle age who is considered wise and experienced and behaves in a civilised and exemplary way. According to Rattray (1916: 23) the term is derived from *nyin* (to grow) and *apa* (old, long-lived). For a more elaborate discussion of the concept of *opanyin*, see Stucki 1985, Van der Geest (1998b).

7   These themes are discussed in various articles (Van der Geest 1997, 1998a, 1998b, 2000, n.d.a, n.d.b, 2001, 2002).

8   Pellow (1977: 162), who studied the lives of women in Adabraka, a suburb of Accra with a high concentration of Kwahu, suggested that many women derived little pleasure from sex in their marriage.

9   All conversations, except the very casual ones, were taped, transcribed and translated into English. Only a few were conducted in English.

10 See for example Klingshirn (1971); Bukh (1979); Fogelberg (1982); Oppong & Abu
(1987); Dei (1994); Avotri & Walters (1999).

Bibliography

Anarfi, J.K., 1993. Sexuality, migration and AIDS in Ghana: A socio-behavioural
study. *Health Transition Review* 3 (Suppl): 45-67.

Ankomah, A., 1998. Condom use in sexual exchange relationships among young
single adults in Ghana. *AIDS Education and Prevention* 10: 303-16.

Apt, N.A., 1996. *Coping with Old Age in a Changing Africa: Social change and the
elderly Ghanaian.* Aldershot: Avebury.

Ardayfio-Schandorf, E. & K. Kwafo-Akoto, 1990. *Women in Ghana: An annotated
bibliography.* Accra: Woeli Publishing Services.

Avotri, J.Y. & V. Walters, 1999. "You just look at our work and see if you have any
freedom on earth": Ghanaian women's accounts of their work and their health.
Social Science & Medicine 48 (9), 1123-33.

Awusabo-Asare, K., J.K. Anarfi & D. Agyeman, 1993. Women's control over their
sexuality and the spread of STDs and HIV/AIDS in Ghana. *Health Transition
Review* 3: 69-84.

Bartle, P.F.W., 1977. *Urban migration and rural identity: An ethnography of a
Kwawu community.* Ph.D. Thesis. Legon, University of Ghana.

Bleek, W., 1976. *Sexual relationships and birth control in Ghana: A case study of a
rural town.* Ph.D. Thesis. University of Amsterdam.

Bukh, J., 1979. *The Village Woman in Ghana.* Uppsala: Scandinavian Institute of
African Studies.

Caplan, P., 1998. Experiencing old age on Mafia Island (Tanzania). In M.I. Aguilar
(ed), *The Politics of Age and Gerontocracy in Africa.* Trenton / Asmara: Africa
World Press, pp. 99-124.

Cattell, M.G., 1992. 'Praise the Lord and say no to men': Older women
empowering themselves in Samia, Kenya. *Journal of Cross-Cultural
Gerontology* 7: 307-30.

Dei, H.J.S., 1994. The women of a Ghanaian village: A study of social change.
African Studies Review 37 (2), 121-46.

Dinan, C., 1983. Sugar daddies and gold-diggers: The white-collar single women in
Accra. In C. Oppong (ed.) *Female and Male in West Africa.* London: George
Allen & Unwin, pp. 344-66.

Fogelberg, T., 1982. *Nanumba Women: Working bees or idle bums. Sexual division
of labour, ideology of work, and power relations between women and men.*
Leiden: ICCS, ICA Publication 53.

Kaye, B., 1962. *Bringing up Children in Ghana. An impressionistic survey.* London: George Allen & Unwin.

Klingshirn, A., 1971. *The changing position of women in Ghana.* Inaugural Dissertation, Marburg

Mill, J.E. & Anarfi, J.K., 2002. HIV risk environment for Ghanaian women: Challenges to prevention. *Social Science & Medicine* 54 (3): 325-37.

Oppong, C. (ed.), 1983. *Female and Male in West Africa.* London: George Allen & Unwin.

Oppong, C. (ed.), 1987. *Sex Roles, Population and Development in West Africa.* Portsmouth / London: Heinemann / James Currey.

Oppong, C. & K. Abu, 1987. *Seven roles of women: Impact of education, migration and employment on Ghanaian mothers.* Geneva: ILO.

Pellow, D., 1977. *Women in Accra: Options for autonomy.* Algonac, MI: Reference Publications.

Rattray, R.S., 1916. *Ashanti Proverbs.* Oxford: Clarendon Press.

Stucki, B.R., 1995. *Managing the social clock: The negotiation of elderhood among rural Asante of Ghana.* Ph.D. Thesis, Northwestern University, Evanston, US.

Vance, C.S., 1991. Anthropology rediscovers sexuality: A theoretical comment. *Social Science & Medicine* 33 (8): 875-84.

Van der Geest, S., 1997. Money and respect: The changing value of old age in rural Ghana. *Africa* 67 (4): 534-59.

Van der Geest, S., 1998a. *Yebisa wo fie*: Growing old and building a house in the Akan culture of Ghana. *Journal of Cross-cultural Gerontology* 13 (4): 333-59.

Van der Geest, S., 1998b. *Opanyin*: the ideal of elder in the Akan culture of Ghana. *Canadian Journal of African Studies* 32 (3): 449-93.

Van der Geest, S., 2000. Funerals for the living: Conversations with elderly people in Kwahu, Ghana. *African Studies Review* 43 (3): 103-29.

Van der Geest, S., 2001. "No strength". Sex and old age in a rural town of Ghana. *Social Science & Medicine* 53 (10): 1383-96.

Van der Geest, S., 2002. From wisdom to witchcraft: The ambivalence towards old age in Kwahu, Ghana. *Africa.* In press.

MAMPRUSI WITCHCRAFT, SUBVERSION AND CHANGING GENDER RELATIONS

Susan Drucker-Brown

The Mamprusi traditional kingdom in north-eastern Ghana is one of a set of loosely centralised kingdoms in the Savannah region of the Volta River system. In the 1960s, during the first decade of its independence, Ghana experienced a remarkable expansion of public services, and expectations of future progress soared. In the 1980s central government disposed of greatly curtailed resources for such communal benefits as education, health, road works or investment in local economic development, all of which had expanded in the immediate aftermath of independence. The mid-1980s were years of grave food shortage and inflation. Armed conflict among neighbouring ethnic groups had become endemic in some areas of the north, and direct army intervention had frequently been used to maintain public order (Drucker-Brown, 1988-89). The suppression of civilian political activity by the military government led, at least in the Mamprusi area, to greater dependence of national government on chiefly courts, which continued to be indispensable centres for gathering and disseminating information locally. At the same time central government provided these rural communities with ever fewer services. In the Mamprusi districts chiefs continued to link national government with the small, dispersed village communities in which Mamprusi people live together with other ethnic groups. Mamprusi have never been more than a numerically and politically dominant minority in this culturally and linguistically heterogeneous area (See Drucker-Brown, 1975).

Thus the historical decay of the Mamprusi kingdom is a complex process, involving a changing balance of power during the past century between a distant central government (be it colonial or independent) and the Mamprusi kingship. In the long term the political powers of king and court undoubtedly diminished and the centralising power of an overriding national government increased. But in the short term there have been oscillations in the balance of power, and these, as well as economic transformation, have been reflected in the theory and practice of witchcraft. It is argued here, following Esther Goody (1970), that witchcraft beliefs reflect an idealised pattern of gender relations in which women are denied legitimate expression of aggressive emotion. However, I argue, further, that political aspects of gender relations are also reflected in Mamprusi witchcraft belief. Mamprusi women are accused of witchcraft not only because their aggressive feelings are denied legitimacy but also because they have no public role in the politico-jural domain, though some women acquire great influence, and all influential men depend on women and ultimately on a female hierarchy. This chapter argues that witchcraft beliefs reflect that hierarchy. It also documents changes in witchcraft belief and practice and argues that these can be seen as a response to the increasing autonomy of women in the sexual division of labour and loss of control by Mamprusi men of the local economy. A changing balance of power is thus reflected, not only between central and local government, but between men and women in the political, domestic and economic domains.

In the pre-conquest Mamprusi kingdom of Northern Ghana witchcraft was a capital offence. The Mamprusi king is said to have had the unique right to order capital punishment and in the 1960s, half a century after British conquest, Mamprusi living in the king's village could still describe the oracles used at the palace to diagnose witchcraft, and the horrible forms of execution suffered by witches, and could point out places where executions had occurred. The executions seem to have been designed as much to terrorise those who might be accused as to punish those found guilty.[1] For Mamprusi, however, the proto typical capital crime associated with public torture and gory execution was adultery, involving the wife of a king or prince. Where discovered, both partners were executed.[2] Women rather than men were always pictured as the victims of execution. I shall return to the connection between witchcraft and adultery with the wives of royals at the end of this chapter.

In the 1960s, as now, witchcraft was a subject hedged about with anxiety. However at that time the subject rarely arose spontaneously in conversation. Then, as now, to mention witchcraft was to admit an interest, and while it was widely believed that all powerful men and old people generally knew about such things, the subject was not to be mentioned casually. Misfortune and death were almost universally attributed to the ancestors or to a distant divinity rather than to the activity of witches. The king, chiefs and powerful household heads were regarded as able to see witches and to protect their dependants from attack. Witches attacked at night, invisibly devouring the bodies of their victims,[3] typically causing lingering illness and death. A victim would often see the witch or witches attacking, and accusations might be made by a victim during an illness, or by the mother of a small child if, as often happened, a child was the victim. To the observer it seemed that a name mentioned by a sick person in a feverish state could easily be taken as an accusation.

In the past, *post-mortem* examinations were performed to reveal the witchcraft substance (*soo*) in a witch's body. This was described as a cotton-like residue in the intestinal tract. As among the neighbouring Tallensi, a propensity to witchcraft is said to be inherited from one's mother, and so the uterine kin (*soog*) of a convicted witch are always suspect. But Mamprusi believe that witchcraft is practised deliberately and stress that the matrikin of a witch need not be witches. Far more significant than any inherited propensity, they argue, are the possession and consumption of medicines (*tiim*). It may happen that an innocent person is fed witchcraft substance by an active witch (*songa*, pl. *sooba*) or even by a group of witches recruiting a novice. The novice will be impelled to act as a witch by medicine which has been secretly added to her food and which she (or, much more rarely, he) eats inadvertently. The novice is then forced to steal flesh from a victim and feed senior witches in a communal feast. The fat is particularly appetising to witches, and persistent loss of weight is a typical sign of attack by witches. It seems that, once eaten, human flesh becomes an addiction, hence medicine becomes deliberate. Variations in the type of attack witches commit depend on the particular medicines consumed. Thus, for example, some witches are said to have 'spears', revealed in the attack of a scorpion or snake. These differ from the more usual lingering illnesses attributed to witchcraft and are said to be the result of different medicines. More recently in the 1990s witches might be described as having 'tanks' and 'missiles', images of modern warfare having been added to the arsenal of witchcraft.

The Mamprusi category of "medicine" *(tiim)* incorporates substances which are prophylactic or curative as well as poisonous, and substances which operate both mechanically and metaphysically. Medicine is used not only by witches but by those who 'see' and defend against witchcraft. Thus the most respected members of the community must be regarded as using the same materials as its most anti-social members, though the goals are presumed to be very different. Among Mamprusi, as among the Azande (Evans-Pritchard, 1937), royals are never publicly accused of witchcraft. In the 1960s I was also told that it was forbidden for a Mamprusi royal to make a public accusation of witchcraft. At commoner funerals public divination, designed specifically to uncover witchcraft as a cause of death, though forbidden from the colonial period, might still be publicly performed, and all commoners' funerals involved some form of public divination to establish the cause of death. Royal deaths, by contrast, male or female, involved no public divination. Royals divined privately to ascertain the cause of death, and I was told that public divination could not be performed, precisely because royal deaths might not be publicly attributed to witchcraft.

In my experience, however, royal deaths, which were inevitably attributed by close kin to 'God' (*Nawuni*) or 'the ancestors', were always believed by some to result from witchcraft. Indeed, royal men are always regarded as vulnerable to the more powerful medicines of their rivals, thus during a king's funeral his death is publicly attributed to God, but an oracle administered secretly to the princes demonstrates that he has fallen victim to the superior supernatural strength of his successor, and this strength is regarded as residing, at least in part, in lethal witchcraft. One might argue that there is no need to execute a royal witch, since, in due course, a rival will perform the task (see Drucker-Brown, 1989, 1991).

The uses of witchcraft medicine when attributed to men and women are appreciably different. In both cases a close kinsperson will be the most likely target. It is said that female novices, trained or coerced by senior witches, are forced to provide food for their seniors, and a mother must kill her own infant not merely to provide meat, but to prove the strength of her commitment. Women are also typically accused of killing a co-wife's child or attacking a husband or brother-in-law. These, normally, are persons with whom the accused resides. Men, by contrast, are not accused of bewitching their spouses or children but are typically held responsible for using witchcraft against rivals -- members of their own patrilineages, who are not normally resident with them and unlike women they may use witchcraft in defence of others.[4]

The Witches' Village

A convicted witch might be executed in the Mamprusi kingdom but there was an alternative manner of dealing with witchcraft. Convicted witches could be, and are still, sent to the market town of Gambaga, a former capital of the kingdom, some five miles west of the present capital. In a special section near the market, immediately behind the large compound occupied by the chief, witches live segregated from the community at large, though they move freely through the market and around the town. The witches' settlement is called *pwaanyankura-foango* – literally, 'old ladies' section' – and it existed prior to the colonial period. Similar witches' settlements have been reported in the Kpasinkpe province of the Mamprusi kingdom and also in the neighbouring Dagomba kingdom.

The theory of the witches' village is similar to that underlying the operation of numerous important shrines in northern Ghana. In all these a protected population is tied in permanent or semi-permanent residence to a shrine, of which the priests mediate for the resident clients with the shrine deities. More commonly than convicted witches, these clients are persons suffering from illness (Field, 1960), but shrines also protected runaway slaves (Maier, 1983), and some combine oracular functions without healing. The chief of Gambaga, like priests at these shrines, provides his clients, the witches, with special medicine, and the ancestors, upon whom he calls at his shrine, activate the medicine the witches drink to render their witchcraft harmless. The medicine is concocted from herbs sought in the bush, combined with water, and drunk by the client in the presence of the chief of Gambaga and his ancestors, who are also called to be present at the shrine. So long as a witch resides in Gambaga and regularly drinks this medicine no one need fear attack. For this reason the population of Gambaga do not avoid the resident witches.

However, segregation in Gambaga is a form of imprisonment. The women have had to leave their homes and families, and though they can trade and work they are uniformly poor and demeaned by their incarceration. The women maintain themselves as they have done in the past, by performing menial tasks in the market; collecting and selling firewood, carrying and selling water. In the 1990s, with the hiring of agricultural labour, some women were also paid to work on farms. However, as the name of the section indicates, many – though not all – of the women were elderly, and all complained of lack of food and the poor condition of their housing. Most of them bitterly denied that they are witches. Some said, resignedly, that they must be witches if everyone says they are. But all the women I spoke to agreed that they were safer in Gambaga than they would have been in the villages from which they had come, and there is no doubt that Gambaga provides a sanctuary for women, who would certainly face ostracism and possibly death, were they not removed from the communities in which they have been accused. In the 1960s I was told that the witches must remain in the village for life and would be released only if they could bribe the chief. In 1991 I was told by the chief that a witch was free to leave if she could find another place to stay, could pay him for the medicines he had given her and could provide him with an animal sacrifice to his ancestor shrine. Some women have done this and been resettled elsewhere.

The Gambaga witches' village is now known well beyond the confines of the kingdom and stories in the national press decrying its existence have merely served to publicise it further. In 1991 the section contained twelve large compounds with a permanent population of at least 140 women and a transient population of perhaps a dozen or more supportive kin, including a few men who were husbands of the resident women. Very occasionally, male witches are also segregated there. In 1991, I was told that a Bimoba man had recently run away. In the 1960s, several male diviners lived among the women but no male witches were resident. In the summer of 1991, a majority of the population were Mamprusi, but it also included Dagomba, Tampolensi, Konkomba and Bimoba women. This is a cross-section of the ethnic groups represented in the population of the central province of the kingdom. Two Dagomba women had come from Karaga, a town some fifty miles away. By contrast, in the 1960s, the population of the witches' village was almost exclusively non-Mamprusi.

Although Mamprusi women were accused of witchcraft they were only rarely sent to Gambaga. I was told that it would be shameful for a Mamprusi woman to be so publicly branded a witch. Equally important, I believe, were a woman to be sent to the Gambaga settlement, it would indicate that her witchcraft could not be controlled by the medicines available to ordinary household heads or village chiefs and that would be a source of further shame. In any case, the ethnic composition of the witches' village at Gambaga had certainly shifted between the 1960s and the 1990s from a population including few Mamprusi to one in which Mamprusi witches are a majority.

Some Implications of Segregating Witches

One of the most obvious implications of segregating witches, rather than executing them is that the women provide useful labour. Prior to the colonial period Gambaga was the largest market and caravan stop in what is now the north-east of Ghana. The slave trade, which operated in the region and through the Gambaga market, must have made labour scarcer and more valuable than it is now. Women's labour was particularly useful in a market town. In the 1960s, whenever the Gambaga witches were mentioned, they were described as suppliers of water and firewood for the market. In the 1990s it was harder to imagine that these women could survive by providing such services alone. Labour by then was far more available and the Gambaga market less important, dwarfed by numerous, newer markets. The women were partially supported by charity, as well as by their own labour. In this context it is noteworthy that, during the famine years of the 1980s, one of the Protestant pastors in Gambaga is said to have made himself (and his church) responsible for helping to feed the women. It would seem, then, that the population of the witches' village has oscillated between being a valuable source of labour and a drain on community resources.

Another obvious result of the witches' survival is that witchcraft cases can be reopened and a witch exonerated, or at least allowed to re-enter normal life. As noted above, women have been removed from Gambaga by their kin and resettled elsewhere. In any case, the witches retain contact with their kin and with their communities of origin. Thus a heterogeneous community is gathered in Gambaga and supervised by the Gambaga chief. Witchcraft cases do not necessarily end in consensus. Indeed, most of the Gambaga witches maintained that they had been wrongly accused.

Anthropologists have often observed that witchcraft accusations do not emerge randomly but arise in relationships where conflict is endemic. Providing a hearing and an alternative to violence in the settlement of disputes is one of the reasons which non-Mamprusi give for accepting Mamprusi chiefs and using Mamprusi chiefs' courts. But much of the authority of chiefs and of the king depends on access to information. The centralised treatment of witchcraft accusations and the congregation of convicted witches are one means, albeit an indirect one, of centrally collecting information about the conflicts which underlie witchcraft accusations. Like the Azande poison oracle which must be manipulated by the representative of a royal, the segregation of Mamprusi witches in a single settlement serves to accumulate information centrally about disputes occurring throughout the kingdom. In 'looking after' witches, and thus providing what is seen as a service to other ethnic groups, Mamprusi reinforce as well as justify the political domination of their chiefs.

Mamprusi reluctance to eliminate witches, their segregation in a single settlement and the use of their labour in the market also publicise an attitude towards witchcraft that might be characterised as sceptical and certainly as stoical. I was struck in the 1960s by the pride with which Gambaga people explained to me that they were not afraid of the Gambaga witches. Their attitude contrasted with a more credulous and fearful view characteristic of those of their neighbours who sent witches to Gambaga. Mamprusi scepticism, it should emphasised, did not normally extend to dismissal of the theory of witchcraft as a source of misfortune. However, in the face of specific accusations Mamprusi often expressed scepticism and did not admit to feeling threatened. The existence of the witches' village, as it was in the 1960s, inhabited mainly by non-Mamprusi witches, and connected with a major market, was thus an exercise in public relations: an assertion of Mamprusi imperturbability in the face of witchcraft.

The indigenous Mamprusi polity contains different classes of chiefs (Drucker-Brown, 1975) and Gambaga, like other villages where in the past witches were gathered together, is not a royal chiefship. Gambaga's chief belongs to the class of earth priests (*tendaan-dima*). Throughout the Voltaic region, the mystical powers of the earth (*tenga*) are opposed to the powers of kingship (*naam*) and lineages of earth priests rather than those of kings deal with witchcraft. Thus, the task of Gambaga's chief, as custodian of witches and owner of the witchcraft antidote, is complementary to that of the chief of Bugiya, a village some fifteen miles north-west of Gambaga. Bugiya's chief is also an earth priest and he controls a powerful witch-finding oracle. The Bugiya oracle is resorted to for divination in witchcraft cases, and suspects are sent there from the king's court. No appeal is possible against a decision of the Bugiya oracle.

The name of this village and of the oracle cannot be uttered in the king's presence. The prohibition was explained to me as part of the prohibition against publicly associating royalty with witchcraft, but I believe it is also consistent with a more fundamental process in which the king is separated from those who hold specialised powers which might rival his own. The segregation of witches, of anti-witchcraft medicine and of the witch finding oracle may thus be seen as manifestations of that division of ritual labour which is a major principle of Mamprusi political organisation (Drucker-Brown, 1975).

Changes in Witchcraft Theory and Practice

Let us look now in more detail at some changes in the Mamprusi theory of witchcraft and associated practice as they appeared in the summer of 1991.

1. Though women of other ethnic groups were segregated there, Mamprusi are now a majority of the women incarcerated in the witches' village.
2. At least one witch-finder, a Tallensi man, and his Kusase assistant were active in the capital. They diagnosed seven cases of witchcraft, and in public seances found five witches whom they physically threatened and ill-treated until the accused revealed where they had hidden their victims.

Several women were then removed to the witch-finder's settlement to receive further treatment. In the 1960s no such enterprising witch-seers operated in the Mamprusi region. The techniques used by the seer, though found in neighbouring areas, contrast radically with Mamprusi methods in the 1960s, in which the diagnosis and treatment of witches were carried out in private, and by separate specialists.

3. During the summer of 1991, the Mamprusi king himself announced, in the presence of the accusing witch-finder, that he had seen the group of women accused of witchcraft in the act of committing their crimes. No witchcraft accusation was brought by any royal in the 1960s, let alone by the king.

Before examining these changes in practice, let us turn to changes in the Mamprusi theory of witchcraft. Theory current in the nineties extended rather than displaced earlier ideas. In the more recent view, witches do not necessarily devour their victims. They may transform them into other creatures, even into vegetable matter, and imprison them in a transformed state for later use. I was told of a witch who changed her victims into the seeds inside a gourd, the better to transport them to a southern market. The king claimed that he had seen the women he accused secreting their victims, transformed into tiny insects, in the hollow of a tree behind the palace. Most often victims are described as changed into small, helpless creatures, usually insects. The reports in 1991 dwelt on transformations wrought upon the victims of witchcraft. In the 1960s, I was told how witches transformed themselves into other creatures, usually predatory nocturnal ones.

I expressed surprise when told that witchcraft had become more frequent and more serious, accounting now for much illness and death. In the 1960s, no one spoke in such general terms about witchcraft. I was then asked:

Haven't you seen those herds of sheep and goats going south to the Techiman market? Those are the people witches have caught and turned into animals. And the smoked bush-meat for sale in the Accra market? Have you not seen it? That too is people caught by witches.

More than one person mentioned those herds of witchcraft victims bound for southern markets. The image is worth examining further. Rather than consuming their victims, witches are now seen as trapping, storing and eventually selling them for money. The need for cash, and the fact that women are trading to accumulate it, is the background of most talk of witchcraft. Women are more mobile than they were, travelling farther away from home on their trading expeditions. They are said thus to have more opportunity to buy witchcraft medicine and to make the contacts needed to dispose of the people they catch. Adduced in evidence of the increase in witchcraft is the fact that women clearly have more cash than they formerly disposed of.

Note that, in this new view of witchcraft, witches are still providing meat. However, that meat is now obtained not to satisfy their own hunger but rather, to satisfy a foreign hunger and their desire for cash rather than meat. This is a trade in which Mamprusi see themselves being consumed by southerners in exchange for the cash they need to buy those very goods which proceed from the south. This deeply shameful witches' commerce resembles another, equally disreputable trade. Those 'herds' of witchcraft victims recall the northerners, trapped as slaves and bound for sale in the south. Witnesses of the slave trade were still alive in the 1960s and Mamprusi participated in the trade as traders and as victims. Those who now speak of the witches' trade have certainly heard descriptions of the slave trade.

The slave trade may have vanished, but the dependence of the north on the south has increased. In 1963, when floods separated the north and south of Ghana for some weeks, the king complained to me that people had become dependent on paraffin, matches and salt, all of which came from the south. Now, many more industrially produced goods have displaced those obtained locally, and all, except what is smuggled or imported across international borders, enter the area from the south. Not only politically but also economically, southern domination of the north has become far more evident to far more of the population. New routes now connect the north with the rainforest markets of Ashanti and the giant coastal capital at Accra. Lorry traffic has greatly increased. Techiman is typical of the new markets opened to northern produce, and its development is a mixed blessing to the north. North-south trade is not in itself new but the volume, and some of the goods exchanged, are. In the 1960s, lorries carrying industrial goods, forest fruit and sugar were almost unknown in the Mamprussi area but they arrived every market day in the summer of 1991, often carrying cereal crops and domestic animals on the return journey. The result of the increased trade is that local prices have risen as livestock is bought up for sale in the south. Local meat consumption has fallen drastically and it seems that in times of poor harvest in the south cereal crops too become scarce in the north as they are bought up to feed southern towns.

At the same time, cash is ever more essential, and the needs of women, who have always been responsible for their own cash outlay, and often that of their young children, may well have increased more dramatically than those of men. In contrast with the 1960s, almost all women now wear some articles of Western clothing; children must pay for school attendance as well as school uniforms, where formerly both were subsidised. Western medicines, much more rarely used in the 1960s, are now routinely bought for cash in the markets.

Simultaneously, with the emergence of these new demands for cash, the economic autonomy of Mamprusi men has been undermined in ways which contrast with women's situation. This is clearest if one looks at trade. Mamprusi women were traders in the 1960s, but with few exceptions they traded locally in small quantities of cigarettes, kola nuts or cosmetics bought from men who controlled the long-distance trade. Women also sold food and beer which they processed from raw materials and sold in local markets or from their home. Women did not, and still never, trade directly in livestock. The livestock trade is traditionally a male preserve. Women are forbidden to kill any living domestic animal, and even fowls bred by women are sold in the market by men. Thus men rather than women are traders in domestic livestock, and it is men who have been most affected by increased demand from the south. Livestock has always been a form of savings but much of the accumulation was wiped out during the famine years 1983-85. It is unlikely that all men were affected equally, but many owners of small herds lost them. Similarly the gradual but notable decrease in bush animals has most directly affected men who hunted them and sold the meat.

By contrast, women have increased not only the spatial range and volume of their trade but also the range of other economic activities. In the 1960s Mamprusi women were not involved in all the phases of farming. They participated only in the sowing and harvesting of the crops. Since the famine period of the 1980s Mamprusi women, following the custom of neighbouring peoples, and partly in reaction to government exhortation, have begun hoeing crops – an activity formerly regarded as men's work. Some women now take full responsibility for their own farms, depending on men only to clear the bush before the initial sowing. Women who have acquired capital through trade may even pay men as hired agricultural labour. Thus some women may now control the sale of their own agricultural produce, where formerly they would have traded for cash to buy cereals, yam or the other foodstuffs they use to produce marketable processed food and beer. Women did not normally buy staple crops for home consumption. The norms of the traditional Mamprusi gender division of labour decree that men should provide staple cereal crops from their farming while women provide soup ingredients, some of which might be obtained from trade but which also might be processed from fruit or leaves collected in the bush. For women to provide cereal crops to make the daily porridge is an indication that men are failing to meet their basic domestic commitments and is a sign of economic crisis. It is not clear whether the increase in women's trading betokens such a crisis. What is evident is that the introduction of modern technology, in the form of irregularly operating piped water and grinding mills, has directly affected women, freeing them from some of their most time-consuming domestic work. Hence, more women have more time for trade and agriculture. Finally, though it still affects only a small sector of the population, there are now young women among the literate population who compete with young men for scarce employment in clerical and teaching jobs.

So horizons in the labour market have widened for women, albeit partly as a result of crisis, while men are experiencing greater competition in areas of trade, farming and even literate employment which they formerly controlled. Simultaneously, of course, the increase in lorry transport which underlies the whole trading process has made everyone more mobile, and the penetration of the northern countryside by commerce controlled from southern towns has made everyone dependent on cash. These changes are neatly mirrored in the image of human flesh, the witches' preferred food, satisfying hunger for meat in the south, whence come the goods Mamprusi buy for cash. The specific changes in practice which I have noted above all show signs of a loss of confidence among Mamprusi in respect of their power to control and defend themselves against the attacks of witches. It is the increased frequency and virulence of these attacks which Mamprusi say has forced them to use new witch-finding techniques and to send Mamprusi women to the witches' villages. A similar increase in the virulence of attack by witches has been widely reported in the past in the anthropological literature in association with similar changes in local economies.[5]

Why Women are Evil Witches

Mamprusi believe that women should play a supportive role in their relations with senior men, never directly opposing or criticism them, much less expressing aggressive emotion. Accordingly female witchcraft may be viewed as female aggression deflected to the supernatural sphere. In contrast they regard male use of witchcraft as directed to legitimate ends.[6] Indeed succession to major royal office is seen as attended by veritable wars of witchcraft, performed by well defended princes who deflect dangerous attack away form themselves, thus harming 'innocent bystanders', that is, victims of these duels or wars who are not directly engaged but simply suffer, as would civilians caught on a battlefield. And they also see the death of major chiefs as resulting from the more powerful witchcraft of their successors.

Among men the ingestion of medicine, which is the basis of witchcraft, is but part of an essential activity. Not only princes but household heads, and even young married men, consume medicines to activate and strengthen all their innate capacities – from sexual potency to the ability to farm, hunt, trade or pass academic examinations. Taking medicine to increase such powers is normal and expected of men. Often implicit in the medication, which may be shared among kin, is the annihilation of rival powers wielded by competitors. For women to consume medicine is anomalous. It runs counter to the ideal image of women as supportive and deferential rather than competitive. Yet, as I will show below, Mamprusi know full well that women are not simply supportive and deferential. Moreover, though men consume their medicines in secret, they may share medicines with trusted daughters, sisters or wives, and women are rarely unaware of the fact, if men in their household are taking medicine.

Mamprusi share a Gonja view which idealises the non-aggressive woman but they invert the Gonja equation in which rank is subordinate to gender.[7] If a Gonja woman chief is a woman first and only then a chief, chiefship, when held by a Mamprusi woman, seems to obliterate gender. For that reason I have translated the term *pwaanaba* (literally *Pwa'a*, woman; *naba*, king/chief) as 'female king'. Mamprusi women chiefs wear male clothing. Unlike the Gonja female chiefs, who do not seem to have unique attributes, the role of the Mamprusi *pwaanaba* is unique (Drucker-Brown, 1975: 84-8, 128). The senior *pwaanaba* of two is responsible for the king's palace during the interregnum and has her own bodyguard of warriors, whose unique titles parallel those attached to the kingship. She also has custody of shrines which were important in the military defence of the kingdom. This association of female chiefship with military defence reverses the normal female role, which holds women to be dependent on men for their defence. In other respects, too, *pwaanaba* reverses women's normal expectations. *Pwaanaba* must leave her husband in order to take up office (married women normally live and are buried in their husband's compound) and she acquires an official 'husband' as part of her court. Most revealing, however, are the attributes of the female king's physical person. No one may enter her presence immediately after having had sexual intercourse lest they become barren, and women become barren if they see her while they are menstruating.[8] The female king is also forbidden to enter the presence of a living king. I believe this is because he is responsible for the fertility of all living things and her power to cause sterility would seem to endanger those powers. Far from being 'above all, a woman' the female king reverses the fertility associated with her sex.

The ways in which rank and gender are related for the Mamprusi are further illuminated by the legend of the first *pwaanaba*, who won her title through her victory over men. It also offers further insight into their reasons why women rather than men are 'bad witches'.

This is the origin of the female kingship:

> *There was once a king who was threatened by a commoner so powerful he was able to defeat all the warriors and princes the king sent against him. Seeing that the princes and warriors had failed, one of the king's daughters begged to be allowed to try her hand at defeating her father's enemy. She dressed in her most beautiful clothes and on market day she passed before the commoner where he sat outside his house. He instantly fell in love with her and married her. She then persuaded her husband to tell her the secrets of all his medicines, and one day, when he was away from home, searched them out of their hiding places and spoiled them all. In one version she literally subverted them: she put on the ground those which had to be kept aloft, and lifted up those which had to be kept on the ground. She put those in water which had to be kept dry and broke those which had to be kept intact. In another version she makes a fire and boils water in a huge pot into which she throws all the medicines. When the power of the medicines was thus destroyed, the princess sent a message to her father that the time had come for him to send his forces against her husband. The commoner was thus vanquished and, in gratitude and commemoration, her father made the princess a female king.*

Note that her feminine charms endeared the princess to her victim and her wit enabled her to learn the secrets of his medicine, but it was her control of the domestic household which gave her access to the medicine and enabled her to spoil them. This is a story about the dangerous dependence of men on their wives. It also illustrates the ways in which women's power in the domestic domain cannot be controlled by men. Men are vulnerable to feminine charms, and at some point every man must travel, entrusting to his wife the possessions he leaves behind.

Other myths of kingship, as well as simple folk tales, tell similar stories. The political significance of men's dependence on women is unmistakably reflected in the Mamprusi foundation myth, explaining the division of the original kingdom which gave rise to the Mamprusi and Dagomba polities. In this sacred legend the old and blind king calls his favourite wife to tell her that he has chosen her son as his successor. Instead a wicked co-wife attends him, pretending to be her rival. Hearing the king's plan, she informs her son, who kills the favourite, thus causing his father's disappearance and unleashing a conflict which divides the kingdom. Mamprusi would certainly agree with the Spanish proverb which asserts that 'Women are the root of all evil' (*No hay mal que por mujer no venga*). Why should it be so? Mamprusi women, with their extremely deferential manner in the presence of men, appear to be less independent than the women of neighbouring, less centralised and less hierarchical societies. The reason lies, I believe, in the unusual powers which some women do attain and in the nature of that power within the hidden hierarchy of the domestic domain.

The Ranking of Women

In the Mamprusi kinship system women's relationships with one another and the segregation of women from men in the Mamprusi household are crucial. The potential conflict among co-wives which exists in all polygynous societies is part here of a highly stratified domestic order. The hierarchy among the wives of a Mamprusi husband is based strictly on the order of marriage. In households with four wives or more there will be a further division between the first three 'senior wives' ranked among themselves, and the junior wives, who are also individually ranked. The authority of the first wife with regard to all others is unquestionable. A Mamprusi senior wife organises the essential domestic activities of junior women, such as carrying water, collecting firewood and preparing food for cooking. She divides and serves the food to be distributed by junior women to the men, the children and to other women. In larger households she may organise and oversee the brewing of beer, the making of shea butter and locust-bean (*dawadawa*) soup, or their production and marketing of other products. Moreover, in all households, a senior wife has authority over the children of junior wives, and young children sleep in her room once they are weaned.

In a well ordered Mamprusi household junior and senior women form cohesive, if hierarchically ordered groups. Ideally, children are separated early from their mothers to join a group of half-siblings, subject to the authority of senior women or young men. Young women, joining such households as junior wives, often rebel by running away. More often than not their male kin return them to their husbands. The vision of such women inadvertently becoming witches may well be a response to the rebellious emotions of junior wives. Certainly the image of a senior witch or witches recruiting a junior woman by surreptitiously feeding her medicine, which then impels her to kill her own child or a co-wife's child in order to feed them all, is a nightmare which encapsulates many of the tensions common among women in the large polygynous Mamprusi households.

Nevertheless, Mamprusi value polygyny highly. Chiefs and important elders often have more than ten wives. It used to be said in the 1960s that a Mamprusi man with only one wife was a bachelor. It is still the case that such a man cannot expect to be an important chief. Traditionally the goal of a man should be to marry many wives, have many children, and prosper through their farming activities and those of their offspring. Women accept this view. Senior women encourage their husbands to take junior wives and may find younger women for them to marry. Though the benefits of education and its increasing cost have led some to question these goals, the demands of the rural agricultural economy continue to reinforce the desire for large polygynous families. But it is well known that it is no easy task to control a polygynous household. A man whose wives fight, who do not show him proper deference or behave with appropriate loyalty – in short, a man who cannot control his household – cannot possibly aspire to chiefship or to any position of political significance, and it is well known that only a man with a well organised, helpful senior wife can control a household.

The manner in which a senior wife controls her household may be well known but it is never publicly demonstrated. The segregation of men and women in the Mamprusi household ensures this. Senior Mamprusi men have rooms in which their wives visit, where they eat and entertain guests. Women occupy their own rooms and the areas of the compound used for domestic tasks. Men visit their wives' rooms more rarely than women enter their husbands' more public space. Only junior men sleep with their wives in the women's rooms. Senior men receive their wives in their own rooms. Only senior men have their own rooms, while a woman has the right to a room of her own once she has borne a child or two. In general, women pass freely through the household space. Unlike Tallensi women, a Mamprusi woman is not forbidden to look into her husband's granary or to enter the places where domestic animals are kept. Men's control of women in the Mamprusi household may well impress the visitor, who sees senior men occupying the more public space and notes the elaborately deferential manner in which women kneel to greet and serve men. However, longer acquaintance reveals the dependence of senior men on their wives for the smooth functioning of a complex household organisation.

A king's wife, as the myth of the origin of the kingdom illustrates, is in a position to influence major political events. Among the wives of the king the first three should be greeted by visitors to the palace, both with conversation and with material gifts. In competition for royal office all gifts pass through the hands of a king's senior wife. The gown and hat used to make a new chief are kept overnight in her room. The senior widow of a dead king is present at the installation rituals performed for his successor. But all these activities and the opportunities for influence they imply are hidden from public view.

By contrast with men, then, the power of women is relatively invisible. Men too use some of their powers secretly but male powers are demonstrated openly in the exercise of office or in the public councils which men attend. On innumerable occasions there is public display of precedence and rank among Mamprusi men. Men are subject to some degree of control through the expression of public opinion in the court councils they so frequently attend. Women have no public role. They do not normally appear in court. Their power is wielded only in the privacy of the domestic domain, in their rooms, which are synonymous with potential divisions of a patrilineage's estate. The blind king, unable to distinguish one wife from another, is not un-like most men, who may be kept in ignorance by their wives. Women, I am suggesting, are potentially subversive, because the power they wield is not publicly recognised and hence is unaccountable.

It can be argued that accusations of witchcraft are directed against vulner-able rather than powerful women. Interestingly this is the path witchcraft accusation is supposed to have taken in the Salem witchcraft trials, where resentment of the most powerful figures in the community is believed to have been translated into accusation against their less powerful associates (Boyer and Nissenbaum, 1974). It is true that, among Mamprusi more vulnerable women are often those to whom the accusations stick, but accusations are frequently directed against women who are outstanding in some way.[9] Often junior women accuse their seniors. In general, however if accusations of witchcraft are to become significant, they must be supported by men. Women are doubly threatened by witchcraft. They must fear both the attack of witches and accusations of witchcraft.

Conclusion

Mamprusi witchcraft accusations appear to be significant attempts to control the behaviour of women. Mamprusi men should be able to defend themselves and their women and children against witchcraft, just as they should be able to control their wives. Both witchcraft and adultery threaten the power of senior men to control women, and the exemplary punishments for witchcraft and for adultery in the past indicate that women were regarded as needing to be terrorised as well as cajoled into submission.

In the nineties however, belief in the increased activity of witches, searching for money rather than meat, seemed to respond to new anxieties. It expressed the increasing difficulty everyone had in finding the cash which had suddenly become essential. Mamprusi men and women have always had independent sources of money. Men have always paid women, including their own wives, for kola nuts or beer. But now, in addition to goods which are relative luxuries, cash is needed for a wide range of goods. In times of food scarcity the staple cereals must be bought. Clothing, Western medicine, school fees, are increasingly regarded as necessities, and women's trading activity – expanded with the general increase in trade – has become more central to the rural economy.

Women have always presented a problem for male control, but it would seem that they are becoming harder to control. As their cash income becomes more important to the survival of the domestic household the increased mobility essential to their trading activities makes it easier for them to evade men. Modern education, like changes in the economy, has introduced new aspirations. Among those Mamprusi who desire an education for their children the very nature of the ideal household is being questioned. The cost to men of maintaining many wives and children is being regarded as problematic. Evangelical Christianity, recently introduced among Mamprusi, also supports new views of family life.

Keith Thomas argued (1970:73-4) that in Tudor England witchcraft prosecutions increased as people were encouraged, by the existence of new though ineffective laws, to avoid the neighbourly charity they would have previously felt obliged to provide for the more vulnerable members of their village communities. Charity and self-interest were in conflict, and the guilt of those who should have been charitable made victims of those who should have been, but were no longer, the recipients of charity. At the same time the Reformation had undermined belief in protection against witchcraft provided by the Church.

One could argue that an analogous conflict exists in the Mamprusi region between changing aspirations and traditional norms. Women are expected to be submissive and subservient to men and to senior women, but economic necessity decrees that they must farm, travel and trade in order to provide for their families. This increasing autonomy is paralleled by frustration among men, who see their own activities threatened as those of their wives expand. Belief in the increased frequency and virulence of witchcraft, as well as new ways of dealing with witches, reflects not so much a change in the nature of female power as a loss of control by Mamprusi men over their own economic and political environment. The need of men for women's economic support, and the increasing autonomy of women which that implies, conflicts with the traditional definition of women as ideally controlled by men. Mamprusi have always regarded women as potentially subversive. I have argued here that the fear of witchcraft has grown as men's dependence on women has increased, and the increasing autonomy of women threatens both men's control of women and the control by senior women of their juniors. Fear of witchcraft can thus be seen as a measure of the importance of that normally hidden female hierarchy, on which relations between men and women in Mamprusi are precariously based.

Acknowledegement

The author is grateful to the ESRC (Grant No. R000232709) for research support and field work in northern Ghana between 1991 and 1993. This enabled her to return to the Mamprusi region and to analyse her data. The article is based on fieldwork from 1963 to 1965 and during brief periods in 1985, 1986, 1991 and 1992. Thanks are also due to the editor of *Africa* for permission to reprint this paper which appeared in issue 63 (4) 1993.

Endnotes

1   Esther Goody (1970) has observed that the horrific public executions of witches in Gonja, a neighbouring kingdom, must have been 'exemplary'.

2   I was more frequently told of the horrific punishments and places of execution in connection with adultery than in connection with the punishment of witchcraft.

3   The verb commonly used is *wobri*, 'to chew and swallow'.

4   Esther Goody's analysis of witchcraft beliefs among the neighbouring Gonja reveals much that is common to the Mamprusi both in the general attribution of evil witchcraft to women and in other particulars. She notes, for example, the significance of dancing with a horse's tail at the annual Damba ceremonies. The horse's tail contains protective anti-witchcraft medicines, and she writes of the Gonja, 'To hold a tail [while dancing] is to be elegant, princely, powerful, and safe', Mamprusi say of the dance, which they too perform, 'Women are also witches but women cannot hold a tail', meaning that women may practise witchcraft but do not use it, as men do, in defence of others.

5   For examples see Nadel, (1952); Ardener, (1970); Strathern, (1982).

6   cf Esther Goody's (1970:207-44) analysis of why the Gonja cast women in the role of evil witches. She argues that Gonja women are ideally benevolent and supportive, aggressive only in defence of their children; but that women are 'denied the legitimate expression of aggressive impulses', and it is this denial which gives rise to the Gonja view that evil witches are women – a view accepted by women as well as men. Goody emphasises that men are widely believed to use witchcraft for legitimate ends, to defend themselves and their dependants and in furtherance of their own goals, particularly in pursuit of office.

7   Esther Goody writes (1970:242) of Gonja women that; "even when they hold political or ritual roles, [they] are above all women. And as such they cannot be permitted to act aggressively without endangering the dominance of men and throwing into doubt the benevolence of the affective relationships on which the domestic group centres."

8   Even her own daughter would not enter her mother's hut because she was menstruating when we visited the *pwaanaba* together in 1991.

9   The women accused in cases reported by Goody include a female chief and healer.

Bibliography

Ardener, E., 1970. Witchcraft, Economics and the Continuity of Belief. In M. Douglas (ed.) *Witchcraft Confessions and Accusations*. Pp. 141-61. ASA Monographs, No. 9. London: Tavistock.

Boyer, P., and Nissenbaum, S., 1974. *Salem Possessed*. Cambridge, Mass.: Harvard University Press.

Drucker-Brown, S., 1975 *Ritual Aspects of Mamprusi Kingship*. African Research Centre Documents 8. African Studies Centre, University of Cambridge.

— 1988-89. Local wars in northern Ghana. In S. Drucker-Brown (ed.), *Local Warfare in Africa, special issue of Cambridge Anthropology*. 13 (2), 86-107.

— 1989. Mamprusi installation ritual and centralization. *Man*. 24: 485-501.

— 1991. Horse, dog and donkey: the making of a Mamprusi king. *Man*. 27: 71-90.

Evans-Pritchard, E. E, 1937. *Witchcraft, Oracles and Magic among the Azande*. Oxford: Clarendon Press.

Field, M. J., 1960. *Search for Security*. London: Faber.

Goody, Esther N., 1970. Legitimate and illegitimate aggression. In M. Douglas (ed.), *Witchcraft Confessions and Accusations*. Pp. 207-45. ASA Monographs, No. 9. London: Tavistock.

Le Roy Ladurie, Emmanuel, 1987. *Jasmine's Witch*. Aldershot: Scolar Press.

Maier, D. J. E., 1983. *Priests and Power: the case of the Dente shrine in nineteenth century Ghana*. Bloomington, Ind.: Indiana University Press.

Marwick, M.G., 1967. The Sociology of Witchcraft in a Central African tribe. In J. Middleton (ed.), *Magic, Witchcraft and Curing*. Pp. 101-27. Austin: University of Texas Press.

Nadel, S., 1952. Witchcraft in four African societies. *American Anthropologist*. 54, 18-29.

Strathern, A., 1982. Witchcraft, greed, cannibalism and death: some related themes from the New Guinea Highlands. In M. Bloch and J. Parry (eds.) *Death and the Regeneration of Life*. Pp. 111-33. Cambridge: Cambridge University Press.

Tait, David, 1967. Konkomba sorcery. In J. Middleton (ed.), *Magic, Witchcraft and Curing*. Pp. 155-71. Austin: University of Texas Press

Thomas, Keith, 1970. The relevance of social anthropology to the historical study of English witchcraft. In M. Douglas (ed.) *Witchcraft Confessions and Accusations*. Pp. 47-81. ASA Monographs, No. 9 .London: Tavistock.

"FEAR WOMAN":
THE IMAGE OF WOMEN IN CONTEMPORARY GHANAIAN POPULAR PERFORMANCE ARTS

Esi Sutherland-Addy

FEAR WOMAN AND LIVE LONG is the full wording of the wry, popular maxim which has found its way into contemporary media, such as the popular culture of putting mottos and sayings on the backs of public buses and wooden lorries (known as "trotro"); naming shops, stalls, houses and domestic animals; and composition of popular song forms such as highlife.

In a few high life songs such as the song **Sii-Sii-Sii** featured on the 2000 CD by Tumi Ebo Ansa entitled **Kente Dress Dance** the full saying appears in the refrain:

Suro basia na nyin kyer oo	Fear woman and live long, indeed,
Kwame Ata, suro basia na nyin	
kyer (Fanti)	Kwame Ata, fear woman and live long.

In the song *Yewo Adze a Oye* by the highlife maestro, A.B.Crentsil, the maxim is stated as a modified form of the initial fragment *Iguee suro basia* (Fanti) (Cape Coast town, fear woman).

The Axiom, **Fear Woman and live long** has been selected here for a number of reasons. Firstly, as a maxim it fits in the realm of popular culture from which we shall be drawing archetypes, secondly it embodies an ideology in a pithy phrase which, being enigmatic, lends itself to a variety of interpretations and thus allows one to explore different facets of its meaning within a number of likely contexts. Finally, we find it apt to project only the initial fragment for symbolic reasons. Like many other maxims and proverbs only the first fragment of the saying is actually verbalized in discourse.[1]

The fragment is deliberately left hanging to be either verbally completed by the listener or to be understood and interpreted as part of the process of communication. Since the speaker and listener share a body of knowledge and a culture of speaking which thrives on cryptic sayings and their interpretation, there is often an encoded subtext, the enigma of which is enhanced by indirection through the technique of partial expression. This invites the decoder to experience emotions such as empathy with the sentiments alluded to (which could take forms such as outrage, or the recall of an experience which tends to exemplify the maxim etc.). The decoders may externalize their reactions by snorting in disgust, laughing at the ingenuity, uttering expressions of affirmation and so on. There is also the possibility of a verbal reaction such as the verbalization of the missing fragment of the axiom. In this case the encoder would say/write/sing "fear woman" and the decoder would say "...and live long". The decoder could also establish a discourse surrounding the maxim.

This is a very pervasive aspect of Akan speaking culture, as it is of many other peoples of Africa. People revel in the art of oblique reference, innuendo and allusion, where what is spoken refers to much that is not spoken but understood within a shared culture of mature language use. The ability to provide the missing piece, even if one does not actually utter it, draws one into becoming a full participant in the discourse surrounding the maxim and sharing the nuances of meaning and often the ideology that it evokes. Therefore, even though it is a common practice in conversation for one person to initiate an aphorism and another to complete it as part of a harmonious discussion, the fact that the second half is not verbally supplied, also gives conversation and discourse a certain flavour of shared but unspoken understanding of the mores, values and ideologies. This is seen as being particularly apt in an ironic way because in the case of women's speech culture, there is much that is established by innuendo and allusion. These are mechanisms for exercising the right to self-expression in situations where it is not encouraged. Thus, even though in the case of the maxim, **fear woman**... women and womanhood are being viewed in a misogynistic light, this essay, in so far as it exposes the view for what it is, interrogates the validity of the assumptions underlying the maxim, from a woman's point of view.

In this chapter, we shall be arguing that it is also an appropriate trope to characterize a misogynistic tendency in the psychology of Ghanaian society, which informs behaviour and attitudes towards women. A number of studies have sought to demonstrate this negative ideology in societies around the world and its emanation in literature and film. Minneke Schipper deduced from her study of African proverbs that women were the source of all evil. She thus entitled her 1991 book on the subject **Source of All Evil: African Proverbs and Sayings on Women**. The chapter will sketch archetypical emanations of this socio-psychological tendency especially as it appears in two forms of popular art, namely highlife lyrics and feature video films. In seeking to establish the entrenched nature of this tendency, we shall refer to other forms of oral literature, such as proverbs and folktales, because they have acted as vehicles carrying these popular ideologies which act as a guide to and a reflector of social attitudes and behaviour. This appears particularly important because the contemporary performance arts refer closely to the traditional forms for archetypes, themes, plots, motifs and literary devices. In order to highlight the misogynistic attitudes which we shall be seeking to establish, we shall begin the discussion by contrasting it with other attitudes towards women that appear to be equally engrained in the social psyche. Ontological thought systems give women then an elevated and primordial role, in contrast with the social view. In the course of the discussion, we shall also acknowledge some emerging trends in the contemporary performance culture which go against the grain of the dominant ideology.

There appear to be perceptibly different, even contradictory tendencies in the view of women and womanhood. In the Akan world view[2] the concept of the African mother placed on a pedestal is illustrated in a number of ways. Firstly, the Earth is revered for being the source of life and its sustenance. She is named Yaa (Twi) or Efua (Fanti) and is evoked during ritual or formal occasions through libation and through classic verse. In a formal dirge from Kwahu Oda we find the following lines,

Grandmother Earth, *Asase Yaa Amponyinamoa*
It is grandmother that is covered with myriads of paths. (Nketia, 1955:194).
In the notes, Nketia describes grandmother as, "Earth, mystical Ancestress. Goddess of fertility". In this apostrophe the ancestress is linked to the primordial feminine principle of the Akan people.
Secondly it is entirely acceptable within the Akan view of the person, to ascribe positive features of motherhood to men who may be praised for being caring, and nurturing leaders, for example. The term *obaatan* (true mother) is the ultimate accolade for one who is deemed to have all the attributes required of a true nurturer. Indeed it is not uncommon for men to also earn this accolade. In the classic forms of praise poetry or dirge poetry imagery may occur which lends virtues associated with the female gender to the addressee. For example,
Although a man, you are a mother to children (emphasis mine). A man who takes another's child for his own. (Nketia 1955:195)

Indeed, a review of the rare anthology of classic Akan dirges from all Akan speaking areas by J.H.K. Nketia reveals that women are frequently the subject of high-sounding classic praise poetry in which their roles are highlighted and given deep significance in public life such as in the following dirge:

Your Grandmother is Akwaa of Hwerebe
The woman that wears a hat, holds a gun and wears ammunition belt.
            * * *
Grandmother Akwaa comes from Hwerebe,
Where mere women use skulls in the Apiredi dance.(Nketia, 1955:152).

Their private role is also highlighted:

Mother Aba, the great Breast that children suck,
Mother Aba, the great wooden Food Bowl around which
children gather,
Mother, you know that when people confer together privately
behind a house,
They do so with people of their own flesh and blood.
Mother, you know our plight:
Don't go too far away from us.
(Nketia, 1955:184)

The idealization of the woman as mother does filter into creative works in popular culture such as highlife particularly in extrapolation of proverbs such as *Ɛna wu a na abusua asa.* (when mother dies, the clan is depleted) or the more metaphorical *"Gyeamerakuku, ɔrebɛwu ama ɛsie adwiri"* (The queen termite: she is going to die for the anthill to crumble)

Again there are a few examples of commemorative songs in the popular domain, which are odes to the lives of extraordinary women. One of these is the song extolling the feats of Yaa Asantewa, queenmother of Effiduase, who led the Asante in a war against the British in 1900, when the Chiefs appeared unable to take up the mantle to defend their nation. The song goes as follows:

Kokrohinkro, Yaa Asantewaa,
The woman who fought at the battlefront
She has indeed left us a legacy

This positive and elevated view of women in Akan classic literary forms of praise poetry, dirge and mythology are countered overwhelmingly by negative perspectives of women which may be found in proverbs, folktales and topical songs.

Akan adages and proverbs for example are quite inter-generic and often form the building blocks for many different forms of literature, including contemporary popular forms such as highlife lyrics. In this rich literary corpus we find observations and reflections about women which dwell on a number of negative facets of the female social persona. The following interpreted sample of proverbs is illustrative of this tendency:

a) It is out of place for women to venture out of the domestic space into the public space "The woman sells garden eggs and not gun powder" or "When a tall woman carries palm nuts, the hornbill eats them"

b) However great a woman may be, she can only be validated through the agency of a man: "If a woman buys a gun, it must lean against the wall of a man's room" or: "The beauty of a woman is attributed to her husband".

c) Stereotypical disdain for elderly women: "If the old lady is quarrelsome, she makes her own fence".

A number of popular sayings and idiomatic expressions intensify the impression that women are feeble minded and inconsiderate and want to gain easy access to wealth and status etc., after the men have toiled to achieve these. For example, "women love affluence and hate debt", or "women love the luxurious life". The phrase *Mmaa Pe Sokoo* is the title of a hit tune by Abrantie Amakye Dede. The first stanza goes

Women love the luxurious life
It is the luxurious life that women love
The women of today, if you have no money they do not love you,
Women love the luxurious life
It is the luxurious life that women love.

In an even less edifying interpretation of this perceived penchant of women for worldly goods, Kwadwo Ahenkan sings the song *Mmaa mpɛ ohia*, the refrain of which is provided here in both the original Twi and English translation because of the intensification of derision and satire achieved by alliteration in Twi.

Mpɛ, mpɛ, ee	Dislike, dislike
Maa mpɛ ohia aa	Women dislike poverty
Cedi na egyee	It is only the cedi that "gets it"[3]

From the heritage of folktales, a number of archetypes of women can also be gleaned. For example, the headstrong girl who insists on choosing her own partner; the wife who cannot keep secrets; the wicked stepmother; the old witch; the jealous co-wife. These archetypical characters then act out motifs which are reinterpreted in contemporary form and provide the building blocks for the highlife song, feature video film, concert party and other forms of theatre, as well as literature.

As indicated above however, we shall be concentrating on the perpetuation and accentuation of the negative aspects of the feminine persona in two main performance genres, the first being highlife and the second, video films.

This chapter takes due cognizance of the observations made by Asante-Darko and Van Der Geest in their essay "Male Chauvinism: Men and Women in Ghanaian Highlife Songs" which appeared in **Female and Male in West Africa** (Oppong ed.: 1983). In this essay, the authors examined the validity of using highlife lyrics as a source of data on gender relations, particularly with respect to polygynous and polycoital relations. They concluded that these lyrics confirm the ideology of male domination in Akan society, but hypothesized that when more women became highlife artistes, they would be able to use the form to make ideological statements that went against the grain of the then dominant view and assert their own view of gender relations. Two decades after the publication of that article, it is not possible for us to firmly support this assertion, which we would have been delighted to corroborate. Women highlife singers have actually declined in number. It would appear that women have chosen not to engage in the arena of highlife music, but to shift into the realm of gospel music and to enter into another realm and discourse. Examining the social and economic factors which may have led to this shift would be the subject of another paper. Suffice it to say that among the few women who have recorded highlife music over the last ten to fifteen years, we can single out Akosua Agyepong for offering an alternative discourse. In her songs, Agyepong questions gender relations and vividly sketches moments in the lives of women.

In her song *Meye Obaa*, the persona is a young woman confidently singing

I am a woman
I am a woman

The Lord God made us women
He made us well

It is significant that in the second stanza the phrase "we are women"....is used indicating that Agyepong identifies completely with other young women and sees herself as a role model. The message of the song is rather conventional, for she importunes young women to listen to their parents, act in a chaste manner and respect their womanhood.

In later songs recorded with the group Nakorex, Akosua, the earnest and coy girl has matured into a defiant woman. These songs are about relations between men and woman in marriage. For example in her song, *Eka bi nie* (What Kind of Debt is This?) she relates the life of a woman who is trying her hand at trading but goes bankrupt because her husband is indebted and not only leaves all expenses to her but borrows her capital until she is over burdened with debt. Here there is a double entendre in the phrase "this type of debt, I cannot pay," which refers to her financial debt and the frustrating burden of a man whom she cannot continue to carry.

The song *Aware Bone* is a total declaration of independence by a young woman who defiantly refuses to be forced into marriage. She openly declares *me ara na mede me ho na me se medi me sigya na adɛn* ("it is I who own myself and I say I shall remain unmarried so what," literally). Given the status of the young unmarried woman in society, this is a truly insolent statement but expresses the inner feelings of many a young woman. Buttressed by the fact that at the time of recording her songs and performing them in public, Agyepong was youthful, beautiful, vibrant and unmarried, she lent a vraisemblance to the personae in her songs.

Unfortunately, Agyepong has not recorded any further albums since the early 1990s. Thus her work can be likened to a flare which flashed brightly and briefly. She has however, indicated that having taken time off to have her children, she will soon come out with another album.[4] Perhaps even in its brevity, Akosua Agyepong's work is the exception which proves the rule.

Next is examined the prevalent way in which women are presented in highlife music. Physical attributes as well as desirable and undesirable personality traits are favorite themes. It is interesting to note that stock phrases related to men are quite difficult to identify.

One framework in which men are depicted associates them with youth and another with money, literally on both sides of the coin. The following expressions which are used frequently by the mega star Abrantie Amakye Dede make the point: **Iron Boy** which is derived from the slang *a – young – boy e* *e* which gained currency in the singing of popular Akan songs and means "young boy". In his album named **Iron Boy,** he has a song called *Sika ne Barima* (Money is Man(hood)). *Onni-Sika Abrantie* (the penniless guy) apears in other works. *Sika Ye Abrantie* (money is the guy) is the title of a song by Super Nana Yaw Ofori. In other words the worth of the young man is weighed in terms of his ability to spend money, preferably publicly or ostentatiously. As regards personal attributes, it would appear that more often than not it is those of the female persona that are dwelt upon and objectified. There are some stock phrases which may be seen as gender neutral, such as *mebroni* which has been interpreted in terms of lightness of skin as "my fair lady/gentleman" or conversely *tuntum se wuo* "dark as a black duiker", which sentiment has been individualized by Amakye Dede as *Tuntum-bracki ee*! a tautology half in Akan and half in an Akan-ised version of the English word "black". It has also been adapted by George Jarah as *obibini ahoɔfɛ* (African beauty). Most others however have to do with women, particularly parts of their bodies. Those most frequently referred to are:

a)   the eyes: *n'ani te sɛ nwira*- her eyes are like white calico;

b)   the legs and feet especially as they appear adorned with footwear;

c)   the neck: *nekon te sɛ adenkum* – her neck is like a gourd or *nekon atwitwa akonakono* – her neck is folded attractively and and *nekon te sɛ abaduaba* – her neck is like that of a fertility doll;

e)   and the teeth: *esi a egyere da mu* – front teeth with a gap in the middle.

f)   The stature of the women is also described: *ɔbaa ahomateaa"* – slender – thread woman.

g)   the hair may also be complemented: *Ne tirewii te sɛ sirikyi ahama* – her hair is like silk thread;

h)   A rare one which may be idiosyncratic of George Jarah is *Wabeti sɛ akyekyedee* – Your shoulder line like that of a tortoise.

In addition to the above are enlightening revelations about desirable personality traits and social behaviour within the culture.

Nowhere are the above traits better woven together with desirable character traits to mould the popular image of the ideal woman than in the 1999 remix of **Seewaa Akoto,** an old song by Yamoah's band on the album **The Best of Yamoah** vol.3. It is worth noting that this song is once again enjoying immense popularity as it did in the early 1970s. Its lyrics set out the paradigm of womanhood, according to the dominant patriarchal ideology, both in terms of physical attributes and personality traits. The very tempo of the melody of the song is slow sensuous and yet sedate;

Se mmaa yinara te sɛ me	If all women were like this sister of mine
nua obaa yi a	
Seewaa Akoto	Seewaa Akoto
Anka nnye ene se yere bre yi	We would not be suffering so much
Se eka ahoofe ne ti nkoara	Were it a matter of beauty and destiny alone,
Anka otuo rennto wo kwae	Never, would there be a gunshot
mu da o	in the deep forest
Nano ne kasa Seewaa Akoto	Her manner of speech, Seewaa Akoto
te se nso wunu	is like cool water
Obue n'ani a Seewa Akoto te	When she opens her eyes, Seewaa
se nwira	Akoto is like white calico
Ne nan ne guarantee⁵ se	With platform shoes on her feet, when you
wo hu no a wo befa no la	see her you will fall for her
Suban papa akyinee nni ho,	A good character, she has without *Ebo*
neho	a doubt
Bayi woano wo badwamu	Come and answer a case in public,
so deɛ	that, she
Onnyee bi da o koraa	has never, ever done.
Seewaa Akoto Ahoofe dua o	Sewaa Akoto, paragon of beauty,
Se eka ahoofe ne ti nkoara	Were it for beauty and destiny alone
Anka otuo rennto wo kwae	Gunshots would never be heard in the
mu da o	deep forest
Ompɛ nkrobo Seewaa	She does not engage in public quarrels,
	Seewaa
Akoto obu no ho	Akoto respects herself
Bayi woano wo badwamu	Come and answer a case in public,
so deɛ	that she
bi da o koraa.	has never, ever done.

These lyrics are quite explicit. They seek to set up a paragon of woman-hood. Seewaa Akoto is set apart from all women in the first line. She is pre-sented as a woman of exquisite beauty. The whiteness of her eyes, the pretti-ness of her feet and her sophisticated appearance contribute to building an image of exquisite physical beauty.

The traits that are given the greatest emphasis though are personality traits. This emphasis is achieved through the technique of repetition by putting the prominent ideas into the refrain "Come and answer a case in pub-lic: that she has never ever done". Seewaa Akoto is depicted as a placid person. She is endowed with saintly sanguinity, self-restraint and dignity especially in the public space.

Pitched against this picture – perfect lady are the personae found in the song *Mmaa Dooso* by Nana Kwame Ampadu. In this song, the composer piles on stereotypical types of behaviour which are deemed unacceptable among married women. Each verse of the song takes up one of these defects:

Ennye Mmaa nyinara na ye ware		It is not all women that one can marry
1)	*Afrakuma pε*	Afrakuma likes
	Akyin-kyin akyin-kyin dodo	To roam about too much
	Onni adagyee nso gya	She has no time to light up the hearth
	Obaa kraman	Dog-woman
2)	*Mekyere no*	When I teach her
	Birirbiara a onnhu	Anything, she cannot grasp it
	Ote hɔ tiboo	She sits there stupidly
	Odwan	Sheep
3)	*Afrakuma*	Afrakuma
	Krono	Thievery
	Obaa agyinamoa	Cat-woman
4)	*Enieden*	hot-headedness
	Ne asoden	and stubbornness
	Obaa abrekyie	Goat-woman
5)	*Obekasa saa*	She will complain incessantly
	Obaa-boniaye	ungrateful woman
	A n'ani nso adee	who is also disrespectful
	Obaa akoko	Chicken-woman
6)	*Neho aye fi*	She is dirty
	Dodo	Too dirty
	Obaa-prako	Pig-woman
7)	*Obaa nipa*	Human-woman
	Nipa ba Afrakuma	Human-born child Afrakuma
	Mmaa ee,	Women!!!
	Kenten woho	Get a grip of yourselves
	Na yemfrε wo	So that you can be called
	Obaa-nipa	Human-woman

This allegorical song portrays every-woman in the persona Afrakuma. With the range of ills that she embodies, Afrakuma is the direct opposite of Seewaa Akoto. She metaphorically takes on a quick succession of bestial natures, quite different from the consistent, cultured nature of Seewaa Akoto. The composer has perfect command of the Akan literary culture and is well known for his adaptation of tales to the highlife genre. In this particular instance he uses stock characters which are often deployed in the narrative culture. Allegory is used to biting effect, both because of what is left unsaid and what is said. Each beast is aptly chosen to trigger in the mind of the listener a set of images by association within the culture shared by the composer and his audience. The emotional impact of the song thus goes far beyond the brevity of the metaphors which are uttered. As we mentioned above, this technique is a key to the culture of speaking and literature in the ethnic cultures of Ghana.

It may be noted that unlike the tone of the author's voice in Seewaa Akoto which is satiated with delight and satisfaction, it can be deduced from the tone of disgust and frustration that the author's voice takes on in the latter song, that it represents the generic long-suffering man, who is obliged to put up with an ungainly and ill trained woman. The worst of his frustrations in stanza 2 is that even though he takes up the duty of the major party in the relationship to train the minor, the woman sits there sheepishly looking at him. In the long run after implying that she is a philandering, stupid, thieving headstrong, nagging, ungrateful, rude, filthy, beast of a woman; he has no choice but to question her humanity. In what appears to be an act of desperation, he commands her to recall that she is born human and to desist from letting down the race by pulling herself together and behaving like a human being. It may be noted once again, that as we have demonstrated in the examples above, womanhood is not only being defined through the agency of men but also almost exclusively from the point of view of their relationship to men.

Mmaa Dooso may be particularly striking because it attempts a startling compilation of the various forms of moral judgement passed on women. The stereotypes portrayed in this song however are treated in a variety of permutations through out the creative arts, not least among which are locally produced video films. After having viewed a considerable sampling of Ghanaian video films, one is likely to come away with the same sense of overwhelming evil, malevolence and at best passive aquiescence to abuse associated with women. These video films have taken a prominent position among the popular creative forms since the mid 1980s. Through their plots, they portray slices of contemporary, (mainly urban) life in Ghana. They are replete with evolving popular thought, stereotypes, norms and values. At the same time, they carry archetypes, motifs and even entire plots from traditional narrative culture. An additional element found in film is the exploitation of the visual properties of the medium to explore the area of myth, mysticism and religion. As we shall attempt to demonstrate, motifs from the mythical and religious world are reinterpreted in a rather melodramatic and distorted form, exploiting the ghoulish and magical rather than the deep "indigenous culture of knowing", which manifests itself in the field of traditional esotericism.

Additionally, being a dramatic form based on conflict, a number of contemporary conflicts are played out on the screen. It is important to note that overwhelmingly, the video films reveal a preference for the didactic moralistic treatment of themes. As we have discussed elsewhere,[6] the intention of these films is to expose social ills. Human character is generally depicted as being distorted by greed, envy, and a lust for sex, power and wealth. The declared intent of filmmakers is certainly didactic and that is all the more reason why the image of women is of great concern. In the 30 or so films studied, the role of the woman in the elaboration of the plot was striking. Women are usually portrayed in a secondary role in plots, limited to a space circumscribed within the life of the male protagonist. Women in the sample viewed are usually victims or the living embodiment of evil.

The woman is often a victim of her relationship with men. She may be subject to both emotional and physical abuse from men who may be cast in the role of husband, partner or gangster. In **Mataa, Our Missing Children** a married woman becomes an abused woman after she abandons her home in pursuit of life with a gangster-lover. She is lured into becoming a drug addict by the anti-hero protagonist. He abuses her physically, rejects her at will and sends her back to the humiliation of her conjugal home with impunity.

There is a significant number of films in which the woman becomes a victim simply because of her biological capacity to bear children. A review of Africanus Aveh's authoritative annotated filmography of over a hundred Ghanaian videofilms demonstrates this very clearly.[7] In this corpus there are at least twenty-two films which turn on a pregnancy or the childlessness of a woman. In all cases the question of pregnancy places the female persona in the position of victim. She must bear the brunt of the negative consequences of a shared act. In some cases such as happens with Shola in **When the Heart Decides,** the pregnant person is in a vulnerable position as domestic worker. She is therefore driven from the house and must fend for herself and her child on her own.

In another twist, the woman as victim appears to be too trusting and may fall victim to confidence tricksters. Akatsi and Akatsa in **Kanana** are two thieves escaping from their own town who seek refuge in a village under false pretenses. They are able to worm their way into the confidence of otherwise independent-minded women. Ignoring their husbands, they give their gold trinkets to Akatsi and Akatsa for safekeeping. The thieves abscond with the loot.

Women are also victims of other women. For example in **Heart of Gold**, Alice a married woman, puts her trust in an unmarried friend and being attracted by the false allure of money and freedom, takes the risk of abandoning the safety of her marriage only to find that her friend has taken her place.

It is highly significant that in all cases reviewed, women as victims bring the victimization on themselves by their repeated inability to judge character. It would appear from the recurrence of this motif that this is perceived as a genetic defect in the women which causes them to lack discernment.

Furthermore, many plots make women victims of their own envy, greed and stubbornness as we find in the storytelling tradition. It is instructive that most of the time the independent-minded woman also pays dearly for her independence, for it is depicted as either a grievous misjudgment or fatal stubbornness. For example a woman insists on going out to work, (**Heart of Gold**) or going to the city (**Dede**). In both of these cases, this decision to mentally and physically step out of the circumscribed domestic space, places the women in the wide wicked world with which they cannot cope. There is a sense in which they appear to be wilful juveniles, whose heedless behaviour brings calamities on themselves and on all associated with them. In **Mataa,** the independent Abena, sister of the protagonist, by refusing adamantly to tell her childhood sweet-heart that they had produced his child, denies herself the obvious opportunity of being spared when he later, as a detective, closes in on her brother. In other words, all these characters breach the bounds of their secure environment, by being adventurous or independent and immediately face irreversible ruin. It is somewhat refreshing to come across Nina in **The Power of Love**, who is forced to marry her father's creditor to save him from ruin but rebels by eloping with her childhood sweetheart on her wedding day.

Women are also viewed as the embodiment of evil. Viewing most of the video features as didactic moral narratives, womankind takes its place in the trinity of deadly traps: Drink, Money and Women. It is worth noting in passing that this approach is absolutely in line with the popular view even promulgated from the pulpit, whereby men are counselled against the false allure of *Nsa, sika, ne mmaa,* (drink, money and women). The irony that the majority of congregations listening to these sermons is made up of women churchgoers cannot be allowed to pass without mention!

The woman as embodiment of evil appears in many permutations. In one, the women victims discussed above may show signs of deep-seated insecurity, against which they may adopt desperate measures. For example the victims may do evil deeds in a vain bid to retain their status. A case in point is the wife of the tycoon, Kodua, in **The Other Side**. She finds herself totally out of her depth with her husband's newfound fortune. She is persistently put down and ignored by him and takes extreme measures to restore her dignity. She prepares a potion, which she puts in his soup to cause him to return to her. This desperate and derisory gesture clearly makes no difference to his attitude towards her as he, on taking a sip of the soup, becomes suspicious and refuses to eat it. She remains a victim and furthermore shares in his disgrace when the law eventually catches up with his dubious business practices. The wife in **The Other Side of the Rich** aided by her mother, puts a concoction containing menstrual blood in her husband's food to keep him on the straight and narrow.

In these films, even the sacred institution of motherhood is not left unscathed. Many mothers, aunts and (not surprisingly,) stepmothers act like monstrous aberrations. Yaayaa's mother in **Harvest At Seventeen** tries to make her commit an abortion after having given her a lot of licence to engage in an affair. **Suzzy I** presents us with a mother who entices her daughter's boyfriend. In the film **The Supreme Force**, Auntie Efua, an aunt who is envious about the marriage of her niece, bewitches her. Where stepmothers are concerned, the less said about them the better for they fall squarely in the stereotypes set up in the traditional tale form. In **Meba**, Danny's new wife who has driven his former wife to her death covers up her malevolent nature with hypocritical sweetness while devising a scheme to drown his son.

Meba, like other films such as **Ghost Tears, Fateful Decision, Suzzy I** and **Suzzy II** features the woman as ghost. She is usually one who has died as a result of rivalry over a man. From the constrained position as victim, they are literally empowered by transition through death to do as they please, unlimited by space, time, conjugal life, or the norms of society. In this ethereal state, the ghosts wreak a ghoulish vengeance on their ex-partners and the women who have betrayed them. Perhaps the most garish of the four ghosts is the one featured in **Ghost Tears**, who enters into the body of her daughter and causes her to stab the ex-domestic worker of the home, who caused her death and took her place as mistress of the home.

It is no wonder that the tail boards of some "tro-tro" or public transport vehicles carry the rubric, "Fear woman ... (and live long)!"

In this paper we have shown how film makers and highlife composers have exploited, amplified and entrenched the view that a woman is to be feared if one wishes to live long. For some artistes interviewed, such as well known actresses Grace Omaboe[8] and Dzifa Gomashie, the films were based on true experiences and a realistic interpretation of the prevalent mind set particularly in urban society, where there is easy permeability between the spiritual and physical dimensions. This leads to situations in which individuals under intensive pressure (emotional, financial, health) will readily assign spiritual causes and seek spiritual remedies. The woman, seen as powerful spiritually, ironically becomes an easy target for blame. It was their consensus that by exposing the negative effectively, they would help people, both men and women to change their attitudes for the better.

This chapter has sought to reflect in some detail both the paragon of womanhood and its antithesis as constructed by society and presented through highlife and film. Because the performance genres in which these images of women are depicted are popular and effective art forms, they are powerful means by which to entrench and amplify the negative image of women. We have however tried to demonstrate that there is a counter discourse, however feeble, led by a determined few within the popular performance forms and that further enquiry is needed into other popular forms, such as the concert party, where a more balanced view on womanhood may emerge. Concert Party is a genre of popular performance which also offers a relief to the relentless vista of evil portrayed in video-films and highlife. Although Concert Party is built around some of the same stock characters, motifs and plots encountered elsewhere, it is not uncommon for female characters who have been wronged to be vindicated. Being morality tales which must end with virtue winning the day, the social situations depicted often place women and children in the position of victim to the irresponsibility of fathers or the heartlessness of uncaring relatives. These characters must be vindicated. In *Mogya Ye Duro* (Blood is Thick) a child born and abandoned by its father brings its parents back together, while in *Hena Bedi Made?* (Who Will Inherit My Property?), a widow prevails against the cruelty of widowhood rites. Both plays by *Kusum Agoromba*[9] enjoyed great popularity in the late 1970s and 80s.

In juxtaposing the social view of women as beings to be feared against the ontological view of women as the source of life, and the beloved mother, we have sought to demonstrate a social psychological dilemma which continues to be very much a part of contemporary Ghana.

End Notes

1   It is interesting to note that Ama Ata Aidoo has succinctly drawn on this use of traditional aphorisms for her own style of cryptic symbolism. "The Tail-less Animal" appears in her short story, "other versions" in **No Sweetness Here** as the name of a passenger truck. It derives its poignancy from the unspoken segment, "...it is God who sweeps around it" (i.e. swots flies for it). The nub of the story rests on a young Ghanaian whose mother does everything to help him get an education. In the United States he discovers the warmth of motherhood through the empathy of an African American woman.

2   We have picked the Akan worldview because it is dominant in contemporary popular culture at the national level. It is also true that in a number of ways, particularly with respect to women, there is some similarity in the worldviews of the peoples of Southern Ghana and indeed a number of ethnic groups in neighbouring countries. The earth-mother concept for example is a prevalent one among the Ga, Ewe, Ibo and so on. On the other hand, the idea of women as wielding spiritual power which can be used mostly for ill is also prevalent. Thus the idea of the woman as a witch is found almost universally in the West African Sub Region.

3   Presumably to get sex from women you must pay them.

4   Personal communication by telephone, December, 12th 2001.

5   "Guarantee" is a term from the 1970s referring to platform shoes.

6   Fontomfrom, Contemporary Ghanaian Literature, Theatre and Film, Kofi Anyidoho and James Gibbs (eds.) Pp.265-282.

7   Ghanaian Video Films of the 1990's An Annotated Selected Filmography in Fontomfrom Contemporary Ghanaian Literature, Theatre and Film. Matatu 21 – 22 edited by Kofi Anyidoho and James Gibbs.

8   Interviews conducted in April/May 1996.

9   Now disbanded Concert Party, established by Efua Sutherland.

REFERENCES

Reading Materials

1. Aidoo Ama, Ata, 1970. *No Sweetness Here*: Harlow Essex: Longmans

2. Nketia, J.H., 1954. *Funeral Dirges of the Akan People*. James Townsend and Sons Ltd.

3. Oppong C. (ed), 1983. *Female and Male in West Africa*. London: Allen and Unwin

4. Schipper, M., 1991. *Sources of All Evil: African Proverbs and Sayings on Women*. Chicago: Ivan R. Doe Inc.

Songs

1. Ampadu Nana, Kwame	*Mmaa Dooso*
2. Ansah Tumi, Ebo	*Sii-Sii-Sii* (Kente Dance 2000)
3. Agyepong, Akosua	*Eka Bi Nie*
	Meye Obaa
	Aware Bone
4. Ahenkae, Kwadwo	*Mmaa Mpe Hia*
5. Crentsil, A.B.	Yewo Adze a Oye – Yewo Adze a Oye
6. Dede Abrantie, Amakye	*Mmaa Pɛ Sokoo*
7. Jarah George	*Obi Abayewa*
8. Ofori, Super Nana Yaw	*Sika Yɛ Aberantiɛ*
9. Yamoah	*Seewaa Akoto* (The Best of Yamoah Vol.3)

Films

1. **A Debut for Dede** Ghana Film Industry Corporation 1992.
2. **A Heart of Gold** Starlight Motion Pictures 1993.
3. **Baby Thief** Ghana Film Industry Corporation 1992.
4. **Bondage** Wericom 1993.
5. **Diabolo** Worldwide Productions 1991.
6. **Fatal Decision** 1993.
7. **Ghost Tears** Hacky Films 1994.
8. **Harvest At Seventeen** National Commission On Culture/Film Africa 1986.
9. **I want Her Blood** Sacky Sowah 1997.
10. **Kanana** Graceland Motion Pictures 1992.
11. **Mataa, Our Missing Children** Galaxy Productions 1992.
13. **Meba** Sid Precious Studios.
14. **Sika Sunsum** Graceland Motion Pictures; 199?
15. **Suzzy I** Vid Productions 1992.
16. **Suzzy II** Vid Productions.
17. **The Other Side of the Rich** Ghana Film Industry Corporation 1992.

18. **The Price of Love** B.M. Imoro 1993.
19. **The Police Officer** Hitline Films 1993.
20. **The Supreme Force** Lustre Pictures 1993.
21. **When The Heart Decides** Hacky Films.
22. **Who Killed Nancy** Hacky Films 1995.

PAWNS AND PLAYERS: THE WOMEN IN AMMA DARKO'S NOVELS

Kari Dako, Aloysius Denkabe and Helen Yitah

According to Amma Darko, it is hazardous, even dangerous to be a female in Ghana – you might end up as Mara in *Beyond the Horizons*, a physical and psychological wreck of a whore addicted to drugs, owned by your pimp, or you may be declared a 'witch', as the old widow in *The Housemaid* and be lucky to survive the ordeal.

> A dejected widow, once upon a time a vibrant *akpeteshie*[1] seller in the village of Braha, now penniless, aged and lonesome, started towards 'witchdom' when one of her grandchildren developed *kwashiorkor*.[2] She had turned herself into a snake and lodged inside the poor child's stomach, they said.
> Then another grandchild got a goitre. And all eyes in Braha saw red.
> (Darko, 1998:3).

This chapter deals with the Ghanaian female, as seen by Amma Darko. It is the story of Mara in *Beyond the Horizon* and the stories of Tika and Efia in *The Housemaid*. All three women end up as tragic examples of the worst fates that can befall a Ghanaian woman. Mara becomes a prostitute hooked on drugs. Tika becomes a barren woman and Efia becomes a poverty-stricken young girl who produces a deformed stillbirth.

Although written by a woman and about women, these are not feminist novels in the sense that their main themes are female solidarity and the suppression of women in a patriarchal society. Even though the exploitation and marginalisation of women is central to her work, the women in Amma Darko's novels all have choices, but they are trapped in a warped society in which everything, including all human relationships are commodified. But as Mitchell (1986) and Hollist (2001) suggest, it is the quality of the relationship between the sexes that determines the humanity of society. If one sex denigrates another, all are losers. It is this additional absence of any dignity, in either the intra-female or the male-female relationships portrayed in the books, that denies them a conventional feminist reading. These novels "force us to look at the reality of women's roles and lives" (Hollist 2001).

Amma Darko's feminism may therefore be described as unconscious in that it lacks a political edge and tends to dwell on the wider issue of the quality of social relations between women and men in contemporary society. Her feminism may thus be taken to be cultural rather than political also in the sense that it is linked to her view of the Ghanaian, male as well as female – a sinister and cynical view related as much in the content as in the form of her narratives. The life-stories of her female protagonists are told with little compassion and with scant show of female solidarity. While the use of a non-intrusive narrator buttresses this by allowing her characters to speak for themselves, make their own choices or let themselves be manipulated into having decisions made for them, it is quite clear that by plot, narrative design and selection of characters Amma Darko is deeply implicated in this cultural criticism of Ghanaian society.

In Amma Darko's novels there is no nostalgia for times gone past, the metaphorical stench from rotten entrails seeps into everything. She is generally concerned with a reality which she sets out to portray with fidelity and without idealisation – the essence of every day 'normal' Ghanaian life, presented not in the classical realist sense of a quest for objective truth and accuracy but with some exaggeration, even sensationalism, in order to establish a motif that then mediates the realistic concerns of the writings. In this respect, her 'realism' is reminiscent of that of her male compatriot Ayi Kwei Armah in *The Beautiful Ones Are Not Yet Born,* whose representation of Ghanaian reality is mediated through metaphors of decay, filth and defecation; what Gikandi (1987:74) describes as confronting 'the rotten underbelly of society'.

The background to this view can be found in Amma Darko's own experience of going to Germany as a young graduate. Once she returned to Ghana she was met with the question 'What did you bring?' This was the same question that confronted Baako in Ayi Kwei Armah's *Fragments* and in answering this question both writers contribute to a discourse that has been going on in the African novel since Achebe's *No Longer at Ease.* In this discourse the story is told of the African abroad in Europe for some time who now comes back home with the 'benefits' of Europe and high expectations of making an impact only to find both himself and his society increasingly 'no longer at ease'.

In Armah's version the protagonist returns home to find an Africa that is nothing more than a vulgar copy of the West with no authentic values, except those associated with money and consumerism. In Amma Darko's version, we are offered an updated version of this story. In this case, the protagonist is not your male all-conquering idealist, making a triumphant return with the trophies of Europe: education, status and economic power. Her protagonist, Mara, is stranded in Europe defeated, victimised and bereft of any ideals. Writing at a much later time in the evolution of the post-colony, she is well positioned to update this discourse, especially with regard to the depth to which the cult of consumerism has eaten into the fabric of African society. As one woman boasts in a quarrel with her neighbour in *The Housemaid*: 'Who told you you can compare yourself to me? How many of your children are in the city?'(p.31). Implying that if you have children in the city, then they are a potential source of income. It is against this background that Amma Darko wrote her first novel, so to speak screaming at Ghanaian society: 'I'll show you how your "successful burgers"[3] earn their money'.

Amma Darko burst onto the literary scene in Ghana in the1990s. Her first novel, *Beyond the Horizon* was first published in German in 1991.[4] *The Housemaid*, her second novel, was published by Heinemann in 1998.

In the context of Ghanaian literature, Amma Darko's novels are not unproblematic. On the one hand they fit into the fiction of disillusionment. This includes Ayi Kwei Armah's *The Beautiful Ones Are Not Yet Born, Fragments* and *Why Are We So Blest*, and Ama Ata Aidoo's *No Sweetness Here* as well as Kofi Awoonor's *This Earth, My Brother.* These have become canonical largely because of their perceived 'seriousness'. On the other hand, she also fits into the very vibrant tradition of Ghanaian popular writing in the way she deals in popular plots and character types, as in her treatment of gendered struggles and coping strategies. While she may be said to problematise these issues in the manner of the canonical tradition, she also offers, in the tradition of the popular writer, positions from which ordinary readers may evaluate and rehearse their stand in the situations and predicaments shown by her characters and plots. Both categories of Ghanaian writers generally do not bemoan a glorious utopian past, so often lauded in early post-independence writing – they lament the loss of essential values in the world they live in now. But they do not perceive the solution to contemporary life and the future in retrospection. Thus the times we live in dictate the strategies for survival. If we compare Amma Darko to Ama Ata Aidoo, another Ghanaian writer, who uses similar material, the differences between the two are startling. The rural-urban dichotomy in Ama Ata Aidoo's characters, as seen in *No Sweetness Here*, reflects layers of complexity and has the saving grace of humour, in that the characters can laugh at themselves in spite of the tragic dilemma of their lives. In Amma Darko's novels there is nothing to laugh about, the characterisation is humourless and the characters are totally cynical in their endeavours.

The two books considered here, already indicate the central concern of her writing: her preoccupation with the body as a site where a relentless and often brutal gendered struggle is taking place. This struggle expresses itself in many varied forms, but common to all is the issue of who gains power over whose body and for what purpose. How do women survive in this hostile environment and what are their strategies in a thoroughly exploitative and materialistic society? This paper argues that women in Amma Darko's novels use essentially the interwoven survival strategies of fertility, sex, subservience, and exploitation. The bitter irony is that the female self is quite often ultimately diminished and devalued by the nature of the gain in these struggles.

Beyond the Horizon is the life story of Mara, her journey from village girl to traditionally married woman eking out a living in Accra serving her husband in all, and then her joining the same husband in Germany, where he has bigamously married a German woman. He forces Mara into prostitution to become her pimp and uses what she earns in the brothel to keep his Ghanaian girlfriend, Comfort, in comfort and style.

We meet Mara, 'this bit of garbage that once used to be me..'(p. 3), in skimpy, red silk briefs sitting in front of her oval mirror in her room in the brothel where she works, 'waiting to be used and abused by strange men' (p.1). She works for an 'Overseer'. 'He is my lord, my master and my pimp. – I am his pawn, his slave and his property.' (p.3). The story Mara narrates is ugly. It is a tale of physical and emotional abuse, as when Mara wants to inform her husband, Akobi, that she is pregnant:

'I was by Mama Kiosk today and I told her that I haven't had my blood for two months and she says I am by all means carrying a baby.'…

…'Did Mama Kiosk sleep with you?' he asked, still in that disregarding tone. I felt cold sweat seep through my pores. I didn't answer. Then suddenly there was this angry roar of, 'Get up!' like an over-irritated boar and the next second I was up at attention on my two feet.

…' And why did you get pregnant?'

...'Pardon?' I replied spontaneously, and before I knew what was happening... Wham! First slap ... wham! wham! wham! three more in succession." (p. 16-17).

and it is a tale of exploitation, broken hopes and promises. It is the story of Mara's downward slide from what she,

> '...was before I was given away to this man who paid two white cows, four healthy goats, four lengths of cloth, beads, gold jewellery and two bottles of London Dry Gin to my family and took me off as his wife from my African village, ... to him in the city.' (p. 3) ...
> ...to our seeing her reflected in her oval mirror.

In *The Housemaid*, we are back in Ghana and the narrative focus shifts somewhat. This novel has a more complex structure. Whereas the stories of Tika and Efia constitute the foregrounded narrative of the novel, the background examines the reaction of ordinary people upon the discovery of a decomposed, newborn baby in the bush. The whys and hows of this find and its accompanying violent and moralistic reactions, seen against the otherwise callous interpersonal relationships in the novel, weave these parallel and intertwining narratives into a whole. The female characters and their stories are still central, but these are not women who are the helpless victims of male exploitation. Used by men, yes, but also users of men. The central female character in *The Housemaid* is not 'the housemaid' but her employer, Tika. She is not a Ghanaian version of Mara – Tika's tragedy is very different:

> It had never been Tika's dream still to be single and childless at the ripe old age of thirty-five.
> Living only with Efia, her maid, in a two-room estate house, and travelling frequently all over Africa to scout for goods to sell in Ghana... (p.17).

How did Tika end up as an infertile, childless woman at thirty-five – the most dreaded fate for any Ghanaian woman?

> 'A very wasted woman.'... 'An unproductive womb is bad enough. But no womb at all? And that is what she is. A walking woman with no womb inside her...' (p. 46).

In Ghana a barren woman is considered neither male nor female, she inhabits an undignified space peculiar to her situation. What makes her situation even more tragic is the popular belief, that successful businesswomen have bartered fertility for wealth. This is also a common theme in popular literature. Akua Julie, for example, the avaricious 'devil' in Asare Konadu (1989) is also barren, but very successful in business. This theme of superstition, of the belief in supernatural power, of the belief in witches causing havoc, permeates the book. It is used as a convenient strategy to shift responsibility of action onto someone or something else, in this case the weakest in society: the old abandoned women. As Ghanaians show no compassion for each other, so there are no constraints on them in their self-serving quest for wealth and power.

Fertility as a tool is employed by almost every female in *The Housemaid*. Thus Tika's mother, Sekyiwa, to get hold of a wealthy man to set her up in business, uses sex and fertility to trap him. She gets herself pregnant to strengthen her hold on him in order to exploit him. When she has achieved what she wants, she discards him. Efia is told by her grandmother to get pregnant in order to inherit Tika's wealth.

In both books, sex is used as a means of control. In *Beyond the Horizon*, the men use sex to manipulate their women. Mara supports Akobi, his girlfriend, Comfort and herself as a prostitute, thus Ghanaian men earn their living by sexually exploiting their women. In *The Housemaid* it is the women who control their men through sex. The matriarchs control Efia's father, who is not reckoned as a man. Sekyiwa controls her emasculated husband and Tika sells herself for expedience and profit – first to Samuel, the customs officer in order to get her goods tax free into the country – then to the factory owner, Attui, "to get good credit rates on the goods she bought" (p. 25), then to Riad, the shop owner with several outlets to whom she can distribute her commodities for sale, then to Eric, the musician, whose elder brother holds a prominent position in Ghana Commercial Bank and can therefore give her credit. In as much as sex is a means of income in Germany, it is as much a means of exchange in Ghana:

'... [this] left sex as the only really affordable entertainment in Kataso. Everyone – young, old, mature and immature – indulged in it freely, making the two midwives the busiest of the village professionals.' (p. 29).

'Thanks to bribes of cash and sex, workers at the building sites regularly tipped [the female porters] on the next place available for occupation.' (p. 32).

'Where to?' The driver asked curtly.

'Kumasi.'
'You have money to pay me?'
'No.'
He grunted. 'So you won't pay me?'
Akua unbuttoned her blouse. The driver's eyes blazed with consent. She removed her pants. He grinned, and stopped the truck in a secluded bend.
(p. 30-31)

Told by her mother and grandmother to get herself pregnant and get a baby who then, they plot, would inherit Tika's wealth, Efia uses sex and fertility in her effort to gain wealth. Sekyiwa uses men to satisfy her sexually, "... she gave [the gold-diggers] good money; they gave her good sex." (p.18). The theme of the female barracuda is not new in Ghanaian writing and popular perception. Asare Konadu's *Devils in Waiting*, set in the 1970s, deals with a typical *kalabule*[5] 'business woman', Akua Julie, who rides roughshod all over Kumasi in her quest for wealth and the men through whom she can obtain this. The term *kalabule* which was coined to refer to unsavoury business practices during the Acheampong regime (1972-78/79), "had been gendered as feminine" (Newell:126) by the time Rawlings had taken over the country in the 1980s. Referring to Victor Amarteifio's *Bediako the Adventurer* Stephanie Newell (126) also argues that there is a "... parallel ... established between a man's loss of control over his wealth and his sexual abandon to a woman". Just as Bediako loses the "control of his conscience, savings and social status" (Newell:122), so Tika's father, who is so insignificant that he is not given a name, suffers the same fate at the hands of his second wife, Sekyiwa. Ama Ata Aidoo's male protagonist in *Anowa*, the infertile Kofi Ako, loses control of his life while blaming it on his wife Anowa. Here the myth of the infertile wealthy woman is reversed – it is the infertile male who has bartered wealth for fertility.

In both *Beyond the Horizon* and *The Housemaid*, subservience is a further strategy women adopt to get their way. The grandmother's advice prior to Efia's departure for Accra is utterly self-serving:

'...So hear me! Be subservient, humble and very dependable...'
'Then get yourself pregnant.'
'... Efia, you will live with her, win her affection, become indispensable to her. So that when you innocently become pregnant...'
'Innocently? How does she become pregnant innocently?' Efia's mother asked.

'By pretending she was forced into the sexual act,' the old lady replied. (p. 46-47)

So the only advice a young girl can get from her mother and grandmother is how she craftily can get herself pregnant and give birth to an illegitimate child so that these same women can benefit from her condition.

Mara also plays the subservient role. When Akobi vetoes Mara's leaving for the station with Mama Kiosk, Mara, anxious to prevent another quarrel acquiesces subserviently only to do what she wants when he is not around. (p. 24). – and in Germany she uses the same strategy, ostensibly to keep peace in Akobi's bigamous household: 'I would be Akobi's hidden wife, so that harmony would prevail in the marriage,...' (p. 26). And once she had accepted that role, she had to play it to the end.

So where Mara is the victim of male exploitation, Tika is the exploiter of males, the chess player par excellence. Amma Darko's feminism radicalises as she focuses on Ghanaian society. Men are here merely as means to an end – they are commodities to be used as studs and for sexual gratification:

> ...Sekyiwa had become one of the wealthy market mummies. Young, good-looking male gold-diggers began to vie for her attention. Her husband's libido was waning anyway,.... She gave [the gold-diggers] good money; they gave her good sex. (p. 18).

They are used for financial expediency. Tika sleeps with four men to get what she wants. Akua offers herself to the truck driver for a free ride. In *The Housemaid* the men become the pawns in a female chess game.

While the female is the victim of male abuse in *Beyond the Horizon*, relationships between females exist that have some redeeming factors: Mara trusts Mama Kiosk and sends money through her for her children; she can also turn to her fellow prostitute, Kaye, when she needs help. In *The Housemaid*, on the other hand, Amma Darko appears to have given up all hope of any redeeming factors in Ghanaian society – everybody exploits everybody else: mothers their daughters, daughters their mothers, girlfriends their lovers, maids their mistresses. Society is a web of exploitation that smothers and stifles any attempt at healthy human interaction. This web is somehow woven around Tika, who is as much the spider as the fly caught in the web as is every other Ghanaian we meet in the book; a manifestation of our earlier argument that the self diminishes as it gains.

The men, considering the role the novels ascribe to them in these struggles, are not explored beyond their emasculated, asocial and absolutely amoral character. They have been written out of the narrative. The women end up with no feminine aspects in the traditional sense, they are not caring and nurturing mothers, nor do they play the expected roles of daughters or wives. For women to survive and be 'free', that is, beyond male exploitation, they must play it by the rules of the cynical world around them. They have to gain power and maintain it and therefore adopt the same exploitative practices as the men. Darko appears not to agree that the oppressed must not adopt the same strategies as the oppressor. Tika's maid, Efia, cast as the stereotypical disloyal employee, is as much a victim as a cunning strategist. She is pawned by her mother and grandmother and used to exploit her employer. With nothing more than the scheming manipulations of these older women to guide her, Efia survives by quickly changing status from pawn to player and back again.

Does Amma Darko blame traditional practices for this? Yes – because the female has now adopted the tools of the male oppressor. The women who traditionally are trusted with the role of raising children have themselves become lured by the trappings of this exploitative web. This is why society is breaking down. Amma Darko's fictional world has become so materialistic that all human relationships are commodified in terms of personal gain. Nugent (1985:3) also argues that 'superior learning, piety and wealth have all harboured the potential to deliver status and power. But Ghanaians have tended to treat wealth as the most reliable route to personal success'. This means deriving material gain from everything and looking at the world in terms of potential gain. Thus you sell what you have: your body, your child, your honour your conscience – as Hooks (1984:83) reminds us 'power is commonly equated with domination and control over people..' so that whereas the reader is persuaded to condemn male exercise of power as domination, in *Beyond the Horizon* the same reader is ambivalently not called upon to attack the same female exercise of power over males in *The Housemaid*.

But the question then is, do women have power in *The Housemaid?* And if they do – is it merely the power obtained by assuming male roles of exploitation? Tika for all her sexual promiscuity has assumed an asexual status by destroying her fertility and denying any female function that society might expect of her. She refuses to be a daughter, a mother or a wife. Mara fulfils the female roles. She is a daughter, and adheres to her father's wishes. She is. a wife and lets her husband use her. She is a mother and uses her predicament as an addicted whore as an alibi to provide for the children she left behind in Ghana – preferring an unreliable husband and the lure of the 'gold in Germany' to the role of mothering and caring for her children in Ghana. Mara thus oscillates between acquiescence, defiance and resignation – from a victim to a woman who shows spunk and fights back – but she lacks the tools to free herself from her predicament. Like Ramatoulaye in *So Long a Letter* (Ba 1981) she finds the marriage stifling but cannot find the courage to leave. This is the dilemma of the contemporary African woman – left out when the rest of the world moved on. She lacks the education, the means, the societal support to carve a role for herself as an individual and not as an appendage. In Amma Darko's novels, schools appear irrelevant. The women do not invest in education neither for themselves nor for their children. Tika drops out of school and is rewarded with financial assistance from her mother to get started in business. Wealth is obviously more important than education.

The strategies in Amma Darko's novels, therefore, are as stark as the reality that spawned them. Thus ten-year old Bibio can throw away her mother as another piece of useless rubbish because, according to her, the mother failed to supply what she wanted, 'she was to blame for their pathetic life' (*Housemaid*:11), which in this case was picking discarded food and clothing from the rubbish dump. There is an erosion of values when a child can discard her mother for not providing materially. There is something sick in a society where a daughter can blame her mother for her father's death and as Tika did, dedicate her whole life to punishing her mother, Sekyiwa. There is also something askew when the market-women in Kumasi can only calculate an increase in their profit by short-changing their all-male truck-pushers. Similarly there is the same 'strategic thinking' in the female porters, the *kayayei*, who sell their bodies to survive and hoard enough money to travel to their rural homes to attend the traditional festivals in order to flaunt their wealth:

> As for Kataso, the ultimate is when the city-dwellers return for the yam festival. The household with the most returnees gets the most honours and attention. And as for the dance at the Quebec Inn... 'The dance that crowns the festival is called 'showtime', because that's when returnees put on their best clothes and compete with each other.' (Housemaid:.31).

Everything is distorted and confounded in Amma Darko's Ghana. Even though some positive traditional beliefs linger – such as the burying of the umbilical cord to bind one's soul to one's birthplace – the predominant traditional beliefs are the ones that are sinister, like the belief in witches, like the belief in the power of curses to kill. Tika's father's first wife:

'..cursed him with leprosy, should he defy her warnings, and had broken six raw eggs at his feet to solicit the powers of the gods to see it through. It had proved too much for his heart'. (p. 20)

Traditional festivals that used to be thanksgivings for a good harvest have been reduced to "show time". Thus even a religious festival has been defiled and commercialised. When Efia's father hears about the plans connected with her going to work for Tika, his immediate response is:

'So, what is in it for us? ....What are we getting out of our daughter's going away to the city to serve somebody?' (p. 43).

Amma Darko's two expositions on her homeland call our attention to the fate of many unresourced Ghanaian women abroad, and open the lid of the proverbial can of worms, in this case, Ghana. Her writing reflects the angst in contemporary Ghanaian society – the themes she chooses echo the stories that we read daily in the Ghanaian press. The headlines scream of abandoned babies, brutalised and murdered women: wives, mothers, daughters, sisters, girlfriends, of ritual executions, of incest and rape, of sale of children, of child labour and of a general degeneration of society into one of oppression and violence.

Beyond the Horizon ends with Mara looking back on her life and concluding unfinished narratives. Akobi is in jail, all he acquired in his German marriage has been confiscated by the bank. She knows there is no hope for her, she can never leave the brothel; money will compensate for her failing as mother and daughter:

Now I can't go a day without sniffing 'snow'. I am hooked on it. I am fast sinking into a place hotter than hell. But I know this. And that is why I have decided that before I sink too deep I will make as much money as possible for my mother and sons back home. (p. 139).

By providing her elder brother with a television and a video deck, and a younger brother with a car and getting a house built for her mother, she has purchased the loyalty of her family and the surety that they will look after her children.

Material things are all I can offer them. As for myself, there's nothing dignified and decent left of me to give them (p. 140).

Mara thus obliterates herself for her children. That is the resolution Amma Darko seems to offer the reader.

The Housemaid ends on a similarly pessimistic note. The final chapter of the book links up with the opening, the belief in witchcraft, the tragedy of old, lonely women being declared witches and blamed for all the ills of society.

Teacher, the woman who initially facilitated Efia being brought from Kataso to Tika's household, has been told the story of how Efia's baby came to be found in the bush in a state of decomposition. Teacher now returns to Tika to narrate what has happened and why it happened. Tika admits that Efia 'was as much a victim of her people's manipulation as I was' (p.105). This should have been the resolution for Tika's dilemma, namely her realisation that Efia's grandmother and mother had caused this tragedy, but this eludes her because she appears not to transcend her own superstitions and fears of the power of the supernatural. Another moment of insight is tossed away when the question, can Tika make peace with her mother, now also old and poor, crops up. Tika evades it, instead wondering what her dead father would have wanted and whether he has been watching over her all these years. She is not able to face her hostility towards her mother and her punishing Sekyiwa for the death of her father so many years ago, so she trivialises it by making the trite comment that she would not have wanted her father to witness '..the business discussions I used to hold in my bedroom!' (p.107).

The conversation between Tika and Teacher now veers into Efia believing that Tika had used juju and that she had cursed her, and that the dead infant was the result of this. This again echoes Tika's infertility – and the suggested demonic trade for material gain. Both Teacher and Tika speculate that if Efia had delivered the baby at home, 'Kataso would have been thrown into a frenzied orgy of witch-hunting' (p. 106). Human error is thus blamed on witches. The implication is that Ghana is unwilling to face its own inadequacies and to accept its own guilt. All failings and all disasters are transferred onto some old women casting them in the role of scapegoats.

This is again seen in Tika and Teacher's typical reaction of pushing the blame for witchcraft onto someone else – in this case a man. The two women prefer to think that the manipulator of the witches is male:

'In which case, the crucial question is why he would want to appoint wrinkled old women as his ambassadors on earth. He certainly seems to, if the rate at which such women are declared witches in our society is anything to go by.' (p. 106).

The issue is of course not whether the chief witch is a man or a women, the issue is that Ghanaian society is paralysed by its own superstitions and evasions. The two women end their conversation by,

laughing and crying away their pain, their disappointment, their anger, their fear. And laughing with hope. (p. 107).

We may wonder what they hope for. Ghana has not resolved any of its problems, it is as caught in its superstitions as ever. It is as crafty in its manipulations as ever. Whether Tika will allow Efia back into her household does not bring a resolution – it just brings the events full circle – we can either laugh or we can cry. It does in the final analysis amount to the same: no solution.

Endnotes

1   A kind of local distilled liquor.

2   An Accra word for toddler sickness associated with under nutrition.

3   The Ghanaian term 'burger' refers to someone who has been abroad and worked there to earn some money. The term is restricted to Ghanaian migrants on the Continent of Europe, especially Germany.

4   By Schmetterling Verlag GbR Paul Sanders & Jörg Hunger with the title *Der Verkaufte Traum* (The Sold Dream). Heinemann published the English manuscript in 1995.

5   From Hausa *kare kabure* (don't open it).

Bibliography

Achebe, Chinua, 1963. *No Longer at Ease*. London: Heinemann.

Aidoo, Ama Ata, 1971. *Anowa*. London: Heinemann.

Aidoo, Ama Ata, 1970. *No Sweetness Here*. London: Longman.

Amarteifio, Victor, 1985. *Bediako the Adventurer*. Accra: Amaa Book.

Armah, Ayi Kwei, 1968. *The Beautyful Ones Are Not Yet Born*. London: Heinemann.

Armah, Ayi Kwei, 1970. *Fragments*. Boston: Houghton Mifflin.

Armah, Ayi Kwei, 1974. *Why Are We So Blest?* London: Heinemann.

Awoonor, Kofi, 1972. *This Earth, My Brother*. London: Heinemann,

Bâ, Mariama, 1981. *So Long a Letter*. London: Heinemann,

Darko, Amma, 1995. *Beyond the Horizon*. London: Heinemann,

Darko, Amma, 1998. *The Housemaid*. London: Heinemann,

Duodu, Cameron, 1967. *The Gab Boys*. London: André Deutsch.

Gakwandi, Shatto Arthur. 1982 *The Novel and Contemporary Experience in Africa*. London: Heinemann.

Gikandi, Simon, 1988. *Reading the African Novel*. London: James Currey,

Hollist, Onipede, 2001. E-mail to Kari Dako, 18th April.

Hooks, Bell, 1984. *Feminist Theory: From Margin to Center*. Boston: South End Press.

Konadu, Asare, 1989. *Devils in Waiting*. Accra: Anowua Educational Publications.

Kwakye, Benjamin, 1998. *The Clothes of Nakedness*. London: Heinemann.

Mitchell, Juliet, 1986. Women and equality. In Juliet Mitchell & Ann Oakley (ed.), *The Rights and Wrongs of Women*. Harmondsworth: Penguin. 378-399.

Newell, Stephanie, 1999. *Ghanaian Popular Fiction*. London: James Currey.

Nugent, Paul, 1995. *Big Men, Small Boys And Politics In Ghana*. Accra: Asempa Publ.

THE VANISHING SEXUAL ORGAN PHENOMENON[1]

Brigid M. Sackey

In January 1997, there were widespread reports in Ghana about people possessing spiritual powers that could cause other persons' sexual organs,
namely, penises, breasts and vaginas, to vanish, shrink or to be sealed respectively, either by a handshake or a touch on any part of the body. This phenomenon, which became known as the vanishing sexual/genital organ syndrome
(VSOS) resulted in a 'ritual' of instant mob lynching and burning of the alleged culprits. In Accra, seven suspects were reported to have been publicly
lynched in the first two days of the genital vanishing scare and an undisclosed
number of people in different parts of the country were executed this way.[2]
    Varied interpretations were given to the phenomenon and the mass hyste-
ria of lynching that accompanied it. These interpretations include medical,
psychological, economic, criminal and supernatural, the latter outweighing
all the others. This paper focuses on the belief in the supernatural as a causative agent for the vanishing sexual organ hysteria. What religious implications does this belief have in a country that strongly claims to be overwhelmingly Christian? In a country where the Ghana Evangelism Committee (1993)
asserted that the relative percentage of traditional adherents is declining and
that by the turn of the millennium the majority of traditional adherents would
either profess to be Christian or Muslim. How credible is this evaluation? Are
traditional beliefs increasing or decreasing? What implications does the
belief in the vanishing-sexual-organs phenomenon have in the re-awakening
of Christian evangelism in the country? We seem to be in a religious dilemma
because, as attempts at evangelization increase, so do traditional beliefs
increase. Historically, this phenomenon is not new to Ghana. A similar phenomenon was rumored in the country in the 1970s though the degree of
publicity and lynching was not as significant as that generated by the 1997
episodes. This means there is a possibility of preventing it from reappearing?
    This chapter collates some of the public views that sought to explain the

phenomenon. Except for newspaper reports, there are no publications on the vanishing sexual organ hysteria in Ghana.[3] Thus data include newspaper reports, live radio interviews of some of the accused who survived the mob actions, and personal conversations with some members of the public, particularly taxi drivers.[4] One major methodological problem has been the inability to interview and examine those who claimed the loss of their organs! Neither did anyone acknowledge the possession of the magical powers under review, though one taxi driver claimed to have seen such a person and the magic substance.

The first episode of the recent shrinking/vanishing sexual organ was reported from Keta in the Volta Region in *The Weekly Spectator* of January 11, 1997 which I quote in detail:

Case One

Nine people have been arrested by the Keta police possessing mystical powers that make one's sexual organ disappear after a handshake or touch. They have been accused of creating fear and panic among the people of the town. Sources in the town said when the organs are restored they became unfunctionable. Mr. Francis Komashie, Assistant superintendent in-charge of Keta District said they would be charged with assault and battery... So far the police have confirmed 10 cases of people having their genitals disappearing... Dr. K.G. Normanyo, Medical Superintendent in-charge of Keta Government hospital said the hospital is able to handle cases involving men, adding that the only woman who had her genitals sealed was transferred to a private clinic for lack of facilities. Meanwhile it has become risky asking questions in the town. One could be lynched if not lucky or taken to the police station. Dr. Normanyo said there is anxiety all over the place... on suspicion one is given severe beatings. In another development a 25-year-old man, Justice Setsoafia... [from] the Volta Region has been arrested by the Kasoa Police [in Central Region] for causing the disappearance of the sex organ of a 17-year-old student.... Setsoafia was said to have suddenly held the hands of the pupil causing the boy to have severe pains in his body. Immediately he held his sex organ, he realised that the organ was not there.

The arrival of the phenomenon in Accra was reported by the *Daily Graphic* and the *Ghanaian Times* of 17/1/97. The two papers give what seemed to be a comprehensive account of VSOS incidents at various parts of Accra.

Case Two

At Laterbiokoshie yesterday morning, James Nii Okine was brutally assaulted when a 17-year-old JSS student (Osbert) Azadagli, raised an alarm that his male organ had disappeared upon being touched by Okine. The boy had gone to fetch water for his father and was returning when Okine came behind, touched him and immediately his penis shrank till it was no longer visible. He therefore shouted for help and a mob rushed on Okine beating him with sticks, stones and cutlasses. When the two were brought to the Graphic offices, Okine was in a critical condition while Osbert's organ was intact and not vanished... Osbert, however, explained that his organ used to be much bigger than what had been left. The father of the boy examined his son's organ and confirmed that it was not the normal size; it is stiffer than normal and he thinks something spiritual had been done to him and demanded a cure from the accused.

Case Three

At Kaneshie, Accra three men whose names were withheld claimed that Tetteh Ahlivia, 32, and a native of Tsiame in the Volta Region had caused their organs to vanish. Ahlivia was lynched to death. The police referred the three men to Kaneshie Polyclinic for examination of their manhood.

Case Four

This story was narrated by Pat Williams on behalf of Abigail Williams, who had been severely brutalized by mob action and was consequently incapacitated to such an extent that she had to be represented by Pat on Joy FM radio's Front Page Live interview on 24/1/97.

Ms. Abigail Williams, a hairdresser who had undergone surgery barely a month ago was accused of causing the penis of a taxi driver whose service she hired to Adabraka to disappear. As Ms. Williams was about to alight from the taxi she observed that the driver had put his hands in his trousers. He got out of the taxi slapped her and robbed her of her jewellery and an amount of 50,000 cedis. When she confronted him the man started shouting 'give me my penis, give me my penis' Undaunted Ms. Williams challenged him to unzip his flap to ascertain the truth but he sped off. Instantly a mob gathered and brutally assaulted her. Stripped her naked and even drove sticks into her. Although she survived she was swollen all over when she was handed to the Adabraka police who later sent her to the hospital.[5]

Case Five

Kwesi Addae was another witness of the Front page live interview to tell his own story. He asked a certain man for direction to the Groove FM radio station where he had an appointment. The man could not help him and just as Addae was about to seek further help he heard the first man he had talked to shout: where is my thing? my prick is missing!

> I was confused; I thought I was dreaming and couldn't say anything. People started rushing towards me so I decided to say my last prayer and face them. Then the people insisted that he (the complainant) remove his pants for them to see if indeed his organ was missing. He claimed that the size had reduced. Surprisingly the people there (Kuku Hill Osu) were very mature in their thinking and they didn't touch me. The guy ran away.

In Kumasi it was reported that a man who was attacked for causing a woman's sexual organ to seal up could not be immediately rescued by the police at post. They needed further police reinforcement before they could quell the mob (see *Graphic* January 20 1997: 1).

Analysis of the Cases

The above cases give some clues, though not enough, about the vanishing sexual organ phenomenon. Although the police and others have asserted that it is not the first time sex organs have disappeared, the current episode we learn, originated from Keta[6] from where it probably spread to Kasoa in the Central Region through a native of the Volta Region.

From other newspaper reports and the live radio interviews, it seems the *modus operandi* of the phenomenon followed the same pattern as that of Keta. A person (usually a male) supposedly has to feel some sensation in his groin and believing that someone has touched him causing his penis to vanish only need to shout: give me back my prick, give me back my penis, or where is my thing? Instantaneously a mob would pounce on the suspect, brutally assault and often lynch or burn him/her to death.

Fear, anxiety and anger which culminate in a retaliatory solidarity characterize the phenomenon. The eagerness of the people to retaliate knows no bounds. From the Kumasi story we can see how furious and uncontrollable the mob could be. The spontaneous lynching action could be seen as a ritual, because it created a state of *communitas* in that short period of liminality in which the crowd were relinquished of their different statuses with a unity of purpose. The mob lynching process supports Turner's (1988: 504) argument that, 'it is in liminality that *communitas* emerges, if not as a spontaneous expression of sociability, at least in a cultural and normative form stressing equality and comradeship.' The state of *communitas* created by the VSOS mob action is amply described by Kwaku Sakyi Addo:

> The taxi driver, the long distant walking newspaper seller, the sweet ditty-singing trader, and the far-sighted, deep-thinking professional picked iron bars, and bricks, sticks and crowbars and clobbered innocent men and women splitting their heads open and setting some of them on fire.[7]

From a psychological point of view:

> people react strangely when there is a panic especially when there is a lot of them together. In such situations normal, ordinary people could turn into beasts because the person they are dealing with is no longer a human being but an object to be destroyed. This becomes more crucial when people are confronted with vital areas of their body such as the sex organ.[8]

In fact when we apply this psychological explanation by Mrs. Phillips to the liminal stage in a ritual process we again see some similarities. In the ritual process the initiate is structurally, if not physically invisible. He/she is in a state of marginality, or liminality, set outside the structural arrangements (Turner 1988: 504). The liminal stage is completed when the initiate (the outsider) is reincorporated into society after going through certain rites which are supposed to transform him/her from one phase of life to another. However, if we take the meaning of ritual to be an outward expression of religion, performed according to laid down procedures with precision, and directed at the specific spiritual being, then the VSOS may not be described as such. On the other hand the VSOS action could be described as a ritual for these reasons: (1) even though the action is not directed at a particular known divinity it is aimed at whatever spiritual forces might be using a particular human being as a vehicle to destabilize society; the action therefore is based on religious ideology; (2) even though the first incident occurred far away in the Volta region the *modus operandi* in other areas followed the same procedures as the first; (3) the acts of beating, insults, robbery and (when not lucky) lynching, could be described as liminal acts, with the aim of transforming or purging the person of the evil magic in order to be reaggregated, though by the spontaneous mob action the individual is sometimes ushered into the spiritual rather than the living world; (4) In our VSOS case, the accused is not seen as part of a normal community but one outside it who intends to harm it. Hence the lynching!

An important basis of this phenomenon is its non-discriminatory, dialectical characteristic, which means that anybody, male or female, adult or adolescent, could accuse anyone, and be accused also by anybody. Nevertheless, a striking observation about the VSOS cases available to me is that while a man can accuse another man or woman of causing his/her organ to vanish/shrink and vice versa, it appears that a woman cannot accuse another woman of VSOS. If this were the case it would mean that only a man's touch can cause a woman's vulva and breasts to recede. Perhaps it would be too hasty to imply that this is an indication of spiritual equality among women. But this is a baffling distinction that needs further investigation.

Some of the several questions that emanate from the above cases are: How did the crowd know that the accused is really the offender and not someone else? Why did it take the form it did? Was the pattern of revenge peculiar to the VSOS or was it preempted by media reports? Why were some of the people taken first to the offices of the media and not the police or hospital? How did the father know the size of the penis of this 17-year old son (case two)? Does it mean he examined his son regularly? Is it a common practice? Is it possible that they bathe together in a compound bathhouse? Could case 4 be described as an intentional robbery disguised in religious beliefs? Was Addae (case 5) just lucky because of the kind of people he encountered? What sort of people were they? Were they more educated than the mob in other areas? Could it be that by that time people had become more aware of the phenomenon or was the mob reaction class-specific? These questions represent some of the questions observation and participation would have helped to clarify.

How real is the Vanishing Sexual Organ phenomenon?

Medical, psychiatric and anthropological literature corroborate the idea of the shrinking and restoration of sexual organs under certain conditions (Kiev 1972, Lander and Marks 1971, Kleineman 1980). The concept has been described as a culture-bound disorder because its clinical features of anxiety states are culturally influenced. Culture determines the specific ways in which individuals perceive and conceive of the environment and strongly influences the forms of conflict and behaviour that occur in members of the culture (Kiev 1972: 9). According to Lander and Marks (1971:35), it is not surprising that 60% of southern Chinese males have anxiety about *koro*, an acute delusional syndrome in which the patient fears his penis is shrinking into the abdomen with potentially lethal consequences. The anxiety about *koro* is based on the fact that Chinese society places a very high premium on the male sexual organ and semen, because they are essential for the preservation of life. Ghanaians hold similar beliefs about the male sexual organ. It is a most important component of the Ghanaian man, which he would do anything to protect and vitalize. First discovered in Malaya among Chinese in 1834, *koro* can be reversed by manually grabbing the penis or tying it with string (Lander and Marks 1971:35).

Religio – Cultural Beliefs

Consideration of religio-cultural beliefs in Ghana will aid in the understanding of the vanishing sexual organ phenomenon. In Africa generally and Ghana specifically, apart from the belief in one God, there is belief also in a pantheon of spirits which man can use positively or negatively. The term magic is usually applied to these forces in the hands of certain individuals. They may use magic for harmful ends as in the case of the VSOS or use it for ends which are helpful to society (see Mbiti 1975:165). In the case of the VSOS, the beliefs that seem to be relevant are witchcraft, sorcery, and *ayera* (Akan). Witchcraft is based on the idea that the spirit of one human being can harm the spirit of another human by means of a remote control mechanism.[9] Though this is a supernatural process, the effect of witchcraft can be physically manifested. Several cases of childlessness, impotence and tampering with one's sexual organs are explained in terms of witchcraft. Sorcery, in contrast, is the ability to use certain tangible objects or materials to harm people through the manipulation of supernatural powers, while *ayera* is a kind of magical power which can cause human beings as well as material possessions to disappear (see Sackey 1997:129). For example, there were also rumours that during the struggle for Ghana's independence Kwame Nkrumah, then imprisoned by the British colonial government, could vanish through the prison walls at night and meet with his political friends in town.[10] In the early 1960s, there was a hysteria about people causing wrist watches of others to vanish when they responded to their request about time. In the light of these beliefs, it was not difficult for Ghanaians to believe that sexual organs can also vanish by touch or handshake.

However in the case of the VSOS, the most appropriate explanation for the phenomenon is to be found in sorcery and *ayera*. This was substantiated by a taxi driver, Sampson, who was an eyewitness to one of the incidents. A man who was arrested for causing someone's organ to vanish was brought to the offices of the Fire Service in Accra. In his pocket was a black powdery substance that he claimed could cause human organs to vanish. When he touches the medicine and then touches a person, the latter's organ vanishes. Sampson thinks the whole vanishing syndrome is economically motivated and organized by a syndicate because the same people who cause the organ to vanish would suggest a cure for it by recommending supposed healers. According to three taxi drivers, including Sampson, the real actor very often evades arrest through the medicine of *ayera,* which makes him invisible immediately after the act. Thus the wrong persons are accused. How then does the person whose organ has vanished become duped by the real actor (the *ayera* man)? Sampson answered that after the hysteria has subsided, the *ayera* man reappears to the person who has lost his organ and offers to help him restore it. It is remarkable that of the three drivers, only one was an eyewitness but the others simply believed in the magic of *ayera*.

Koro and VSOS

Koro and the Ghanaian VSOS appear to be related in so far as they both involve the retraction of the sexual organs of predominantly male members of the society. Both conditions are reversible and both syndromes are culturally based. However, *koro* and VSOS are different with regard to causation. While the former is said to be viral and usually sporadic (Lader and Marks) 1971:35), the Ghanaian VSOS was an epidemic induced by a supernatural force. The victim needed to have been touched by someone with supernatural power. Also, death can occur in both cases but while with *koro*, it is the person with retracted sex organs who dies as a result of the disease, in the VSOS cases, it is rather the alleged agent of the supernatural, who is believed to have caused the loss of the organ, who could die by instant mob execution.[11] Unlike *koro*, the VSOS cannot really be classified as a disease in a biomedical sense, since it does not exhibit any systematic and consistent symptoms such as vomiting, palpitation, bodily pain and fainting that accompany *koro*. In the VSOS attack, some of the sufferers claimed to have experienced only some sharp pains in the abdominal area. However, the VSOS could fit in African classifications of sickness or disease, since the causative agents of disease are spiritually induced. Hence diseases must also be treated through spiritual means. In case two above the father of seventeen year old Osbert attributes the shrinkage of his penis to the spiritual realm, which also needs a spiritual solution.

The Police

There seems to have been a general consensus that blamed the police for what happened. Some argued that the police were not as responsive as they should have been; that they acted most unprofessionally, and that if they had acted promptly after the first report from Keta, they could have arrested the phenomenon from spreading. Suffice it to say that a representative of the police admitted their fault to some extent, but also explained their difficulty in handling the case, mainly due to the lack of basic logistics such as vehicles, communications equipment etc. to facilitate their work.

Public opinion, however, thinks otherwise. The main argument behind the seeming insensibility of the police to the whole issue is said to be real fear, based on religio-cultural beliefs. According to Ms. Pat Williams, the police who rescued her sister were afraid and did not examine her closely in spite of the fact that she was bleeding from the nose, mouth and head. 'The police were even afraid to touch her because they feared they might lose their something [sic]'. She claimed that it was only after one policeman had gathered courage to examine closely the extent of her sister's assault and exclaimed, 'you see, I haven't lost anything?' that the police felt relieved. From the Keta report, we learn that for fear of losing their genital organs people were keeping a safe distance from others. Fear is also indicated in another incident reported to have occurred in one of the banks in Accra. A well-dressed woman's hand accidentally hit the abdomen of a gentleman behind her, while she was keeping safe the money she had just withdrawn. Immediately, the man grabbed the woman with one hand, and the other hand resting on his sex organ, he anxiously cautioned the lady in Twi, *twen ansa* (implying wait till I check myself that everything is intact). After satisfying himself that his penis was in place he smiled and let go of the woman's hand. According to eyewitnesses, the woman left the bank, panting and thanking God for her life.

These seemingly interesting stories were deadly serious events at the time they occurred, and from all indications, many people did believe the reality of the phenomenon. Among the questions posed by the public were, how could this happen when we claim to be Christians?

How can these beliefs and mob action be reconciled with the peaceable, non-violent, friendly Ghanaian? At this juncture it is worthwhile to investigate the religious direction of Ghanaians at the turn of the millennium. What are the prospects of Christianity and traditional beliefs at the beginning of the third millennium? Deep down in our conscience and volition, are we becoming more Christian and less traditional or are we becoming more oriented to traditional religious beliefs and practices? Where are we going? Does the strong reawakening of Christian evangelization and the fact that we are moving in to the twenty-first century mean anything at all to people in this country? There are two schools of thought. While some people believe that the country has never been more Christian than at the present time, others think Satan and for that matter African indigenous religion is at work more than ever before. Considering certain events in recent imes one might admit that both arguments are valid.

Renewed Christian Evangelism

Apart from the mushrooming of Christian churches of some kind and the increase in born-again Christians, there are other indicators which give ample evidence that there is a strong re-awakening of evangelization in Ghana. These include new methods of evangelization through revivals and crusades by both indigenous and foreign ordained Christian ministers, radio-evangelism and the blasting of gospel music everywhere – in the radio stations, in markets, private shops, government offices, banks, and in some of the hospitals. In fact, the establishment of FM radio stations (both private and state-owned) in 1995 initiated radio-evangelism in Ghana.[12] A tune-in to any of the stations in the morning hours will give you some kind of religious devotion, thought for meditation, moments of inspiration etc. by different Pentecostal-/charismatic church pastors. These are interspersed with Ghanaian and foreign gospel tunes. An array of religious programs is heard at night. Also, the recent release of *trokosi* or female vestal virgins in certain parts of the country seems to suggest that African religions are losing their hold while Christian religions are thriving. The following statistical survey by the Ghana Evangelism Committee (1993: 103), which observed a changing pattern in religious affiliation, seeks to portray both an obscure future for African indigenous religions and an increase in the Christianization and Islamization of Ghanaians. The Evangelism Committee (GEC 1993:103) wrote in the early nineties that the relative percentage of traditional adherents was declining as they were becoming either Christian or Muslim. It went on to prophesy that by the end of the millenium the majority of traditional adherents would profess to be either Christians or Muslims, publishing figures to support this apparent trend.[13] The question then arises, if Christianity in particular is on the ascendancy, does it mean both culprits and victims were Christians or was it the few non-Christian Ghanaians who were responsible? Can we really extrapolate our cultural beliefs from our new faiths? Perhaps there can be no better words to describe our dilemma than the statement by the former Catholic Archbishop of Tamale, P.P. Dery (1973: 53):

> Christianity cannot unmask the mythical and superstitious man completely. The African is a good Christian only when all is well with him. He resorts to mythical healing whenever he is in serious trouble.

Looking at the contemporary religious behaviour of Ghanaians it seems that the more Christianity intensifies its evangelization process, the more Ghanaians resort to the more familiar traditional beliefs to explain the inexplicable.

With regard to African indigenous religions the statistics by the Ghana Evangelization Committee appear to assume changes that do not correspond to the observed reality. For example, in the 1980s and early 1990s Ghanaian newspapers reported an influx of people from both inside and outside the country to the Kwaku Firi Shrine, whose priest, Nana Drobo, was said to have had a cure for Aids. The concerns of the Christian communities have been reflected in conference themes such as, "The Challenge of Evangelisation in West Africa Today in the Light of African Traditional Religion", "The New Religious Movements and the Renewed Islamic Presence"; "Christianity and African Culture in Contemporary Ghana"; "Religions in Ghana: Co-existence and Conflicts".

There has been dialogue between Christians and representatives of indigenous religions in attempts at indigenization of Christianity in order to retain their Christian congregation (see Sackey 1996). This shows that there is still some insecurity and anxiety on the part of the Christian churches. A very high-ranking mission clergyman expressed his concern to me about how some of his clerical colleagues have African protective medicine prepared and brought to them even at their hospital bedsides. It is therefore difficult to determine who adheres to African religion and who does not. Such events, among others, should be considered when assessing the evangelization process, rather than relying solely on statistics which do not represent reality.

Precipitating Factors

Anthropological literature emphasizes that cultural practices of every sort can induce stress: from toilet training to puberty, religious beliefs etc. Culture and personality studies, cognitive theories, as well as theories of social change (e.g. the death of a person, loss of status, loss of culture) and adaptation have been described as variables that produce stress (Spradley and Phillips 1972, Wallace 1970). In the light of these, an evaluation of public opinion may be based on the social stresses prevailing at the time of the vanishing organ scare:

Political and Economic Stressors

It was a period, indeed barely a month after the general parliamentary and presidential elections in December 1996, and there were mixed feelings about the election results. There was a general feeling of discontent with regard to some public officials who should have been justly punished for serious fraud offences, but a government white paper sought to exonerate them. It was an economically lean period when the already deplorable financial situation of the average Ghanaian was worsened by expenses during the past Christmas celebrations – a celebration which has become more materialistic and expensive. This reality, together with the impending financial angst of back-to-school expenditures and increases in the prices of household utilities such as the LP Gas, could have contributed to the way people conducted themselves during the vanishing organ scarce.

Religious stressors

It was a period when Christian religious re-awakening was apparently flourishing, as evidenced in the rapid mushrooming of newer versions of Pentecostal and charismatic movements and the presence of various evangelists, prophets and reverends from both within and abroad. However, the presence of VSOS indicates that the religious fervor or faith might have changed but the functions of indigenous beliefs – as a source of solving current existential problems, as a unifying factor in times of distress – are consciously or unconsciously still prevalent.

Ethnicity factor

It was a period when people were ready to vent ethnic sentiments that had been brewing in the country. A *Graphic* (January 25, 1997: 5) columnist did not rule out the possibility of people seeking and taking revenge on other people, whom they had had in view for some time. Because this phenomenon is said to have originated in Eweland and some of the accused were Ewe, it could be argued that it was a moment of expressing disapproval of the alleged Ewe hegemony which people have hitherto been unable to fight against.

Lawlessness

Lawlessness, which seems to have consistently characterized the Ghanaian society and culture since the Rawlings led AFRC military coup in 1979, and his revolution in 1981 is a precipitating factor for the VSOS hysteria and lynching. These events had to their discredit several cases of lynching, including the murder of the three high court judges and a senior army officer; the indecency and brutality of lashing naked women (traders) in public; and the burning down of Makola no. 1, one of the largest markets in Accra (see also Sackey 1996). In recent times people have taken the law into their own hands, since the law enforcement agents and courts do not perform their expected duties. One Jimmy who phoned-in to Joy FM Front Page program on 24/1/97 thought the VSOS was 'symptomatic of an increasingly lawless society' and that the police did not seem to fulfil their role adequately and thought maybe the police need a shrinkage (of their sexual organs). The *Chronicle* (August 27-28, 1997:8) also wrote that lawlessness resulting in lynching is becoming a cultural syndrome in urban areas of the country where one needs only to shout 'thief' and people will set on the person with an assortment of weapons to batter them.

Conclusions

It appears Ghanaians are not prepared for any eventualities in life, be they droughts, famines, floods, disease etc. If we cannot handle these very important tangible things of day to day existence, how much less can we deal with supernatural phenomena such as the vanishing organ syndrome?

That the fear of the vanishing sexual organ was prevalent among men could imply a strong power relationship between the genders. The angst of the VSOS might also have sprung from the masculinized self-construction of sexual and gender superiority and domination. Any idea therefore that impinges on this powerful ideology tends to humiliate masculinity. There was therefore a need to avert and preserve a loss of power.

A word of caution has also been suggested for the general public (*Graphic* January 25, 1997: 5). If the victims and passers-by will be patient enough (when such an incident occurs) and then calmly cause the arrest of those doing the 'touching', it will end the mystery. It seems this advice has been heeded to by the police because according to a police source[14] seven persons who claimed that their organs had vanished after the suspects shook hands or touched them were detained together with the accused to be examined for the veracity of the phenomenon. Just after this, the VSOS quickly moved out of Ghana traveling through Ivory Coast to Senegal where it proceeded to cause distress and havoc. Finally, the police must be well equipped with the basic logistics needed, such as riot-control material at all police stations to enable them to deal effectively with mob action. It might be advisable for both the police and victims to mount a strategy that would effectively prove whether or not the seeming hoax is real. (*Graphic* January 25, 1997:5).

As Ghanaians, our cultural beliefs are generally inseparable from everyday life. Our essence is embedded in our culture and we shall continue to resort to the known whenever we want to make sense of the unknown. However, I hope now that we are also more aware of the VSOS, we would be more vigilant and level-headed to be better able to handle it the next time it should recur in Ghana.

Endnotes

1 This chapter has appeared earlier in an edition of the Pan African Anthropological Association's Journal. *African Anthropology* vol. IV (2) 1997: 110-125. The author and editors are grateful for permission to reprint.

2 Statistics on the total number of deaths were not available.

3 At the time of writing, police dockets on those arrested in connection with the phenomenon had already been sent to the courts.

4 These have become my daily companions and partners in conversation in the absence of a personal car and other reliable means of transportation.

5 The police action has been recorded at the Central Police Station, Accra where I was kindly allowed to view some of their documentation on the VSOS.

6 However, it was later found out that this phenomenon is widespread rather than localized. It is believed to have entered Ghana from Cameroon. From there it got to Ivory Coast and currently it is said to have reach Senegal where it has also claimed human lives.

7 Addo on his live interview, Front Page, on Joy FM radio, 24/1/97.

8 Comments by Mrs. Rachel Phillips, a psychologist at the University of Ghana on Kwaku Sakyi Addo's Front Page live program on Joy FM radio, January 24, 1997.

9 Although witchcraft is believed to be inherited, it can also be acquired in various ways. One can buy or receive it as a gift from strangers (see Sarpong 1974)

10 This type of *ayera* or magic could be described as a good one, if the assertion about Nkrumah were true. This would imply that Nkrumah used this power to liberate his people from colonial bondage.

11 As already indicated, the real actor or offender often evades arrest through spiritual means.

12 Formerly, there were only a few minutes of religious broadcast in the form of religious worship and prayer solely by mission churches and the revivalistic 'Hour of Visitation' program.

13 The figures given raised many questions as they lumped together traditionalists and atheists and implied that traditional adherents would disappear by the year 2000.

14 An officer at Criminal Investigation Department CID at the Central Police Station, Accra, disclosed this to me in a conversation on 30/8/97.

Bibliography

Chronicle, 1997. Lynching is barbaric. August 27 – 38

Daily Graphic, 1997. Panic Drama in Accra January 17. How sex organs are said to vanish. January 22.

Daily Graphic, 1997. Of satanic seals, ignorance and superstition. January 25. Accra

Dery, Peter P., 1973. Traditional Healing and Spiritual Healing in Ghana; Christian Attitudes. *Ghana Bulleting of Theology*. 4(4): 53-64.

Ghana Evangelism Committee, 1993. *National Church Survey Update*. Kumasi: Ghana Evangelism Committee.

Ghanaian Times, 1997. Seal of Satan Reaches. Accra, January 17.

Kiev, Arik, 1972. *Transcultural Psychiatry*. Hamondsworth: Penguin Education.

Kleinman, Arthur, 1980. *Patients and Healers in the Context of Culture*. Berkeley: University of California Press.

Lader, Malcolm and Isaac Marks, 1971. *Clinical Anxiety*. London: Heinemann.

Mbiti, John S., 1975. *Introduction to African Religion*. London: Heinemann.

Sackey, Brigid M., 1996. *Women, Spiritual Churches, and Politics in Ghana*. Ph.D. diss. Temple University.

Sackey, Brigid M., 1997. 'Don't Think of me as a Woman because He that is me is a man' The story of Sofo Mary Owusu of the Great I am that I am Church. In R. Mahlke et al. (eds.), *Living Faith, Festschrift fuer hands-Juergen Greaschat*. Frankfurt: Peter Lang. Pp. 125-136.

Sakyi Addo, K., 1997. Front Page Program, Joy FM Radio January 24.

Sarpong Peter K., 1974. *Ghana in Retrospect. Some Aspects of Ghanaian Culture*. Accra /Tema: Ghana Publishing Corporation.

Spradley, James and Mark Phillips, 1972. Culture and Stress. A Quantitative Analysis. *American Anthropologist* 74:518-529.

Turner Victor, 1988. Passages, Margins and Poverty: Religious Symbols of Communitas. In Paul Bohannan and Mark Glazer (eds.), *High Points in Anthropology*. New York: McGraw-Hill Inc. Pp. 503 – 528.

Weekly Spectator, 1997. The Mystery of Keta. Accra, January 11.

EPILOGUE

GHANA'S ATTEMPTS AT MANAGING THE HIV/AIDS EPIDEMIC: A REVIEW OF EFFORTS

Phyllis Mary Antwi & Yaa P. A. Oppong

The AIDS[1] epidemic in Ghana has spread *relatively* "slowly" and "steadily" over the past two decades. Currently, the national prevalence rate stands at 3.0% and at the end of 2001 approximately 360,000 Ghanaians were living with HIV/AIDS and 200,000 children were orphaned (UNAIDS 2002). In comparison with her immediate neighbors and with other African countries, Ghana's prevalence rate is *relatively* low. Nevertheless, according to the Ghanaian Ministry of Health (MOH), the prognosis is *"grim"* and efforts to achieve the country's development goals are being thoroughly eroded and undermined by this deadly virus (ibid.). Despite efforts to date, "evidence suggests that the epidemic is still expanding throughout the country," and the epidemic has yet to stabilize. Indeed, analysis of the sentinel surveillance data from 1994 through 2000 indicated that HIV prevalence increased from 2.7% in 1994 to 4.6% in 1997 to 3.0% today. Although there appears to have been a slight dip in prevalence this is not being reported as such, but is rather accounted for by changes in the manner in which prevalence is calculated.[2] In short, the future is uncertain and the very survival of the nation is threatened (MOH 2001).

Over the past two decades, several entities have been involved in HIV prevention efforts. First and foremost, the Government of Ghana (GOG) has spearheaded the national response and the government has increasingly partnered with international and local NGO's. The NGO community has been very much a part of the national response, indeed increasingly so, as have some faith-based institutions.[3] This epilogue to the volume describes the Government of Ghana's response to the AIDS epidemic over the past two decades. It outlines the various institutional arrangements/responses that have been developed by the government over time, as well as the partnerships that the government has developed with various international institutions. In addition, the chapter details the various components of the emerging national response and outlines the efforts to date in prevention, care and latterly treatment. In sum this chapter reviews the accomplishments to date and offers suggestions for the difficult and uncertain road ahead.

AIDS Cases

In 1985 the laboratory diagnosis of human immunodeficiency virus (HIV) infection began at the Noguchi Memorial Institute of Medical Research (NMIMR), in Accra, when Professor Masanori Hayami, of the Institute of Medical Science of Tokyo, introduced the Indirect Fluorescent Antibody Test (ITAT) for HIV. His donation of the reagents made it possible for the Institute to provide HIV screening to the Korle Bu Teaching Hospital Blood Transfusion Unit in Accra and Clinicians for the whole of 1986.[4]

Since the first recorded case in March 1986 – through 2003 – only 89,000 cases were officially reported to the Ministry of Health; two-thirds of *all* these cases were female. In truth, the number of cumulative AIDS cases in the country is unknown and unknowable and the vast majority of those infected do not know that they are. For a variety of reasons, including cost and access (social, economic and geographic), some individuals do not seek hospital care when they are sick. In addition the MOH notes that, 'some physicians or nurses may not want to record a diagnosis of AIDS because of the stigma attached to the disease.' Furthermore, private laboratories are not required to report their figures to the government and many choose not to do so.[5]

HIV and AIDS surveillance began with the reporting of AIDS cases. However, it soon became apparent that this was not sufficient, and in order to provide information for planning, targeting and evaluating preventive activities, community-based surveys needed to be carried out. Given the resources required, both human and financial, the National AIDS Control Programme (NACP) opted for annual Sentinel Sero Surveillance. In 1992 the HIV Sentinel Sero Surveillance was established in five regions. The number of sites included in the national surveillance system has gradually expanded over time and today each of Ghana's ten administrative regions has designated two hospitals or health centers as sentinel surveillance sites. In 1999 two further sentinel sites were added to Greater Accra, in order to, 'reflect the diversity of population in that region', bringing the total number of surveillance sites in Ghana to 22 (MOH 2001).

According to the Ghanaian Ministry of Health (MOH) and to USAID, 'The HIV Sentinel surveillance system in Ghana, with a sample size of 500 at each site... and consistent reporting each year, ranks among the best sentinel surveillance systems in any African country.' (MOH 2001:70; USAID 2002). Surveillance data is not without its limitations however, since it only captures sexually active female populations who attend antenatal clinics.[6] Therefore, males are excluded, as are women who are not pregnant and not in the reproductive age group.

HIV/AIDS in Ghana: Gender and Geography

Sex & Age

Several 'outstanding' (Anarfi et al. 1997:227) and 'rare' (Oppong, J.R. 1998) features of the epidemic in Ghana were apparent from the outset, and distinguished it from other countries. The first outstanding feature of the Ghanaian epidemic was that initial cases were predominantly – over 80% – female. Indeed, the initial female/male sex ratio was 6:1 and the epidemic remained primarily a female epidemic until the late 1990s (Anarfi et al. 1997). By 1996/1997 the female/male sex ratio began to narrow. As a result women were particularly blamed for, and stigmatized by, the epidemic.

The majority of early cases – both female and male – were aged between twenty and forty, although cases were reported in all age groups. Today, 'the peak ages for AIDS cases are 25-34 for females and 30-39 for males' (MOH 1999b: 15). More than 90 percent of AIDS cases in Ghana today are found among adults between the ages of 15 and 49.

Economic Migrants

In the early 1970s, Ghana's compromised economic situation fuelled an exodus of economic refugees to other countries in the sub-region and to parts of Europe and North America. The economic crisis reached its peak in 1983 with massive food shortages and the adoption of structural adjustment. It has been noted that, '...risky sexual behavior, including commercial sex work, became increasingly viable among these economic refugees' (Oppong J.R. 1998: 446). During the early days of the Ghanaian epidemic, close to, '*98% of...cases were found in people with a history* of recent residence or an extended visit outside the country, particularly former residents of Cote d'Ivoire' (Oppong, J. R. 1998: 440). Thus, the second exceptional feature of the disease was that initially, close to 100% of infected women had a history of travel outside the country.

Several studies have documented and described the unique vulnerabilities of commercial sex workers and female itinerant traders in Ghana. The latter constitute an important element in the national economy and both may have unwittingly contributed to the spread of the disease (Anarfi et al. 1997; Anarfi et al. 2000; Oppong, J.R. 1998). Anarfi et al. note that, 'itinerant women traders appear highly vulnerable, as women and as highly mobile people' (Anarfi et al. 1997). Specifically, migration ties between the Eastern Region of Ghana and Abidjan are believed to have fuelled the high rates of HIV in the early years of the epidemic (Oppong J.R. 1998).

During this period (late 70s to late 80s), La Côte d'Ivoire had the highest HIV/AIDS prevalence rate in the sub-region and does to this day. Today, La Côte d'Ivoire has a national prevalence rate of 9.7%. Significantly, it has been estimated that approximately one-quarter of La Cote d'Ivoire's population were migrants from neighboring countries (Decosas et al. 1995). More Ghanaian women than men migrated to Abidjan at this time. Indeed, two-thirds of all Ghanaian migrants in Abidjan were female and a significant proportion were commercial sex workers (Decosas et al. 1995). In a 1995 review of Migration and AIDS in West Africa, Decosas et al. (1995) noted that, 'more than half of all professional prostitutes in Abidjan are Ghanaian.'

The proportion of new HIV/AIDS cases in Ghana with a history of travel has subsequently declined. Nevertheless, in popular perception, migrant women are still to be feared. To this day, studies have documented that returning female migrants are 'completely [shunned]' by their village community upon return from their travels and branded as HIV carriers (Anarfi et al. 2000:113).

Geographical Disparities

As noted in the introduction Ghana is a very diverse country due to a number of different factors. Today, HIV infection exists in all parts of the country, nevertheless the geographical distribution of cases throughout the country is considerably uneven and specific regional patterns have developed (Agyei-Mensah 2001). Of Ghana's ten regions, the Eastern Region has consistently reported the highest levels of infection. The northern third of the country presently reports a lower prevalence rate (1.4%) than the middle (2.6%) and southern regions (3.6%) (MOH 2001:15).

Initially, the Ghanaian epidemic was predominantly rural. This is in contrast to other African countries where the highest HIV prevalence rates were usually, observed in major urban areas, typically the largest cities. This is the case in Burkina Faso, Mali, Nigeria, and Sierra Leone, but not Ghana. (Oppong, J. R. 1998: 437). In the early years of the epidemic, Greater Accra (home to the capital city, Accra) had one of the lowest rates in the country; Accra's prevalence rate has gradually increased.

The social geography of Ghana has shaped the HIV epidemic in the country. The early story of AIDS in Ghana – linking as it does issues of gender and geography – illustrates, that, 'HIV diffusion patterns...reflect[ed] the spatial distribution and social networks of vulnerable social groups' (Oppong, J. R. 1998). As the epidemic has matured, infection has spread from the, 'original core of high risk, migrant, commercial sex workers into the general adult population as an endemic problem' (Oppong, J. R. 1998: 441). The differences between the regions has narrowed.

Complex Processes

Over time, various models and hypotheses have been put forward to account for the spread of HIV/AIDS in Africa. These models, often focusing on different processes implicated in the spread of the disease, are not mutually exclusive (Agyei-Mensah 2001). Indeed, several of these theories would appear pertinent to the Ghanaian case and go some way to shedding light on the complex social, economic and political processes fueling the epidemic.

The sexual behavior *model* suggests that frequent sexual contact and frequent changes in sexual partner fuel the epidemic. Although this model, 'downplays the importance of [the] historical, social, political and economic contexts within which such risk behaviors are played out' (Agyei-Mensah 2001), it is widely acknowledged, and accepted, that certain sexual behaviors and preferences (specifically such factors as rates of multi-partner sex and the age disparities between partners) have profound implications for the nature and prevalence of the epidemic. In Ghana for example, there are significant differences in the rates of HIV/AIDS infection between northern Moslem populations and southern Christian populations. These differences can partly be accounted for by differences in the nature of polygamous unions among these populations. Broadly speaking, polygynous unions among Moslem peoples tend to be 'closed' while Christians are more likely to have 'open' polygynous relationships making the latter more vulnerable.[7]

A vulnerability interpretation of the epidemic (Tarantola 2002) suggests that a range of situations, contexts and conditions renders individuals and certain groups (by virtue of their position/roles in society) susceptible (in other words vulnerable) to infection. These vulnerable individuals and groups engage in 'risky' survival strategies such as commercial sex. Thus, this theory suggests that the diffusion of the disease reflects the social networks of these vulnerable people, such as returning commercial sex workers, the unemployed and poor as well as those engaging in 'non-formal' polygamous unions (Oppong, J.R. 1998). Vulnerability theory also ties in with another highly pertinent perspective, which suggests that the asymmetrical nature of gender relations is a contributory factor. Gender issues are at the core of the Ghanaian – and sub-Saharan – epidemic and three distinct gender-related aspects of the disease can be identified. In the first place, risk and 'vulnerability' to HIV/AIDS differ significantly by sex and age. As outlined above, although the sex ratio has narrowed somewhat in Ghana, the initial AIDS cases in Ghana were almost entirely female and the ratio of female infections still exceeds the number of male infections to this day. Following on from the first assertion, (that women are disproportionately infected) they are also disproportionately *affected* and impacted by the disease. This reflects the different roles and responsibilities that men and women in Ghana bear in family, household and society affairs/issues. Additionally, the epidemic is basically fuelled by sexual behavior and women often have little or no decision making power in sexual relations.

From a geographical perspective, issues of migration and diffusion would appear to be highly pertinent in explaining the Ghanaian situation and the migrant labor hypothesis (Agyei-Mensah 2001) undoubtedly goes some way towards explaining the spatial configurations of the epidemic, both now and in the past. This theory posits that HIV is spread through intra and international labor migration, which spatially diffuses the epidemic over time. As discussed earlier in this chapter, economic migrants – including itinerant female traders – accounted for significant numbers of initial cases. Additional explanations are offered by political ecology approaches, which relate the epidemic to socio-economic contexts and to local and global political developments. In applying this political ecology approach to the Ghanaian situation one could relate the harsh economic climate and uncertain political situation, experienced in the late 1970s/early 1980s, to the exodus of economic migrants and political refugees. These uncertainties, and the economic migrants created, are squarely implicated in fuelling the epidemic in Ghana. More recently, the present political and economic crisis in Cote d'Ivoire has fuelled a refugee crisis and thousands of individuals have crossed into Ghana. With Cote d'Ivoire's elevated HIV prevalence figures one could hypothesize that these refugees could contribute to an elevation of Ghana's HIV prevalence rate.

In sum, many factors have contributed to the spread of HIV/AIDS in Ghana. These include a compromised economic and political situation, asymmetrical gender relations, international labor migration and certain high-risk sexual behaviors among vulnerable populations.

Impacts on National Development

What makes AIDS so important to national development is that it affects virtually all sectors of the economy and all sections of society. In the worst affected countries, the economic and social impact of HIV/AIDS is very visible and its qualitative and quantitative impacts have been appraised. In Ghana however, the economic[8] and social impacts are yet to be experienced on a national scale and subsequently very few studies have catalogued the impacts of the epidemic on society and the economy. The few analyses that do exist consistently use the *future* tense in describing the impacts of the epidemic. The MOH notes that HIV/AIDS is a, 'killer disease of increasing seriousness that will have a significant impact on the country' (MOH 2001: 31). Elsewhere the MOH states, 'The economic effects will be felt first by individuals and their families then ripple outwards to firms and businesses and the macro-economy'. In other words, these are the likely scenarios – based upon experiences gleaned from other parts of the continent – but at present the relatively low prevalence rates have not translated into observable/measurable impacts.

Institutional Response: The National Program and the National Policy on HIV/AIDS

Early National Response

In 1985, the Ghanaian Government established a National Technical Advisory Commission on AIDS and shortly afterwards – in 1987 – created the National AIDS/STD Control Program (NACP) to coordinate the national response to the epidemic. More recently, in 2000, all government sectors were brought under the umbrella of the multi-sectoral Ghana AIDS Commission. One of the specific goals of this latter agency is to ensure that all government Ministries incorporate a separate budget for HIV/AIDS activities. In the section that follows these various institutional arrangements will be described before some of their specific AIDS prevention initiatives are analyzed.

In 1985 the Ministry of Health appointed a group that was designated as the National Technical Committee on AIDS (NTCA). It was assigned the responsibility to a) define the extent of the AIDS problem and its epidemiology in Ghana; b) establish a prevention and control programme; c) and advise Government on the disease and related matters. The NTCA was in fact established a year before the first case of HIV-seropositivity was officially diagnosed. The Ministry of Health also purchased ELISA machines and testing reagents and established HIV screening at four regional hospitals.[9] The NTCA, in fulfillment of its mandate, initiated a wide range of activities, such as educational programmes to increase public awareness and studies of the disease pattern in some high-risk sections of the population, notably, commercial sex workers. One of the initiatives put forward, in the initial NTCA document was the formation of District AIDS Committees.

National AIDS Control Program: Short and Medium Term Plans

In 1987, the government created a National AIDS Control Programme (NACP) to which the Ministry assigned a full-time Programme Manager, at the request of the Ministry of Health. A short-term plan (STP) for the Prevention and Control of AIDS was formulated during the implementation of which (1987 and 1988) an intensive health promotion campaign was mounted using various channels including radio and television. Part of the STP activities were to make blood transfusions safe and increase the capabilities of health and non-health workers at the national and regional levels. In addition to promoting a broad range of activities, for the prevention and control of AIDS, the STP served as preparatory assistance for the development of the five year Medium Term Plan (MTP) for the Prevention and Control of AIDS. The general objectives of the MTP were to a) prevent further transmission and spread of human immunodeficiency (HIV) infection; b) to reduce the impact of AIDS on affected individuals, families, groups and communities at large. The MTP, 'guided HIV/AIDS prevention and control efforts over the 1989 – 1993 period' (MOH 2001: 53).

The strategies of the Medium Term Plan were a) surveillance to determine the extent and pattern of distribution of HIV infection and sexually transmitted diseases (STD's) in Ghana; b) assuring the safety of blood transfusion: c) providing adequate laboratory services for the detection of HIV infection and diagnosis of AIDS and STD's: d) providing adequate clinical management to AIDS and STD's patients: e) providing psychosocial support to both affected individuals, their families and their communities: f) providing information and education to the general public and various target groups on the dangers of HIV. The organizational framework for the implementation of the MTP included a) The Programme Management Unit; b) The National Advisory Council on AIDS; c) Regional and District AIDS Committees.[10] The Program Management Unit was expected to provide the mechanism for planning and coordinating all AIDS programme activities in the country. It also provided policy direction, technical strategies, and assisted in resource mobilization and programme monitoring and evaluation. The NACP was seen as an integral part of the Primary Health Care Programme and the Ministry of Health was primarily responsible for oversight and implementation of HIV programs. Over time however, other public sector ministries and private sector organizations as well as NGO's and People Living with HIV/AIDS (PLWHA) have become involved in programme implementation

Government Efforts at Expanding the Response

In 1994, a Consensus Workshop was organized to sensitize all Ministries and Departments about the need to have a multi-sectoral approach to the prevention and control of AIDS.[11] It was recognized that AIDS could no longer be considered a health problem, as originally thought, and it was acknowledged that AIDS was going to affect the overall development of the country, hence the need for all departments and agencies to be involved. The Workshop sought commitment from the various sectors and urged them to look at their relevant activities and provide resources and the needed manpower to combat the epidemic.

It had become quite clear that the public sector, that is the Ministry of Health alone could not spearhead the response to HIV/AIDS. Some NGOs and private sector organizations, which had a comparative advantage, came on board and implemented activities relevant to the AIDS response. Organizations such as Ghana Social Marketing Foundation (GSMF) and the Christian Health Association of Ghana (CHAG) implemented programs. GSMF launched a number of initiatives, which included a mass media campaign on HIV/AIDS and condom promotion targeted at the youth. In the year 2000, a major HIV/AIDS awareness campaign was launched named *'Stop AIDS. Love Life'* – GSMF was one of the main collaborators in this campaign. Today many Ministries have HIV/AIDS programs in place. For example the Ministry of Youth and Sports, 'has an AIDS Programme directed at the youth', the Ministry of Agriculture, 'has developed a very comprehensive plan aimed at reducing the spread of HIV/AIDS among its extension workers and the country's farmers' (IPAA 1999:9).

The National Policy on HIV/AIDS and STIs

The second medium term plan (1993) attempted to incorporate the plans of actions of all ministries. However this did not work since it was widely believed that the Ministry of Health needed to organize AIDS activities. In 1997 the NACP began drafting a Policy Document on HIV/AIDS. It was elaborated in 1999. In the document, Government had recognized the threat that AIDS posed to national development goals. The HIV/AIDS and STI's policy document provided,

> the necessary statement of policy commitment for which a legislative framework shall be built for the protection of people infected with HIV/AIDS and in creating an Expanded Multi-sectoral Response to combat any further spread of the epidemic in Ghana. It is expected that this National Policy will evolve with new scientific knowledge and information as well as changes in our attitudes and behaviors. The policies and guidelines will therefore need to be revised periodically. (MOH 2000a: ix-x)

In order for the policy to be owned, by as many of the concerned organizations as possible, six task forces wrote the relevant sections of the document. Secondly the initial draft was circulated widely for initial review and comments and then consensus workshops were organized at the regional levels where representatives of various communities, Ministries and Departments reviewed the document and made the necessary changes. The guiding principles are stated as follows,

'The Government and people of Ghana affirm that this National Policy on HIV/AIDS and STI's is :

> Premised on and complementary to the 1992 Constitution of Ghana, Ghana's Vision 2020 document, the Revised Population Policy and the Medium Term Health Strategy of the Ministry of Health.

Based on the principles of social justice and equity.[12]
Derived from the recognition that adequate health care is an inalienable
right of every Ghanaian, and this includes those infected with HIV or
other STI's.
Based on the view that appropriate legislation will be enacted to com-
plement the provisions in this Policy. (MOH 2000a: 4)

'The national policy emphasises information and education leading to
behavioural change, specially among youth, and the widespread
availability and promotion of condoms as keys to limiting the spread
of the virus.' (MOH 2001: 54)

National Strategic Framework

A National Strategic Framework on HIV/AIDS was prepared for the period
2000-2005 in order to provide an overarching framework for mobilizing all
sectors. The framework outlines the goals, principles and prioritized strategies on HIV prevention and care provision in the country. Five key intervention areas were proposed (Bosu et al. 2001): prevention of new transmission of HIV;[13] care and support for PLWHA;[14] creating an enabling legal,
ethical and policy environment for national response; decentralized implementation and institutional arrangements;[15] research, monitoring and
evaluation including surveillance (ibid.)

The draft policy document has implicitly guided HIV/AIDS policies in
Ghana since it was drafted during the government of J.J. Rawlings, whose
party lost power in the December 2000 elections. The subsequent government, presided over by J. A Kuffour, based much of its HIV/AIDS program
on this draft policy. After its submission to the Cabinet, President Kuffour
gave approval for the policy to be implemented in August 2004.

Ghana AIDS Commission

A supra-ministerial body, known as the Ghana AIDS Commission, was
established in 2000 by an Act of Parliament. This commission, under the
office of the President, is chaired by the Vice President and is the 'highest
policy-making body in HIV/AIDS' (MOH 2001: 57). The Commission has a

secretariat responsible for the day-to-day coordination, management of funds, monitoring and supervision of *all* national HIV/AIDS related activities.[16] The Commission's mandate is to: advise the Government of Ghana on policy issues relating to HIV/AIDS; expand and coordinate the national HIV/AIDS STI response; monitor and evaluate all on-going HIV/AIDS activities; identify and mobilize various resources for programs.

From the preceding section we see that the Government of Ghana appears to have put much time and effort into creating appropriate institutional mechanisms for managing the epidemic. These arrangements have changed over time and have expanded to include all Ministries/Sectors of the government. Indeed they have also included many partners from the international community.[17] Ghanaian leadership has been very much engaged and successive presidents have taken public leadership roles in discussing HIV/-AIDS in Ghana. This history of institutional arrangements and policy interventions would appear to contradict a recent JHU/USAID statement claiming that there had been a, 'virtual silence and absence of a coordinated and sustained national response to HIV/AIDS issues in Ghana' prior to 2000 (JHU/USAID: 2002). We now turn our attention to the main HIV/AIDS prevention activities that these various institutional mechanisms have overseen and implemented.

HIV/AIDS Interventions: Policies & Priorities

Prevention through behaviour change, condom promotion, and STD treatment is many times more cost-effective than either providing hospital treatment for AIDS patients or trying to prevent the spread of the virus with anti-retroviral therapy (MOH 2001:48).

The priorities of the Government of Ghana's HIV interventions have essentially been three-fold. In the first instance HIV/AIDS interventions have been implemented with a view to limiting HIV transmission through heterosexual contact. A secondary set of activities aims at HIV/AIDS management (care for people living with AIDS (PLWHA)) and prevention of mother to child transmission (MTCT). A third – more recent – focus is on treatments and vaccines. However, from the above quotation we see that priorities are firmly with behaviour change interventions.

HIV/AIDS Prevention Activities: Behavior Change Initiatives

Almost two decades since the outbreak of the epidemic in Ghana, information, education and communication initiatives continue to predominate in AIDS prevention activities. Although there has been public education on the epidemic since 1985, the kinds of messages disseminated have changed. Initially, 'IEC on HIV/AIDS gave basic information about the aetiology and mode of transmission of the disease. Subsequent messages have been geared towards achieving behavioural change, and dispelling rumours and misconceptions about the disease' (Awusabo Asare 1995:231).

In addition to campaigns geared towards the general population, various targeted interventions have been implemented. These have been aimed at groups with the highest levels of infection and highest "risk" of acquiring the disease. For example, after a MOH study of Commercial Sex Workers (CSW's) in the Accra-Tema municipality estimated a prevalence of 75.95%, CSW's were targeted for specific interventions including condom promotion (MOH 2000). In addition, specific faith-based organizations have also become exceedingly active and are receiving considerable funding from the donor community.

Overall, the Ghanaian government has prioritized the following objectives in a bid to limit the sexual transmission of HIV/AIDS (MOH 2001: 43): promoting abstinence and faithfulness; reducing the overall number of sexual partners; delaying the onset of sexual activity among adolescents; promoting the use and consistent availability of condoms, including female condoms; strengthening programs for STD control; encouraging voluntary counseling and testing (VCT). These objectives have been promoted through a variety of strategies. For example, mass media campaigns, counseling and education programs, social marketing campaigns etc. have been variously used. As the section on institutional arrangements illustrates the government has – through various means – attempted to curtail the increase of the epidemic over time. However, it was not until 1999/2000 that efforts were stepped up and a coordinated nation-wide campaign was implemented. We now turn our attention to the largest and most comprehensive HIV/AIDS awareness/social marketing campaign organized in Ghana and will review its efforts and achievements to date.

Stop AIDS. Love Life
Partners

In February 2000 a major nation-wide HIV/AIDS campaign was launched in Ghana called, 'Stop AIDS. Love Life'. The campaign involved a consortium of partners including the Ghanaian Ministry of Communication and the

Ministry of Health/National AIDS Control Program, the Ghana Social Marketing Foundation (GSMF) and the Johns Hopkins University Center for Communication Programs (JHU/CCP). According to the USAID Mission Director, the campaign was a synthesis of the, 'lessons learned from fighting AIDS in Africa over the past decade'. The prevention programs have focused on a 'trilogy of protective behaviors to successfully slow the epidemic, including abstinence, fidelity and condom use – the ABCs of prevention.' (JHU/USAID: 2002: vi).

According to USAID, when the program was first designed in 1999, 'the data suggested that Ghana had been in a good position relative to many other African countries with respect to the first two elements of this trilogy' (ibid.). In other words, the data suggested that compared with many other African contexts the average age at sexual debut was *relatively* late – 17.6 years for women and 19.4 for men (1998 GDHS). Additionally, the DHS noted that the proportion of men and women reporting multiple partner sex was *relatively* low.[18] The decision was therefore taken to promote all three ABC's but to place more emphasis on the C, namely condom promotion, since condom use was relatively low. Johns Hopkins and USAID sources additionally state that, 'research conducted with Ghanaian Youth prior to the intervention suggested that "social risks" of using abstinence, faithfulness or condoms were perceived as much greater than the "health risks" of not using them" (JHU/-USAID 2002: 2). Messages that focused exclusively on health issues were therefore not perceived as *'credible or relevant'* (ibid.). The campaign's efforts therefore focused on the 'social barriers' to preventive behavior.

Shattering the Silence

The campaign has been 'rolled out' in three successive phases – over a five-year time-line (JHU/PCS). The first phase, launched in February 2000 ran through June 2001 and was called **'Shattering the Silence'**. As the name implies, the campaign aimed to promote increased national dialogue about HIV/AIDS. It also had as its focus the aim of slowing the epidemic in Ghana by 'promoting greater use of HIV-protective behavior – abstinence, faithfulness, and condoms'. The campaign used an innovative 'combination of electronic media, community-based activities and print materials to maximize exposure and impact'[19] (JHU/PCS 2002). The campaign is seeking to increase risk perception among Ghanaians, increase social support for positive behavior (such as condom use) and increase compassion for those living with AIDS. A 'Love Life' Music Video and song were created – and the country's leading artists donated their time for free. Inventive television and radio spots[20] focused on three basic issues: "1) Modeling positive peer pressure for the ABC's of prevention, 2) convincing people of the urgency and magnitude of the problem in Ghana, and 3) testimonials from Ghanaians living with HIV and AIDS." (JHU/PCS 2002). More than 400,000 people are believed to have participated in Community rallies nation-wide in more than 200 Ghanaian cities, towns and villages. Twenty audio/video vans from the Information Services Department conducted rural outreach showing videos on AIDS in 5 local languages followed by question and answer sessions. Over four million people were reached this way – mainly poor, rural-dwelling populations. (JHU/CCP: 2003).

Interestingly, the GSMF is more explicit than JHU in its description of the phases of the campaign. Of phase 1, the GSMF say, "Phase I aggressively promotes the triad of Abstinence, Fidelity and Condom use, with emphasis being placed on condom use." No other source makes the point that the over-all emphasis is on condom use. JHU/CCP on the other hand suggests that during the first phase the focus was on abstinence *and* condom use as opposed to fidelity.

Journey of Hope

The second phase of the **'STOP AIDS Love Life'** campaign was launched in 2001. It was called the 'Journey of Hope' and continued with the dissemination of information and materials begun in phase 1. Additionally, it had as its focus the aim of helping people to move away from judgmental attitudes about safe sexual behaviour. Prominent chiefs and queen mothers – respected elders in many communities – were featured on television and radio spots addressing the subject of HIV/AIDS. Over 70% of the population is believed to have heard or seen these messages. A 'Journey of Hope' life skills kit was launched in September 2001. It was a tool to, 'assist organizations with participatory ways to enhance dialogue and behavioral change at the community level.' (JHU/CCP)

Some initiatives have been targeted at specific groups, for example a workplace initiative called Lifeshield was implemented in March 2001 with a goal to 'propel a paradigm shift from the perception of HIV/AIDS as a welfare issue to a human resource investment protection plan'. Eleven organizations from six regions in Ghana were initially enrolled in the programme. Participating companies include financial institutions, factories and plantations to name a few. Another prevention initiative has been implemented with commercial drivers – *Drive Protected*. A CIDA funded program has concentrated on providing treatment for sexually transmitted diseases for commercial sex workers. This has been on-going in Greater Accra and Ashanti Region since 1996. The initial phase of the campaign was in seven strategically selected hubs in five regions in Ghana. Peer educators were trained to carry out HIV/AIDS preventive education, as well as sell condoms in the hubs.

Reach out, Show Compassion

Phase three of the **Stop AIDS Love Life** campaign was launched in November 2002. Dubbed *'Reach out, Show Compassion,'* its aim is to work with religious leaders – both Christian and Moslem – to reduce the stigma surrounding HIV/AIDS. This phase aimed to train 900 clergy, Imams, and other religious leaders in Ghana. In addition television and radio spots are being used to support a compassionate response by quoting directly from the Bible and the Koran.

'I know my Goal'

The latest phase of the ongoing campaign is a programme aimed at empowering adolescent girls. It is called, *'Sara – "I know my Goal"*. The Programme, launched in April 2003, is being coordinated by the Ghana Education Service's Girls Education Unit and involves all primary and junior secondary schools in Ghana and child welfare NGO's operating at the community level.[21] The aim of the initiative is to, 'enable Ghanaian girls to develop self-esteem, self-efficacy, decision-making skills, and personal risk perception that will enable them to stay in school, develop positive boy-girl relationships, abstain from sex, and avoid *HIV/AIDS.'* (JHU 2003) While girls aged 11-15 years are the primary audience, boys, teachers, parents and community members are the 'secondary audience' (ibid.) Activities will involve the establishment of Sara clubs in schools and the facilitation of Sara initiatives in communities.[22]

In sum, over the past two decades, the government of Ghana has developed a series of institutional mechanisms and promoted a combination of interventions. These efforts were stepped up on a massive scale in 2000 with the launch of the **Stop AIDS Love Life** campaign. It is the view of the MOH that, 'each of the intervention packages…can make an important contribution to controlling the spread of HIV. Alone, none is likely to solve the problem completely; some people will respond to or be affected by one type of intervention while others will respond to or be affected by another.' (MOH 2001:46) We now turn our attention to the initiatives promoted in treatment, care and support.

HIV/AIDS Management: Treatment, Care and Support

It does not appear that either drugs or vaccines will contribute much to reducing the spread of HIV by sexual contact in Ghana in the next several years. (MOH 2002: 50)

In the third edition of the Ghanaian Ministry of Health's policy document, published in December 2001, *HIV/AIDS in Ghana: Background, Projections, Impacts, Interventions, and Policy,* a significant shift in the HIV/AIDS program in the country was noted, "from an almost exclusive focus on prevention to a Programme which still puts a priority on prevention but which has now been broadened to include a comprehensive programme on prevention, care and support" (MOH 2001: iv). Although HAART (Highly Active Anti-Retroviral Therapy) is 'not widely available' in Ghana, 'efforts to make these drugs more available and affordable to the clients will be strengthened' (ibid.) Some of the small-scale efforts in treatment, care and support are described below.

Home Care

Since the early 1990's, the Christian Health Association of Ghana (CHAG) – an umbrella organization for the health programs of sixteen churches (Catholic, Protestant, Pentecostal, etc.) has carried out Home-Based Care for Persons Living with HIV/AIDS (PLWHAs) as an extension of hospital services (Price et al. 2002). Home-based care was established in order to help families take care of their sick relatives and the activities included infection prevention, administering drugs and providing for the spiritual needs of the patients. During the implementation of home-based care it became apparent that the persons living with AIDS had various needs, the primary one being financial assistance. Therefore some of the programs implemented income-generating activities and provided seed money to the PLWHAs.[23] Due to issues related to stigma and discrimination, it was observed that many PLWHAs did not want home-care and the volunteers who visit the PLWHAs are now called 'friends of the sick' with no mention made of HIV or AIDS.

Treatment

Anti-retroviral treatment has only recently become available in Ghana. Although the drugs are available in the country for those who can afford it, large-scale systematic efforts to provide ARV therapy began in 2001. In February 2002 the START (Support, Treatment and Anti-Retroviral Therapy) Program was launched in Manya and Yilo Krobo districts in the Eastern Region. The program was a collaboration between Family Health International and the Government and implemented by FHI[24] (and funded by USAID) in Manya Krobo – a high prevalence area in the Eastern Region – where 18,000 out of an estimated population of 240,000 are HIV positive. The 'Start' program is a five-year, 'comprehensive prevention, care and treatment program that is designed to define, refine and document approaches to HIV/AIDS service delivery in resource-poor settings' (USAID 2002). Services being provided include VCT, clinical management of HIV-related conditions, opportunistic infections and AIDS; prevention of MTCT and community programs for home-based care; orphan care and community-based prevention activities (USAID 2002). At the end of 2003 voluntary counselling and testing, prevention of mother to child transmission and the provision of ART was expanded to the Korle Bu Teaching Hospital and provision of ART to Komfo Anokye Teaching Hospital. Patients who qualify to receive antiretroviral drugs have been receiving treatment since December 2004. Almost two thousand patients had been put on ARVs at the four sites (Agomanya, Atua, Komfo Anokye and Korle Bu hospitals), by September 2004.

Mother-to-child-transmission

The FHI pilot project has a MTCT component and 'interventions under this program include counselling, medical management, counselling on feeding options and the provision of Nevarapine. Under this program home-based care is also being encouraged.' (MOH 2001) Plans are afoot to scale up this initiative to 'include all districts in Ghana in the future'. (MOH 2001:49). According to the MOH, 'in the course of the first half of 2002, mothers who had tested positive for HIV received drug treatment during labour and the same drug was then given to their babies after birth. Boehringer Ingleheim, a pharmaceutical company, has offered to provide drugs for the Programme. At the close of May [2002] 49 mother-baby pairs had received treatment. The Programme has been extended to twenty-four other sites (MOH 2003).

The Global Fund to Fight AIDS, TB and Malaria

To support the provision of ART and other activities for the effective response to HIV/AIDS, the Government of Ghana submitted a successful proposal to the Global Fund to fight AIDS, TB and Malaria (GFATM). In addition to support for capacity building, expansion of VCT and PMTCT sites, GFATM funds are being used to purchase ARVs, HIV test kits, and other commodities needed to provide comprehensive HIV/AIDS prevention, treatment and care services. (MOH 2004)

Changes in A, B, C?

Phase one of the **Stop AIDS Love Life** campaign was evaluated in 2002 using a number of different data sources. The 1998 Ghana Demographic and Health Surveys (GDHS) as well as the Ghana Youth Survey (GYS) were used as baseline assessments. In July 2001 a household survey (the Ghana Reproductive Health and Child Survival Survey – GRHCSS) provided measures, 'following the initial phase of the campaign.' Impact assessments also included data on trends in condom sales between 1996 and 2001 as an independent measure of program effect. (JHU/CCP: 2003).[25]

According to these evaluations, the first phase of the campaign successfully reached a large proportion of the Ghanaian population. Overall, 83% of males (aged 15-59) and 77% of females (aged 15-49), 'recalled hearing or seeing the campaign logo or slogan.' (JHU/CCP: 2003). In addition, individuals exposed to the campaign were more likely to know of ways to avoid HIV/AIDS and more likely to have discussed condoms and abstinence. Awareness of abstinence as a method of HIV prevention increased during Phase One but it is unclear that 'usage' of this method changed (ibid.) What is clear though is that, 'young men, but not young women, exposed to Stop AIDS Love Life had more favorable attitudes towards abstinence' (JHU/USAID: 2002). The same source notes that 'reported' faithfulness did increase among married men with high exposure to the campaign (ibid.). As a result of these findings the campaign aims to 'intensify its efforts in promoting abstinence and in reducing the number of partners, especially for single people' (ibid.). Attitudes to condoms were more favorable among those individuals who had been exposed to the campaign. Regarding condom use, JHU/CCP conclude that, 'The campaign accomplished its objective of increasing the use of HIV-protective behaviors, particularly regarding the use of condoms. Among sexually active men, condom use at last sex increased from 13% in 1998 to 24% in 2001. Among sexually active women, condom use at last sex increased from 4% to 12% during that period.' (JHU/CCP: 2003)

The evaluation also concluded that sexually active men and women who had been exposed to the campaign were more likely than unexposed individuals to have used a condom at last sex.[26] Clearly, these figures do not in any way prove a causal link between exposure to the first phase of the campaign and condom use but the figures do suggest an association. The report noted that, 'although condom use increased, age at first sex and multiple partnerships were largely unchanged by the campaign among the population at large. This lack of change in sexual behavior may have been due to the relatively late age at sexual debut and the relatively low level of multiple partnerships in Ghana.' JHU/CCP: 2003).

A commonly used "measure" of the success of recent education and condom social marketing efforts is data on the increased sale of condoms in Ghana. It is not uncommon to come across statements such as, 'Sales have more than doubled to 1.8 million condoms a month since the campaign began'. (USAID Brief 2002). In the print media as well as in JHU's own evaluation materials great weight is attached to the fact that condoms sales in Ghana have 'soared' since the start of the campaign. It is always implied that this increase in sales is clear evidence that the campaign is succeeding and that protective behaviors have increased. An article by Goodrich et al. (1998) reminds us of the caution required in interpreting condom sale data. As more condoms are promoted larger packages, containing more condoms are sold, and little is *really* known about condoms after they are bought. They caution that, 'where condoms are heavily promoted, people may feel compelled to report their use, to conform to the perceived expectations of the researchers.' (Goodrich et al. 1998).

Challenges & The Way Forward

Despite the concerted and immense efforts to date, there are still a number of serious challenges that require attention.

Continuing Feminization of HIV/AIDS

At the beginning of the epidemic in Ghana, AIDS was seen as an epidemic that primarily affected women. The epidemiological information prevailing at the beginning of the epidemic supported that popular opinion. As the epidemic has unfolded it has become quite clear that all sections of the population are at risk of acquiring the infection. However, women's vulnerability still remains an issue to be addressed, since the factors that prevailed in the 1970s and 1980s are still relevant. There are marked gender differences in access to economic opportunities in Ghana. There are also cultural practices that promote the transmission of HIV/AIDS such as the acceptance of extra-marital relationships for men and the low levels of education for young girls, which increases their dependence on men. In the year 2000, women formed 57% of HIV/AIDS cases, nevertheless in popular perception HIV is still perceived as a women's epidemic. Indeed, from time to time law enforcement agencies round up 'prostitutes' and prosecute them in the court, perpetuating the myth that AIDS is *caused* by women. (NACP 2000).

Indifference & Denial

Another challenge is posed by the existence of denial about HIV/AIDS in many sections of Ghanaian society. This can partly be explained by the fact that Ghana is still experiencing an HIV epidemic rather than a full-blown AIDS epidemic. The epidemic is not visible on a massive scale and many people have yet to see and experience AIDS cases first hand, as they have in Eastern African countries. Some people feel that AIDS is still other people's problem and not their own. There is evidence that some segments of Ghanaian society are indifferent to the fact that AIDS is a killer disease. This issue has been well documented in various sources, including a recent 1999 article by Awusabo-Asare et al. entitled, 'All die be die'. This phrase translates as 'every death is death' and reflects the commonly stated perception that, 'people are going to die anyway, and it may not matter much what they die from' (Awusabo-Asare et al. 1999:125). The authors of this particular study of behavioral change (or rather the lack of) among young people in the Central Region of Ghana note that, 'HIV infection was one of the many things confronting people and, therefore, death from AIDS was not different from death from other conditions' (ibid.).

Discrimination

Another challenge is stigmatization and discrimination against people with HIV/AIDS.[27] The PLWHAs have repeatedly reported subtle and sometimes overt discrimination against them in the workplace, in the community[28] and sometimes by health care workers. As a result, in the year 2002, the Ministry of Health, the religious bodies and the JHU/CCP launched a campaign to promote compassion for PLWHAs. It is unclear as to what kind of a difference the campaign is making. The media continues to use language that is discriminatory against PLWHA, for instance instead of talking about PLWHAs they talk about AIDS 'victims' and they also say that AIDS is a killer disease. However, with the advent of anti-retroviral therapy AIDS is now (or at least it ought to be) considered a chronic disease. The current thinking in the country is that efforts need to be doubled to avert the gloom and doom message, hence VCT is being used as an entry point to care and people are being encouraged to find out their HIV status to be able to access care, since it has been shown that when people know their HIV status early they can be helped to prevent opportunistic infections by having prophylaxis for TB and other opportunistic infections.

Ownership & Acceptance

A major challenge is for employers to have specific programs for HIV/AIDS and fund these programs from their internal corporate resources and not from external funding. The companies in Ghana that have their own HIV/AIDS work programs tend to be companies that are affiliated to multinational companies. Ghana Social Marketing Foundation (GSMF) is currently working with some employers to develop workplace policy and programs (GSMF 2002). Clearly, GSMF is taking the lead and not the employers *per se*, but homegrown workplace programs are few and far between because employers have yet to feel the impacts on their businesses.

Scaling up Interventions

Since 2002 voluntary counseling and testing has become available in several sites in the whole country. These sites have demonstrated that given the right community sensitization, training of health care workers and establishing a friendly facility, the general population will patronize these services. There is therefore the need to identify resources, both human and financial to make these services widely available in the country. With the support of the Global Fund it is envisaged that VCT will be available in a total of 24 sites in the next five years. Clearly this will be inadequate and hence every attempt should be made to make this widely available, particularly to young people. Prevention of mother to child transmission is an intervention (if implemented properly) that can easily reduce the number of children born with HIV. Again, this needs to be scaled up. A major challenge facing this intervention is the low level of medically supervised deliveries – 50%. For this intervention to be implemented properly there is a need to find a way for women to have medically supervised deliveries and to have Nevirapine at the time of delivery.

Capacity Building

Attrition rates of trained staff (both clinical and project staff) is very high in Ghana. In the year 2001 alone, '662 health personnel comprising 60 doctors, 363 general nurses and 238 pharmacists left the country to seek greener pastures abroad.' (*Graphic* 2002) Even as the number of AIDS patients grows there are fewer and fewer nurses to care for them. Key personnel are being lost in prevention and care programs and finding replacements is proving difficult. Now that Ghana wants to use Voluntary Counselling and Testing as an entry point to care and support, it is imperative that the counselors trained remain at post. Capacity building is one of the major challenges and the rapid attrition of trained staff needs to be addressed. Many trained staff are leaving due to economic incentives elsewhere. Ways will have to be found to pay nurses realistic salaries and to find other incentives (such as assistance with transportation, housing, clearly defined career development etc.) to make nursing attractive for those who choose to stay and to avert future losses.

Conclusions

The trends, portrayed in the Sentinel surveillance data, clearly show that Ghana is still in the midst of the epidemic. The MOH cautions that, 'it will require several more years of careful monitoring before any definitive statements could be made about stabilization or decline in HIV prevalence in Ghana.' (MOH). Given the relatively modest prevalence rate and given the intensity and scope of the interventions reviewed in this paper, the epidemic can still be contained. Nevertheless, 'Ghana will need to mount an expanded programme of care and support and will need to develop a comprehensive Programme to mitigate the social and economic impacts of this epidemic' (MOH 2001:26). In addition to mitigating the social and economic impacts of the disease, concerted efforts ought to be placed into defining and comprehending the socio-cultural norms and contexts that promote HIV/AIDS in Ghana in the first place. Norms that promote transmission – gender inequities, 'open' polygamous unions etc. – as well as cultural practices that could well aid in the prevention of HIV/AIDS – such as using puberty rites as an entry point for adolescent education – all such require serious and concerted attention.

Endnotes

1   Both HIV-1 and HIV-2 exist in Ghana with HIV-1 being the predominant type; information on HIV prevalence by type is not available. (UNAIDS 2002)

2   The estimate of 4.6% was based on 1997 sentinel-surveillance data adjusted for several factors. In 1997 it was the standard practice to define adult HIV prevalence, 'as prevalence among the population age 15 and over. It was also standard scientific practice at that time to adjust the ANC data to account for the lower fertility of HIV-positive women. The ANC data were reduced to account for the lower prevalence among older adults, and increased to account for lower fertility of HIV-positive women.' Today, the adult HIV prevalence rate is calculated as the percentage of the adult population between the ages of 15 and 49 infected with HIV.

3   There have been literally, 'hundreds of community groups and thousands of individuals that have been working endlessly and tirelessly throughout the nation.' (JHU/USAID: 2002) While these entities are fundamentally important to the story of HIV/AIDS initiatives at the community level, they are not the focus of this chapter.

4   Heterosexual sex was – and remains – the predominant mode of transmission, accounting for 75-80% of all infections. Mother-to-child transmission and transmission through blood and blood products account for 15% and 5% respectively (MOH 2000a: 1). Between 30 – 40% of babies of HIV positive mothers are infected.

5   In 2002 only 6 of Ghana's 10 regions reported their AIDS case data to the Ministry of health. Of these 8 regions a total number of 8,000 cases were reported

6   At the designated sites, 'health workers take blood samples from pregnant women as part of their standard antenatal care. These blood samples are then tested anonymously for HIV infection.' (MOH 2001)

7   According to Islamic tenets, a man may marry up to four wives concurrently. Therefore although there may be five individuals in the marriage, a "closed" polygynous system implies that the individuals remain faithful to one another. "Open" polygyny implies that a man may be married but may have other 'wives' or girlfriends and may change these partners from time to time – thus widening the pool of sexual partners and increasing the 'risk' of infection.

8   There are only a few studies on the social and economic impacts of HIV in Ghana and one such study, conducted in 2001, found that there was little demonstrable economic impact of HIV/AIDS on the selected businesses studied. The financial costs to AIDS were relatively low. For the companies studied it cost between $5 to $55 per episode of illness per employee and there were very few employees who were ill (Nabila et al 2001). Although the impacts appeared to be relatively minor, of the six organizations studied, only one had developed a comprehensive workplace program on HIV/AIDS. In addition, the costs of anti-retroviral treatment for the, *few patients for whom this was available, amounted to 45 million Cedis per patient per year.'*– a considerable amount, far beyond the reach of the majority of employers.

9   The Korle Bu Teaching Hospital in Accra (Greater Accra Region), the Komfo Anokye Teaching Hospital in Kumasi (Ashanti Region) the Effia-Nkwanta Hospital in Sekondi-Takoradi (Western Region) and the Tamale Regional Hospital (Northern Region).

10   Recognizing that District-level initiatives are central for decentralized development and grassroots participation, the government and IPAA – working through the Ministry of Employment and Social Welfare (MESW) has expanded HIV/AIDS prevention initiatives to the district level.

11   In 1989, a similar exercise had been attempted with the establishment of the National Advisory Council on AIDS (NACA). It was a multi-disciplinary body established with representatives from other government sectors besides the Ministry of Health and interested parties from health professional bodies and NGO's. The NACA was to advise the Government on AIDS and to promote research activities and educational activities relating to AIDS. However the body, *'failed to make any meaningful impact and has since become defunct.'* (IPAA 1999: 7)

12   The National Policy explicitly focuses on the issues of: stigma reduction; the promotion of voluntary counselling and testing; the promotion of ethical codes regarding confidentiality; the support of efforts aimed at empowering women and, 'recognising their vulnerability to HIV infection' (MOH 2001); worker protection.

13   Promote safer sex particularly among vulnerable groups; Provide effective management of STDs; minimize the risk of transmission through blood and blood products; reduce MTCT; promote VCT

14   Provide cost-effective institutional care; provide home-based care

15   Strengthen national program coordination and implementation; mainstream HIV/AIDS into Ministries, Departments and Agencies (MDAs); scale up the District Response Initiative; implement at the Community level

16   The Commission is composed of the following membership: representatives of ministries, departments and agencies (MDAs), organised labour, National Union of Ghanaian Students, Ghana Employers Association, PLWHA, National House of Chiefs, and selected individuals and co-opted members.

17   Various partnerships have been formed over the years. For example the IPAA (International Partnership against HIV/AIDS) was introduced to Ghana in 1999. It has as its aim an acceleration of the response to the African HIV/AIDS epidemic. 'With AIDS fast becoming the number one killer in Africa, the UNAIDS co-sponsors (UNICEF, UNDP, UNESCO, WHO, UNDCP, UNFPA and the World Bank)...resolved in 1999...to create and support an International Partnership Against HIV/AIDS in Africa (IPAA). For example, Family Health International/ (FHI/IMPACT) with USAID support is, 'working with three of the largest churches and several Muslim groups to sensitize faith leaders and train priests, imams, marriage counselors, and grass roots women's and youth groups in discussing HIV/AIDS. This activity led JHU/CPCS to support a national dialogue among leaders and faith-based organizations.' (USAID 2002)

18   56.7% of women said that they restricted sex to one partner in order to avoid AIDS. 54% of men likewise. (GDHS 1998: 134 – 135).

19   According to JHU/PCS, large quantities of informational and promotional materials were produced including: 2 million leaflets, 200,000 Q & A booklets, 50,000 stickers, 30,000 posters, 25,000 t-shirts, and 25,000 caps (JHU/CCP: 2003). These materials were distributed through a demand-driven distribution network that includes hundreds of organizations from a wide spectrum [of] sectors including government ministries

and agencies, local and international NGO's, religious organizations, schools, community groups, trade organizations.' This distribution mechanism ensures that the materials will be distributed efficiently to the community level and be used effectively.' (JHU/PCS) 2001

20   The award winning radio show, 'Speakeasy' proved so popular that it was turned into a television drama, 'Things We Do For Love.' 'Speakeasy' is a pre-recorded serial radio drama followed by discussion with a live youth audience. According to a survey conducted by the African Broadcast Network, this show became the number one rated television show in Ghana (JHU/CPU).

21   The Sara initiative was originally developed in East Africa by UNICEF.

22   USAID has supported the development of 5,000 Sara Club kits that contain videos, books, posters, stickers, Sara Game boards, and facilitation manuals. The kit materials deal with the following subjects: 1. The Special Gift: Girs retention in School; 2) Sara saves her friend: Sexual harassment and HIV/AIDS; 2) The Trap: Sexual exploitation by Sugar daddies; and 4. Choices: Teenage pregnancy and positive girl-boy relationship. (JHU 2003).

23   Since many of the AIDS patients were women, activities that were introduced included tie-dye making, seed money for trading, bee keeping and preparation of food for sale. It became quite clear that giving money individually to PLWHA for trading was not a very good idea because as they became ill they used the money to buy food, drugs and other necessities. Those who sold also found that because of stigma and discrimination, people did not patronize their wares and they became bankrupt.

24   FHI's partners in Ghana include: Church of Pentecost, Salvation Army, Ghana Red Cross Society, Lady Pharmacists of Ghana, Paediatrics Society of Ghana, Presbyterian Church of Ghana, Ghana Girl Guides Association, National AIDS Control Programme, Muslim Relief Association of Ghana, National Public Health and Referenec laboratory, Manya Krobo Queenmothers Association of Ghana, Ghana Uniformed Services (Police, Armed Forces, Prison Service).

25   It is worth noting that this was an internal (JHU) review.

26   'While only 10% of male non-viewers used a condom at last sex, 34% of men with high campaign exposure had done so. Among sexually active women, 4% of female non-viewers reported using a condom at last sex, compared to 22% of women with high campaign exposure' (JHU/CCP: 2003).

27   A recent report, 'The Economic Impact of AIDS in Ghana' (Bollinger et al. 1999) quoted J. Gasu from a paper presented at the 1996 African Youth Alliance on Sexual Health held in Accra. It was alleged that, *some insurance companies and churches are exceeding their rights by demanding HIV tests before issuing insurance or allowing marriages, despite the fact that there are no mandatory statutes in the country."*

28   "The 6-year old boy who had been HIV positive since birth and had been on [admission] at the Korle-Bu teaching hospital from the time his mother died of AIDS in 1987, was put into a foster home. This was because none of his mother's relations was willing to take care of him." (NACP 1991:26)

Bibliography

Agyei-Mensah, S., 2001 Twelve Years of HIV/AIDS in Ghana: Puzzles of Interpretation. *Canadian Journal of African Studies.* 35 : 441-72

Anarfi, J. K., 1993. Sexuality, Migration and AIDS in Ghana – A Socio-behavioural Study. *Health Transition Review.* Vol. 3 Supplementary Issue.

Anarfi, J. K. E. N. Appiah., K. Awusabo-Asare, 1997. Livelihood and the risk of HIV/AIDS infection in Ghana: the case of female itinerant traders. *Health Transition Review.* Vol. 7 Supplementary Issue

Anarfi, J. K., K. Awusabo-Asare, 1993. Experimental Research on Sexual Networking in Some Selected Areas of Ghana. *Health Transition Review.* Vol. 3 Supplementary Issue.

Anarfi, J.K., K. Awusabo-Asare., E. N. Appiah, 2000. Female emigration, AIDS and their socio-demographic impact: a case study of a Ghanaian rural community. In J. C. Caldwell et al. (eds.), *Towards the Containment of the AIDS Epidemic: Social and Behavioural Research.* Health Transition Centre, Canberra.

Antwi, P., 1992. *An Overview of the AIDS Control Programme.* Unpublished

Awusabo-Asare, K., 1995. HIV/AIDS education and counselling: experiences from Ghana. *Health Transition Review,* Supplement to Volume 5, 229-236.

Awusabo-Asare, K., J. K. Anarfi., D. K. Agyeman, 1993. Women's Control over their Sexuality and the Spread of STD's and HIV/AIDS in Ghana. *Health Transition Review* .Vol. 3 Supplementary Issue.

Awusabo-Asare, K., A. M. Abane., D. M. Badasu., J. K. Anarfi, 1999. "All die be die": obstacles to change in the face of HIV infection in Ghana.In Caldwell, J. et al (eds.) *Resistances to Behavioural Change to Reduce HIV/AIDS Infection in Predominantly Heterosexual Epidemics in Third World Countries.* Health Transition Centre Books, Canberra

Bollinger, L., J. Stover., P. Antwi, 1999. *The Economic Impact of AIDS in Ghana.* The Futures Group International.

Bosu, W. K., A. Dzokoto, 2001. Situational Assessment of HIV/AIDS in Ghana: A Report Prepared for the Family Health International START Initiative Assessment Visit. Unpublished.

Decosas, J., Kane, F., Anarfi, J.j., Sodji, K. D. R., Wagner, H. U., 1995. Migration and AIDS. *The Lancet* 346: 826-28.

Ego, M. L., M. Moran, 1993. HIV/AIDS Counselling Program: A Rural Ghana Experience. *Health Transition Review.* Vol. 3 Supplementary Issue.

FHI, 2003. *Ghana: Ghana Program Overview.* https://www.fhi.org

Graphic 2002. Health Sector faces crisis. In Ghanaweb.com: General News of Thursday, 04 July 2002. https://www.ghanaweb.com

JHU 2002. JHU/PCS *Ghana HIV/AIDS & STIs Communication Component.* Unpublished

JHU 2003. *Ghana Launches National Program to Encourage Adolescents to Develop Skills to Fight HIV/AIDS infection.* http://www.jhuccp.org/pressroom/2003/04-09.shtml

JHU/CCP 2003. "Stop AIDS Love Life" Campaign in Ghana Shatters the Silence. *Communication Impact.* Number 15.

JHU/USAID 2002. Ghana's *Stop AIDS Love Life* Program. Phase 1: Evaluation Report, February 2000 – June 2001.

Ministry of Health 2004a *The National HIV/AIDS and STI Policy.* National AIDS/STD's Control Programme. MOH. Accra.

Ministry of Health 1991. *HIV Sero Sentinel Surveillance Report.* MOH. Accra.

Ministry of Health 1992. *HIV Sero Sentinel Surveillance Report.* MOH. Accra.

Ministry of Health 1993. *HIV Sero Sentinel Surveillance Report.* MOH. Accra.

Ministry of Health 1994. *HIV Sero Sentinel Surveillance Report.* MOH. Accra.

Ministry of Health 1995. *HIV Sero Sentinel Surveillance Report.* MOH. Accra.

Ministry of Health 1996. *HIV Sero Sentinel Surveillance Report.* MOH. Accra.

Ministry of Health 1997. *HIV Sero Sentinel Surveillance Report.* MOH. Accra.

Ministry of Health 1998. *HIV Sero Sentinel Surveillance Report.* MOH. Accra.

Ministry of Health 1999a. *HIV Sero Sentinel Surveillance Report.* MOH. Accra.

Ministry of Health 2000b. *HIV Sero Sentinel Surveillance Report.* MOH. Accra.

Ministry of Health 1991. *Annual Report of the Epidemiology Division.* MOH. Accra.

Ministry of Health 1991. *Annual Report of the National AIDS Control Programme.* MOH. Accra.

Ministry of Health 2000. *Annual Report of the National AIDS Control Programme.* MOH. Accra.

Ministry of Health 1999b. *HIV/AIDS in Ghana: Background Projections Impacts Interventions.* MOH. NACP. Accra.

Ministry of Health 2000. *Draft National HIV/AIDS and STI Policy Document* MOH. Accra.

Ministry of Health 2001. *HIV/AIDS in Ghana: Background Projections Impacts Interventions.* MOH. NACP. Accra.

Ministry of Health 2003. Official website.

Nabila, J. S., P. Antwi., K. Yeboah., S. O. Kwankye, 2001. *A Study of the Economic Impact of HIV/AIDS on Selected Business Organizations in Ghana* POLICY PROJECT, Accra. Unpublished Document.

NACP 2001. *HIV/AIDS in Ghana: Background, Projections, Impacts, Interventions, and Policy.* 3rd Edition.

Oppong, J. R., 1998. A Vulnerability Interpretation of the Geography of HIV/AIDS in Ghana 1986-1995. *Professional Geographer*, 50 (4) 437-448.

Price, M. P., A. Navele, 2002. Report on Assessment of Home Based Care Programme in 10 CHAG Institutions. CHAG INST. MONITORING REPORT.doc.

Tarantola, D., 2002. Reducing HIV/AIDS risk, impact and vulnerability. *Bulletin of the World Health Organization.* 2000, 78 (2).

USAID 2002. HIV/AIDS in Ghana: A USAID Brief.

USAID 2002a. *USAID Announces Introductory Anti retroviral Treatment Sites* Press Release http://www.usaid.gov

World Bank 2002 *The Gender Dimensions of HIV/AIDS: Putting Gender into the MAP* Africa Region Gender Team. World Bank. Washington DC.

Appendix: A Chronology of Major Political Events

1482 – Portuguese set up trading settlement.

1874 – British proclaim coastal area a crown colony.

1877 – Accra becomes capital of the Gold Coast Colony

1925 – First legislative council elections take place.

1957 – March – Ghana becomes independent with Osagyefo
Dr. Kwame Nkrumah as prime minister.

1960 – Ghana proclaimed a republic; Dr Nkrumah elected president.

1964 – Ghana becomes a one-party state.

1966 – Nkrumah overthrown in military coup; Russian and Chinese
technicians expelled.

1969 – New constitution facilitates transfer of power to civilian
government led by Kofi Busia.

1972 – Busia ousted in military coup led by Colonel Ignatius Acheampong.

1978 – Acheampong forced to resign; General Frederick Akuffo takes over.

1979 – Akuffo deposed in coup led by Flight Lieutenant Jerry J. Rawlings.
Acheampong and Akuffo tried and executed on charges of
corruption.

1979 – September – Rawlings hands over power to an elected president,
Hilla Limann.

1981 – Limann ousted in military coup led by Rawlings after two years

1983 – Rawlings abolishes subsidies and price controls, privatizes many
state enterprises and devalues the currency.

1992 – Referendum approves new constitution introducing a multiparty
system. Rawlings elected president.

1996 – Rawlings re-elected president.

2000 – December – John Kufuor wins in the presidential election.

2001 – February – Petrol prices rise by 60% following the government's
decision to remove fuel subsidies.

2001 – April – Ghana accepts debt relief under a HIPC scheme designed
by the World Bank and the IMF

Map of Ghana

FIG.   NAME OF TOWNS AND PLACES IN THE BOOK

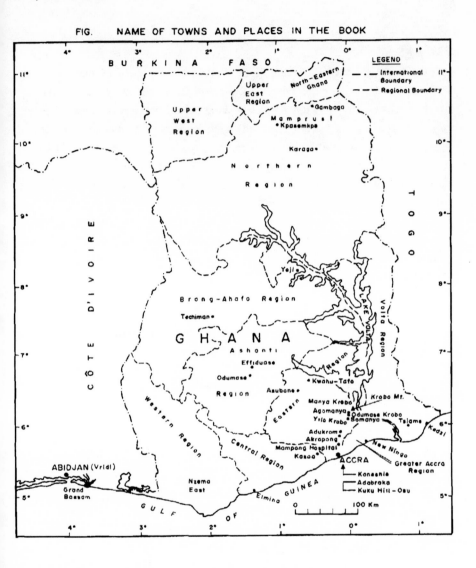

BIODATA

EDITORS

Irene Korkoi Odotei (B.A. and Ph.D. History, University of Ghana), Associate Professor and formerly acting Director of the Institute of African Studies, University of Ghana has visited many universities in Europe and North America to lecture and carry out research. She has designed and directed a number of collaborative research programs, including most recently projects on *Chieftaincy, Governance and Development* and *Tradition and Modernity*. Several of her recent publications focus on the death, burial and installation of Asante kings. In 2002 she became the President of the Historical Society of Ghana. With support from the UN Food and Agriculture Organization (FAO) she has in the past carried out extensive studies of coastal fishing communities and has published several monographs and papers on fishing themes. She has been actively involved in several types of educational extension work, including the design and holding of exhibitions, the editing of video documentaries and capacity building workshops. She is a Member of the Judicial Council of Ghana.

Christine Oppong (B.A. MA. Ph.D. Social Anthropology Cambridge.; M.A. African Studies, University of Ghana; Fellow of the Ghana Academy of Arts and Sciences), is Professor of Applied Anthropology at the Institute of African Studies University of Ghana. She was for some time the gender specialist in the UNFPA supported Population and Labour Policies Program of the Employment and Development Department of the International Labour Organization (ILO), Geneva, during which time she served as collaborating agency scientist on the Committee of the Task Force on Social Science of the Human Reproduction Program of the World Health Organization (WHO). She is an Associate of the African Studies Centre, Cambridge. In 1997-8 she held a Mellon Fellowship in Anthropological Demography at Brown University and in 2000-2001 and again in spring 2003 she was a visiting Fellow at the Netherlands Institute for Advanced Study (NIAS), where work on this volume commenced, among other things. She has written and edited a number of books and published many essays on aspects of family, gender, population and development in Sub Saharan Africa in general and Ghana in particular. Some of her recent publications on infants' entitlements and gendered aging have appeared in the Institute of African Studies Research Review and Occasional Research Papers series.

M. Yaa P. A. Oppong, (B. A. Social Anthropology and Geography, University of Durham; Ph. D. Social Anthropology, SOAS, University of London) was for some time a Research Fellow and Research Associate at the Harvard Centre for Population and Development Studies (CPDS), (Harvard School of Public Health). While at CPDS, Dr. Oppong worked on a range of issues relating to gender, HIV/AIDS and reproductive health. Her monograph *Moving Through and Passing on: Fulani Mobility, Identity and Survival in Ghana* was published by Transactions Publishers, New Jersey in 2002. Dr. Oppong recently joined the World Bank in Washington DC.

CONTRIBUTORS

Akosua Adomako Ampofo (B.Sc. Architecture; M.Sc. Development Planning UST Kumasi Ghana; Ph.D. Sociology Vanderbilt University, Tennessee) is an Associate Professor at the Institute of African Studies, University of Ghana, and until recently was the coordinator of the Development and Women's Studies Programme (DAWS). Her recent publications include, "Framing Knowledge, Forming Behaviour; African Women's AIDS-Protection Strategies." in *African Journal of Reproductive Health* 2(2): 151-174 (1998); "Nice guys, Condoms and Other forms of STD Protection; Sex Workers and AIDS protection in West Africa", in Becker, C, J. Dozon, C. Obbo and M. Touré (Eds.), *Vivre et Penser le SIDA en Afrique/Experiencing and Understanding AIDS in Africa,* Paris: CODESRIA, IRD, Karthala, PNLS: 559-588 (1999); and 'When men speak women listen'; Gender Socialisation and Young Adolescents' Attitudes to Sexual and Reproductive Issues, *African Journal of Reproductive Health.*(2002).

Emmanuel Akyeampong (B.A. History and the Study of Religions University of Ghana & Ph.D. in African History, University of Virginia) is a Professor of History of Africa and African American Studies, Harvard University and in 2004 he was named Harvard College Professor. He is the author of two monographs: *Drink, Power, and Cultural Change: A Social History of Alcohol in Ghana, 1800 to Recent Times* (Heinemann, 1996); and *Between the Sea and the Lagoon: An Eco-Social History of the Anlo of Southeastern Ghana, c.1850 to Recent Times* (James Currey, 2001). His book in progress examines the history of disease and towns in English-speaking West Africa from the mid-nineteenth century to the present. He currently serves as the chair of the Committee on African Studies at Harvard University. He is Vice President of the West African Research Association, and a Corresponding Fellow of the Royal Historical Society (U.K.).

Samuel Agyei-Mensah (B.A. Ph.D.) is a Senior Lecturer at the Department of Geography and Resource Development, the University of Ghana. He is the author of several articles as well as *Fertility Decline in Developing Countries 1960-1997: An*

Annotated Bibliography (Greenwood Press, 1999); and is the co-editor of *Reproduction and Social Context in Sub-Saharan Africa: A Collection of Micro-Demographic Studies* (Greenwood Press, 2003). He has also recently published on the subject of HIV/AIDS in West Africa.

John Anarfi (B.A. Hons) Geography, University of Cape Coast, Graduate Diploma, M.A. and Ph.D. in Population Studies from the Regional Institute for Population Studies (RIPS, Legon). He is a Social Demographer and an Associate Professor at the Institute of Statistical, Social and Economic Research (ISSER) at the University of Ghana, Legon. He is one of the few people who have done field work on migration of Ghanaians in the West African sub-region. His many publications on the subject make him one of the leading researchers on the social dimensions of HIV/AIDS in Ghana. His other research interests include sexuality, adolescent reproductive health and street children.

Phyllis Antwi (MB Ch.B; University of Ghana; MPH; University Surgeons of Ghana; MSc; University of London, Maternal and Child Health) is a Fellow of the West Africa College of Physicians (Community Health) and a Fellow of the Ghana College of Physicians. She is currently doing research and teaching in the School of Public Health, University of Ghana and has been at various times coordinator of a comprehensive HIV /AIDS prevention, care and treatment program in Manya Krobo and Yilo Districts of Eastern Region Ghana; Public Health Specialist, Ministry of Health and Programme Manager of the National AIDS Control Programme. Dr Antwi has written and edited a number of publications on Family Health, including on AIDS, teenage pregnancy and infant morbidity and mortality. She is currently researching maternal care in the Ashanti Region.

Kari Dako (BA MA Department of English University of Ghana) is an Associate Professor in that Department. She has written extensively on Ghanaian pidgins and varieties of English. She has also several publications on Ghanaian literature. Among her recent books are the translation from Danish of Thorkild Hansen's trilogy on the Danish/Norwegian participation in the slave trade, published by Sub-Saharan Publishers, and *Ghanaianisms: a glossary,* published by the Ghana Universities Press. She has also published a volume of short stories and edited a Ghanaian novel.

Aloysius Denkabe (B.A.; MA) was educated at the University of Ghana and St John's College Cambridge. He teaches literature at the department of English, University of Ghana. He has held fellowships at various universities in Europe and the

United States and has published several books and articles in the areas of literary studies, development and gender issues.

Susan Drucker-Brown (Licencia Escuela Nacional de Antropologia e Historia Mexico; Ph.D. Cantab, Social Anthropology) has taught in the Department of Brazilian Studies, University of Goias; Departments of Social Anthropology at the University of Cambridge, and of Sociology and Anthropology, University of Hull. She is Chair of the West Africa Seminar at the University of Cambridge, Centre of African Studies and Chair of the editorial board, *Cambridge Anthropology*. Her initial field research was carried out in Mexico (See *Cambio de indumentaria en Santiago, Jamiltepec,* 1963, and the edited volume, *Malinowski in Mexico*, 1982) From 1963 however, the main focus of her research has been in Northern Ghana with the Mamprusi people. (See *Ritual Aspects of Mamprusi Kingship* 1979 and numerous papers in MAN, or the JR AI).

Doris Essah (B.A. and M. Phil. African Studies University of Ghana) is studying history for a Ph. D degree at the University of Michigan. Her interests include labour relations, gender issues and education.

Douglas Frimpong Nnuroh (BA Hons. Religions and Philosophy Legon, PGCE Religious Education, University College Cape Coast, M.Phil. African Studies Legon, M.Phil. Gender and Development University of Bergen) is a teacher by profession. He is currently a Ph. D. candidate working on child care in Ellembelle Nzima. His wider research interests are in family, gender and development issues and he has published an article "Conjugal Morality and Sexual Vulnerability: the Ellembelle case." In the Institute of African Studies *Research Review Legon Vol. 18 No. 1 2002 pp 27-32.*

Brigid Sackey (M.A. Non-Western Religions, Marburg; Ph.D. Cultural Anthropology, Temple University, Philadelphia) is an Associate Professor at the Institute of African Studies, University of Ghana. In 2002-2003, she was a research fellow and visiting professor at the Women's Studies in Religion Program, Harvard Divinity School. She has researched and published extensively on African Religious Movements, women in religion, health and sexuality. Her recent publications include: *Apuskeleke*: Youth Fashion Craze, Immorality or Female Harassment? *Etnofoor*, XVI (2) 2003: 57-69; African-American Youth, Adolesence, *Encyclopedia of Primary Prevention and Health Promotion*, edited by Thomas Gullotta and Martin Bloom. New York: Kluwer Academic/Plenum Publishers, 2003: 165-169; Women, Religion, and Health: Faith Healing in Accra, *Occasional Research Paper Series 2000*, Institute of

African Studies, University of Ghana, Legon, 2002, 68 pp;Cultural Responses to the Management of HIV/AIDS: Repackaging Puberty Rites, *Research Review*, N.S. Institute of African Studies, University of Ghana, Legon. 17 (2) 2001: 63-82.

Esi Sutherland-Addy (B.A. French and Linguistics U. of Ghana; M.A. African Area Studies UCLA; D. Litt. *Honoris Causa* Winneba) is a Senior Research Fellow, and head of the Language, Literature and Drama Section, of the Institute of African Studies. She is also associate director of the African Humanities Institute Program at the University of Ghana. She has been a Senior Fellow and visiting lecturer at several universities abroad, including the Institute of International Education at Manchester University; the University of Indiana; the Centre for African Studies, University of Birmingham; and L' Institut des Hautes Etudes en Sciences Sociales, Paris. She has conducted studies for several African governments and national and international organizations and has served on a number of national and international boards and commissions. She was Founding Chair of the Management Committee of The W.E.B. Dubois Memorial Centre for Pan African Culture, Accra. She has also made many appearances on radio and television, including Ghana Broadcasting Corporation, the BBC World Service and Radio France Internationale She has held portfolios in the Ghana Government as Deputy Minister for Higher Education and Culture and Tourism. She has many, well known publications.

Marijke Steegstra (Ph.D. University of Nijmegen, The Netherlands, 2004) currently holds a post-doctoral research position in the anthropology department of the University of Nijmegen. She has spent several fieldwork periods in Ghana. Her present research focuses upon the role of 'development chiefs' and 'development queens' in Ghana. Her publications include: – *Re337silient rituals. Krobo initiation and the politics of culture in Ghana*, Münster: LIT Verlag, 2004 and "*A mighty obstacle to the gospel*": Basel missionaries, Krobo women, and conflicting ideas of gender and sexuality, *Journal of Religion in Africa*, vol. 32.2, 2002 and 2005 *Dipo and the Politics of Culture*, Woeli.

Sjaak van der Geest studied sociology and African Studies at the University of Ghana (Masters 1972) and defended his PhD dissertation, based on Ghanaian field work, at the University of Amsterdam (1976). He has been teaching cultural and medical anthropology at the University of Amsterdam from 1975 until today. He has been professor of Medical Anthropology since 1994. He has carried out fieldwork in Ghana and Cameroon and published books and articles on the following subjects: marriage and kinship, perceptions and practices concerning birth control, witchcraft beliefs, anthropological field research, Ghanaian Highlife songs, missionaries and anthropologists, as well as various topics in medical anthropology; in particular the perception and use of Western pharmaceuticals in Non-Western communities. Currently he is involved in research into the social and cultural meaning of old age in the Kwahu area of Ghana and in perceptions of hygiene and human waste.

Helen Atawube Yitah B.A., English and Linguistics, M.Phil. English, University of Ghana, where she is a Lecturer in the Department of English. She is at present a Fulbright scholar working on a Ph.D. in English at the University of South Carolina, Columbia. Her educational extension work includes the presentation of book reviews on Radio Universe, the F.M. radio station of the University of Ghana. She has published in the African Studies *Research Review*, and has entries in the Routledge Encyclopaedia for Postcolonial Literature in English. Her interests include postcolonial and women's literature.

These essays are written by male and female scholars, from several disciplines and fields, including anthropology, demography, history, literature, medical geography, public health and sociology. The writers use statistics, surveys, historical records, novels, songs, films and ethnographic observations to depict people's changing sexual behaviour and aspects of gender roles and relationships, including perceptions, expectations, communication and associated rites and risks, in rural and urban communities in various regions of the country in the last decades of the millennium.

The several essays are ultimately set within the context of an expanding HIV/AIDS epidemic, the impacts of which are yet to be fully felt on a national scale and the potential of which could challenge the very existence of the state. Accordingly the collection ends appropriately by discussing some of the responses and reactions of the Government of Ghana to this escalating crisis of communicable disease and death.

Printed in the United States
205292BV00001B/256/A